26917

# GODS, GRAVES, AND SCHOLARS

## The Story of Archaeology

## by C. W. Ceram

Translated from the German
by E. B. Garside and Sophie Wilkins

Second, Revised and
Substantially Enlarged Edition

Vintage Books
A Division of Random House
New York

Library of Congress Cataloging-in-Publication Data

Ceram, C. W., 1915-1972.
  Gods, graves, and scholars.

  Translation of: Götter, Gräber und Gelehrte.
  Reprint. Originally published: New York: Knopf,
1967.
  Bibliography: p.
  Includes index.
  1. Archaeology—History.    I. Title.
CC100.C4213  1986      930.1      86-11131
ISBN 0-394-74319-9

There is no such thing as a patriotic art or a patriotic science. Both art and science belong, like every higher good, to all the world and can be fostered only by the free flow of mutual influence among all contemporaries, with constant regard for all we have and know of the past.

—Goethe

He who wants to see his time rightly, must look upon it from a distance. How great a distance? Quite simply, just far enough away so that he cannot discern Cleopatra's nose.

—Ortega y Gasset

# FOREWORD TO THE SECOND, REVISED AND ENLARGED EDITION

Since the original German edition of this book was published in 1949, it has been translated into twenty-six languages and read by millions of people, even though I have never permitted a reprint edition to be issued. While *Gods, Graves, and Scholars* was originally written for the widest general reading public, its strict adherence to scientific standards has led long since to its being made required reading for some college courses. University and college libraries often stock as many as ten copies or more in order to be able to satisfy the demand for the book, which my publisher and a number of critics have called a classic.

In the meantime, archæology has marched on. New discoveries have been made, new interpretations advanced, and above all, remarkable new techniques for archæological researches developed. To cover these new developments, I have revised the original edition and concluded the book with a summary of the important new findings and methods. The extensive additions to the original American text have been translated from the German by Sophie Wilkins, to whom I particularly wish to express my appreciation also for her painstaking work in comparing texts and making necessary rearrangements in the revised edition.

*Gods, Graves and Scholars* was followed by *The Secret of the Hittites: The Discovery of an Ancient Empire* (1956), *The March of Archæology* (1958), a pictorial history of archæology, and *Hands on the Past* (1966), a documentation. Together these four volumes,

with their combined total of nearly a thousand biblio-
graphical items and picture sources, constitute the most
comprehensive history of archæology ever published for
the general reader, containing numerous facts and
stories long forgotten even by the specialists, as well as
the latest developments and scientific thought in the
field.

C. W. C.
July 1967

# FOREWORD TO
# THE FIRST AMERICAN EDITION

My book was written without scholarly pretensions. My aim was to portray the dramatic qualities of archæology, its human side. I was not afraid to digress now and then and to intrude my own personal reflections on the course of events. Nor have I shied away from prying into purely personal relationships. All this has produced a book that the expert may condemn as "unscientific."

But I wanted the book to be that way. Archæology, I found, comprehended all manner of excitement and achievement. Adventure is coupled with bookish toil. Romantic excursions go hand in hand with scholarly self-discipline and moderation. Explorations among the ruins of the remote past have carried curious men all over the face of the earth. Yet this whole stirring history, I discovered, was hopelessly buried in technical publications that, however great their informative value, were never written to be read. I also learned that not more than three or four attempts had ever been made to bring this dramatic story to light. Yet in truth no science is more adventurous than archæology, if adventure is thought of as a mixture of spirit and deed.

Though my method allows little scope for pure description, I am still deeply obligated to learned writings on antiquity. It could not be otherwise. Inded, my book is a hymn of praise to the archæologist's brilliant accomplishments, his penetration and indefatigability. Above all, it is a memorial to those investigators who, out of genuine modesty, have hidden their light under a bushel. With a sense of responsibility toward these little-known people who make up the backbone of the archæological profession, I have tried hard to avoid false groupings and false emphases.

I realize that the specialist who reads my book will probably discover certain defects. To some extent this is inevitable. When I began writing, for example, the mere spelling of proper names loomed as an almost insurmountable obstacle. More than once I had a choice among a dozen different spellings of the same name. I finally decided to follow the commonest usage and eschew any scientific principle that, in places, might have led to complete unintelligibility: If the great German historian Eduard Meyer, faced with a similar problem in his *History of Antiquity*, could say, speaking to the scholars themselves, "... here I saw no other way than to proceed without any principle whatever," the author of a mere report may surely do likewise.

Beyond this, of course, simple factual mistakes have undoubtedly crept into the text. Some delinquency, I believe, is quite unavoidable, considering the tremendous amount of material drawn from four specialized fields that I have tried to compress.

I am indebted, moreover, not only to archæology, but to the writers of sound scientific popularizations, who have showed me what can be done in this form and whom I have earnestly attempted to emulate. To the best of my knowledge it was Paul de Kruif who first undertook to trace the development of a highly specialized science so that one could read about it with genuine excitement, with the sort of response too often produced, in our times, only by detective thrillers. De Kruif found that even the most highly involved scientific problems can be quite simply and understandably presented if their working out is described as a dramatic process. That means, in effect, leading the reader by the hand along the same road that the scientists themselves have traversed from the moment truth was first glimpsed until the goal was gained. De Kruif found that an account of the detours, crossways, and blind alleys that had confused the scientists—because of their mortal fallibility, because human intelligence failed at times to measure up to the task, because they were victimized by disturbing accidents and obstructive outside influences—could achieve a dynamic and dramatic quality capable of evoking an uncanny tension in the reader. The title of his book, *The Microbe Hunters*, transforming as it did the dryly scientific term *bacteriologists* into a dramatic human image, in itself contains the program for a new literary category created by his revolutionary approach. This new form is the narrative of facts currently called the nonfiction or documentary novel.

Since Paul de Kruif's pioneering effort there is hardly a science that has not been skillfully popularized at least once. It is natural that most of these popularizers should be dilettantes by scientific reckoning. They cannot be dismissed on that account. In my opinion, a critical principle to apply in measuring the value of this type of book is this: what relation is there in the book between science and literature? Specifically, which preponderates, the factual element or the literary? It seems to me that the best works of the genre are those in which the literary effect is derived from the factual "arrangement," those in which fact is consistently of prime concern. I have tried to approximate this ideal.

Finally I should like to express my thanks to all those who have helped me with this considerable task. Dr. Eugen von Mercklin, Professor of Classical Archæology at the University of Hamburg; Dr. Carl Rathjens, Professor of Near East Geography at the University of Hamburg; and Dr. Franz Termer, Professor of American Archæology and Director of the Anthropological Museum at the University of Hamburg, were kind enough to examine the manuscript, each from his point of view as specialist. Dr. Kurt Erdmann, Professor of the History of Art at the University of Hamburg; and Dr. Hartmut Schmökel, Professor of the Old Testament and Biblical Culture at the University of Kiel, gave me some important supplementary corrections. I should also like to record my gratitude for something more than technical aid: namely, for the complete understanding that they, as specialists, showed for my book.

C. W. C.

# CONTENTS

# GODS, GRAVES, AND SCHOLARS

PART ONE

# THE BOOK
# OF THE STATUES

Pompeii, Troy, Mycenæ, Crete

*What marvel is this? We begged you for drinkable springs,*
*O earth, and what is your lap sending forth?*
*Is there life in the deeps as well? A race yet unknown*
*Hiding under the lava? Are they who had fled returning?*
*Come and see, Greeks; Romans, come! Ancient Pompeii*
*Is found again, the city of Hercules rises!*

—Schiller

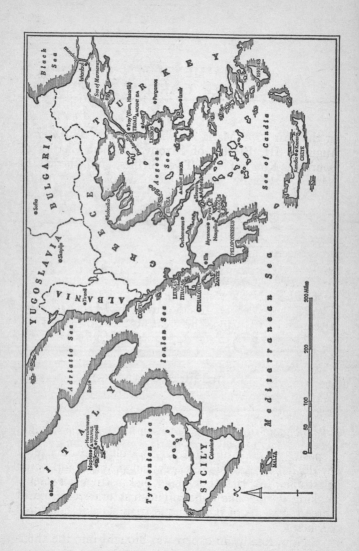

# 1/THE QUEEN OF NAPLES: FROM HER GARDEN TO POMPEII

In the year 1738 Maria Amalia Christine, daughter of Augustus III, Elector of Saxony, married Charles of Bourbon, King of the Two Sicilies, and moved to Naples. The lively young Queen, who was of artistic bent, explored the spacious precincts of her palace gardens and discovered there a wealth of statuary and other carved works. Some of these had been found accidentally before the last eruption of Vesuvius, and others were dug up later on the initiative of a certain General d'Elbœuf.

Delighted by the beauty of these antiquities, she begged her royal husband to let her look for new pieces. The King gave in because Vesuvius had been quiet for a year and a half since the great outbreak of May 1737.

The likeliest place to continue the search was where d'Elbœuf had left off on the side of the volcano. The King sought the advice of a certain Cavaliere Rocco Gioacchino de Alcubierre, commanding officer of the Royal Engineers. This Spaniard organized a labor force and equipped it with tools and blasting powder. The difficulties were formidable, for at the outset the diggers had to penetrate 49.5 feet of stony-hard lava deposit. Working outward from a well shaft discovered by d'Elbœuf, Alcubierre's crew cut passages and bored blastholes. At last the men's picks struck on metal, making it ring like a bell. The first find consisted of three fragments of bronze equestrian statues sculptured on heroic scale.

Now, finally, an expert was brought into the enterprise. The Marchese Don Marcello Venuti, humanist and royal librarian, henceforth supervised the handling and disposition of further discoveries. Three marble sculptures of Roman figures in togas, some painted columns, and the bronze torso of a horse were next unearthed. The royal couple came to inspect the finds. The Marchese had himself lowered down the shaft on a rope, and discovered a flight of stairs. Its construction gave him some clue to what sort of edifice it was into which they were tunneling. Several weeks later, on December 11, 1738, an inscription was found indicating that a certain Rufus had built, with money of his own, the "Theatrum Herculanense."

It now appeared that a buried city had been revealed, for almost certainly a theater could only have been in an inhabited place. By luck, it seemed, d'Elbœuf, the first excavator, had struck the very middle of the stage. This stage was littered with statuary. It was the one spot on the whole site where it was possible to find sculpture piled up literally one piece on top of another. The enormous stream of lava had rolled against the back wall of the theater, which had been richly decorated with carved works, and toppled it down upon the stage. For seventeen hundred years the stone figures had lain undisturbed.

The inscription gave the name of the city as Herculaneum.

Lava, a liquidly flowing stone, is a mixture of several kinds of minerals, which hardens as it cools into glass and new kinds of rock. Herculaneum was covered to a depth of 65 feet by this material.

Lapilli, on the other hand, consist of small fragments of glassy volcanic rock. When spewed out of a volcano together with greasy ashes, these little stones descend as a relatively light rain, and form a loose cover not too resistant to light tools. Pompeii lay under a blanket of this kind and, moreover, was not nearly so deeply buried as its sister city, Herculaneum.

In history, as in the life of the individual, it often happens that the difficult course is chosen in preference to the easier one, and the longest way mistaken for the shortest. Thirty-five years passed after d'Elbœuf's initial efforts at Herculaneum before the first spade-cut was made which ultimately led to the uncovering of Pompeii.

The Cavaliere Alcubierre became dissatisfied with results at d'Elbœuf's site, even though these had already yielded to Charles of Bourbon a collection of antiquities superior to any other in the world at the time. King and engineer agreed that excavation activities ought to be moved to areas indicated by scholars, instead of blindly hacking away at the lava debris and trusting to luck. Ancient sources reported that Pompeii was destroyed on the same day as the city of Hercules.

On April 1, 1748, the new excavations were started. By April 6 the first marvelous wall painting had already been found and on April 19 the first body was uncovered. Stretched out full-length on the floor was a skeleton, with gold and silver coins that had rolled out of bony hands still seeking, it seemed, to clutch them fast.

But now, instead of continuing to dig systematically and evaluating what had already been found in order to facilitate further progress, the pits were filled in. No one appears to have had any notion that the very middle of Pompeii had been breached. Instead, more holes were started.

The royal couple's interest, after all, was superficial, the passing enthusiasm of cultured laymen. Moreover, Charles's intellectual and æsthetic preoccupations did not amount to much. As for Alcubierre, his only interest was to master a technical engineering problem. All others connected with the project simply hoped for another sudden stroke of luck which would bring them another haul of gold and silver. Of the twenty-four men employed at the diggings on April 6, twelve were criminals. Neither they nor their miserably remunerated fellow workers could be expected to take a detached view of the proceedings.

The auditorium of the amphitheater was now laid open. But when no statues, gold, or ornaments of any kind were turned up, the diggings were again moved elsewhere. A little more patience and they would have struck it rich. Near the Gate of Hercules they came upon a villa that—on what justification no one seems to know—was declared to be Cicero's house. On the walls of the villa were wonderful frescoes, which were cut out and copied. Then the excavated dirt was promptly shoveled back into place. To climax this bizarre procedure, for four whole years thereafter the area around Cività (the earlier Pompeii) was quite neglected, in favor of richer diggings at Herculaneum. There was discovered one of the most interesting treasures known up to that time, the villa containing the library of the philosopher Philodemus, the "Villa dei Papiri."

Finally in 1754 excavations were again undertaken on the south side of Pompeii, and the remains of some tombs and ancient masonry were unearthed. From that time up to the present, digging has been in progress, with few interruptions, in both Pompeii and Herculaneum.

The catastrophe that overwhelmed the cities of Pompeii and Herculaneum turned out to be of tremendous significance to archæology.

In the middle of August A.D. 79, there were signs that Vesuvius was again about to erupt, but since Vesuvius was often active, at first there was no alarm. On the forenoon of the 24th, however, it became clear that a disaster of unparalleled dimensions was in the making. The top of the mountain split apart with a thunderous explosion. Smoke mushroomed into the sky, darkening the sun. A rain of volcanic cinder and ashes began to sift down, amid terrific crashes and terrifying flashes of light. Birds tumbled dead out of the air, people ran about screaming, animals slunk into hiding. Meanwhile torrents of water rushed through the streets, and no one could tell whether they came from the sky or out of the earth.

This violence descended on the two cities of Pompeii and Herculaneum during the busy, sunny hours of early morning and worked their total destruction in two different ways. An avalanche of mud—a mixture of volcanic ash, rain, and lava—poured massively over Herculaneum, forcing its way into streets and alleys, rising higher and higher, and always increasing in pressure. The flow covered roofs, ran in through doors and windows, and eventually filled Herculaneum as water fills the interstices of a sponge. Everything and everyone not immediately evacuated were buried deep.

At Pompeii it was different. Here there were no flood of muck; disaster began with a light fall of ash, so light that people were able to brush the powdery dust off their shoulders. Soon, however, lapilli began to come down, then occasional bombs of pumice weighing many pounds. The extent of the danger was only gradually revealed, and only when it was too late. Clouds of sulphur fumes settled down on the city. They seeped through cracks and crevices and billowed up under the cloths that the suffocating townsfolk held up to their faces. If they ran outdoors seeking air and freedom, they were met by a thick hail of lapilli that drove them back in terror to the shelter of their homes. Roofs caved in, whole families were buried. Others were spared for a time. For a half hour or so they crouched in fear and trembling under stairs and arched doors. The fumes reached them, and they choked to death.

The sun came out forty-eight hours later, but by this time Pompeii and Herculaneum had ceased to exist. For a distance of eleven miles around, the landscape had been destroyed. Clouds of ash were borne by air currents as far as Africa, Syria, and Egypt. Yet now nothing but a thin column of smoke issued from Vesuvius, smudging the lovely blue dome of sky.

Almost seventeen hundred years passed. New generations, with other customs and new forms of knowledge, struck spades into the earth and brought forth the dead cities from oblivion. It was almost like a resurrection, a miracle.

The archæologist, infatuated with his work to the exclusion of the usual pieties, is quite capable of praising this sort of catastrophe as a stroke of luck. Even Goethe, the author of immortal tragedies, in his capacity as a scientist said of Pompeii: "I hardly know of anything more interesting . . ." and did not realize he was being callous. It is indeed hard to imagine a better way of preserving a whole city for the benefit of posterity, of catching it fairly in the midst of its everyday activity, than by sealing it beneath a great blanket of ash. Pompeii was quite different from the ruins of a city which had died a natural death by a process of withering away. The living community was touched with a magic wand, and the laws of time, of becoming and of fading, lost their validity.

Before the first excavation nothing but the bare memory of the two cities' entombment remained. But once digging began, little by little the whole dramatic event took shape in men's minds, and information on the catastrophe left by the authors of antiquity came to life. The full frightfulness of the disaster was realized. The daily round had been cut off so abruptly that the suckling pig was found where it had been left to roast in the oven, and bread discovered half done on the baker's peel.

What a story of death in debacle these poor bones could tell, bones still wearing the fetters of the slave! The sifting, seeping flow of ash and lapilli had steadily risen higher and higher, lifting a chained dog with it. And at last, when it filled the room, he had perished, still fastened to his leash, next to the ceiling.

The excavators' shovels revealed all manner of family tragedies, scenes of mothers, fathers, and chil-

dren caught in absolute extremity. Mothers were found
still holding their children in their arms, protecting
them with the last bit of veil as they both suffocated.
Men and women were dug up who had gathered their
valuables together, got as far as the city gate, and there
collapsed under the stony hail, still clinging to their
gold and precious things. "Cave canem," reads a sign
in mosaic at the gate of the house in which Bulwer-
Lytton lodged his Glaucus in *The Last Days of Pompeii*. At the threshold of one house two young women
were found who had hesitated until it was too late,
intending to go back into the house and salvage some
of their treasures.

Body after body was found at the Gate of Hercules, bodies all heaped together, and still encumbered
with the household gear that had grown too heavy to
drag any farther. In a sealed room the skeletons of a
woman and a dog were uncovered. Close examination
revealed a grisly incident. Whereas the skeleton of the
dog had remained intact, the woman's bones were scattered about the floor. Apparently crazed by hunger, the
dog's wolfish nature had come to the fore and he had
fallen on his dead mistress and eaten her. Not far from
this house was another in which funeral rites had been
in progress when cataclysm fell. There they were,
the funeral guests, after seventeen hundred years still
sprawled on their benches about the table bearing the
funeral feast, mourners at their own obsequies.

In an adjacent building seven children had been
surprised by death while innocently playing in a room.
In still another structure thirty-four bodies were found,
with them the remains of a goat that, in his fright, had
rushed indoors to find safety among humankind. Neither
courage nor a cool head nor brute strength helped those
who delayed their flight too long. The remains of a
truly gigantic man were uncovered. In vain he had tried
to protect his wife and their fourteen-year-old child, who
were hastening along ahead of him. Apparently with a
last, despairing surge of strength he had tried to pick

them up, but just then the fumes had stupefied him, and slowly he crumpled, rolled over on his back, and stretched out, in which position ashes buried him and preserved his tremendous form. The excavators poured plaster of Paris into the depression where he had lain, and in this way secured the proportions of a dead Pompeian.

The rows of houses, the Temple of Isis, the amphitheater—all were there exactly as they had looked on the fateful August day. The wax tablets still lay on the study table, the papyrus rolls were still in the library, the tools in the work-sheds, the scrubbing brushes still in the baths. Vessels and dishes were found on inn tables, likewise the money left by departing guests who had hurriedly paid their accounts to proprietors who had already left. On tavern walls verses were found, scurrilous or sentimental, written by lovers, and beautiful frescoes on villa walls (see Plate I).

It was the cultured man of the eighteenth century who first saw this richly detailed museum of the past. The Renaissance had prepared him for the æsthetic appreciation of antique splendors. But he also sensed the incipient power of science and was eager to dedicate himself to facts rather than rest content with mere contemplation of the beautiful and strange. To do justice to both these viewpoints someone was needed who combined a love for the art of antiquity with a talent for systematic investigation and criticism. At the time the excavation of Pompeii was first attempted, the man who would fill this dual role was employed as librarian by a German count and at thirty had yet to accomplish anything of note.

# 2/WINCKELMANN:
# THE BIRTH OF A SCIENCE

A famous sketch of J. J. Winckelmann made in Rome, in 1764, shows him sitting over an open book, quill in hand. Huge, dark eyes shine out from under an intellectual brow. The nose is large, almost a Bourbon nose in this portrayal. The mouth and chin are soft and rounded. Altogether the drawing suggests an artistic rather than an academic personality.

Winckelmann, a cobbler's son, was born in 1717 in Stendal, a small town in Prussia. As a boy he tramped the countryside looking for the prehistoric barrows of the district and lured his comrades into helping him dig for old urns. By 1743 he had made himself senior assistant master of a grammar school in Seehausen.

In 1748 he found a post as librarian for the Count of Bünau, near Dresden, in Saxony, and left the Prussia of Frederick the Great without regret. He had early realized that Prussia was a "despotic land," and in later life he looked back on the years spent there with a shudder, remarking that "I at least felt the slavery more than others." The future course of his life was determined by this move. He landed in the midst of a circle of important artists, and in Dresden found the most comprehensive collection of antiquities then extant in his native Germany. The opportunity to study these relics put out of his thoughts half-serious plans to go abroad, perhaps to Egypt. When his first writings appeared, they evoked echoes throughout all Europe. In order to get a chance to work in Italy, he turned Catholic, but with the passage of the years he became,

if anything, more spirtually independent than before
his conversion, and in religion he was never dogmatic.
Rome, he thought, was worth a Mass to him.

In 1758 he became the librarian of Cardinal Al-
bani's collection of antiquities. And in 1763 he was
appointed Chief Supervisor of all antiquities in and
about Rome, and in this capacity he visited Pompeii
and Herculaneum. In 1768 he was murdered.

Three of Winckelmann's voluminous works contributed
basically to the introduction of scientific methods in
the investigation of the past. These are his *Sendschreiben*, or *Open Letters*, on the discoveries at Herculaneum; his main work, *History of the Art of Antiquity*;
and his *Monumenti antichi inediti*, or *Unpublished
Relics of Antiquity*.

Excavations at Pompeii and Herculaneum during
the early years were haphazard. But worse than plan-
lessness was secrecy. An atmosphere of exclusiveness
was generated by prohibitions imposed by self-seeking
rulers on all foreigners, whether mere travelers or students of the past, who sought permission to visit the
two dead cities and tell the world about them. The
only exceptions made by the King of the Two Sicilies
had been to allow a bookworm by the name of Bayardi
to prepare a catalogue of the finds. But Bayardi plunged
into an introduction to his catalogue without even
bothering to visit the excavations. He wrote and wrote,
and by 1752 had completed five volumes, totaling some
2,677 pages, without even getting to the essentials.
Meanwhile he spread malicious reports about two new-
comers who showed signs of going straight to the heart
of the matter, and was able to have them denied permission to visit the sites.

And when a bona fide scholar managed to get hold
of one or another excavated piece to inspect at first
hand, as often as not total lack of preparation would
lure him into such devious theories as the one advanced
by Martorelli. This Italian savant wrote a two-volume

work running to 652 pages in order to prove, by inspection of an inkwell, that the ancients did not use scrolls, but regular books of rectangular shape. And this when the papyrus rolls of Philodemus stared him in the face.

The first large folio volume on the antiquities of Pompeii and Herculaneum finally appeared in 1757, written by Valetta, and subsidized by the King to the extent of twelve thousand ducats. Meanwhile Winckelmann entered this atmosphere of envy, intrigue, and moldly bookishness. After countless difficulties, during which he was treated like a spy, Winckelmann obtained permission to visit the Royal Museum. He was expressly forbidden, however, to make the smallest sketch of the sculptures stored there.

The embittered Winckelmann now found a friend of somewhat his own disposition. In the Augustine cloister where he had been given lodgings, he became acquainted with Father Piaggi, whom he found engaged in a most peculiar task.

When the Villa of the Papiri was discovered, everyone had been delighted with the rich find of ancient writings. But delight faded into dismay when the papers were handled, for on handling they began to crumble into carbon dust. All sorts of expedients were tried in an attempt to save the rolls. No one had the least success, however, until one day Father Piaggi appeared with "a frame almost like the kind used by wigmakers in preparing hair" and claimed to be able to unroll the scrolls with his instrument. He was allowed to experiment, and when Winckelmann arrived had already spent years on this painstaking task. He had, it seemed, been successful enough in preserving the manuscripts, but a dismal failure in his relations with the King and Alcubierre. They, he said, did not appreciate him.

As Winckelmann crouched beside Father Piaggi at his worktable, the angry cleric vented his spleen on everything that passed within view of his window. Meanwhile, with an incredibly delicate touch, as if he were sorting fluff, he turned the scorched papyrus a millimeter at a time on his little machine. He grumbled about the King, he deplored his sovereign's lukewarmness, the incapacity of royal officials and working crews. Showing Winckelmann a freshly recovered column from an essay by Philodemus on music, he ranted in his pride against the impatient and envious ones who did not give him his due.

Winckelmann was all the more receptive toward Father Piaggi's censures after the authorities persisted in denying him permission to visit the diggings. They restricted his research to the museum, and even there he could not copy. He bribed the foremen at the excavations, and they let him look at odd pieces here and there. In the meantime objects had been exhumed that were of real importance in an inclusive survey of antique culture such as that conceived by Winckelmann. The new findings were carvings and pictures of a highly erotic nature. The narrow-minded King, shocked by a statue showing a satyr coupled with a goat, had all the new material shipped off to Rome and there put under lock and key. And so Winckelmann did not get to see these latest and significant discoveries.

Despite these frustrations he was able, in 1762, to publish his first open letter, "On the Discoveries at Herculaneum." Two years later he paid a second visit to the city and to the Royal Museum, which trip resulted in another commentary. Both these productions contained harshly critical allusions to situations that Winckelmann had heard discussed in Father Piaggi's cell. When the second open letter reached the Neapolitan court in French translation, a storm of indignation arose against the German who had so shabbily repaid the authorities with abuse for their kindness in letting him work in the Royal Museum. Winckelmann's sarcasms were, of course, justified, and his anger based on a real grievance. Yet the contentious side of his *Sendschreiben* no longer has any relevance. The value of the letters derives from the fact that for the first time they gave the world a clear, objective description of the antiquities taken from the slopes of Vesuvius.

About the same period Winckelmann's chef-d'œuvre appeared, the *History of the Art of Antiquity.* In this masterpiece he succeeded in impressing a recognizable order of an immense accumulation of antique material that hitherto had languished as the loosest sort of aggregation. The book was written, as he proudly remarks, "without a model" to go by. It broke first ground in approaching the subject of ancient art from a developmental point of view. Winckelmann built his system out of the meager accounts bequeathed to posterity by the ancients. With unerring sensitivity he groped toward original insights, and expressed them with such power of language that the cultured European world was carried away by a wave of enthusiasm for the antique ideal. This rush of surrender was of prime importance in shaping the course of archæology in the following century. Winckelmann's book excited a lively interest in tracking down beautiful objects wherever they lay hidden. It demonstrated means of understanding ancient cultures through their artifacts; it awakened the hope of uncovering new treasure trove, as replete with wonders as Pompeii.

With his *Monumenti antichi inediti,* published in 1767, Winckelmann produced a real tool for the new science of antiquity. "Without model," he became the model himself. To interpret the meaning of Greek sculpture he traced out the whole range of Hellenic mythology. He showed a rare genius for drawing inferences from the smallest hints. Before his advent such archæology as there was had been strongly affected by philological bias and dominated by the historian. Winckelmann completely altered the canons.

Many of Winckelmann's notions were false, and many of his conclusions overhasty. His image of antiquity was highly idealized. Not only "men like gods" had lived in Hellas, but ordinary mortals as well. Despite a plethora

of material, Winckelmann's acquaintanceship with
Greek works of art was rather limited. What he had
seen for the most part consisted of copied material dating no farther back than Roman times, sculptures of
immaculate whiteness, scored by billions of raindrops
and abrasive grains of sand. Hellas had not characteristically expressed itself in severely conceived and blind-
ingly white forms set off against a luminous landscape.
The plastic works of the ancient Greeks were gaily
colored. Statuary was deeply dyed with garish pigments.
The marble figure of a woman found on the Athenian
Acropolis was tinctured red, green, blue, and yellow.
Quite often statues had red lips, glowing eyes made of
precious stones, and even artificial eyelashes.

And so Winckelmann's service consists in his having imposed a provisional order on what before had
been outright chaos, in replacing, so far as lay within
his power, conjecture with real knowledge. His systematic approach was to prove valuable in rescuing
much older cultures from the abyss of time.

Returning to Italy in 1768, Winckelmann stopped over
at a hotel in Trieste, and there innocently fell into the
company of an Italian criminal who had served several
jail sentences.

We can only assume that Winckelmann consorted
with this former cook and pimp, and even shared a
meal with him in his room, because his archæological
interest had been somehow beguiled. Winckelmann, of
course, was one of the hotel's most important guests
and attracted notice. He wore fine clothes, he had a
worldly manner, and occasionally he liked to show off
the gold coins that he kept as souvenirs of an audience
with Maria Theresa. The Italian, very inappropriately
named Arcangeli, equipped himself with a noose and
a knife.

The murder took place on the evening of June 8,
1768. Winckelmann, intending to write some directions
to his publisher, had removed his outer clothing and

was seated at work at the writing table. The Italian came in, threw his garrotte about Winckelmann's neck, overpowered him after a brief struggle, and inflicted severe knife wounds.

The victim had a robust physique, however, and despite his mortal wounds was able to drag himself downstairs. But his blood-soaked clothing and terrible pallor so paralyzed the waiters and servant girls with fright that by the time they had summoned help it was too late to save his ebbing life.

The famous scholar was dead a few hours later. On his writing table a sheet of paper was found, on it the last words from his pen: "It should—" After these two words the murderer had knocked the quill from Winckelmann's hands. So perished one of the most learned men of his time, founder of a new science.

After his death Winckelmann's work bore ample fruit. His children, so to speak, are scattered all over the face of the earth. Nearly two hundred years have elapsed since his death, and still on December 9, his birthday, students of antiquity celebrate his memory in the great archæological institutes of Rome and Athens.

# 3/INTERLUDE:
## WHY SEARCH FOR THE PAST?

The aim of this book is to describe the evolution of archæology; that is, to describe, without anticipating, a process of development; to answer questions that present themselves in the course of our daily intellectual lives.

Often, in search of whence we have come, we wander through museums and see yellow, half-decayed leaves of papyrus, and fragments of vases, reliefs, and columns, all covered with wonderful signs and pictures called cuneiform characters or hieroglyphs. We know there are men who can read these signs as easily as we read newspapers and books in our own languages. We wonder how the mysteries of these ancient scripts and languages that had ceased to be written when Europe was still virgin forest were revealed. We ponder how it was possible even to read sense into the dead signs.

We leaf through the works of our historians. We read about the history of ancient peoples whose heritage we carry with us, in linguistic fragments, in many of our customs and usages, in the artifacts of our culture, and in traces of a common blood stream though these same peoples may have lived out their lives in distant zones and have disappeared from view in grayest antiquity. We read about their history not in terms of saga and legend but of dates and numbers. We learn to know the names of their kings, we find out how they lived in peace and in war, we see them in their homes and in their places of worship. We are instructed concerning their rise and their decline, a cultural pulsation

18

of fixed duration to the year, the month, and the day. Yet all this may have ocurred when our own time-reckoning had not even begun, before our very calendar had come into being.

Where, then did this knowledge of the past come from?

But when all is said and done, what does it matter to twentieth-century man, who drives a car and flies a plane, who worries about the future, not about the past, what an Assyrian king wrote to his son in cuneiform writing, or what the ground plan of an Egyptian temple may be? This is a fair question, and deserves a fair answer.

In Chapter twenty-four of this book the idea is developed that one cannot look at the numbers on the face of one's clock without taking into account the old Babylonian method of reckoning time. This indicates that anyone who occupies himself with the study of ancient cultures no longer can be justly compared to a seaman pressing forward through unknown waters not knowing whence he comes or whither he is going. Rather he is like the navigator who has suddenly become aware of the current he is sailing, and of his course from a definite past to a recognizable future. Yes, he even has some sense of the future, for the science of the past uniquely provides him, in its five thousand years of history, with a model, in terms of which he can extrapolate the future.

All of us live within our heritage of five thousand years of history. Were this not so, we would be no different from the ahistorical Australian bushman. The white construction-worker in an Australian city may never have heard of the name Archimedes. This is of no importance. Important is the fact that he makes use of the laws formulated by Archimedes.

It may be that the learned men of the Middle Ages who called themselves "humanists" completely misunderstood Greek and Roman antiquity. But the important thing to remember is that through their intervention the dead doings and thought processes of ancient Greek and Rome became a social stimulus. Perhaps the men and women of the *Mayflower* in 1620, and the Spaniards under Cortés and Pizarro who came to Middle and South America in 1519–32, were able to imagine beginning a new life on a new soil because the old and customary had been written down for them. It turned out that in migrating they did not lose their old life, but instead brought it along with them. To new continents came men who, in thought and feeling, in religion and in customs, in their attitudes toward life's basic institutions of love, marriage, work, and duty, and toward the principles of good and evil, of deity and devil, were at one with their past—and this regardless of whether they were conscious or unaware of the fact.

This has become the archæologist's grandiose task: to make dried-up wellsprings bubble forth again, to make the forgotten known again, the dead alive, and to cause to flow once more that historic stream in which we are all encompassed, whether we live in Brooklyn or Montparnasse, Berlin-Neukölln or Santiago de Chile, Athens or Miami. This stream is the great human community of the Western world which for five thousand years has swum with the same flood tide, under different flags, but guided by the same constellations.

On this account archæology is everybody's concern and is not in the least an esoteric special branch of science. When we busy ourselves with archæology, life as a whole has become our subject. For life is not an occasional affair, but a constant balancing on the point of intersection where past and future meet.[1]

In his memoirs the Roman antiquarian Augusto Jandolo tells how, as a boy, he participated with his father in the opening of an Etruscan sarcophagus. "It was no

[1] See "The Ideal Archæologist" by Leonard Woolley, in C. W. Ceram, ed.: *Hands On the Past* (New York: Alfred A. Knopf; 1966), p. 13.

easy matter, moving the cover," he writes, "but finally it was lifted upright, then allowed to fall heavily on the other side. And then something happened that I have never forgotten and that will remain before my eyes as long as I live. I saw resting within the coffin the body of a young warrior in full military panoply, with helmet, spear, shield, and greaves. Observe that it was not a skeleton that I saw, but a body, complete in all limbs, and stiffly outstretched as if freshly laid in the grave. This apparition endured but a moment. Then every thing seemed to dissolve in the light of the torches. The helmet rolled to the right, the round shield fell into the now sunken breast-piece of the armor, and the greaves suddenly collapsed flat on the ground, one to the right, one to the left. The body that had remained untouched for centuries had suddenly dissolved into dust when exposed to the air ... a golden dust was suspended in the air and about the flame of the torches."

In this sarcophagus described by Jandolo had lain a member of that mysterious Etruscan people whose origin and descent remain to this day undetermined. Yet the discoverers had only a passing glimpse of the body before it fell apart, never to be restored. Why? Gross carelessness caused this irreparable misfortune.

When the first statues were dug out of classic ground, long before the discovery of Pompeii, there

Singing reveler, decorative picture from inside a bowl attributed to the school of Epictetus.

existed even at that time people of sufficient enlightenment to see things of beauty as well as heathen idols in
the naked marble forms. Even so, as often as not when
they were put on display in the palaces of Renaissance
princes and cardinals and in the villas of doge, con-
dottiere, and parvenu, they were regarded as little more
than curiosities that it was the fashion to collect. It
could very well happen that in private museums of this
sort an antique statue of wondrous beauty would be
shown beside the dried embryo of a two-headed child.
Next to an antique relief it was quite possible to find
the skin of a bird that reputedly had lit on the shoulder
of St. Francis.

Up to the last century there was nothing to prevent the greedy and the ignorant from enriching themselves on whatever finds they chanced to discover, or to
stop them from inflicting great incidental damage in
their exploitations.

In the sixteenth century lime kilns were operated
in the Forum Romanum, the Roman place of assembly
and site of the most splendid buildings grouped about
the Capitol. The Roman temples were razed to provide
stone for building material. Pieces of marble were used
indiscriminately by the popes to decorate their fountains. The Serapeum was blown apart with gunpowder
to get stone for embellishing the stables housing the
stud horses of a pope named Innocent. For four centuries the Colosseum was used as a stone quarry. Even
as late as 1860 Pius IX continued this work of destruction to obtain cheap decorative materials for a Christian
building project.

Nineteenth- and twentieth-century archæologists
who studied ancient Rome had wreckage left to work
with, whereas had the monuments been intact, it would
have vastly facilitated their task.

Even where no incompetent hand had wantonly
destroyed, where no thieves had sought hidden treasure,
where the past lay untouched—and how rare this was—
still there were difficulties of another sort. For even

with perfect material the problem of interpretation has to be reckoned with.

In 1856 a cave was opened in Düsseldorf, and from it was taken the skeleton of a man who, according to the geological circumstances of the find, must have lived in remotest prehistory. Today we call this skeleton the Neanderthal man. At the time, however, it was thought to be the remains of an animal. Only a certain Dr. Fuhlrott, a secondary school teacher in the provincial town of Elberfeld, interpreted this find correctly. A Professor Mayer of Bonn declared that the bones belonged to a Cossack killed in 1814. Wagner, of Göttingen, maintained that the skeleton was that of an old Hollander; and Pruner-Bey, of Paris, that of an old Celt. The great German pathologist Virchow, whose too rashly accepted authority retarded so many sciences, said that the skeleton was that of a gouty old man.

It took about fifty years for the scientific establishment to decide that the schoolteacher from Elberfeld had been right.

This example, of course, more properly belongs to prehistoric and anthropological research than to archæology. A more apt illustration, perhaps, is the early attempt to date the Greek sculpture called the Laocoön. Winckelmann placed the statue in the period of Alexander the Great. Experts of the last century believed it to be a masterpiece of the Rhodian school, and dated it c. 150 B.C. Others contended that it had been created in early imperial days. Today we know that actually it was the composite work of the sculptors Agesander, Polydorus, and Athenodorus of the Rhodian school, a group of artists who flourished about the middle of the last century before Christ.

And so it is obvious that even when material is found intact, interpretation is difficult enough. How much more difficult, then, when the genuineness of the artifact itself is in doubt!

Into this category of the dubious falls the sort of tomfoolery that victimized Professor Beringer of Würz-

burg. In 1726 the professor published a book with a
Latin title that I shall not give here for the reason that
it covers one and a half pages. The book tells about the
fossils that Beringer and his students found in the
vicinity of Würzburg. The text describes petrified flowers, frogs, a spider in the act of catching a fly (spider
and fly petrified simultaneously); also a petrified star, a
half-moon, tables with Hebraic characters, and other
curious objects. The book was richly illustrated. The
reader could see engraved on copper the very things
described verbally in the text. This work was comprehensive in scope and contained a running commentary
in which the professor's intellectual enemies were subjected to invective and counter-attack. It was widely
read and came in for much praise—until the horrid
truth was revealed. Schoolboys had been playing an
elaborate practical joke on the innocent Beringer. Working at home, they had carefully manufactured "fossils,"
and these they had planted where the professor was
sure to dig.

Beringer's name brings to mind that of Domenech.
This French abbé published in 1860 a curious volume
that is preserved in the Paris Arsenal Library. It contains 228 plates showing, in facsimile, what the author
called the "*manuscrit pictographique américain.*" These
supposedly Indian drawings later turned out to be the
crude products of a child of Low German settlers in
the American backwoods.

Even the great Winckelmann was duped—by Casanova's brother. This Casanova, an artist, had been engaged to illustrate Winckelmann's *Monumenti antichi.*
In Naples Casanova produced three paintings, one of
which showed Jupiter and Ganymede, the others dancing female figures. These he sent to Winckelmann,
boldly claiming that they had been taken from walls in
Pompeii. To make his story more credible he embellished it with romantic details. An officer had secretly
stolen the paintings piece by piece. Mortal danger, dark

nights, shadows of the tomb—Casanova made a production. And Wickelmann was completely taken in.

He believed not only in the genuineness of the paintings, but in Casanova's story as well. In the fifth section of his *History of the Art of Antiquity* he wrote an exact description of the find and maintained that the Ganymede in particular was a painting "the like of which had never been found before." In that he was not far from wrong, seing that after Casanova he was indeed the first ever to look at it. "Jupiter's favorite," he wrote, "is undoubtedly one of the most beautiful figures to come down to us from ancient times. I know of nothing to compare with the face of this figure; it is instinct with sensual bliss, as if all life were but one long kiss."

If the hypercritical Winckelmann could be fooled by such deceptions, who could ever be sure to escape them? In our own times a Russian archæologist has shown how confusing interpretation can be. For what appeared to be a relatively simple marble statue from Herculaneum he listed nine different identifications, all of them arguable.

The art of not being fooled, the method of determining the genuineness, the mode, and the history of an artifact from a diversity of signs, is called hermeneutics. Whole libraries are filled with literature devoted exclusively to the interpretation of known classic finds. It is possible to track down a single line of interpretation from Winckelmann's initial attempt to the controversies of modern scholars over the same object. Archæologists are pathfinders. With a detective's sharpness of observation they fit stone to stone—often literally—until the logical conclusion stands out clear and irrefutable.

Is their task easier than the criminologist's? They deal with dead objects, which offer no resistance, which do not purposely mislead or leave false trails behind. And, true enough, dead stones are open to anyone's

inspection. But how much error is already inherent in
them? How many mistakes have been made in the first
reports of the find? No archæologist can closely examine all remains in the original, scattered as they are
throughout Europe and all the museums of the world.
Today photography can give a precise copy, but in fact
much material has yet to be photographed. Drawings
must still be used in many cases, and these may be
subjectively miscolored and misconceived, especially
when made by persons unversed in mythology or archæology.

On a sarcophagus kept in the Louvre in Paris is an
Amor and Psyche group in which the right forearm of
Amor is broken off, but with the right hand still caress-
ing Psyche's cheek. Two French archæologists published
a work with an illustration in which this hand is shown
as a beard. Psyche with whiskers!

Despite the patent absurdity of the drawing, another Frenchman, author of the Louvre catalogue,
writes: "The sculptor who worked on this sarcophagus
did not understand the theme, for his Psyche, though
dressed like a woman, wears a beard."

In Venice there is a relief that, in a series of
scenes, shows two boys leading two oxen harnessed to
a cart in which stands a woman. This relief was restored
about one hundred and fifty years ago. The interpreters
of the period considered the relief to be an illustration
for a tale from Herodotus. Herodotus tells hows Ky-
dippe, priestess of Hera, had two sons, who, the usual
oxen not being available, harnessed themselves to the
cart used to bear her to the temple. The mother,
touched by this act of filial devotion, prayed that the
gods would grant her sons the greatest happiness known
to mortals. Hera, with the questionable approval of the
other gods, caused the boys to fall gently asleep, never
to awaken; for easy death in early youth was the sweet-
est boon available to mankind.

The relief was restored in terms of this legend. A
lattice at the woman's feet was made into a wagon with

a wheel, and a rope-end in one boy's hand became a
wagon-tongue. The ornamentation was enriched, the
contours of the sculpture developed, the depth of the
carving deepened. All manner of detail stemmed from
the new interpretation. The relief was dated on the
basis of the restoration—falsely dated. What had originally been pure ornamentation was assumed to be representative sculpture and treated accordingly. What
had been a temple was falsely identified as an ædicula,
or shrine. Herodotus' fable was inaccurately decked out
in many ways. The whole concept of the restoration
was wrong. Indeed, the relief had never illustrated a
story from Herodotus. Herodotus had never been "illustrated" at all in the works of antiquity. The cart was a
free invention on the restorer's part. It was provided
with ornamental spokes such as never had existed in
ancient times. The wagon-tongue and the strap about
the oxen were also pure inventions. And so this single
example shows how many misconstructions can arise
once one has strayed off the right track.

The writings of Herodotus are a bubbling spring
of information on antique works of art, their creators
and their dates. The works of ancient authors of all
periods are the foundation pillars of hermeneutics. Yet
how often archæologists have been misled by them!
For, after all, are not creative writers rightly concerned
with a higher truth than that of literal reality? Are they
not justified in using historical fact—and myth, of
course—as so much raw material subject to alteration
and reshaping according to their personal whim in order
to achieve an artistic form?

Authors lie, the literal man says. And if we conceive poetic license to be a lie, we must admit that the
ancient authors have erred quite as much in this respect
as later ones. The archæologist must use great effort to
cut his way through the thicket of data provided by
the ancients. For instance, to date the Olympian statue
of Zeus, most famous gold and ivory piece by Phidias,
it is important to know the circumstances of the sculp-

tor's death. Ephorus, Diodorus, Plutarch, and Philochorus all give different accounts. He is supposed to have died in prison, to have escaped, to have been executed in Elis, to have died peacefully in that city. Philochorus' version was finally confirmed by a papyrus published in translation at Geneva in 1910.

The above account gives some idea of the contrarieties the archæologist must oppose with shovel and much exercise of good judgment. To explain archæology's critical methods; the accepted ways of seeing, drawing, and describing; the interpretation of myths, literature, inscriptions, and coins; the correlative interpretative approach, which takes into account other sculptures, the location, physical arrangement, and mileu of the find—to go into all these matters would exceed the bounds of a single volume.

Take, for instance, the object illustrated below this paragraph. For the sake of those who find pleasure in testing their wits, I ask: What is it?—hastening to add that archæologists themselves have yet to agree on an answer.

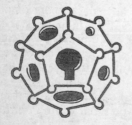

The mysterious dodecahedron
with the pentagonal ends.

Judging by its external appearance as shown in the picture, it is a bronze object shaped like a pentadodecahedron. Round openings of various sizes are found in the center of each face. The interior of the object is hollow. All specimens of this artifact have been found north of the Alps, which indicates a Roman origin.

One interpreter sees this mysterious thing as a mere toy; another as a die used in games of chance; a third as a model used in teaching the measurement of cylindrical bodies; a fourth as a candleholder.

What is it?

Since this book was first published, I have received over a hundred answers to this question from both experts and laymen all over the world. The experts' explanations tend to be quite authoritative in tone, though they contradict each other. The most probable solution—though far from established—is that we have here a musical instrument.

# 4/SCHLIEMANN (I):
## A MERCHANT DIGS FOR TROJAN GOLD

Now comes a fairy tale, the story of the poor boy who at the age of seven dreamed of finding a city, and who thirty-nine years later went forth, sought, and found not only the city but also treasure such as the world had not seen since the loot of the conquistadors.

This fairy tale is the life of Heinrich Schliemann, one of the most astounding personalities not only among archæologists but among all men to whom any science has ever been indebted.

It began this way: A little boy stood at a grave in the cemetery of the little village where he was born, far up in the North German state of Mecklenburg. The grave was that of the monster Hennig. He was said to have roasted a shepherd alive, then to have kicked the victim for good measure after having broiled him. For this misdeed, it was said, each year Hennig's left foot, covered with a silk stocking, grew out of the grave like some strange plant.

The boy waited by the grave, but nothing happened. He went home and begged his father to dig up the grave and find out where the foot was that year.

The father, a poor clergyman, told the boy fables, fairy tales, and legends about, among other things, the battles fought by Homer's heroes, about Paris and Helen, Achilles and Hector, about mighty Troy, which was burned and leveled. For Christmas 1829 he gave his son Jerrer's *Illustrated History of the World*, which contained a picture showing Æneas holding his son by the hand and carrying his old father on his back as he

fled the burning citadel of Troy. The boy looked at the
massive walls and the great Scæan Gate. "Is that how
Troy looked?" he asked. The father nodded. "And it
is all gone, and nobody knows where it stood?" "That
is true," the father replied.

"But I don't believe that," said the boy, Heinrich
Schliemann. "When I am big, I shall go myself and
find Troy and the King's treasure."

The father laughed.

The prophecy of a seven-year-old became a reality. And
at the age of sixty-one, by which time he had become
a world-famous archæologist, he was still an enthusiast.
During a chance visit to his native village he actually
considered digging into the grave of the wicked Hennig.
And in the preface to his book *Ithaca* he wrote:

"When my father gave me a book on the main
events of the Trojan War and the adventures of Odysseus and Agamemnon—it was my Christmas present for
the year 1832—little did I think that thirty-six years
later I would offer the public a book on the same subject. And do this, moreover, after actually seeing with
my own eyes the scene of the war and the fatherland
of the heroes immortalized by Homer."

A child's first impressions stick with him throughout his life, but in Schliemann these impressions soon
passed beyond those left by parental recitals of classic
deeds. His schooling was finished at the age of fourteen, whereupon he was signed on as apprentice in a
grocery business in the little city of Fürstenberg. For
five and a half years he retailed herring, brandy, milk,
and salt. He ground up potatoes for distillation, and
swept up the shop at night. His work lasted from five
in the morning until night.

He all but forgot his father's stories. Then one day
a drunken miller's helper came into the store, hung
about the counter, and in a resounding voice declaimed verses filled with the scornful pathos that the
once-educated are wont to show toward intellectual
inferiors. Schliemann was enchanted, though not a

word did he understand. When he found out that the man was reciting from Homer's *Iliad*, he scraped a few pfennigs together and bought the drunkard a schnapps to get him to say the verses all over again.

Schliemann's youth was filled with adventure. In 1841 he went to Hamburg and was signed as cabin boy on a vessel bound for Venezuela. After fourteen days at sea the ship ran into a wild storm and foundered off the Dutch island of Texel in the North Sea. He made shore, but landed in a hospital, exhausted and in rags. A recommendation from a family friend enabled him to get employment as an office boy in Amsterdam.

In a miserable, unheated garret room he began his study of languages. Within two years, by an unusual method of self-teaching, he had mastered English, French, Dutch, Spanish, Portuguese, and Italian. "These exacting and strenuous studies," he says, "within a year had so strengthened my memory that the effort of learning Dutch, Spanish, Italian, and Portuguese seemed very easy. Six weeks spent on any one of these languages, and I could speak and write it fluently."

After being promoted to correspondent and bookkeeper with another Amsterdam firm doing business with Russia, in 1844, when only twenty-two years old, Schliemann began to learn Russian. But no one in the city, he found, could speak this most difficult of European languages. The only teaching aids he could pick up were an old grammar, a dictionary, and a poor translation of *Telemachus*.

He carried on imaginary conversations so loudly that he disturbed his neighbors. The walls shook when he declaimed pieces he had learned by heart from *Telemachus*. Other tenants complained, and twice he was forced to seek new lodgings. Finally he hit on the idea of providing himself with a critical audience and for this purpose hired a poor man, whom he paid four francs a week. This unfortunate fellow was required to sit on a chair and hear out long passages from *Telemachus*, not a word of which he understood. After six hectic weeks Schliemann was conversing fluently with

Russian merchants come to Amsterdam to attend the indigo auction.

He was as successful in business as in his language studies, though here luck undoubtedly played a part. Yet in fairness to Schliemann it must be said that he belonged to the few who know how to hold fast to the luck that comes everyone's way sooner or later. The indigent minister's son, the apprentice, the shipwrecked cabin boy, the office worker—and master of eight languages—became first a small wholesaler, then, with dizzying speed, a royal merchant. Invariably he picked the shortest road to commercial success. When only twenty-four years old he went to St. Petersburg as agent for his firm. This was in 1846. A year later he founded his own export-import business, all of which took time and a great deal of hard work.

"It was not until 1854 that I was able to learn Swedish and Polish," he writes. He made extensive trips, one to North America in 1850. During that year, while he was there, the admission of California into the United States automatically gave him American citizenship. Like so many others, he was carried away by the gold-rush fever. He set up a bank for dealing in gold. Already he was a man of sufficient status to be received by the President of the United States. "About seven o'clock I was driven to visit the President of the U.S.A. I told him how my desire to see this splendid country and to make the acquaintance of its great leader had led me to travel here all the way from Russia. My first and most important duty was to pay my respects to him, I said. He received me warmly, introduced me to his wife and daughter and father, and I talked with him for an hour and a half."

But soon thereafter Schliemann came down with a fever. In the end, uneasiness over the weird, lawless customers he had to deal with drove him back to St. Petersburg. In those years he was indeed a gold seeker, just as one of his biographers, Emil Ludwig, described him.

Yet his letters of that period and his two autobiographies reveal him always and everywhere in the relentless grip of that childhood dream to find and explore the distant scenes where Homer's heroes had performed their great deeds. This obsession even gave him, probably the most gifted student of languages in his century, a peculiar inhibition regarding the study of Greek. Fearing that he might fall under its spell and abandon his business before he had created a sound foundation for the free pursuit of his quest, he did not begin his study of modern Greek until 1856. He achieved it within his usual six weeks; in another three months, he had mastered the intricacies of Homeric hexameters. How did he do it? "I have thrown myself so wholly into the study of Plato that, if he were to receive a letter from me six weeks hence, he would be bound to understand it."

Twice in the following years he was on the verge of actually treading on earth hallowed by Homeric song. On a trip to the second cataract of the Nile, by way of Palestine, Syria, and Greece, only a sudden illness prevented him from visiting the island of Ithaca. On this journey he learned Latin and Arabic. His diaries are written in the language of the country where he chanced to be. In 1864 he was again on the point of paying a visit to Trojan lands, but instead decided on a two-year trip around the world, the fruit of which was his first book, written in French.

By this time he was financially independent. The pastor's son from Mecklenburg had developed an uncanny busines sense. "My enterprises had been wonderfully blessed by Heaven," he says with unconcealed pride, "to such a degree that by the end of the year 1863 I was already in possession of means far beyond my most ambitious expectations." And to this he added, in a casual tone that would sound overweening in anyone but Heinrich Schliemann: "I [now] retired from business so that I could devote myself entirely to the studies that so completely fascinated me."

In 1868 he went to Ithaca, through the Peloponnesus and the Troad. The introduction to his *Ithaca* is

dated December 31, 1868. The subtitle reads: *Archæological Investigations of Heinrich Schliemann.*

A photograph of Schliemann taken during his St.
Petersburg days shows him as a prosperous gentleman
wearing a heavy fur cloak. On the back of this picture,
which he sent to a forester's wife whom he had known
when she was a little girl, is an inscription that reads:
"Photograph of Henry [*sic*] Schliemann, formerly apprentice with Herr Hückstaedt in Fürstenberg; now
wholesale merchant in the Imperial Guild of St. Petersburg, hereditary honorary freeman, Judge of the St.
Petersburg Commercial Court, and director of the Imperial State Bank of St. Petersburg."

Is it not a fairy tale? That a highly successful businessman should burn all his bridges behind him in
order to make a youthful dream come true? That,
armed with little but his knowledge of Homer, he
should dare challenge the science of his day? That he
should pit his beliefs against the doubters and the
philologists, preferring pick and shovel to the bookish
approach?

In Schliemann's day, Homer was thought of as the
legendary bard of a prehistoric age. Scholars took no
more stock in his facts than they did in his very existence. Until that much later time when someone
boldly called Homer the first war correspondent, his
reporting of the struggle for Priam's citadel was rated,
for historical accuracy, about on a par with the ancient
sagas, if not relegated to the shadow realm of myth.

For does not the *Iliad* begin with the story of "far-
darting Apollo," who set a deadly sickness into the
Achæan ranks? And did not Zeus himself intervene in
the Trojan War, and likewise "lily-armed Hera"? And
did not gods turn into mortals, susceptible to fleshly injury? Even Aphrodite was not immune from the cut of
a bronze spearpoint. Myth, saga, legend—illuminated
by the divine spark of one of the world's greatest poets!

In the *Iliad* Greece is portrayed as a highly cultured land. Yet when the Greeks appeared in recorded

history they were a simple and numerically small people. Their kings were not powerful, they did not have great fleets of vessels. And so in Schliemann's day it was much easier to believe that Homeric Greece was a poetic myth than to give credence to the idea that a Homeric epoch of high culture had preceded the youthful barbarism out of which, by historical record, the noble Hellenic culture unfolded.

Such considerations failed to shake Schliemann's belief, dreamer as he was in Homeric mists. He read Homeric poetry as bare reality. He believed implicitly. This was as true when he was forty-six as it had been when, as a boy, he had been fascinated by the picture of the fleeing Æneas.

When Schliemann read Homer's description of the Gorgon shield of Agamemnon and was told that the buckler strap had been decorated with a figure of a three-headed snake, he accepted all this as gospel truth. The chariots, weapons, and household articles portrayed in detail by Homer were for him part and parcel of ancient Greece. Were all these heroes—Achilles and Patroclus, Hector and Æneas—and this pageant of friendship, hate, love, and high adventure, nothing but mere invention? Schliemann did not think so; to his mind such people and such scenes had actually existed. He was conscious that all Greek antiquity, including the great historians Herodotus and Thucydides, had accepted the Trojan War as an actual event, and its famous names as historical personages.

Carrying his belief in Homer before him like a banner, in his forty-sixth year the millionaire Heinrich Schliemann set forth directly for the kingdom of the Achæans, not even bothering, en route, to explore modern Greece. It is of symbolic interest that almost the first native Greek he got to know was an Ithacan blacksmith whose wife was introduced to him as Penelope, his sons as Odysseus and Telemachus. We can only imagine how he must have been fired by this auspicious omen.

Incredible as it may seem, this actually happened: the rich and eccentric foreigner one evening sat in the village square and read the Twenty-third Book of the *Odyssey* to the descendants of those who had been dead for three thousand years. Overcome by emotion, he wept, and the villagers wept with him.

The majority of contemporary scholars believed that the site of ancient Troy—if Troy had existed at all—was near a little village called Bunarbashi. This remote hamlet was distinguished, as it still is today, by the odd fact that each house had as many as twelve stork nests on its roof. At Bunarbashi were two springs, on which account some more daring archæologists were inclined to give credence to the idea that eventually ancient Troy might possibly be located thereabouts. For it is written in Homer, in the twenty-second song of the *Iliad* (verses 147–52):

> "...And [they] came to the two fair-flowing springs, where two fountains rise that feed deep-eddying Skamandros. The one floweth with warm water, and smoke goeth up there from around us as it were from a blazing fire, while the other even in summer floweth forth like cold hail or snow or ice that water formeth."

For a fee of forty-five piasters Schliemann hired a local guide and rode out bareback to have his first look at the land of his boyhood dreams. "I admit," he says, "that I could scarcely control my emotion when I saw the tremendous plain of Troy spread out before me, a scene that had haunted my earliest childhood dreams."

But this first impression was enough to convince him, believing literally in Homer as he did, that Bunarbashi was not the site of ancient Troy. For the locality was fully three hours away from the coast, and Homer describes his heroes as able to travel back and forth several times daily between their moored ships and the beleaguered city. Nor did it seem likely to Schliemann that a great palace of sixty-two rooms would ever have been built on such a small knoll. The setting was not right for cyclopean walls, breached by a massive gate through which the crafty Greeks entered in a wooden horse.

Schliemann examined the springs of Bunarbashi, and was surprised to find that in a space of 1,650 feet he could count not merely two—the number mentioned by Homer—but thirty-four of them. Even so, his guide assured him that he had miscounted. Actually there were forty. For that very reason, the guide pointed out, the region was called "Kirk Giös"—that is, "Forty Eyes."

Schliemann made a careful survey of the country-side in his *Iliad* and reread the verses telling how Achilles, the "brave runner," chased Hector three times around the fortress of Priam, "with all the gods looking on." Following Homeric directions as best he could, Schliemann traced out a likely course about the hill. At one point, however, he encountered a drop so steep that he had to crawl down it backwards on all fours. Since, in Schliemann's view, Homer's description of the landscape was as exact as a military map, surely the poet would have mentioned the incline had his heroes scrambled down it three times "in hasty flight."

With watch in one hand and Homer in the other, he paced out the road between what were purported to be the two hills securing Troy, this road winding through the foothills to the shore off which the Achæan ships were supposed to have been anchored. He also re-enacted the movements of the first day of battle in the Trojan War, as portrayed in the second to the seventh songs of the *Iliad*. He found that if Troy had been located at Bunarbashi, the Achæans would have had to cover at least fifty-two miles during the first nine hours of battle.

The complete absence of ruins clinched his doubts about the site. He could not even turn up any potsherds. Elsewhere, in Ithaca, potsherds had been found in such quantity that someone had remarked: "Judging by the archæologists' findings in graves, the ancients must have spent most of their time patching up broken vases. Low creatures that they were, before going out of existence they smashed everything to smithereens, to be sure to leave their finest pieces behind in the form of jigsaw puzzles."

"Mycenæ and Tiryns," Schliemann wrote in 1868, "were destroyed 2,335 years ago, but their ruins are of such solid construction that they can last another 10,000 years." And Troy was destroyed only 722 years earlier. It seemed highly unlikely that the cyclopean walls described by Homer would have disappeared without a trace. Yet in the environs of Bunarbashi there was not a sign of ancient masonry.

Ruins there were aplenty, however, in other not too distant places. Even the untrained eye could not miss them at New Ilium, now called Hissarlik—which means "Palace"—a town some two and a half hours northward from Bunarbashi and only one hour from the coast. Twice Schliemann examined the flat top of the mound at Hissarlik, a rectangular plateau about 769 feet long on each side. This preliminary survey pretty well satisfied his mind that he had located ancient Troy.

He began to cast about for proof and discovered that others shared his opinion, among which minority was Frank Calvert, American vice-consul, but English by birth. Calvert owned a part of the mound of Hissarlik and had a villa there. Having excavated on his own account, he was inclined to agree with Schliemann, but had never given much thought to the consequences of the idea. The Scottish scholar C. MacLaren, and Eckenbrecher, a German, were other voices that had called out unheard in the wilderness.

And how about the wells mentioned in Homer, which were the main prop of the Bunarbashi theory? For a short while Schliemann wavered when he found no springs at all at Hissarlik, in striking contrast to his discovery of thirty-four at Bunarbashi. It was Calvert who helped him over this difficulty. Calvert pointed out that in this volcanic region he had heard of several hot springs suddenly drying up, only to reappear after a short period. And so Schliemann casually cast aside everything that hitherto had seemed so important to the scholars. Moreover, the running fight between Hector and Achilles was plausible enough in the Hissarlik setting, where the hill sloped gently. To circle the city three times at Hissarlik they would have had to run nine miles. This feat, Schliemann thought, was not beyond the powers of warriors caught up in the heat of a grudge fight.

Again Schliemann was more influenced in his thinking by the judgment of the ancients than by the scholarship of his day. He recalled how Herodotus had reported that Xerxes once visited New Ilium to look at the remains of "Priam's Pergamos," and there to sacrifice a thousand cattle to the Ilian Minerva. According to Xenophon, Mindares, the Lacedæmonian general, had done the same. Arrian had written that Alexander the Great, after making an offering at New Ilium, took weapons away with him and ordered his bodyguard to carry them in battle for luck. Beyond this, Cæsar had done much for New Ilium, partly because he admired Alexander, partly because he believed himself to be a descendant of the Ilians.

Had they all been misled by a dream? By the bad reporting of their day?

At the end of a chapter in which he has piled up evidence in support of his views, Schliemann abruptly abandons his scholarly argument to gaze, enchanted, at the ancient landscape. He writes, as he might have cried out when a boy: ". . . and this I should like to add, that no sooner has one set foot on Trojan soil than one is astonished to see that this noble mound of Hissarlik seems to have been intended by Nature herself to be the site of a great citadel. If well fortified, the location would command the whole plain of Troy.

In the whole region there is no point comparable with this one.

"Looking out from Hissarlik, one can see Ida, from whose summit Jupiter looked down on the city of Troy."

And now a man possessed went to work. All the energy that had made him a millionaire, Schliemann concentrated on realizing his dream. Ruthlessly he squandered his material means and strength.

In 1869 he had married a Greek girl named Sophia Engastromenos, who was as beautiful as his image of Helen. Soon Sophia, too, was absorbed in the great task and was sharing his fatigues, hardships, and worries. He began to dig at Hissarlik in April 1870. In 1871 he dug for two months, and another four and a half months in the two succeeding years. He had a hundred workers at his disposal. All this time he was restlessly active. Nothing could hold him down, neither deadly mosquito-borne fevers and bad water nor the recalcitrance of the laborers. He prodded dilatory authorities, he ignored the incomprehension of narrow-minded experts who mocked him as a fool, and worse.

The Temple of Athena had stood on the highest ground in the city, and Poseidon and Apollo had built the walls of Pergamos—so it was recorded in Homer. Therefore the temple should be located in the middle of the mound, Schliemann reasoned, and somewhere round about, on the original level ground, would be the walls constructed by the gods. He struck into the mound, boldly ripping down walls that to him seemed unimportant. He found weapons and household furnishings, ornaments and vases, overwhelming evidence that a rich city had once occupied the spot. And he found something else as well, something that for the first time caused Heinrich Schliemann's name to speed around the world. Under the ruins of New Ilium he disclosed other ruins, under these still others. The hill was like a tremendous onion, which he proceeded to dismember layer by layer. Each layer seemed to have been inhabited at a different period. Populations had lived and died, cities had been built up only to fall into decay. Sword and fire had raged, one civilization cutting off another, and again and again a city of the living had been raised on a city of the dead.

Each day brought a new surprise. Schliemann had gone forth to find Homeric Troy, but as time went on he and his workers discovered no less than seven buried cities, then two more; nine glimpses, all told, of primitive ages that previously had not been known to exist.

The question now arose which of these nine cities was the Troy of Homer, of the heroes and the epic war. It was clear that the bottommost level had been a prehistoric city, much the oldest in the series, so old that the inhabitants had not known the use of metals. And the uppermost level had to be the most recent, and no doubt consisted of the remains of the New Ilium where Xerxes and Alexander had made sacrifice.

Schliemann dug and searched. In the second and third levels from the bottom he found traces of fire, the remains of massive walls, and the ruins of a gigantic gate. He was sure that these walls had once enclosed the palace of Priam, and that he had found the famous Scæan Gate.

He unearthed things that were treasures from the scientific point of view. Part of this material he shipped home, part he gave over to experts for examination, material that yielded a detailed picture of the Trojan epoch, the portrait of a people.

It was Heinrich Schliemann's triumph, and the triumph, too, of Homer. He had succeeded, the enthusiastic amateur, in demonstrating the actual existence of what had always counted as mere saga and myth, a figment of the poetic fancy.

A wave of excitement coursed through the intellectual world. Schliemann, whose workers had moved more than 325,000 cubic yards of earth, had earned a breathing spell. Presently, his interests meanwhile having turned to other projects, he set June 15, 1873 as the date for the termination of the diggings. On the day before the last shovelful of earth was to be turned, he found a treasure that crowned his labors with a golden splendor, to the delight of the watching world.

It happened dramatically. Even today, reading about this amazing discovery takes one's breath away. The discovery was made during the early hours of a hot morning. Schliemann, accompanied by his wife, was supervising the excavation. Though no longer seriously expectant of finding anything, nevertheless out of habit he was still keeping close watch on the workmen's every move. They were down twenty-eight feet, at the lower level of the masonry that Schliemann identified with Priam's palace. Suddenly his gaze was held spellbound. He began to act as if under compulsion. No one can say what the thievish workers would have done if they had seen what met Schliemann's astonished eyes. He seized his wife by the arm. "Gold!" he whispered. She looked at him in amazement. "Quick," he said. "Send the men home at once." The lovely Greek stammered a protest. "No buts," he told her. "Tell them anything you want. Tell them today is my birthday, that I've just remembered, and that they can all have the rest of the day off. Hurry up, now, hurry!"

The workers left. "Get your red shawl!" Schliemann said to his wife as he jumped down into the hole. He went to work with his knife like a demon. Massive blocks of stone, the debris of millennia, hung perilously over his head, but he paid no attention to the danger. "With all possible speed I cut out the treasure with a large knife," he writes. "I did this by dint of strenuous effort, and in the most frightful danger of losing my life; for the heavy citadel wall, which I had to dig under, might have crashed down on me at any moment. But the sight of so many immeasurably priceless objects made me foolhardy and I did not think of the hazards."

There was the soft sheen of ivory, the jingle of gold. Schliemann's wife held open the shawl to be filled

with Priam's treasure. It was the golden treasure of one
of the mightiest kings of prehistory, gathered together
in blood and tears, the ornaments of a godlike people,
buried for three thousand years until dug from under
the ruined walls of seven vanished kingdoms. Not for
one moment did Schliemann doubt that he had found
Priam's treasure-trove. And not until shortly before his
death was it proved that Schliemann had been misled
in the heat of enthusiasm. Troy lay neither in the second nor in the third layer (see page 479). The treasure
had belonged to a king who antedated Priam by a
thousand years (see Plate III).

Like thieves the Schliemanns spirited their find
into a wooden hut on the site, and there spread everything out on a rough wooden table. There were diadems
and brooches, chains, plates, buttons, golden wire and
thread, and bracelets. "Apparently someone in Priam's
family had hastily packed away the treasure in boxes
and carried them out without even taking time to remove the keys from the locks. Then, on the walls, this
person met his death either directly at enemy hands or
when struck down by a flying missile. The treasure lay
where it fell, and presently was buried under five or six
feet of ashes and stones from the adjacent royal house."

Schliemann, the fantast, took a pair of earrings
and a pendant and put them on his young wife, ornaments three thousand years old for the twenty-year-old
Greek. He stared at her. "Helen!" he breathed.

What to do now with this golden hoard? Schliemann allowed news of the find to get out, but by various adventurous means, aided by his wife's relatives,
was able to smuggle the treasure to Athens, thence out
of the country. When Schliemann's house was searched
and sealed on orders from the Turkish Ambassador, not
a trace of gold was found.

Was he a thief? The law regulating the disposal
of antiquities found in Turkish territory was loosely
framed, and highly subject to interpretation according
to the caprice of local officials. Having sacrificed his

whole career to the fulfillment of a dream, Schliemann could hardly be expected to be excessively scrupulous at this point in the game. He was determined to preserve his hoard of golden rarities for the delectation of European scholarship. Seventy years before, Thomas Bruce, Earl of Elgin and Kincardine, had set a precedent of sorts when he deliberately removed invaluable sculptures from the Parthenon. In Elgin's day Athens was still Turkish, as was Hissarlik in Schliemann's. Elgin had been given a Turkish firman, or license, that contained a clause stating that "nobody may hinder him from removing carved figures from the Acropolis, or inscribed blocks of stone." On the strength of this clause Elgin acted boldly. Two hundred cases filled with material from the Parthenon were shipped to London. The legal battle over ownership of this incomparably beautiful collection dragged on for years. The marbles had cost Elgin £74,240, but the compensation voted him by Parliament amounted to only £35,000, not even half of his expenses.

When Schliemann retrieved the "treasure of Priam" from its hiding place, he felt that he had reached the pinnacle of his life. Could such brilliant success be improved on?

# 5/SCHLIEMANN (II):
## THE MASK OF AGAMEMNON

Certain lives are played out almost entirely on the level of hyperbole, lives in which successes accumulate so improbably that they defy belief. This is particularly true of the career of Heinrich Schliemann. His exploits were consistently fabulous. His archæological success reached three peaks, the first of which was the discovery of "Priam's treasure," the second the exploration of the royal tombs of Mycenæ.

One of the darkest and most sinister chapters in the semi-legendary history of ancient Greece is the impassioned story of the Pelopidæ of Mycenæ, especially that part of it dealing with Agamemnon's return and death. For ten years Agamemnon had been away, laying siege to Troy, and Ægisthus had made good use of his absence.

> *We were yet*
> *Afar, enduring the hard toils of war,*
> *While he, securely couched in his retreat*
> *At Argos, famed for steeds, with flattering words*
> *Corrupted Agamemnon's queen.*

Ægisthus ordered a lookout to be kept for the returning husband and then lay in wait with twenty men. He invited Agamemnon to a banquet—"thinking shameful knavery"—and "struck him down at the banquet, as one slaughters the ox at the crib. None of Agamemnon's friends escaped, all following him." Eight years passed before Orestes, the filial avenger, appeared to kill his adulterous mother, Clytemnestra, and Ægisthus, his father's assassin.

Tragic poets have often dramatized this famous theme. Æschylus' most powerful play deals with the story of Agamemnon. In our own time Eugene O'Neill and Jean-Paul Sartre, among others, have written plays based on the story of Orestes and his family. The memory of the "king of men," ruler of the Peloponnesus, one of the mightiest and richest of historical characters, has remained forever green in posterity's mind.

Mycenæ had golden as well as sanguinary connotations. According to Homer, Troy was rich, but Mycenæ even richer, and the word *golden* was the adjective that he characteristically used in describing the city. Enchanted by his discovery of Priam's treasure, Schliemann was eager to find new riches. And—contrary to universal expectation—this he actually did. Mycenæ lies "in the farthest corner of Argos, pasture land of horses," halfway to "the Isthmus of Corinth." Viewed from the west, the former royal citadel is seen as a field of ruins, among them the remains of heavy walls. Behind these ruins, rising at first gently, then steeply, is Mount Eubœa, capped by the Chapel of the Prophet Elijah.

About A.D. 170 the Greek travel writer Pausanias visited the spot and described what he saw there. Then there was still more than what greeted Schliemann's nineteenth-century eyes. Yet the archæological problem at Mycenæ was simpler than at Troy. There was no doubt whatever about the site of the city called Mycenæ. The dust of thousands of years covered the ruins, and sheep were grazing where once kings had held sway. Still, the ruins were there to behold, mutely testifying to the splendor and majesty of yesteryear.

The Lion Gate, main palace entrance, stood high and open in full view. Accessible, too, were the so-called "treasuries," once thought to be bakers' ovens, the most famous of which was that of Atreus, first Pelopid and father of Agamemnon. This subterranean room is fifty feet high, and shaped like a dome. It is constructed of concentric rings of stones laid flat, and crowned by a single capstone (see cross section, below).

Schliemann found that several ancient authors had located the graves of Agamemnon and his murdered friends at Mycenæ. The citadel site was obvious enough, but the graves were another matter entirely. Schliemann had found Troy by depending on his Homer. In this instance he staked his claim on a certain passage in Pausanias, which he declared previous archæologists had incorrectly translated and misunderstood. Up to this it had been assumed—and two of the greatest experts of the day, Dodwell, an Englishman, and Curtius, a German, supported the idea—that Pausanias had pictured the graves as outside the walls of the citadel of Mycenæ, but Schliemann maintained that they must be inside the walls. He had already expressed this opin-

Cross section and ground plan of the
"Treasŭry of Atreus."

ion in his *Ithaca*, in keeping with his tendency to place more stock in the writings of the ancients than in scientific deliberation. In any event, speculation, as he saw it, was irrelevant. He went ahead and dug, and his diggings shortly proved that again he was on the right track.

"I began the great work on August 7, 1876, with 63 workers. . . . Since August 19 I have carried on the excavating with 125 laborers and four carts, on the average, and have made good progress."

Indeed, the first important find, after he had uncovered an enormous number of vases, was a curious circular structure, made of a double row of stone slabs set on edge. Schliemann believed immediately that the stone circle was a bench on which the elders of the Mycenæan citadel had sat in the agora while addressing assemblies, taking counsel, and dispensing justice. Here, he believed, Euripides' herald had stood—as recorded in *Electra*—while he called the people to the agora.

"Learned friends" confirmed his view. Presently he found the following sentence in Pausanias, relating, to be sure, to another agora: "Here they built the place of senatorial assembly, in such fashion that the heroes' graves would be in the midst of the meeting-place." Thereafter he knew with the same somnambulistic certainty that had led him safely through six layered cities to the "treasure of Priam" that he was standing on Agamemnon's grave.

And when, in short order, he found nine stelæ, four of them with well-preserved bas-reliefs, his last doubt vanished, and with it, too, all scholarly restraint. "Indeed, I do not hesitate for a moment," he wrote, "to announce that here I have found the graves that Pausanias, following tradition, ascribes to Atreus, to Agamemnon, king among men, to his charioteer, Eurymedon, and to Cassandra and her companions."

Meanwhile the work on the treasuries near the Lion Gate progressed slowly. Masses of stony rubble aggravated the difficulties of excavation. But here, too, Schliemann's mystical certainty would not be shaken. "I am convinced," he wrote, "of the absolute validity of the tradition which says that these mysterious structures were used as storage places for the treasure of primeval kings." The first find, taken from the debris that he had heaped to one side in an attempt to gain entrance, exceeded in delicacy of form, beauty of execution, and quality of material anything of a similar sort discovered in Troy. There were fragments of friezes, painted vases, terracotta idols of Hera, stone molds for casting ornamental articles, ("these apparently of gold and silver"), as well as glazed clay objects, gems, and beads.

The amount of work involved in the project is suggested by Schliemann's following observations: "So far as the diggings have progressed to date, nowhere do I find debris piled deeper than 26 feet, and this extreme depth only near the big circular wall. From that point the rock rises rapidly, and farther along the depth of the rubble notably diminishes, being anywhere from less than 13 to approximately 20 feet in thickness."

But the effort paid dividends.

The discovery of the first grave was noted in Schliemann's journal on December 6, 1876. The grave must have been opened with great care. For twenty-five days Sophia, the tireless helper, explored the earth with fingers and pocket-knife. Eventually five graves were found, in them the skeletons of fifteen dead. On the strength of this revelation Schliemann sent a cable to the King of Greece:

"It is with extraordinary pleasure that I announce to Your Majesty my discovery of the graves which, according to tradition, are those of Agamemnon, Cassandra, Eurymedon, and their comrades, all killed during the banquet by Clytemnestra and her lover, Ægisthus."

One skeleton after another came to light, the bones of heroes who had fought before Troy, only to be banished to the realm of fable by posterity. One can only imagine Schliemann's emotions when he looked into their faces, eaten away by time, but still recognizable as such, the eye sockets empty, noses gone, mouths twisted into a terrible smirk as if remembering some last frivolity. Flesh still clung to some of the bones.

Schliemann did not entertain the least doubt about his discoveries. "The bodies were literally covered with gold and jewels," he wrote at the time. Would such valuables have been interred with the bodies of ordinary persons, he inquired. He found expensively fashioned weapons, seemingly placed in the grave so that the dead would be armed against any contingency in the shadow world. Schliemann pointed to the obviously hasty burning of the corpses. The burial crew, it appeared, had hardly taken time to let the fire do its work before piling gravel and earth on the scorched victims. This implied the haste of murderers frantic to hide their crime. True, the corpses had been furnished with funerary gifts and accouterments, but this concession could be explained by the force of custom. As for the graves as such, they were anything but pretentious—indeed, as unworthy, one might imagine, of the rank of the deceased as hatred could make them. Had it not been said that the murdered were "thrown like the carcasses of unclean animals into miserable holes"?

Schliemann sought to buttress his identification of the graves by recourse to his beloved authorities, the writers of antiquity. He quoted from the *Agamemnon* of Æschylus, from Sophocles' *Electra*, from Euripides' *Orestes*. It simply did not occur to him to question the correctness of his notions. Today, however, we know that his theory was false. He had, it is true, found royal graves under the agora of Mycenæ; they were not, however, the graves of Agamemnon and his followers, but of people who most likely had lived some four hundred years earlier.

This discrepancy did not really matter. The important thing was that Schliemann had taken a second great step into the lost world of prehistory. Again he had proved Homer's worth as historian. He had unearthed treasures—treasures in a strictly archæological as well as material sense—which provided valuable insight into the matrix of our culture. "It is an entirely new and unsuspected world," Schliemann wrote, "that I am discovering for archæology."

Schliemann was a proud man, yet never arrogant or inconsiderate of others. Even at the height of success, when he was exchanging telegrams with kings and ministers, he was in touch with the humble side of his affairs. He could become violently incensed over an injustice done those whom he liked and trusted. Typical of this is the occasion when the Emperor of Brazil, among countless others, came to look at Mycenæ. Upon his departure the Emperor gave the police commander Leonardos the niggardly tip of forty francs to distribute among the police. The commander had always been loyal to Schliemann, and so Schliemann was much upset when it came to his ears that envious officials were spreading the story that Leonardos had actually been given a thousand francs, all of which, excepting forty, he had pocketed. When Leonardos, on account of this accusation, was relieved of his post, Schliemann moved into action. The world-famous investigator used all his influence in the interest of the obscure policeman, striking straight into the heart of the matter. Immediately he sent a wire to the Greek Minister of the Interior: "As countervalue for the many hundreds of millions by which I have enriched Greece, I pray you to do me the kindness of pardoning my friend the policeman Leonardos of Nauplion and of returning him to his post. Please do this for me, Schliemann." When he failed to get an immediate reply, he sent off a second telegram: "I swear the policeman Leonardos is honest and efficient. Nothing but calumny. Guarantee that he got only forty francs. I demand justice." And more than this, he did the most extravagant thing possible. He also sent a telegram to the Emperor of Brazil, who meanwhile had landed in Cairo. This telegram said:

"Upon leaving Nauplion, Your Majesty gave the police commander Leonardos forty francs to divide among the police. The mayor, in order to defame the brave fellow, claims that he received a thousand francs from Your Majesty. Leonardos has been removed from his office, and it was with difficulty that I was able to keep him out of jail. Since I have known him for ten years as one of the most honest people in the world, I beg Your Majesty in the holy name of truth and humanity to telegraph me, saying how much Leonardos got, forty francs or more."

Heinrich Schliemann, archæologist, in the name of justice put the Emperor of Brazil in the awkward position of having publicly to admit his stinginess. But the policeman Leonardos was saved.

The golden relics found by Schliemann were of enormous value, and not exceeded in opulence until Carnarvon's and Carter's finds in Egypt. "All the museums of the world taken together," Schliemann said, "do not have one fifth as much."

In the first of the five graves he found on each of three skeletons five diadems of pure gold, laurel leaves, and crosses of gold. In another grave, containing the remains of three women, he collected no less than seven hundred and one thick golden leaves, also wonderful ornaments in the shape of animals, flowers, butterflies, and cuttlefish. Besides these he found golden decorative pieces showing figured lions and other beasts, and warriors engaged in battle. There were precious pieces shaped like lions and griffons, others showing deer at repose, and women with doves. One of the skeletons wore a golden crown, on the fillet of which were fastened thirty-six golden leaves. The head wearing the crown had almost completely crumbled to dust. In another grave was a skeleton so near dissolution that only a fragment of the skull was still stuck to the elegant diadem at its head.

Most important of all, he found certain gold masks and breast-plates, which, according to tradition, were used in outfitting dead kings to protect them against malign influence after death. Down on his knees, his wife hovering over him ready to lend a helping hand, Schliemann scraped away the layers of clay sheathing the five corpses in the fourth grave. After a few hours' exposure to the air the heads of the skeletons dissolved into dust. But the shimmering golden masks kept their shape, each mask representing completely individual features, "so utterly different from idealized types of god and hero that unquestionably each of the same is a facsimile of the dead person's actual appearance."

Evenings, when the day was done and the shadows of night were creeping over the acropolis of Mycenæ, Schliemann had fires lit "for the first time in 2,344 years." Watchfires—recalling those which once had warned Clytemnestra and her lover, Ægisthus, of the approach of Agamemnon, but this time serving to frighten thieves away from the greatest treasures ever taken from the grave of dead kings.

# 6/SCHLIEMANN (III):
## CONFLICT WITH THE SCHOLARS

Schliemann's third series of excavations failed to reveal any more buried gold. However, they brought to light an ancient castle at Tiryns. Schliemann's discoveries here, together with what he had already turned up at Mycenæ, and the additional finds made a decade later by Arthur Evans on Crete, made possible the world's first picture of the prehistoric Minoan culture that once dominated the Mediterranean littoral.

But something must first be said about Schliemann's situation in his own time. Then as now, the pioneer in any field may find himself in a crossfire between the public and the specialists. Schliemann's reports were addressed to an audience very different from that to whom Winckelmann sent his communications. The eighteenth-century man of letters wrote for an elite, the chosen few who either owned museum collections or, as members of a court circle, had access to one. This exclusive little world was staggered by the discovery of Pompeii, and thrilled to hear of even a single statue unearthed. But its interest never moved beyond the parquet level of polite æstheticism. Winckelmann's influence was far-reaching, but only because poets and other writers as self-appointed intermediaries spread it from the rarefied sphere of the cultured aristocrats to all the levels and distances of his time.

Schliemann had no intermediary. He went directly to the nineteenth-century public. He publicized each one of his discoveries, being himself their greatest admirer. His letters went out to all the world; his articles into all the papers. Schliemann would have been a natural user of radio, film, and television had they existed in his time. His finds on the site of ancient Troy created a furore not only within the enclave of the cultured but everywhere. Winckelmann's descriptions of statues had appealed to æsthetes and connoisseurs. Schliemann's discoveries of gold electrified an era of industrial empire builders enjoying a wave of prosperity, entrepreneurs who had made their own way and whose natural sympathies and common sense placed them on the side of the "self-made" pioneering layman against the purists of the academic establishment who might turn away from him.

Regarding Schliemann's newspaper reports of 1873, a museum director wrote a few years afterward: "At the time of these reports great excitement prevailed among scholars and public alike. Everywhere, in the home and on the street, in the post coach and the railway car, the talk was of Troy. People were filled with astonishment and questions."

If Winckelmann, in the words of Herder, showed us "the mystery of the Greeks from afar," then Schliemann had now uncovered their prehistory. He had dared to bring archæology out from under the scholar's oil lamp into the sun of the Hellenic sky, to solve the problem of Troy with his spade. With one step he moved from the guarded precinct of classical philology into the very life of prehistory, incidentally enlarging and enriching an academic discipline with the gift of that life.

The tempo in which this revolution was accomplished, his mounting achievements, Schliemann's ambiguous image—not quite a businessman, not quite a scholar, and yet such an extraordinary success at both—and the "notoriety-seeking" air of his publications all shocked the world of scholarship, especially the German one. The extent of the disturbance may be gauged by the fact that ninety publications about Troy and Homer were fired off by scholars during the years of Schliemann's activity. The prime target of their philippics was his dilettantism. In the history of archæological excavations we will encounter, time and again, the academic archæologists who made life miserable for outsiders daring to provide the impetus for a fresh leap into the unknown. Since the attacks on Schliemann were made "on principle," a few relevant words must be said and cited at this point. First, let a rather disgruntled philosopher, Arthur Schopenhauer, have the floor:

> "Dilettantes, dilettantes!—is what those who pursue a science or an art for love and the delight they take in it, *per il loro diletto*, are disdainfully called by those who pursue it only for gain, because *they* delight only in the money that is to be made by it. Their disdain is based upon their vile conviction that no one will devote himself seriously to anything if he is not driven to it by necessity, hunger, or greed. The general public has the same outlook and the same opinion: hence its wholehearted respect for the 'professionals' and its distrust of dilettantes. But the truth is that to the dilettante the subject is an end in itself, while to the professional it is only the means to an end. But only the man who cares about something in itself, who loves it and does it *con amore*, will do it in all seriousness. The highest achievement has always been that of such men, and not of the hacks who serve for pay."

Professor Wilhelm Dörpfeld, Schliemann's collaborator, adviser, and friend, one of the few specialists that Germany placed at his side, wrote as late as 1932: "Yet he never did understand the scorn and derision with which several scholars, German philologists in particular, accompanied his work in Troy and Ithaca. I also found this derision, which a number of great scholars later on vouchsafed to my own excavations at Homeric sites as well, always regrettable and not only unjustified, but really quite unscientific."

The professional's mistrust of the successful out-

sider is the mediocrity's mistrust of the genius. The man
of ordered life looks down his nose at the rover of un-
trodden, uninsured pathways who, in the words of
Martin Luther, "has banked on nothing in this world."
And the mediocrities are in the majority and, usually,
on the seats of power.

No matter how far back we go in the history of
science, it seems that an extraordinary number of great
discoveries were made by dilettantes, amateurs, outsiders—the self-taught who were driven by an obsessive
idea, unequipped with the brakes of professional training and the blinkers worn by the specialists, so that
they were able to leap over the hurdles set up by
academic tradition.

Otto von Guericke, the greatest German physicist
of the seventeenth century, was a jurist by profesion.
Denis Papin, eighteenth-century pioneer in the development of the steam engine, was a medical man. Ben-
jamin Franklin, son of a soapmaker, without even a
secondary education, not to mention university training, became not only a great statesman but a scientist
of note. Luigi Galvani, the discoverer of electricity, was
another medical man who owed his discovery, as Wilhelm Ostwald shows in his history of electrochemistry,
precisely to the deficiencies of his knowledge in the
field in which he made it. Joseph von Fraunhofer, the
author of distinguished works on the spectrum, could
not read or write before he was fourteen years of age.
Michael Faraday was the son of a smith, a bookbinder's
apprentice, and almost completely self-educated. Julius
Robert Mayer, who discovered the law of the conservation of energy, was a physician, not a physicist. Another
physician, Hermann L. F. von Helmholtz, published
his first work on the same subject at the age of twenty-
six. Georges, Comte de Buffon, a mathematician and
physicist, published his most significant work in the
field of geology. The man who built the first electric
telegraph was a professor of anatomy, Thomas Söm-
mering. Samuel Morse was a painter, as was Louis

Daguerre; yet the first created the alphabet for the telegraph, the second invented photography. The fanatics who created the dirigible, Ferdinand Count Zeppelin, Gross, and Parseval, were military officers without a trace of technical training. The list is endless. If these men and their work were excised from the development of the sciences, the entire structure would collapse. Yet they all, in their time, had to endure the scorn and derision of the experts.

Archæology, with its auxiliary sciences, has its own list of such amateurs. William Jones, the first man to turn out good translations from the Sanskrit, was not an Orientalist but a high justiciary in Bengal. Grotefend, the first decipherer of cuneiform, was a classical philologist; his successor, Rawlinson, a military officer and political leader. A medical doctor, Thomas Young, took the first steps on the long road toward the decipherment of the Egyptian hieroglyphics. The man who completed this work, Champollion, was a history professor. Humann, the excavator of Pergamon, was a railway engineer.

No one would wish to contest the value of what is achieved by professionals as such. Yet, if it is results that count in the end, providing the means to that end remain unexceptionable, is not our special gratitude due to the "outsiders"?

Schliemann, it is true, made some serious blunders in the course of his early digs. He tore down ancient structures that should have been preserved; he destroyed walls that might have yielded some important clues. But Eduard Meyer, the great German historian, has this to say: "Schliemann's unmethodical way of going directly to the original floor of his site turned out to be most fruitful for science. A more systematic type of excavation would hardly have penetrated to the older strata within that hill, and thus would have left undiscovered what we now consider the true Trojan culture."

It was of course unfortunate that almost all of his earliest interpretations and datings were in error. But when Columbus discovered America he thought he had reached the Indies—yet his error does not seem to have lessened the value of his actual accomplishment.

And there is no doubt that in the interval between the time he attacked the mound of Hissarlik like a child smashing at a toy with a hammer and the time he excavated at Mycenæ and Tiryns, Schliemann had grown immensely in archæological stature. Both Dörpfeld and Evans attest to this.

Nevertheless, like Winckelmann harassed by "despotic" Prussia, Schliemann found a painful lack of appreciation in his own country. Despite the evidence of his excavations, there for all the world to see, a scholar named Forchhammer published, as late as 1888, a second edition of his *Erklärung der Ilias* (*The Iliad Explained*), an unfortunate attempt to see the Trojan war as a poetic metaphor for the conflicting tides of the sea and the rivers, the fogs and rains in the Trojan plain. Schliemann always fought back. When a certain Major Boetticher, a querulous fool and a vociferous antagonist of Schliemann's, accused him of having deliberately destroyed the remnants of ancient walls that might have contradicted Schliemann's hypothesis, the latter invited the man to Hissarlik at his own expense. Experts present at the ensuing encounter confirmed the views of Schliemann and Dörpfeld. The Major took a careful look around, assumed a grim expression, went home and declared that the "so-called Troy" was no more than a vast ancient crematory. Thereupon Schliemann invited an international roster of scholars to his hill for a fourth dig in 1890. He put up wooden cabins on the hills surrounding the Scamandros Valley to house fourteen scholars who came from England, America, France, Germany (Virchow among them). They too, overwhelmed by the evidence, confirmed all that Schliemann and Dörpfeld had said.

Schliemann ended up with collections of incalculable value. His testament provided that they should go to the national museum of that country "which I most love and esteem." He offered them first to the Greek government, then to the French. To a Russian baron in St. Petersburg he wrote in 1876: "A few years ago, when I was asked the price of my Trojan collection, I set it at 80,000 pounds sterling. But since I have spent twenty years of my life in St. Petersburg, all my sympathies are with Russia, and I sincerely desire my collections to go there, I am asking only £50,000 from the Russian government and would be prepared, if necessary, to go as low as £40,000 . . ."

His real, most openly expressed love, however, belonged to England, where he had found the greatest response, where the columns of *The Times* had always been open to him when none of the German publications were, and where even the Prime Minister, Gladstone, had written a foreword for his book on Mycenæ, as the famous A. H. Sayce of Oxford had done previously for Schliemann's work on Troy.

That the collections at last went to Berlin nevertheless, "to be owned and held there in perpetuity and in their entirety" is again due—and how ironically!—to a man who was an archæological dilettante, the great physician Virchow, who succeeded in having Schliemann made an honorary member of the Anthropological Society and finally an honorary citizen of Berlin, together with Bismarck and Moltke.

Schliemann had once been forced to hide and guard his treasures, like a thief, from the grasp of officialdom. After many detours, important pieces from his Trojan collection finally landed in the Berlin prehistorical museum. There they lay for decades, surviving one great war. Even after the bombs of the second great war had fallen, parts of the collections remained unharmed and were taken to places of security. The "Golden Treasure of Priam" went first to the Prussian State Bank for safekeeping, then into the air raid shelter at the Berlin Zoo. Both these places were demolished.

Most of the ceramics went to Schönebeck on the Elbe, to Petruschen Palace near Breslau, and to Lebus Palace in East Germany.

Of Schönebeck, nothing remains. Nothing has been heard from Petruschen—the area is now under Polish sovereignty. Lebus Castle was plundered at the war's end, and later the East German government ordered the ruin pulled down. Subsequently word leaked to Berlin that there were still some ceramics to be rescued at Lebus. When a woman scholar managed to get permission to see Lebus she found the local authorities uncooperative. She then bought fifty pounds of candies and with these bribed the children to bring her any pottery they could find. Even though the children quickly learned to smash those pots that were yet un-broken, so as to increase their take in candies by bringing the shards separately, a few undamaged things did come to light—from the homes of local rustics who had been putting to their own uses the pots and plates and pitchers off which the ancient Trojans and the royal race of the Atrides had dined and drunk.

And then she learned something far worse than this. The survivors of the German defeat at Lebus had no inkling what those boxes full of clay vessels were worth. When new life began to stir in the village, and there was to be a wedding, for example, the young men went off to the castle, loaded a wheelbarrow full of urns and amphoræ, the irreplaceable finds of Heinrich Schliemann, and with joyful shouts and yells smashed them upon the bridal pair's threshold for luck!

In this way parts of ancient Troy were once again destroyed in 1945, and the remnants once again collected with the aid of half a hundredweight of sweets.

# 7/SCHLIEMANN (IV):
## MYCENÆ, TIRYNS, AND CRETE

In 1876, at the age of fifty-four, Schliemann first drove a spade into the ground at Mycenæ, and in 1878–9, with Virchow's assistance, he dug for the second time at Troy. In 1880, at Orchomenos, Homer's third "golden" city, he uncovered the Treasury of Minyas. In 1882, with Dörpfeld, he dug for the third time in the Troad, and two years after this began his excavations in Tiryns.

Once more the familiar pattern unfolded: the masonry of the citadel at Tiryns, laid open to view, showed that a conflagration had calcined the stones and turned the clay that bound them to brick. The archæologists held these walls to be medieval remains, and Greek guides told Schliemann that there was nothing special to be seen at Tiryns.

Schliemann preferred to rely on his ancient Greeks. He began to dig with such zeal that he destroyed the caraway plantings of a peasant at Kophinion and had to pay 275 francs in damages.

Tiryns was the reputed birthplace of Heracles. Its Cyclopean walls were considered a marvel by the ancients and ranked by Pausanias with the pyramids of Egypt. Proetus, legendary King of Tiryns, was said to have sent for seven Cyclops to build him those walls. They were later copied elsewhere, particularly in Mycenæ, so that Euripides called all of Argolis "the Cyclopean land."

Schliemann kept digging and discovered the foundation walls of a palace that exceeded in grandeur anything of its kind found so far, giving one an awe-

inspiring sense of the prehistoric people that built it
and the kings who dwelt in it.

Gradually there appeared the outlines of a citadel
crowning the limestone crag. The walls were built of
huge, hammer-dressed stone blocks, some as much as
10 feet long by 3 feet 3 inches or 3 feet 6 inches wide.
On the outer, lower levels, where there were chiefly
housekeeping rooms, storerooms, stables and the like,
the wall was 28 to 32 feet thick, but in the upper part
where the ruler lived its thickness reached nearly 43
feet and rose to a height of 63 feet or more. What a
splendid sight this interior must have been when it was
swarming with armed warriors! Nothing had been
known, up to this time, of the plan of such a Homeric
palace; nothing had been left of the royal home of
Menelaus, Odysseus, or the other rulers; even the remains of Troy, Priam's citadel, gave no idea of the plan.

Here for the first time the spade brought to light
the outlines of a true Homeric palace, with pillared
walls and chambers, the men's court with the altar, the
stately megaron with porch and antechamber, and even
the bathroom—its floor a single block of limestone
weighing about 44,000 pounds—where Homer's heroes
had bathed and anointed themselves. Thanks to Schliemann's spade the scenes familiar from the *Odyssey*,
such as that of the wily hero's homecoming, the ca-
rousals of Penelope's suitors, the blood bath in the great
hall, were endowed with a new physical reality.

But there was something even more interesting—
the character of the pottery and wall paintings. Schliemann immediately recognized the similarity of the pottery, the vases, and the jars to those he had found in
Mycenæ, and pointed to their relation to those found
by other archæologists at Asine, Nauplia Eleusis, and
the islands, most notably Crete. In the ruins of Mycenæ he had found an ostrich egg (at first, to be sure,
he mistook it for an alabaster vase), which pointed to
Egypt. Here he found also vases displaying the so-called
"geometric pattern," which had allegedly been brought

by the Phœnicians to the court of Thotmes III as early as 1600 B.C.

So he set out to establish in detail that he had discovered traces of a cultural complex of Asiatic or African origin, a culture, indeed, which had spread over the whole east coast of Greece, which embraced most of the islands, but which probably had a cultural focus in Crete. We now call this culture Minoan-Mycenæan. Schliemann had found the first traces of it. Its actual discovery was to await another.

All the chambers of the palace were whitewashed. All the walls were decorated with frieze paintings, usually bordered with a blue and yellow band that probably encircled the room at eye level, dividing the walls into two parts horizontally.

One of these frescoes was exceptionally striking. Upon a blue ground it showed a powerful red-spotted bull in mid-career, with an upraised whiplash tail, and a perfectly circular eye suggesting his ferocity. Upon this bull a man was poised in a dancer's leap, one hand clutching the bull's horn.

In Schliemann's book on Tiryns he cites a Dr. Fabricius: "... one might think that the man on the bull's back is meant as a bare-back rider or bull tamer, showing his virtuosity by vaulting upon the beast's back in mid-career, like the horse-tamer of that well-known incident in the *Iliad* leaping from back to back of four horses wildly racing along side by side." This explanation, to which Schliemann apparently had nothing to add at the time, was incomplete. If Schliemann had only yielded to a persistent wish to visit Crete, he would have found there confirmation of a great many of his ideas relating to this fresco, and would have been able to add the crowning touch to his life's work.

Schliemann's plan to dig on Crete, specifically at Knossos, occupied his mind until the end of his life. Where there was so much rubble, he felt, much might be found. A year before his death he wrote: "I should like to conclude my career with one great piece of work: the excavation of the ancient, prehistoric royal palace at Knossos, on Crete, which I believe I discovered three years ago."

But too many obstacles were put in his way. He had managed to obtain permission from the Governor of Crete, but the owner of the site was opposed to any "poking around," and demanded the absurd price of 100,000 francs for the property. Schliemann dickered with him and finally got the price down to 40,000 francs. But when he returned from a trip to close the deal he found that the area had been measured out differently from the original stipulations, leaving him with only 888 olive trees instead of the expected 2,500. He then withdrew his offer. For once, Schliemann's business sense damped his archæological ardor. He had poured a fortune into his searches—yet, because of 1,612 olive trees, he gave up the chance to find the key to prehistoric riddles his own discoveries had posed but were still far from answering.

In 1890, death took the spade from his hand and buried the great excavator himself.

Schliemann had planned to be home with his wife and children for Christmas. He was tormented by an ear ailment. But, preoccupied with new plans, he did no more than consult some obscure physicians on his way through Italy. They apparently reassured him. But on Christmas Day he collapsed on the Piazza della Santa Carità in Naples and, while retaining consciousness, lost his power of speech. Sympathetic bystanders took the millionaire to a hospital, but were turned away. At the police station, his next stop, they found in his pocket the address of a doctor, who was duly fetched. He identified the patient and ordered a carriage to move him. The curious stared at the broken man lying on the ground in his simple attire, looking rather poor to them, and someone asked the doctor whom he expected to pay for the carriage. "Why," cried the doctor, "he is a rich man!" and reaching into the invalid's pocket, drew out a pouch full of gold.

Through the long night Heinrich Schliemann struggled for his life, never losing consciousness. Then he died.

When his body was brought to Athens, the King and the Crown Prince of Greece, the diplomatic representatives of foreign powers, the Greek minister of state, and the heads of all the Greek scientific institutes came to pay their respects at the bier. A bust of Homer looked down on this ardent lover of all things Greek, who had enriched the knowledge of Hellenic antiquity by a thousand years. Beside the coffin stood his wife and his two children.

They were called Andromache and Agamemnon.

It was Arthur Evans, an Englishman, who succeeded in revealing fully the Minoan culture glimpsed by Schliemann. Born in 1851, Evans was thirty-nine years old when the great German student of antiquity died.

Evans was the complete antithesis of Schliemann. Educated at Harrow, Oxford, and Göttingen, he became interested in hieroglyphics and found certain characters that pointed to Crete. There he began to dig in 1900. In 1909 he was made Extraordinary Professor of Prehistoric Archæology at Oxford, steadily rose to become the acknowledged authority in his field, was knighted and showered with honors to the end, receiving the distinguished Copley Medal of the Royal Society as late as 1936, when he was eighty-five. In a word, he was in character and education the exact opposite of the roving, impetuous German.

But for all the respectability of his career, the results of his researches are no less interesting. He had come to Crete to confirm his theory of hieroglyphic interpretation. He had not expected to stay long. But he wandered over the island and saw the vast piles of rubble and ruins that had fascinated Schliemann before him. And one day he laid aside his theories about the origin of writing and reached for a spade. A year later, in 1901, he announced that he would need at least another twelve months to lay bare everything of archæological interest. He was mistaken. A quarter of a century later he was still digging on the very same spot.

Like Schliemann, Evans was guided in his quest

for buried cultures by old legends and other folklore. Like Schliemann, he dug up palaces and treasures. He provided the frame for the picture Schliemann had drawn, and added sketches of his own for many more pictures in which we have not yet filled in the colors.

Crete lies on the periphery of a great curve of mountains running from Greece through the Ægean Sea to Asia Minor. The sea in which these peaks are drowned did not, as one might think, act as a cultural barrier. Schliemann had demonstrated this fact when he found objects at Mycenæ and Tiryns that must have come from distant parts. Later Evans found ivory from Africa and statuary from Egypt on the island of Crete. Commerce and war are the prime movers of social intercourse, and in this regard the little world of antiquity was no different from the greater world of today. The islands of the Ægean were culturally and economically coextensive with their two motherlands. With their motherlands? Motherland in this case was not a continental entity. The real matrix of the ancient Ægean culture, its creative source, may have been one of the islands in the complex—namely, Crete.

According to myth, Zeus himself was born on Crete, of Rhea, the Earth Mother, in a cave on Mount Ida. He was nourished with honey brought him by bees. The goat, Amalthea, gave him suck from her udders, and he was attended the while by nymphs. Youths of military age banded together to protect him from his own father, the pædophage (child-eater) Cronus.

Minos is said to have ruled Crete, Minos, the legendary king, son of mighty Zeus, a figure regarded with awe by the ancients.

Evans dug at Knossos.

The masonry walls lay close to the surface of the ground. A few hours of work sufficed to yield some results. After a few weeks the astonished Evans found himself looking at the remains of buildings covering an

area of 8,480 square feet. As the year passed, the ruins
of a palace extending over an area of two and a half
hectares (equals 5½ acres) were exposed.

The ground plan of the structure was clearly de-
fined, and showed a certain relationship with the palaces
of Tiryns and Mycenæ. But the greater massiveness
and splendor of the Cretan buildings strongly suggested that Crete had been a cultural headquarters,
whereas the mainland citadels of Mycenæ and Tiryns
had been the capitals of outlying provinces, or colonies.

About the gigantic rectangle of the largest courtyard on all sides rose the wings of various buildings,
their walls made of stone rubble, their flat roofs held
up by columns. The rooms, corridors, and halls of the
various stores were laid according to a confusing plan.
So many were the opportunities to go astray in moving from room to room that the term *labyrinth* came
naturally to mind, even to those who had no inkling
of the legend surrounding King Minos. This legend
tells of a labyrinth built by Dædalus for Minos, a model
for all subsequent structures of its kind.

Evans promptly announced to the world that he
had found the palace of Minos, son of Zeus, father of
Ariadne and Phædra, master of the Labyrinth and of
the terrible monster, the Minotaur, that it housed.

Thereafter he revealed a whole series of wonders.
The people who had lived in Knossos—a people known
to Schliemann only by their colonial offshoots, and to
the world at large only as described in legend—had evidently reveled in riches and lived lives of elegant de-
bauchery. At the height of their development they had
apparently reached a state of sybaritic decadence that
contained the seeds of decline; for those who habitually
lie in bed, even on a mattress of rose petals, in time will
suffer from sores.

An economic golden age made this decadent culture possible. Then, as today, Crete was a land of wine
and olive oil. But in its ancient heyday it was a com-

mercial center, an island entrepôt for the Ægean area. A puzzling fact was gradually revealed by the excavations. The most pretentious palace of Greek prehistory had completely lacked any sort of protective walls or fortifications. The paradox was resolved by the discovery of the relics of a Cretan fleet, useful both in commerce and as a mobile weapon to repel invaders, a weapon far more effective than static defenses.

Reconstruction of the south palace steps at Knossos (after Thomas Fyfe).

The palace of Minos did not look like a fortress to the seafarers of the period as they sailed into the harbor of Knossos. They saw it as a marvel of the coast. Its columns were chalky white, its decorated walls shone under a burning Cretan sun. It was a maritime jewel flaunting Crete's riches and superiority from every sparkling facet.

Evans discovered, among other things, the old storerooms of Knossos. In them were rows of huge vaselike oil-containers, richly ornamented vessels, elegantly decorated in a style already known from Tiryns. Evans took the trouble to measure the capacity of this oil store and judged it to be about 19,000 gallons. And this was the oil supply for a single palace (see Plate IV).

Who were the beneficiaries of this opulence?

Presently Evans discovered that his finds did not all stem from the same period. Walls were of various ages; the ceramics, faïence, and painting showed a variety of styles. After making a close survey of Cretan artifacts Evans was able, he believed, to distinguish the different periods of the cultural whole. He divided Cretan history into three parts: an Early Minoan period from 3000 to 2000 B.C.; a Middle Minoan period, lasting until 1600 B.C.; and a Late Minoan period, shortest of the three, which lasted until about 1250 B.C. Evans found signs of human occupation prior to the

Old Cretan goddess with a lion. The imprint of a seal ring from Knossos (about 1500 B.C.).

earliest period, indeed, dating back to neolithic times, when the use of metals was unknown and implements were made entirely of stone. He assigned an age of ten thousand years to these prehistoric traces, but later investigators have reduced this figure to five thousand years.

How were these dates arrived at? How was it possible to work out such a scheme of periods?

In each epoch Evans found objects of foreign origin, particularly ceramics and pottery ware from Egypt that belonged to exactly dated Pharaonic times. He named the period of transition from the Middle to Late Minoan—that is, the decades around 1600 B.C.— as the golden age of Crete. It was at this time, apparently, that a Minos lived, commander of the fleet and ruler of the sea. It was a time when splendor and luxury were generated by a high degree of economic well-being. The cult of beauty was in universal vogue. The wall paintings show youths wandering through the meadows, gathering saffron flowers, which they placed in Kamares bowls, and maidens wading through fields of lilies. During this transitional period the Minoan æsthetic was on the verge of becoming sheer ostentation. Painting, which hitherto had been strongly bound by conventional forms, showed a tendency to erupt in a riot of color. Luxury was becoming a prime consideration in the appointments of habitations, of equal importance with utility. The style of dress was no longer dictated by the needs of protection against the weather and of modesty. On every hand the whims of a refined leisure class made new demands.

It is not surprising that Evans used the word *modern* to describe what he saw. The palace of Minos was as large as Buckingham Palace. The great structure contained drainage sumps and luxurious bathrooms, ventilation systems, ground-water conduits, and waste-chutes. But the parallel with modernity is even more strikingly evident in the people themselves, in their manner, clothing, and modes.

The "bull-dancer."
Impression of a gem
from Crete.

At the beginning of the Middle Minoan period the women were still wearing high peaked caps and a long, gaily figured gown, slit in front and held in with a belt. The collar of the bodice was high and stiff, and in front the breasts were exposed (see Plate IV).

At the high point of Cretan history this traditional costume became much more refined. The originally simple arrangement developed into a tightly bodiced affair with sleeves. The buttocks were closely sheathed, so as to show the curves of the figure as boldly as possible, and the breasts were now exposed with as much thrust and coquetry as could be devised. Skirts fell in long, brightly figured folds, covered with designs showing hillocks of earth out of which grew stylized lotus blossoms. Over the skirt a bright apron was worn. The old peaked cap had now become a sort of helmet.

Among the pictures found by Evans, paintings that, as he says, had "a magic and enchantment felt even by our uneducated workers," one in particular is very familiar, that of the bull-dancers (see Plate V).

Dancers? Performers? So Schliemann had thought when he discovered similar representations at Tiryns, though in that obscure outpost there was nothing to remind him of Cretan legends centered on bulls, sacrifices, and smoking blood in the temples.

As for Evans, he was standing on the very ground where Minos had held sway, the King with the Minotaur, the taurine monster. And the legends spoke about these dim scenes from the past.

Minos, King of Knossos, Crete, and all the Ægean, sent his son, Androgeus, to the mainland as a contestant in the Athenian games. Being stronger than any of the Greeks, Androgeus was consistently victorious. Out of jealousy, he was murdered by Ægeus, King of Athens. The enraged father thereupon sent his fleet to Athens, took the city by storm, and imposed a fearful reparation. The Athenians were ordered to send every nine years the pick of their youth, seven young men and seven virgins, to be sacrificed to the monster of Minos. When this expiatory obligation was about to fall due for the third time, Theseus, son of Ægeus, recently returned from a long journey filled with heroic deeds, offered to sail with the victims to Crete, and there kill the monster.

> Through the Cretan sea rushed the ship's
> Blue-streaming prow. With it went Theseus
> And seven pairs of Ionic youth.

The boat was outfitted with black sails, which were to be exchanged for white ones on the homecoming if Theseus was successful in his mission. Ariadne, daughter of Minos, seeing the doomed youth Theseus, lost her heart to him. She gave him a sword with which to do battle, and a ball of wool to guide him out of the Labyrinth, she holding the other end, when Theseus went in to seek the Minotaur. In a terrible battle Theseus killed the monster. Using the woolen thread, he found his way out of the maze and made haste to flee homewards with Ariadne and his companions. But he was so excited at having got away that he forgot to change sails as previously agreed. Ægeus, his father, seeing the black sails, believed his son dead, and in anguish threw himself into the sea.

Does this legend offer any solution to the mystery of the bull-dancers? Two girls and a boy are shown playing with a bull. But were they actually playing? Could this not have been a representation of the sacrifice to Minotaur? And was not the monster simply a large bull owned by Minos?

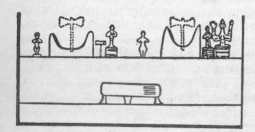

Cult niche in Knossos. After a sketch by Evans.

When the legend is checked still further against the reality of the excavations, other arguable points arise. The fact that there was an actual labyrinth indicates that the story definitely has a kernel of truth. It could be assumed that Theseus' victory over the Minotaur in the legend is a symbol of the conqueror who came from the mainland and destroyed the palace of Minos. It seems highly improbable, however, that a personal act of revenge on the part of Minos could ever, by itself, have occasioned the retaliatory destruction of the Cretan kingdom.

Yet there is no doubt that the kingdom of Crete was wiped out. It was annihilated with such suddenness and thoroughness that apparently the destroyers themselves had no time to see or hear or learn anything of the Minoan culture. The debacle was as complete as that visited three thousand years later on Moctezuma's kingdom by a handful of Spaniards. In sum, nothing afterwards remained but ruins and dead stone, which could not speak.

Where did this civilization spring from, and what were the circumstances of its disappearance? The genesis and fall of the Cretans is to this day one of archæology's most teasing problems, of central interest to all students of prehistory.

According to Homer, five linguistically separable peoples lived on the island. According to Herodotus, Minos was not a Greek, though Thucydides maintains that he was. Evans, who more than any other man has delved into these mysteries, believes that the Cretan culture had an African-Libyan origin. Eduard Meyer, the profound historian of antiquity, is content to make the observation that probably it did not stem from Asia Minor. Dörpfeld, Schliemann's old collaborator, in

This discus remains a mystery. Even after Ventris, it is not yet decipherable.

1932, as an octogenarian, took up the cudgels against the Evans theory. Dörpfeld held that Cretan-Mycenæan art derived from Phœnicia and did not develop indigenously in Crete, as Evans claimed.

Where is the Ariadne's thread that will lead us out of the labyrinth of conjecture?

Minoan writing may some day provide the clue. It will be recalled that Evans' original purpose in Crete was to study Minoan script. By 1894 he had already described the first Cretan characters. As the years went by he discovered countless hieroglyphic inscriptions. At Knossos he found two thousand small clay tablets covered with the symbols of a linear system of writing. Schliemann's "learned friend" Émile Burnouf, in reference to the writing on Trojan vases, once said: "The symbols are neither Greek nor Sanskrit, nor are they

Phœnician, nor . . . nor . . ." This sort of negative definition was the only one anyone had yet been able to apply to the Minoan script. In 1910 the Egyptologist Erman entertained some mild hopes of solving the riddle. "These Cretan inscriptions have yet to be deciphered," he wrote, "but at least we see much more clearly into the matter." In a most exhaustive work on ancient forms of writing, *Die Schrift* by Hans Jensen, published in 1935, the author flatly stated: "The deciphering of Cretan writing is still completely in the rudimentary stage, and we are not at all clear about its real nature."

The end of the Cretan kingdom is a mystery as dark as the mystery of the Minoan script. There are many daring theories on the subject, however. Evans, for example, believed that Crete was destroyed three different times. Twice the palace was rebuilt, but the third time it fell not to rise again.

If we scan the history of this distant period from the broad viewpoint, we note that hordes of fair-skinned Achæans drifted down into Greece out of Danubian country or perhaps out of southern Russia. These nomads overcame the citadel cities of darker races and destroyed Mycenæ and Tiryns. This same barbaric invasion may well have extended across the sea itself and so spelled the finish of prehistoric Crete. A little later we see new campaigns, waged by the Dorians, as a result of which the Achæans, in their turn, were overcome. The Dorians brought even less culture with them than had the Achæans. Whereas the Achæans were plunderers who at least knew how to hold onto and make use of their booty, a race worthy of being memorialized in Homeric song, the Dorians were brute destroyers, who permanently wrecked whatever they touched. From their midst, however, sprang a new Greece.

Thus it was with Crete, says one school of thought. But what do the others say?

Evans discovered evidence suggesting that the palace, the focal point of Minoan life, might have been destroyed by geological rather than human intervention. Pompeii was the classical example of such an occurrence. In the chambers of the Minoan Palace Evans found signs of sudden death analogous to those first found by d'Elbœuf and Venuti at the foot of Vesuvius. Tools had been left lying about, there were unfinished objects of art and utility, and evidence of suddenly interrupted domestic activity.

On the basis of these findings Evans formulated a theory that was later dramatically confirmed. On June 26, 1926, at nine forty-five in the evening, Evans was lying in bed reading when without warning he was tossed about by a heavy earth tremor. His bed shook; the walls of the house trembled; things fell on the floor; water was spilled out of a bucket; the earth emitted sighing sounds, which became groans, then curious bellowing roars, as if the Minotaur, the mythical bull, had come to life. When the earth had stopped quaking, Evans jumped out of bed and ran to the palace. His work of reconstruction had withstood the shock, for through the years he had installed steel pillars and props wherever possible. But throughout the villages of the district, and as far away as the capital city of Kandia, the earthquake had caused great devastation.

Even before this demonstration of the destructive power of natural forces, it had been well established that Crete is one of the most active quake areas in Europe. But Evans' experience certainly gave point to his notions. Many centuries ago the earth had shuddered, causing man's architectural monuments to split asunder and tumble down. Nothing less than a very heavy tremor, he maintained, could account for annihilation so complete that throughout succeeding millennia nothing but miserable huts ever rose on the ruins of the palace of Minos.

So much for Evans. Most archæologists do not subscribe to his interpretation. A later day may clear

up the mystery. Evans, at any rate, was able to define
the cultural pattern first suspected by the credulous
Schliemann when he explored the ashes of Mycenæ.
Both these men were pioneers, breaking the trail for
the current phase of research, which may succeed in
unraveling Ariadne's thread.

The preceding paragraph was written in 1949. Midway
in 1950 came the news that Ernst Sittig, professor at
the University of Tübingen, had solved the problem on
which the Finnish scholar Sundwall had been laboring
for forty years, followed by the German Bossert, the
Italian Meriggi, the Czech Hrozný (who had deciphered
the Hittite cuneiform scripts from Bogazköy), and Alice
Kober of New York, who said resignedly, in 1948, that
"an unknown language, written in an unknown script,
cannot be deciphered."

Apparently a great triumph had been achieved.
Sittig was the first philologist to apply consistently the
art (and science) of the decipherment of military secret
codes, based on statistical frequency studies, which had
been perfected in the course of two world wars. He
believed that he had deciphered eleven signs, and later
on, as many as thirty signs of the so-called Cretan
Linear-B script.

A second development came in 1953, when a clay
tablet dug up by Blegen in Pylos came into the hands
of an Englishman, Michael Ventris. It showed a grouping of symbols such as Sittig had not yet seen, and which
the brilliant Ventris, another outsider, could indisputably read as Greek. This invalidated part of Sittig's interpretations: only three of his thirty readings had been
correct. And so there began a new effort that will probably go on for a long time. While ancient philology is
approaching the final solution of its problem, a far
greater problem has come to confront us regarding the
entire history of antiquity. Why should the language
of the Greeks, a far from highly developed people at
the time, be written in Cretan script on Crete, the cen-

ter of an independent, highly advanced culture, about 600 years before Homer? Did these two languages exist side by side? It is possible that our entire chronology of early Greece is all wrong? Is Homer becoming problematic again?

# PART TWO

# THE BOOK
# OF THE PYRAMIDS

## The Empires of Egypt

*Soldiers! Forty centuries gaze down upon you!*
*—Napoleon*

*They who built with granite, who set a hall in-*
*side their pyramid, and wrought beauty with*
*their fine work... their altar stones also are*
*empty as are those of the weary ones, the ones*
*who die upon the embankment leaving no*
*mourners.*

*—Ancient Egyptian Saying*

*O Mother Nut! Spread your winds above me*
*like the imperishable stars!*
*—Inscription on the coffin of Tutankhamen*

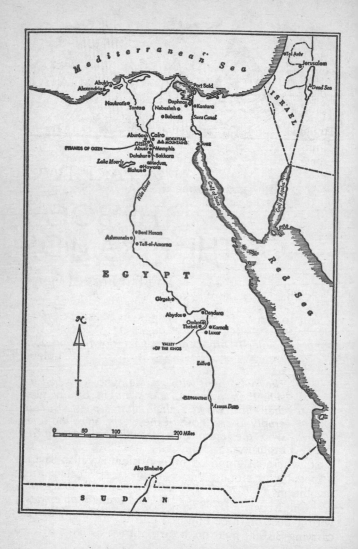

# 9/NAPOLEON:
## IN THE LAND OF THE PHARAOHS

Napoleon I and Vivant Denon dominate the very beginning of the archæological discovery of Egypt. Emperor and baron, general and artist—for a short distance they traveled together and knew each other well, though by nature they had nothing in common. For the one the pen was useful only in writing down commands, decrees, and legal codes; the other used the pen to write facile, immoral—indeed, pornographic—*novelle* and to make drawings that today belong among the most curious of erotica.

On October 17, 1797, the Peace of Campo Formio was signed, ending the Italian campaign and allowing Napoleon to return to Paris. "Napoleon's heroic days are over!" said Stendhal. He was wrong. Actually the Corsican's heroic phase was only about to commence. But before he swept across Europe he embraced "a mad chimera, sprung from a sick brain." Restlessly pacing back and forth in a narrow room, consumed by ambition, inwardly comparing himself with Alexander, despairing of the vast works yet to be accomplished, Napoleon wrote: "Paris weighs me down like a cloak of lead!—This Europe of ours is a molehill. Only in the East, where six hundred million human beings live, is it possible to found great empires and realize great revolutions."

On May 19, 1798 Napoleon sailed from Toulon with a fleet of three hundred and twenty-eight vessels, carrying 38,000 men on board, almost as large a force as Alexander had commanded when he embarked on his Eastern campaign. The goal was Egypt.

The French plan was worthy of Alexander. Napoleon's seeking gaze traveled far beyond the valley of the Nile to the immense peninsula of India. The purpose of this initial overseas campaign was to strike a deathblow at one of the main appendages of Britain, imponderable in the European balance. Nelson, commander of the English fleet, for a month vainly scoured the Mediterranean, but failed to trap Napoleon's force, though on two occasions French vessels were almost within sighting distance.

On July 2 Napoleon stepped onto Egyptian soil. After horrible desert marches the soldiers bathed in the Nile. On July 21 Cairo took shape before French eyes, a vision from *The Thousand and One Nights*, with its four hundred minarets and the great cupola of Jami-el-Azhar, central mosque of the city. In powerful contrast to this abundance of filigreed ornament lightly traced against the pearly morning sky, there rose, out of the arid desert wastes, silhouetted against the violet-gray slopes of the Jebel Mokattam, the profiles of enormous structures of stone, cold, massive, and forbidding. These weer the Pyramids of Gizeh, geometry petrified, silent eternity, symbols of a world already long dead before Islam was born.

The soldiers had no time for gaping. Round about them lay the enormous relics of a dead past, but Cairo, symbol of an enchanting future, beckoned. Between them and their glittering goal stood the army of the Mameluke sultans. This colorful force was made up of ten thousand horsemen, brilliantly drilled, armed with glittering yataghans, mounted on prancing steeds of noble stock. The commander was the ruler of Egypt himself, Maurad. Accompanied by twenty-three of his beys, he rode at the head of his swarm on a swan-white horse, his green turban glistening with precious stones. Napoleon pointed to the pyramids. He exhorted his men, as a general, a master of mass psychology, and as a European face to face with world history. "Soldiers," he said, "forty centuries are looking down upon you!"

The collision was frightful. The elan of the Mamelukes could not hope to prevail against European bayonets. The battle became a bloody rout. On July 25 Bonaparte entered Cairo, and half the great trek to India seemed to have been safely accomplished.

But on August 7 came the sea battle of Abukir. Nelson had finally located the French fleet and descended on it like an avenging angel. Napoleon was in a trap. Abukir put a quietus on the Egyptian adventure, though actually it dragged on for another year. During this interval General Desaix overran Upper Egypt, and Napoleon won a land victory at the same Abukir where his fleet had been cut to pieces. Despite these successes, misery, hunger, and pestilence dogged the French. Great numbers of soldiers were blinded by the Egyptian eye disease. The malady became such a prominent feature of the expedition that it was called "ophthalmia militaris."

On August 19, 1799 Bonaparte fled from his army. On August 25, from the frigate *Muiron*, he watched the coast of the land of the Pharaohs sink into the sea behind him.

Napoleon's expedition, ill-advised as it was from the military standpoint, had the long-range effect of politically awakening Egypt; also of setting in motion a scientific examination of its antiquities that continues to this day. For Napoleon had taken one hundred and seventy-five "learned civilians" to Egypt. The soldiers and sailors called this brain trust "the donkeys." The intellectual contingent brought along a large library, containing practically every book on the land of the Nile available in France, and also dozens of crates of scientific apparatus and measuring instruments.

Napoleon first gave notice of his cultural interest in Egypt at a meeting of scientists held, in the spring of 1798, in the big assembly hall of the Institut de France.

While explaining the duties of science in the Egyptian project, for emphasis he occasionally rapped with the knuckle of his forefinger on the leather back of a copy of Niebuhr's *Arabian Journey* that he held in his hand. A few days later the astronomers, geometers, chemists, mineralogists, Orientalists, technicians, painters, and poets went aboard ship with him at Toulon. And among them was an extraordinary man whom the gallant Josephine had recommended as an illustrator.

Dominique Vivant Denon was his full name. Under Louis XV he had been supervisor of a collection of antique gems, and he had the reputation of being one of Pompadour's favorites. In St. Petersburg he had filled the post of embassy secretary, and had been much liked by Catherine. A man of the world, fond of women, a dilettante in all the arts, his conversation sparkling with malice, banter, and wit, Denon somehow managed to keep on good terms with the whole world. As a diplomat assigned to the Swiss Confederation he had often been Voltaire's guest, and had painted the famous *Breakfast at Ferney*. For a drawing called *Adoration of the Shepherds*, done in the manner of Rembrandt, he had been made a member of the Academy. News of the outbreak of the French Revolution came to him while he was living in Florence, where he was a familiar figure in the art-saturated salons of the city. He rushed to Paris. From the rich and independent life of a diplomat and *"gentilhomme ordinaire,"* he found himself suddenly reduced to the emigrant list. He saw his real-estate and financial holdings confiscated.

Poor, forsaken, betrayed on all sides, he vegetated in the slums of Paris, eking out a bare existence by the sale of his drawings. He wandered about the markets, saw many heads roll in the Place de Grève, including some of his friends', until at last he found an unexpected patron in Jacques Louis David, the great painter of the Revolution. He was given work engraving David's costume sketches, which were intended to revolutionize French dress. His labors won him the goodwill of the "incorruptible one." Scarcely was he once more treading familiar parquet floors, having splashed on foot through the mud of Montmartre to scenes of splendor, when he unfolded his tested diplomatic abilities to public view under conditions where they would do the most good. Shortly his properties were restored to him by order of Robespierre, and his name was removed from the list of the banished. He got to know the beauteous Josephine Beauharnais, made an impression on Napoleon, and in due course was taken on the Egyptian expedition.

He returned from the land of the Nile a proved and highly honored man, and was made director-general of all museums. As Napoleon proceeded to demonstrate his power on the battlefields of Europe, Denon held fast to the bull's tail. He filched works of art in the name of collecting, and he persisted until the first few nondescript pieces had grown into one of France's most noble ornaments. Remembering how successfully he had dabbled at painting and drawing, he thought he might do the same in literary fields. At a social gathering the point was argued that it was impossible to write a love story realistically without the use of obscenity. Denon made a bet that he could do it. Twenty-four hours later he had finished *Le Point de lendemain*. This long short story earned him a niche in literature. Connoisseurs pronounced it one of the most delicate examples of its genre. Balzac later judged it to be "an education for married men, and for young people an excellent picture of the customs of the last century."

Denon also produced the *Œuvre priapique*, which appeared in 1793. This collection of etchings, as the title suggests, was brazenly phallic in concept. In this regard it is interesting to note that archæologists who have written about Denon seem to be quite unaware of this pornographic side of his activities. On the other hand, even such a knowledgeable historian of culture as Eduard Fuchs, who in his *History of Morals* devoted a whole section to pornography, apparently had no idea that Denon played an important role in the early days of Egyptology.

This many-sided and in some respects astonishing man unquestionably deserves remembrance by posterity for one unique acomplishment. Napoleon conquered Egypt with bayonets, and held it for one short year. But Denon conquered the land of the Pharaohs with his crayon, and held it permanently. It was through the power of his trained eye and hand that Egypt again came to life in the modern consciousness.

From the moment he first felt the hot breath of the desert, Denon, effete creature of the salons, was lifted up by a rapturous enthusiasm for all things Egyptian. As he wandered from ruin to ruin, this enthusiasm never waned.

He was attached to the army of Desaix, and with this general went off in reckless pursuit of Murad Bey, the escaped Mameluke leader, through the wastes of Upper Egypt. At this time Denon was fifty-one years old, old enough to be Desaix's father. The general was fond of Denon, who was also popular among the ranks. The soldiers marveled at his indifference to the rigors of the climate. One day he would spur his old nag on far ahead of the van of the army, the next straggle at the rear. He was out of his tent by dawn, he made drawings on the march and during the nightly bivouac. Even while he ate his scanty meals his sketch pad was beside him. Once, amid bugled alarms, he discovered he had run squarely into a skirmish. As the soldiers returned the enemy's fire, Denon encouraged them to the fray by waving his drawing-paper. Then, realizing that a paintable scene was spread before his eye, he forgot the bullets and began to sketch.

Eventually he came upon the hieroglyphics. He knew nothing at all about them, and no one in Desaix's army was able to satisfy his curiosity. Regardless, he drew what he saw. And immediately his acute, if untutored, gaze distinguished three different hieroglyphic modes. The hieroglyphics, he saw, were either deeply engraved, done in low relief, or *en creux*, hollowed out. In Sakkara he sketched the Step Pyramid (see Plate VI), and in Dendera the gigantic remains of the late Egyptian period. Tirelessly he rushed hither and thither among the extensive ruins of Thebes of the hundred gates, and was in despair when orders came to break camp before he had caught everything with his crayon. Cursing angrily, he summoned some soldiers from their packing and had them scrape encrusted dirt off the head of a statue that had caught his attention. He continued to sketch while the van of the camp was already on the move.

Desaix's adventurous campaign took him as far as Aswan and the first cataract of the Nile. At Elephantine, Denon drew the charming, pillared chapel of Amenophis III. His excellent sketch is the only picture of it extant, for in 1822 the structure was torn down. When the troop column turned homeward, after the victorious battle at Sediman had been fought and Murad Bey annihilated, Baron Dominique Vivant Denon, with his innumerable sheets of drawings, brought back to France a richer booty than did the soldiers who had despoiled the Mameluke army. His sensibilities might have been inflamed by Egypt's strangeness, but this excitement had not affected the precision of his draftsmanship. His drawing was as realistic as that of the old etchers who lavished infinite care on detail, ignoring both impressionism and expressionism, and blissfully unaware of derogatory connotations in the word *craftsman*. Denon's drawings became an invaluable source of material for the archæology of the times. They were to provide the basis of a fine work on Egyptology, the first of its kind, the famous *Description de l'Égypte*, in which the science blossomed out as a systematic intellectual endeavor.

Meanwhile in Cairo the Egyptian Institute was started. While Denon was busy drawing, the other artists and scientists of the Napoleonic party were measuring,

counting, investigating, and collecting whatever the surface of Egypt had to offer. And only the surface, for so
abundant was the material open to casual view that
there was no incentive to excavate. Besides plaster
models, masses of memoranda of all kinds, transcripts,
drawings, and collections of animal, plant, and mineral
specimens, Napoleon's brain trust brought home with
them several sarcophagi and twenty-seven pieces of
carved stone, mostly fragments of statuary. Included in
these findings was a stele of polished black basalt, bearing an inscription in three different forms of writing.
The heavy plaque became famous as the Rosetta Stone,
key to the mysteries of Egypt.

But in September 1801, upon the capitulation of
Alexandria, France had to hand over to the English the
conquered regions of Upper Egypt, and with them the
expedition's collection of Pharaonic antiquities. General Hutchinson undertook their transport to England.
By the instructions of George III the pieces, at that
time rarities of the first order, were housed in the British
Museum. A whole year of effort by the French appeared to have gone for naught, a year in which several
scholarly adventurers had lost their eyesight in the
cause. Then it was realized that notwithstanding the
loss of original pieces to the English, every single thing
in the vast collection had been faithfully copied. Enough
material would reach Paris to occupy the minds of a
whole generation of scholars.

The first member of the expedition to make use
of its findings was Denon. In 1802 he published his
interesting *Voyage dans la Haute et la Basse Égypte*.
Simultaneously François Jomard began to edit his great
work, basing it upon the material collected by the scientific commission, and particularly upon Denon's voluminous drawings. This work, a unique event in archæological history, at one stroke impressed on the modern
world's attention a culture hitherto known but to a few
travelers, a culture as remote and mysterious, if not so
completely hidden from view, as that of Troy.

One of the first products of Egyptian art, the so-called "Narmer palette," shown front and back. It is about 5,000 years old, and possibly shows the great Menes himself, founder of the first dynasty, after his victory over enemies from Lower Egypt.

Jomard's *Description de l'Égypte* was published through the four years between 1809 and 1813. The interest evoked by the publication of these twenty-four volumes can be compared only to that occasioned, at a later date, by Botta's first work on Nineveh and Schliemann's book on Troy.

In this age of the rotary press it is not easy to appreciate the significance of Jomard's choice and comprehensive compilation, with its many engravings, a number of them colored, and its costly bindings. The books were accessible only to the rich, but by them were preserved as a treasure of knowledge. Today, when every scientific discovery of importance is almost immediately disseminated all over the globe, multiplied a millionfold in effect by its being chronicled in pictures, film, word, and sound, the excitement of great discoveries has been very much diluted. One publication follows on the heels of the next, always competing for attention, contributing to a process whereby everybody knows a little about something, but nothing in particular. And so it is not easy for moderns to understand how Jomard's first readers felt when they picked up the *Description*. They saw in it things never seen before, they read of absolute novelties, they became aware of a mode of life the existence of which had previously not even been suspected. Having more capacity for reverence than ourselves, these first readers must have experienced a shuddering sensation as they were carried back thousands of years.

For Egypt was old, older than any other culture known at the time. It was already old when the political policy of the future Roman Empire was being framed in the first meetings on the Capitoline Hill. It was already old and blighted when the Germans and Celts of the north European forest were still hunting bears. When the First Dynasty came into power, about five thousand years ago, so fixing Egyptian history in calendrical time, marvelous cultural forms had already been evolved in the land of the Nile. And when the Twenty-sixth Dynasty died out, still five hundred years separated Egyptian history from our era. The Libyans ruled the land, then the Ethiopians, the Assyrians, the Persians, the Greeks, the Romans—all before the star shone over the stable at Bethlehem.

Of course, the stone marvels of the Nile had been known to some, but knowledge of them was more or less legendary. Only a very few Egyptian monuments had been carried away to museums in foreign lands and were accessible to public view. In the Napoleonic period the tourist in Rome could gape at the lions, since gone, on the steps of the Capitol. He could also see the statues of some of the Ptolemaic kings—that is, very late works, finished during a period when the splendor of ancient Egypt had been replaced by the new glories of Alexandrian Hellenism. Among the monuments truly representative of ancient Egyptian times still in Rome were twelve obelisks, in addition to some reliefs in the gardens of the cardinals. More common were Egyptian scarabs, representations of the dung beetle held sacred by the people of the Nile. These scarabs were at one time used throughout Europe as amulets, later as ornaments and ring seals. That was all.

And little, too, that could be called genuinely informative scholarly material was to be found in the bookshops of Paris; but an excellent translation in five volumes of Strabo's works appeared in 1805, thus making more generally available the observations of an authority hitherto known only to scholars. Strabo traveled through Egypt in the time of Augustus. More information of value was contained in the second book of Herodotus, that most wonderful traveler of antiquity. But who read Herodotus? And how many were acquainted with the handful of even more esoteric and scattered references to Egypt found in the ancient writers?

"Who coverest thyself with light as with a garment," says the Psalmist. Early in the morning the sun rises up into a steely blue sky, and pursues its course, yellow and glaring, kiln-hot, reflected from brown, ocherous, and whitish sands. The shadows are sharply etched, poured over the sand like ink in silhouettes of the original. And toward this eternally sunny waste, which knows no weather, no rain, snow, fog, or hail, which seldom hears the rumble of thunder or sees the flash of lightning—toward this desert which makes the air bone-dry, seedless, where the ground is unfruitful, granulated, frangible, its clods all crumbly, rolls the mighty Nile, the father of rivers, the "All-Father Nile." The river rises in the country's remote depths and is nourished by the lakes and tropical rains of the distant Sudan. In flood it overflows its banks, spills out over the sand, swallows up the wasteland, and spits out mud, fertile July muck. This it has done for thousands of years, each year rising fifty-two feet. On this account sixteen children, one for each ell of flood, play about the river god in the symbolic marble group in the Vatican. When the Nile sinks back into its bed, it has saturated the dry earth and burning sands. Where its brown waters have stood, green things germinate. Shoots of grain appear, to bear double and quadruple fruit and bring "fat years" to nourish the people during the "lean years." Each year a new Egypt arises, "the present from the Nile," as Herodotus described the event 2,500 years ago, the breadbasket of antiquity. Far away Rome either hungered or ate in a glut, depending on the Nile's bounty.

In minareted cities rising out of sun-blistered landscapes people of divers races and colors—Nubians, Berbers, Copts, Bedouins, Negroes—crowd through the narrow streets, shrilling in a babel of tongues, saluting a world of ruined temples, columned halls, and tombs.

In the shadowless wastes the pyramids lift their heads. Sixty-seven of them stand in the open land about Cairo, lined up about the "Drill Ground of the Sun," monstrous tombs for kings. One of them alone required for its construction two and a half million blocks of stone, carried into place by more than a hundred thousand slaves working steadily for twenty years.

There crouches the Sphinx of Gizeh, greatest of its species, half man, half animal. His lion's mane has been demolished, his eyes and nose are nothing but holes, for the Mamelukes used his head as a target when they practiced shooting their cannon. But there he has rested for thousands of years, broadly reclining as he waits out eternity, so mighty in mass that Thotmes, dreaming to gain the throne, found space for a large stele between his paws.

There, too, the obelisks stand out in the crystalline air, needle-sharp, guardians of the temple gates, honoring gods and kings. Some of these fine stone fingers point ninety-one feet into the sky. There are also rock tombs and mastabas, statues of "village magistrates" and of the Pharaohs, sarcophagi, columns and pylons, sculptured reliefs and paintings. The people who once ruled the ancient kingdom march in endless procession across the friezes, stiffly posed, breathing greatness in every gesture, always shown in profile and directed toward some goal. "The life of the Egyptian," it has been said, "was a journey toward death." The teleological principle is so strongly emphasized in Egyptian wall reliefs that a modern cultural philosopher designated "the way" as Egypt's most fundamental symbol, on a par in depth of significance with European "space" and Greek "body."

Practically every object in this vast graveyard of the past was covered with hieroglyphs. These hieroglyphs consisted of signs, pictures, outlines, hints, all manner of secretive and mysterious forms. The symbolism of this strange system of communication drew inspiration from human beings, animals, plants, fruits, mechanical apparatus, pieces of clothing, wickerwork, weapons, geometrical figures, undulant lines and flames. There were hieroglyphs on the walls of temple and burial chamber, on memorial plaques, coffins, stelæ, on statues of gods and mortals, on boxes and clay vessels. Even inkstands and canes bore hieroglyphic signs. The Egyptians seem to have been fonder of writing than any other ancient people. "If someone set about copying the inscriptions on the temple at Edfu and wrote from morning till night, he would not be done in twenty years!"

Jomard opened up this magnificent world to a Europe swiftly awakening to the wonders of science and the wonders of the past. Thanks to Caroline, Napoleon's sister, the excavations at Pompeii were being pressed with renewed zeal. Through Winckelmann, scholars were learning the rudiments of archæological method and were eager to try their hand at deciphering the mysteries of antiquity.

Though the *Description* indubitably contained a wealth of drawings, copies, and descriptions, the authors could not explain them, for this was beyond their power. When, occasionally, they attempted interpretation, it was wrong. For the relics chronicled in the book themselves were silent, and remained so obdurately. Whatever order was imposed on them had to be purely intuitive, for no one had any notion how to make empiric, concrete explanations. The hieroglyphs were simply unreadable, as were their hieratic and demotic or simpli-

Façade of the temple of Edfu.

fied scripts.[1] The written language was utterly strange
to European eyes. The *Description* introduced an entirely new world, which, in respect to its inner relationships, its natural order and significance, was a complete
riddle.

What would one not give, it was felt in Jomard's
day, to be able to solve the puzzle of the hieroglyphs!
But was this possible? De Sacy, the great Parisian Orientalist, said that "the problem is too complicated,
scientifically insoluble." On the other hand there was
no denying that a little German schoolteacher by the
name of Grotefend, from Göttingen, had published a
paper that correctly pointed the way to deciphering the
cuneiform writing of Persepolis. Already his method
was showing results. And whereas Grotefend had had
extraordinarily little material to work with, now innu-

[1] Demotic writing was a simplified or popular form of hieratic writing,
which in turn was an abridged form of hieroglyphic writing that had
assumed a cursive character. Hieratic was used for all literature, both
secular and religious, until the demotic became prevalent, when hieratic
was reserved for religious writing.—Ed.

merable hieroglyphic inscriptions were available for examination. Furthermore, one of Napoleon's soldiers by sheer good luck had found a remarkable slab of black basalt. Even the journalists who first reported this find realized that the Rosetta Stone was the key to the solution of the Egyptian hieroglyphics. But where was the man who knew how to make use of this tablet?

Shortly after the discovery of the famous stele an article about it appeared in the *Courrier de l'Égypte*, under a dateline that read, in Revolutionary style: *"le 29 fructidor, VIIᵉ année de la République"* ("Fructidor 29, Year 7 of the Republic"). By the rarest coincidence this Egyptian newspaper turned up in the parental home of the man who, in a work of unparalleled genius, some twenty years later was actually to read the inscription on the black slab and so solve the riddle.

# THE MYSTERY OF THE ROSETTA STONE

When Dr. Franz Joseph Gall, the famous phrenologist, was touring France in order to popularize his skull-bump theory of personality—during which itinerary he was marveled at and laughed at, now honored, now slandered—at a certain home in Paris he was introduced to a young student who immediately interested him. Gall's professional glance fell on the young man's head. He was staggered by its conformations. "Ah," he exclaimed, "what a linguistic genius!" Whether or not the skull doctor had got his information beforehand, at this time the sixteen-year-old boy had already mastered half a dozen Oriental languages as well as Latin and Greek.

No less astounding is the account of Champollion's birth as recorded in one of the highly imaginative biographies so fashionable in the nineteenth century. Since there is no evidence to contradict the colorful tale, however, it must be included in the portrait of the controversial man to whom the science of archæology owes so much.

In the little French town of Figeac the wife of the bookseller Jacques Champollion lay abed, crippled, unable to move. Sometime in mid-year 1790 Jacques, after the regular doctors had given her up as incurable, called in the magician Jacqou. The town of Figeac, incidentally, is in the Dauphiné, in the southeastern part of France, and is known as the Province of the Seven

Miracles. The Dauphiné is one of the most beautiful sections of the country, a place where God might reasonably be expected to linger. The Dauphinois are a hard, conservative race, not easily aroused from their lethargy, yet, once awakened, capable of excessive fanaticism. They are Catholic in religion and highly susceptible to the mystical and miraculous.

The magician, Jacqou—and this on the evidence of several sources—had the sick woman lie on heated herbs, and drink hot wine. If she followed his instructions, he said, she would be promptly cured. Moreover, to the astonishment of the family, he prophesied she would give birth to a boy child, now in her womb, and added that the child would achieve fame and be remembered down through the centuries.

On the third day the sick woman rose from her bed. On December 23, 1790, at two o'clock in the morning, Jean-François Champollion was born, he who was destined to decipher the hieroglyphs.

If the devil's children, as they say, have cloven feet, it is not surprising to find some modest signs of prenatal influence where a magician has been at work. Examination of the young François revealed that the corneas of his eyes were yellow, a peculiarity commonly found only among peoples of the East and certainly a curiosity of the first order among western Europeans. Moreover, he had a strikingly sallow, almost brown pigmentation, and the whole cut of his face was decidedly Oriental. Twenty years later he was known everywhere as "the Egyptian."

Jean-François Champollion was a child of the Revolution. The advent of the Republic was proclaimed in Figeac in September 1792. From April 1793 the Terror reigned. The Champollions lived in a house situated only thirty paces or so from the Place d'Armes—the square subsequently named after the boy—where a liberty pole had been set up. The first sounds that Jean-François remembered hearing were the noisy music of the carmagnole and the weeping of refugees seeking protection from the aroused mob in his father's house, among them the priest who became his first tutor.

Jean-François was five years old, an impressed biographer notes, when he accomplished his first feat of decipherment: he taught himself how to read by comparing a list of words he had learned by heart with the written text. He was barely seven years old when he first heard the magical name of Egypt, a name that for the sensitive boy had the deceptive shine of a fata morgana; for his brother, Jean-Jacques, Jean-François's senior by twelve years, had hopefully planned to accompany Napoleon's expedition to the land of the Nile, only to be left behind at the last moment.

The young Champollion, according to both hearsay and eyewitness accounts, did not do so well in his studies at Figeac. To remedy this situation his brother, already a gifted philologist much interested in archæology, in 1801 took him to Grenoble and there took personal charge of his education. When the eleven-year-old François quickly showed a rare talent for Latin and Greek and began to devote himself with astonishing success to the study of Hebrew, his brother then and there made a decision to hide his own light under a bushel in order that the younger brother's might shine that much the more brightly. From this time on he called himself Champollion-Figeac, later simply Figeac. His modesty and fixed conviction that the younger brother would do more than himself for the family name is all the more remarkable in view of his own indisputable abilities.

That same year Jean-Baptiste Fourier, the famous mathematician and physicist, had a conversation with the lad who knew so much about languages. Fourier had acompanied the Egyptian expedition and later served as secretary of the Egyptian Institute in Cairo. He had also been commissioner in the French military government in Egypt, chief of jurisdiction and prime mover in the scientific commission. At this time he was prefect of the department of Isère and had taken residence in the provincial capital of Grenoble, where he had quickly drawn about him a circle of enlightened spirits. During a school inspection he entered into a little debate with François and was so taken by his superior intelligence that he later invited him to his home, where he showed him his Egyptian collection. The dark-skinned little boy was enchanted by his first sight of papyrus fragments and hieroglyphic inscriptions on stone tablets. "Can anyone read them?" he asked. Fourier shook his head. "I am going to do it," little Champollion announced with absolute certainty. "In a few years I will be able to. When I am big." In after years he himself often referred to this incident.

Inevitably this anecdote calls to mind the other boy who said to his father: "I will find Troy." Both showed the same sureness, the same somnambulistic certainty. Yet how differently were their boyish dreams realized! All his life Schliemann remained the autodidact; but Champollion never departed so much as an inch from the paths of orthodoxy in matters educational, though his mind developed with a speed that soon left his fellow students far behind. Whereas Schliemann began his work without any technical equipment whatever, Champollion armed himself with all the knowledge that the century could place at his disposal.

The brother supervised his education. He tried to curb the boy's ravening hunger for knowledge, but without success. Champollion explored the most esoteric fields of learning, leaping from peak to peak. At the age of twelve he wrote his first book, a *History of Famous Dogs*. Finding his historical research hindered by a lack of orderly digests, he made his own chronological table, which he called "Chronology from Adam to Champollion the Younger." When the older brother had retreated so that the limelight would fall exclusively on Jean-François, the boy repaid the compliment

by calling himself "Champollion the Younger," to remind the world that there was a Champollion to whom
he deferred.

At thirteen he began to learn Arabic, Syrian, Chaldean, and finally Coptic. It is remarkable, in this regard, that everything he learned or did, and indeed
everything that chanced to come his way unasked, was
somehow related to the Egyptian theme. No matter
what he turned his mind to, he seemed to be led in-
sensibly to some Egyptian problem. He took up Old
Chinese in order to seek out a connection between it
and Old Egyptian. He studied textual excerpts from
the Zend, Pahlavi, and Parsi—rare linguistic material
available in Grenoble only through Fourier's intervention. Having used every source he could lay hands on,
in the summer of 1807 Champollion, then seventeen
years old, drew up the first historical chart of the kingdom of the Pharaohs.

The daring of this attempt can be appreciated only
when it is realized that he had no other source material
to draw on excepting Biblical references, garbled Latin,
Arabic, and Hebraic texts, and comparisons with the
Coptic, the only language providing a link with the
Old Egyptian. The Coptic tongue had actually been
spoken in Upper Egypt as late as the seventeenth century.

Learning that Champollion wished to transfer his
studies to Paris, the *lycée* authorities asked him to write
a paper on a subject of his own choosing. They expected the usual schoolboy essay; instead Champollion
sketched out a whole book for them: *Egypt under the
Pharaohs.*

On September 1, 1807 he read the introduction to
this projected work. The whole teaching staff of the
*lycée* of Grenoble had assembled to listen to the slender
boy. He stood before them very erect and serious, his
face aglow with the feverish beauty of prodigy. His
ideas unfolded in a series of bold theses, impelled by

powerful logic. The professors were overwhelmed to such degree that on the spot they elected the boy to join them on the faculty. Renauldon, the president, got up and embraced Champollion. "In making you a member of the faculty, we of the *lycée* are taking into account your accomplishments to date," he said. "Yet beyond that we are counting on what you will do in the future. We are convinced that you will justify our hopes, and that when you have made a name for yourself, you will not forget those who first recognized your genius."

And so overnight Champollion was graduated from student to teacher.

Leaving the *lycée* building, Champollion fainted away. At this time he was a hypersensitive youth, an intense personality prone to elegiac moods. Already he was recognized in many quarters as a genius, and his precocious intellectual development was well known. Physically, too, he was old beyond his years. (When, for example, he made up his mind to marry just after leaving school, it was not at all a case of calf love.) He knew that he was moving into a new phase of his career. He visualized the metropolis of Paris, hub of all Europe, focal point of politics and adventures of the spirit.

By the time the heavy coach in which he and his brother had been riding for seventy hours drew near Paris, Champollion was quite lost in feverish visions, poised between dream and reality. Yellowed papyri swam before his eyes, words from a dozen different languages whispered in his ears. He thought of the Rosetta Stone, a copy of which he had seen while taking leave of Fourier. The hieroglyphs incised into the basalt haunted his racing, disjointed thoughts.

It is said on good authority that while the brothers were riding along together on this trip to Paris, Champollion suddenly blurted out his secret thoughts. He told Figeac what he had hoped to do, and now sud-

denly knew that the consummation of this hope lay
within his power. The dark eyes gleamed in the sallow
face as he said: "I am going to decipher the hieroglyphics. I know I will."

A man called Dhautpoul is usually credited with the
discovery of the Rosetta Stone. Other sources name
Bouchard, but close investigation reveals that Bouchard
was merely the officer in direct charge of a gang of
men working on the ruins of Fort Rachid; he personally did not find the stone. This fort—the French re-
named it Fort Julien—was located four or five miles
northwest of Rosetta, on the Nile. This same Bouchard
took charge of shipping the tablet to Cairo.

The Rosetta Stone in actual fact was dug up by
some unknown soldier. Conceivably he may have had
some education, or at least enough common sense to
recognize the rarity, or curiosity value, of the stele. Or
he may have been ignorant and superstitious, to such
degree that he mistook the signs on the stone for witchcraft, so creating a disturbance that brought Bouchard's
attention to the find.

The Rosetta Stone was about the size of a table
top, three feet nine inches in length, two feet four
and a half inches in breadth, and eleven inches in thickness. It was made of fine-grained basalt, "hammer-hard."
On one polished side were three columns of writing,
partially weathered and worn away by two thousand
years of sandy abrasion. The first of these columns,
fourteen lines in length, consisted of hieroglyphs; the
second, thirty-two lines long, was in the demotic script;
and the third, fifty-four lines long, in Greek.

Greek! Therefore, it would seem, readable, understandable.

One of Napoleon's generals, a Hellenist by avoca-
tion, immediately undertook the translation of the
Greek column. The message, he found, recorded a
decree of the Egyptian priesthood, issued in 196 B.C.,
praising Ptolemy Epiphanus for benefits conferred.

Together with other French booty, the tablet, after the capitulation at Alexandria, reached the British Museum. Fortunately the "commission" had caused plaster copies to be made of it and of all the other pieces. These reproductions were sent home to Paris. The scholars crowded round and began their comparisons.

Comparisons, for the very arrangement of the columns suggested that all three contained the same text. The *Courrier de l'Égypte* had already proposed that here lay the key to open the gates of the dead kingdom, the possibility of "explaining Egypt through the Egyptians." Once the Greek inscription had been properly translated, it seemed unlikely there would be much difficulty in establishing a connection between the hieroglyphic signs and the Greek words.

The best minds of the day applied themselves to the task, in England (using the original Rosetta Stone) and also in Germany, in Italy, and in France. With no result. One and all they built on false premises. Their mistake was to read into the hieroglyphs ideas that, in part, went back ultimately to Herodotus. It was one of those typical misconceptions which persist through the historical development of the human mind. To pry into the secret of Egyptian writing a virtually Copernican change of viewpoint was needed, an inspiration that would break the bonds of tradition.

The older brother, Champollion Figeac, had a former teacher named de Sacy who lived in Paris. De Sacy, despite his unprepossessing appearance, was a scholar of international repute. When Figeac took his younger brother, then aged seventeen, to meet de Sacy, the boy acted as if he were in the presence of an equal. Indeed, with de Sacy he behaved much as he had with Fourier when introduced to this other great man at Grenoble some six years before.

De Sacy was rather suspicious of the prodigy from the provinces. Aged forty-nine, and an intellectual leader of his times, at first he hardly knew what to make of this stripling who, in his *Egypt under the Pharaohs,* of which de Sacy had seen only the introduction, visualized a plan that the author himself admitted would not be realized in his day. Yet much later, recalling his first meeting with Champollion, de Sacy spoke of the "deep impression" the young man had made on him. And small wonder! This same book had almost been finished by the end of the year in which they met. Already the seventeen-year-old was earning the right to the public recognition so richly accorded him seven years afterwards when the book had finally been published.

Champollion threw himself into his studies. Holding himself completely aloof from the distractions of Paris, he buried himself in the libraries, ran from institute to institute, studied Sanskrit, Arabic, and Persian—the "Italian of the Orient," as de Sacy aptly called it. In sum, he immersed himself in all the Oriental languages, laying the groundwork for an understanding of their idiomatic developments. Meanwhile he wrote to his brother asking for a Chinese grammar, "for amusement," as he put it.

He felt his way so perfectly into the Arabic that his voice actually took on a different quality. At a social gathering an Arab salaamed to him, mistaking him for one of his own. Through bookish contact alone he acquired such an extensive knowledge of Egypt that the then famous African traveler Somini de Manencourt, after a conversation with the young man, exclaimed: "He knew the countries we were talking about as well as I do myself!"

Only a year later he spoke and wrote Coptic so well—"I speak Coptic to myself," he said—that for practice he kept journals in Coptic. This eccentricity, forty years later, resulted in a famous *gaffe.* A French scientist mistook these notes for Egyptian originals from the time of Marcus Aurelius Antoninus and wrote a commentary on them as such. This was the French counterpart of the German Professor Beringer's solemn finding that certain bones planted as a joke by the schoolchildren of Würzburg were fossils of vast antiquity.

During the Parisian period Champollion ran into hard times. But for his brother's selfless generosity and support, he would have literally starved to death. He lived in a miserable little room near the Louvre, for which he paid eighteen francs a month. Unable to raise even this small sum, he wrote begging letters to his brother, saying that he was at his wits' end and could not make ends meet. His brother wrote back that he would have to pawn his library unless François cut down expenses. Cut down? Still more? His shoes were worn through, his shirts in rags. Things got so bad that he was ashamed to appear in public. The winter was unusually severe, and he fell sick. As he lay in his damp, cold room, the seed was sown of the disease that eventually was to take his life. But for two small successes he would have completely succumbed to despair.

To add to his tribulations, the Emperor needed more soldiers and in 1808 issued an order making all males over sixteen liable to conscription. Champollion was terrified. His whole nature rebelled against coercion. Though capable of the strictest intellectual discipline, he shuddered when he saw marching squadrons of guardsmen, the pawns of a type of discipline that leveled off all individual differences. Had not Winckelmann suffered the same pangs under the threat of being swallowed up in the military? "There are days," François wrote in dejection to Figeac, "when I completely lose my head."

The brother, ready as always to lend a helping hand, moved into the breach to protect Champollion. He enlisted the aid of friends, he drew up petitions, wrote countless letters. The outcome was that Champollion finally was able to continue with his studies of dead languages in times deeply infected with martial unrest.

Another matter that occupied his attention, which now began to fascinate him so much that at times he even forgot the threat of being inducted into the army, was the study of the Rosetta Stone. In this regard he was much like Schliemann, who put off learning ancient Greek until he had taught himself to speak and write all the other European languages. Like Schliemann with the Greek language, so Champollion with the Rosetta Stone. Always the young man's thoughts reverted to the enigmatic slab, yet always, up to now, he had hesitated, believing himself not to be properly equipped to tackle a problem so definitive.

Now, however, after seeing a new copy of the Rosetta Stone made in London, he could suddenly no longer restrain himself entirely. Yet he contented himself with comparing the stone with a certain papyrus instead of plunging into actual decipherment. His first try at the black stele enabled him "to find independently the correct values for a whole row of letters." "I submit my first step to you for examination," he wrote to his brother on August 30, 1808. He was then eighteen years old. For the first time one can sense the pride of the youthful discoverer lurking behind the typically modest explanation of his methods.

Even as he made this initial contact and, having made it, knew himself to be on the road to success and fame, he was dealt a stunning blow. He had anticipated toil and denial and did not complain; but now news came to him that seemed to destroy his laborious preparations and his soaring hopes: the hieroglyphs had been deciphered.

Though at first the news completely cast down Champollion, its effect proved to be only transitory. Champollion was walking along the street on his way to the Collège de France when he ran into the friend who broke the news to him, unaware of the havoc he was causing. Champollion turned pale, swayed, and had to cling to his friend for support. Everything he had lived and worked and gone hungry for had vanished in smoke.

"It is Alexandre Lenoir," the friend said, "His book

is just out, a brochure. He calls it the *Nouvelle Explication*. In it he deciphers all the hieroglyphs. Think what this means!"

Indeed, think what it means!

"Lenoir?" asked Champollion. He shook his head. Then he saw a gleam of hope. Only yesterday he had seen Lenoir. He had known him for about six months. Lenoir was a competent scholar, but far from a genius. "Impossible," said Champollion. "Nobody said anything about deciphering to me. Even Lenoir himself didn't mention it."

"Does that surprise you?" his friend asked. "Who wouldn't keep mum about such a discovery?"

Champollion suddenly pulled himself away. "Where is the bookshop?" he asked. He rushed off at breakneck speed. With trembling hands he counted out the francs on the dusty counter. Very few of Lenoir's brochures had yet been sold. Then he ran home, threw himself on his shabby couch, and began to read. . . .

In the kitchen the widow Mécran set her pan on the table, almost startled out of her wits. From her lodger's room came a hellish racket. She listened for a moment in horror, then ran to the door and looked in. François Champollion was lying on the sofa, his whole body shaking. He was laughing and laughing, in hysterical peals.

He had Lenoir's book in his hand. Decipher the hieroglyphs? The flag had been planted a little too soon! Lenoir's book was sheer nonsense, freely invented, a quixotic mixture of fantasy and misguided scholarship. Champollion knew enough about the possibilities to realize that.

Still, the blow had been terrible, and Champollion never forgot it. His reaction showed him just how deeply he was given over to the task of making the dead symbols talk understandably. That night when he fell asleep from sheer exhaustion he dreamed wild dreams. Egyptian voices spoke to him out of the phantasmagoria. In the dream his true being stood forth clearly, untrammeled by the press and distractions of everyday, revealing him as a man possessed, maniacally fixed, bewitched by the hieroglyphs. His dream was fraught with intimations of triumphs. Yet more than a dozen years separated him from his goal.

# 11/CHAMPOLLION (II):
## TREASON AND HIEROGLYPHICS

At the age of twelve, while studying the Old Testament in the original, Champollion wrote an essay arguing that a republic was the only reasonable form of state. Having grown up amid intellectual influences that paved the way for the century of enlightenment and released the forces of the French Revolution, he suffered under the renascent depotism that crept in with decree and edict and ultimately showed its face openly after Napoleon's coronation as Emperor. Unlike his brother, Champollion did not succumb to Napoleon's charm.

Yet it was the Egyptologist Champollion who, impelled by a tremendous need for freedom, stormed the Bourbon citadel of Grenoble, banner in hand. He tore the lilied flag from the citadel tower, and in its place raised the tricolor, which for a decade and a half was to fly before Bonapartist armies as they swept over Europe.

Champollion was again in Grenoble. His appointment to a professorship of history at the university dates from July 10, 1809. At the age of nineteen, then, we find him lecturing to young men, among whom were many who had shared school bench and classroom with him at the *lycée* only two years earlier. It is quite understandable that he should have made enemies. Almost at once he fell afoul of a net of intrigue woven by older professors whom he had too easily surpassed and unwittingly humiliated.

And what curious ideas the young history professor championed! He proclaimed a jealous regard for the truth to be the highest ideal of historical research, meaning by that the absolute truth, not any Bonapartist or Bourbon version. To attain this ideal he demanded intellectual freedom, and this at a time when inquiry was limited by all kinds of political prohibitions and dispensations. Historians, he felt, should pay no heed to the powers that be. He demanded the continuance of the liberties that had been shouted from the housetops during the initial ferment of the Revolution, but that already were being consistently betrayed.

Champollion's politicking necessarily brought him into conflict with the timeservers of his day. He never deviated from his convictions, though often he was discouraged enough. At such times he would cite to his brother a thought that might have been taken from Voltaire's *Candide*, but which he, the Orientalist, found expressed more to his liking in one of the secred books of the East. "Make your fields arable! In the Zend-Avesta it says: better make six acres of poor land arable than win twenty-four battles. That is also my opinion." Ever more hopelessly entangled in academic scheming, sick in spirit, deprived of a fourth of his stipend by professorial machination, he wrote: "My lot is decided. I must be poor as Diogenes. I must try to buy myself a barrel to live in, and sacking to wear on my back. Then perhaps I can hope to subsist on the well-known generosity of the Athenians."

He wrote satires on Napoleon. Still, when Napoleon finally fell from power, and when, on April 19, 1814, the Allies marched into Grenoble, Champollion wondered bitterly whether a government of laws would now actually replace Bonapartist tyranny and saw little hope of any such consummation.

His intense concern for freedom of government and science, however, in nowise diminished his passion for Egyptology. His labors continued to be incredibly fruitful, though he scattered his attention among a variety of remote and sometimes unimportant subjects. He worked up a Coptic dictionary for his own use, and at the same time wrote plays for production in the salons of Grenoble, among these one on the Iphigenia theme. In a French tradition which began with Peter Abelard in the twelfth century he wrote political songs, which were taken up by the people in the streets as fast as he could turn them out. He also continued on his main work, which was to pry deeper and deeper into the mystery of Egypt. No matter what the cry in the streets, "*Vive l'Empereur!*" or "*Vive le Roi!*" his mind never relinquished this central preoccupation. He wrote countless essays, he laid plans for books, gave generously to all who came to him seeking help in their own compositions, worried his head about the needs of mediocre students. So much activity frayed his nerves and undermined his health. In December 1816 he wrote: "Every day my Coptic dictionary is getting thicker. The author, meanwhile, is getting thinner." He groaned when he found that he had reached page 1069 without finishing the project.

Then came the Hundred Days, when Europe again stiffened under Napoleon's grip. Overnight the persecuted became the persecutors, the rulers subjects, the erstwhile King a refugee. Champollion himself was so excited he could do no work. "Napoleon is coming back!" The phrase was on everyone's lips. The reaction of the newspapers of Paris was shamelessly opcratic. Their headlines, milestones of falseness, reflected the chameleon mood. "The Monster has Escaped" evolved progressively into: "The Werewolf has Landed at Cannes"; "The Tyrant Is in Lyon"; "The Usurper Is Sixty Hours away from the Capital"; "Bonaparte Approaches at Top Speed"; "Tomorrow Napoleon will Be within Our Walls"; and finally "His Majesty Is in Fontainebleau."

On March 7 Napoleon entered Grenoble at the head of his army. With his snuffbox he rapped on the city gates, torchlight playing on his face. Highly conscious of his melodramatic role in this historic scene, for one spine-tingling minute Napoleon stood alone facing the cannon on the walls. Up above, the cannoneers were running about in confusion. Then "Long Live Napoleon!" the cry rang out, and "the adventurer marched in, and marched out an emperor." For Grenoble, the heart of the Dauphiné, was the most important base of operations to be won over along the itinerary of Napoleon's trumphal return.

Figeac, Champollion's brother, in the past had always openly expressed his sympathy for Napoleonism. Now his enthusiasm knew no bounds. When Napoleon inquired after a competent private secretary, the mayor brought in Figeac, having slyly misspelled his name "Champoléon." "What a good omen!" the Emperor exclaimed. "The man has half my own name!" Champollion himself was present when the Emperor interviewed the older brother. Napoleon asked the young professor about his work and was told about the Coptic grammar and dictionary. Though Champollion, for his part, remained cool, the Emperor was fascinated by the boyish savant. He conversed with him at length. He promised him, with imperial gesture, to have his Coptic works published in Paris. Still not satisfied, the following day he visited Champollion in the university library, and there reopened the subject of the youthful professor's linguistic studies.

Two conquerors of Egypt stood face to face. One had included the land of the Nile in his plan for global conquest and had hoped to restore the country's economy by the construction of a great irrigation system. The other had never actually set foot on Egyptian soil, but with the eyes of the spirit had viewed the ancient ruins a thousand times, and eventually would make them live again by sheer power of intellect. Napoleon's imperial imagination was so keenly stimulated by his meeting with Champollion that on the spot he announced his decision to give Coptic the status of the official Egyptian language.

But Napoleon's days were numbered. His collapse was as catastrophically abrupt as his passing restoration.

Elba had been a place of exile; St. Helena was to be a grave.

Again the Bourbons returned to Paris. They lacked strength, and their vengefulness was correspondingly mild. Still, it was inevitable that hundreds of death sentences should be decreed. "Punishments rained down like manna on the Jews," it was said at the time. Figeac was among those selected for reprisal, for he had completely exposed himself by following Napoleon to Paris. In the summary political proceedings started against Figeac, no distinction was made between him and Champollion, an error that those who rancorously envied the young professor at Grenoble took pains not to correct. To make matters worse, Champollion, during the last hours of the Hundred Days period, had been unwise enough to help found the Delphinatic League, the program of which was to promote liberty in all directions. This program naturally had now become highly suspect. Champollion made this serious tactical mistake when he was struggling, without hope, to raise a thousand francs to buy an Egyptian papyrus.

When the Royalists marched on Grenoble, Champollion presented himself at the city walls to help the defenders, quite failing to recognize where the greater freedom lay. But what happened? The moment that General Latour began to bombard the city, thus endangering Champollion's precious manuscripts, the young man rushed from the walls, forgetting politics and war, and up to the third floor of the library. There he stayed through the bombardment, hauling water and sand to put out fires, all alone in the big building, risking his life to save his papyri.

It was after he had been banned from the university for traitorous activities that Champollion finally set about actually deciphering the hieroglyphs. The ban lasted for a year and a half, and was followed by additional tireless labors, at Paris and Grenoble. Then a fresh indictment on charges of treason loomed. In July 1821 he fled from the city in which he had risen from student to professorial rank. One year later he published his famous *Lettre à M. Dacier relative à l'alphabet des hiéroglyphes phonétiques*—that is, the *Letter to M. Dacier in regard to the Alphabet of the Phonetic Hieroglyphs*. This monograph outlined the rudiments of a successful decoding method, and evoked a great deal of comment in circles interested in solving the mystery of Egyptian pyramid and temple.

Several ancient writers had mentioned the hieroglyphs, and during medieval times a number of fanciful interpretations of them had appeared. Herodotus, Strabo, and Diodorus, all of whom had traveled through Egypt, refer to the hieroglyphs as an unintelligible form of picture writing. Horapollon, in the fourth century B.C., left a detailed description of the Egyptian script. (Allusions to Egyptian writing in Clement of Alexandria and Porphyry do not make sense.) Horapollon's comments were usually taken as a point of departure by later writers, for lack of any better source on which to base an opinion. And Horapollon thought of the hieroglyphs as picture writing. On this account the dominant tendency throughout later centuries was to look for a purely symbolic meaning in the pictures. This tradition permitted the non-scientific to give full rein to their imagination and drove the scholarly to despair.

Not until Champollion had deciphered the hieroglyphs was it realized just how far from the truth Horapollon had been. Egyptian writing actually had developed far beyond the original symbolism, in which three wavy lines stood for water, the outline of a ground plan for a house, a banner for a god, and so on. This literally ideographic interpretation, when applied to later inscriptions, resulted in serious misapprehensions, some of which were absurd.

Athanasius Kircher, the Jesuit, who is credited with inventing the magic lantern, between 1650 and 1654 published in Rome four volumes containing "translations" of the hieroglyphs, not one of which even remotely fitted the text. For instance, the group of signs standing for *autokrator*, title of the Roman emperor, in Kircher's reading appeared thus: "The creator of all vegetation and fruitfulness is Osiris; whose generative force holy Mophta draws into his kingdom from heaven." In spite of this colossal mistake, Kircher had at least anticipated Champollion and others in recognizing the value of studying Coptic, the latest form of the Egyptian language—a value that a dozen other scholars denied.

A hundred years later de Guignes, speaking before the members of the Paris Academy of Inscriptions, proclaimed a theory, based on comparative hieroglyphology, that the Chinese were Egyptian colonists. Yet almost every mistake of this sort contained some germ of truth. De Guignes, for instance, correctly read the name of the Egyptian King "Menes," which an antagonist changed to the reading "Manouph." Voltaire, most spiteful critic of the time, thereupon turned his invective on etymologists, "who have a low opinion of vowels and place little value on consonants." English students of the same period, reversing the thesis mentioned above, declared that the Egyptians came from China!

One might think that the discovery of the Rosetta Stone would have brought unbridled conjecture to a halt, but just the opposite proved to be the case. The solution of the problem now seemed so obvious that even lay folk began to play the game. An anonymous contributor from Dresden read the whole Greek text into its fragmentary hieroglyphic equivalent on the Rosetta Stone. An Arab by the name of Ahmed ibn Abubekr "unveiled" a text that the otherwise serious Orientalist Hammer-Purgstall went to the trouble of translating. An anonymous Parisian said he recognized the Hundredth Psalm in a temple inscription found at Dendera. In Geneva appeared the translation of inscriptions found on the so-called "Pamphylitic obelisks," which supposedly comprised "a report of the victory of the good over the wicked four thousand years before Christ."

Fantasy outdid itself. Imagination combined with extraordinary arrogance and stupidity in Count Palin, who claimed that he had recognized the sense of the Rosetta Stone at a glance. Leaning on Horapollon, on Pythagorean doctrines, and on the cabala, in one night's work the Count achieved complete results. Eight days later he offered his interpretation to the public, saying that speed of attack had "preserved him from the systematic errors that must arise from excessive contemplation."

Detail from the Narmer Palette, of the end of the fourth millennium B.C. The Horus falcon symbolizes the king, holding a conquered land (represented by the oval with the head of a bearded man) on a leash—that is, in subjection. The conqueror stands on six lotus blossoms. The lotus blossom being the sign for a thousand, these represent six thousand prisoners. The harpoon below probably indicates the name of the country. The square filled with wavy lines may mean the country is located on the seacoast. Both symbols probably refer to Syria.

Champollion sat unmoved among these fireworks, patiently ordering, comparing, testing, slowly climbing the long hill. Meanwhile he was told in a pedantic brochure from the hand of Abbé Tandeau de St. Nicolas that the hieroglyphs were not a system of writing at all, but a kind of decorative device. Undeterred, Champollion, as early as 1815, said in a letter on the subject of Horapollon: "This work is called *Hieroglyphica*, but it does not contain an interpretation of what we know as hieroglyphs, but rather of the sacred sculptural symbols—that is, the emblems of the Egyptians—which are quite different from the real hieroglyphs. My idea runs counter to general opinion, but the evidence I adduce for it is found on Egyptian monuments. The sacred sculptures distinctly show the emblematic scenes mentioned in Horapollon, such as the snake biting the swan, the eagle in characteristic posture, the heavenly rain, the headless man, the dove with the laurel leaf, etc., but there is nothing emblematic in the real hieroglyphs."

During these years, then, the hieroglyphs became a catchall for notions about a mystical Epicureanism. All manner of cabalistic, astrological, and gnostic doctrines were attributed to them, as well as agricultural, mercantile, and administrative allusions to practical life. Biblical quotations were discovered in them, even an antediluvian literature, not to mention excerpts from the Chaldean, Hebrew, and Chinese. "It was as if the Egyptians," Champollion remarks, "had nothing to express in their own language."

All these interpretative sallies were more or less based on Horapollon. There was only one way to decipherment, and this path led away from Horapollon. This was the direction that Champollion took.

The great intellectual discoveries are seldom fixed exactly in time. They are the result of innumerable findings of a protracted process of training the mind to deal with a single problem. They represent the intersection of the conscious and the unconscious, of purposeful observation and the errant dream. Only rarely is solution achieved at one sudden stroke.

Great discoveries, too, lose much of their glamour when dissected in the light of their historical background. In retrospect, to those who already understand the principle involved, the errors are likely to seem a little ridiculous, the false conceptions the result of downright blindness, the problems simple. Today it is difficult to imagine how daring it was for Champollion to offer a dissent from the tradition of Horapollon. It must be remembered that both the specialists and the informed public held fast to Horapollon for two weighty reasons. First, he was revered as an ancient authority, in much the same spirit as medieval thinkers had revered Aristotle, and as later theologians esteemed the early church fathers. Second, though they may have been privately skeptical, they simply could not visualize any other way of looking at the hieroglyphs except as symbols, conventionalized pictures. The very evidence of the eyes, unfortunately, strongly supported this thesis. Also, Horapollon had lived one and a half millennia closer in time to the period of the last hieroglyphs, and this seeming advantage tipped the scale in favor of his conception, a conception that confirmed what everybody could plainly see—pictures, pictures, and more pictures.

We are unable to say exactly when this occurred, but the moment that Champollion hit on the idea that the hieroglyphic pictures were "letters" (or, more precisely, "phonetic symbols"—his own earliest formulation says: "without being strictly alphabetical, yet phonetic") the decisive turn away from Horapollon had been made, and the right track to eventual decipherment found. It is possible to speak of inspiration after so many years of toil? Was it a case of one happy minute of perfect insight? The fact is that when Champollion was first toying with the idea of a phonetic interpretation, he decided against the notion. He even identified the sign of the horned viper with the letter *f* and still mistakenly resisted the idea of a completely phonetic system. Other investigators, among them the Scandinavians Zoëga and Akerblad, the Frenchman de Sacy, and, above all, the Englishman Thomas Young, all recognized the demotic inscription on the Rosetta Stone as "alphabetic writing" and, so doing, arrived at a partial solution of the problem. Yet beyond this point they were unable to progress. They either gave up or retracted. De Sacy announced his full capitulation. The hieroglyphic writings, he said, still remained as "untouched as the Holy Ark of the Covenant."

Even Thomas Young, who achieved outstanding

results in deciphering the demotic inscription on the Rosetta Stone, for the reason that he read it phonetically, modified his own theory in 1818. In decoding the hieroglyphic for *Ptolemy* he arbitrarily divided up the characters into letters, monosyllables, and disyllables.

Here the difference between two methods and two results comes clearly to light. On the one hand there was Young, the naturalist. Though undoubtedly a man of genius, he was unschooled in philology. His approach was schematic. He compared, he interpolated ingeniously. Though actually he deciphered only a few of the hieroglyphs, the extraordinary power of his intuition is proved by the fact that Champollion confirmed the correctness of Young's rendering of 76 out of a list of 221 groups of characters, despite his ignorance of their phonetic value. Champollion, however, had mastered more than a dozen ancient languages. Through the Coptic he had approached much closer than Young ever could to the spirit of the old Egyptian language. Whereas Young correctly guessed the meaning of a few single words or letters, Champollion recognized the underlying linguistic system. He went far beyond an interpretation of fragments; he made the Egyptian script readable and teachable. Once he had grasped basic principles, he saw that decipherment must begin with the names of the kings. This idea had been lying dormant in his mind for a long time.

But why with the names of Egyptian kings? The inscription on the Rosetta Stone, as already related, consists of an announcement in three different forms of writing that the priesthood has granted special divine honors to King Ptolemy Epiphanes. The Greek text, which could be read straight off, made this much clearly evident. And in the hieroglyphic section of the text was a group of signs enclosed in an oval ring, which ring came to be known as a cartouche.

It seemed reasonable to suppose that these cartouches, since they were the only signs in the text show-

ing evidence of special emphasis, might contain the
Egyptian word for the king's name. For the king's name
was the only element in the text seemingly meriting
distinction. One might think, too, that anyone of ordinary intelligence should be able to pick out the letters
of the name Ptolemy (as written in ancient style) and
so correlate the eight hieroglyphic signs with eight
letters.

All great ideas are simple in afterthought. Champollion's accomplishment was to break away from the
tradition of Horapollon that for fourteen centuries had
fogged the whole subject of Egyptian writing, and as
such was no mean triumph. By sheer luck, moreover,
Champollion's theory was brilliantly confirmed by study
of the inscription on the Obelisk of Philæ, which was
taken to England in 1821 by the archæologist Banks.
This obelisk bore a message also written in hieroglyphics
and Greek, and was in effect a second Rosetta Stone.
And here again the name Ptolemy was framed in a
cartouche, as was also another unfamiliar group of hieroglyphs that through comparison with the Greek
were shown to be the Egyptian word for Cleopatra.

Champollion wrote down the groups of signs one
above the other in this fashion:

The two "cartouches"
from the obelisk of
Philæ which put
Champollion on the
road leading to the
ultimate decipher-
ment of the
hieroglyphics.

Cleopatra

It was obvious that the second, fourth, and fifth signs
in the hieroglyphic group for Cleopatra coincided with
the fourth, third, and first signs of the equivalent group
for Ptolemy. With that the key to the hieroglyphs had

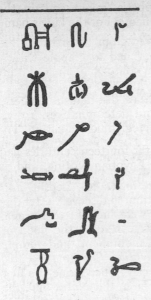

Showing how the already
highly developed
hieroglyphics evolved
into a hieratic and then
into a demotic script.

been found—the key, too, to all the locked doors of
Egyptian antiquity.

Today we know how endlessly complicated the hieroglyphic system of writing really is. Today the student
learns as a matter of course all sorts of detail that
Champollion, basing his attack on his original insight,
was able to master only by a supreme effort. The language in his day, despite his contribution to its understanding, still offered great difficulties, for, of course, it
was shot through with variations generated during the
passage of three thousand years. Today we know a great
deal about these variations, which divide "classical"
from "new" Egyptian, and "new" from "late." Before
Champollion no one had seen this development. A discovery that helped the scholar decipher one inscription
failed to solve the next. Today to the uninformed the
decorative initial letter of a medieval script almost cer-

tainly indicates a letter and nothing more. Yet medieval writing lies within our own cultural sphere and is not even a thousand years removed from us in time. But the pioneer in hieroglyphology had to grapple with a developing script evolved by a completely alien culture three thousand years away in time.

Today it is easy enough to distinguish phonetic characters from ideographs and determinatives, a division that is the first step in hieroglyphic evaluation. Today we are no longer irritated when one inscription reads from right to left, the next from left to right, the third from top to bottom. Rosellini in Italy, Leemans in the Netherlands, de Rougé in France, Lepsius and Brugsch in Germany, all contributed discovery after discovery. Ten thousand papyri were brought to Europe; eventually the cryptologists were reading the flood of new inscriptions from tomb, monument, and temple with ease. Champollion's *Egyptian Grammar* (Paris, 1836–41) appeared posthumously. Then came the first dictionary of Old Egyptian, later the *Notes* and the *Monuments*. Building on these results and on still later investigations, the Egyptologists were able in time not only to decipher but to write in Old Egyptian. The names of Queen Victoria and the Prince Consort Albert were inscribed in hieroglyphs in the Egyptian Court of the Crystal Palace at Sydenham. The dedication of the courtyard of the Egyptian Museum in Berlin was written in Old Egyptian characters. Lepsius affixed on one of the Pyramids of Gizeh a tablet on which the name of the expedition's sponsor, King Friedrich Wilhelm IV, was memorialized in ancient script.

The bookworm type of scholar is not always granted the boon of proving his theories firsthand. Often he never even has an opportunity to see the places that for decades he may have roamed in spirit.

As it happened, Champollion was not fortunate enough to add excavational successes to his great theoretical conquests. But at least he was able to see Egypt with his own eyes and had the satisfaction of proving in the field theories worked out in the seclusion of his study. Even as a youth Champollion had studied the chronology and topography of ancient Egypt. Through the years, while he succeeded in fixing a statue or inscription in space and time as best he could with such slight foothold, hypothesis after hypothesis had welled up from his train of thought. Once actually on the Egyptian scene, Champollion was in much the same position as a zoologist would be who, having reconstructed a dinosaur out of bones and fossils, suddenly found himself in the Cretaceous period face to face with the living beast.

Champollion's expedition, which lasted from July 1828 to December 1829, was a march of triumph. By this time everyone in Egypt but French officialdom had forgotten that Champollion had once been charged with high treason. The natives came in droves to look at the man who could "read the writing on the old stones." Champollion's warm reception by the Egyptians inspired the expedition to sing the "Marseillaise" and the "Freedom Song" from *La Muette de Portici* in honor of the Governor of Girgeh, Mohammed Bey. The excited Frenchmen also got some work done. Champollion went from one discovery to the next, and found his ideas confirmed on every hand. At a glance he was able to classify the architecture of different epochs found in the ruins of Memphis. At Mit Rahina he discovered two temples and a cemetery. At Sakkara —a site that several years later was to prove a great source of finds for Mariette—he discovered the royal name Onnos and forthwith correctly dated it as belonging to the earliest Egyptian times.

Then he had the sweet satisfaction of proving a claim that six years before had made him the laughingstock of the whole Egyptian commission. The expedition's boats were tied up at Dendera. In the foreground, ashore, was one of the great Egyptian temples built by a succession of kings and conquerors. The kings of the

| | Character | Phonetic Transcript | Object Represented | Remarks |
|---|---|---|---|---|
| 1 | 🦅 | ꜣ | Hawk | hard aspirate (Hebrew ℵ) |
| 2 | 𓇋 | j | Reed | |
| | 𓇋𓇋 or \\ | jj.j | | since the Middle Kingdom in the final sound for j |
| 3 | —🖑 | ꜥ | Forearm | mute glottal stop |
| 4 | 🐦 | w | Quail | |
| 5 | 𓃀 | b | Leg | |
| 6 | ☐ | p | Chair | |
| 7 | ⬿ | f | Horned Snake | |
| 8 | 🦉 | m | Owl | |
| 9 | 〰〰 | n | Water | |
| 10 | ⬯ | r | Mouth | |
| 11 | ⬜ | h | Court (yard) | |
| 12 | 💈 | ḥ | Braided Flat plait | more roughly sounded than h |
| 13 | ⊙ | ḫ | Placenta (?) | like German ch in ach |
| 14 | ⚬—⚬ | ẖ | Animal belly with teats | similar to above sound |
| 15 | — | s | Bolt to lock a door | originally voiced s |
| 16 | 𓏭 | ś | Folded Cloth | originally unvoiced s | s |
| 17 | ⬭, ⬭ | š | Pond, Lake | like German sch |
| 18 | △ | ḳ | Hill (slope of) | deep guttural k-sound |
| 19 | ⌣ | k | Basket with a handle | |
| 20 | ⧄ | g | Stands for pitchers | |
| 21 | ⌂ | t | Bread | |
| 22 | ⚊ | t̠ | Line to lead cattle | either like English th or like German tsch |
| 23 | ⬭ | d | Hand | |
| 24 | 𓆓 | d̠ | Snake | either like ds or like dj |

The hieroglyphic alphabet of twenty-four consonants. It was never used by itself, but always supplemented by signs signifying two or three consonants and by determinatives.

Twelfth Dynasty of the Middle Kingdom had shared in the construction of the Temple of Dendera, and so had Thotmes III and the great Ramses, mightiest rulers of the New Kingdom, and also Ramses's successor. The Ptolemies also had had a hand in its building, and later the Romans, Augustus and Nerva, and finally Domitian and Trajan, these last two remembered for putting up the gate and the surrounding walls.

Napoleon's troops, after a terrible march, arrived at Dendera on May 25, 1799, and there were overwhelmed by the spectacle of the ruins. Here, a few months before this, General Desaix and his division had interrupted their pursuit of the Mamelukes to stare, fascinated, at the might and splendor of a dead kingdom. Here, at last, stood Champollion, knowing beforehand almost every detail of the prospect through descriptive accounts, drawings, and copied inscriptions. Now it was night, a bright, gleaming Egyptian night under a full moon. The fifteen members of the Champollion expedition begged their leader for permission to go ashore. Finding he could not restrain them, he led the way, and they stormed the temple. "An Egyptian would have taken us for Bedouins," he writes, "a European for a gang of well-armed Carthusians."

L'hôte, who took part in this incident, fairly stammers with excitement when he tells about it. "We ran helter-skelter through a stand of palm trees—a fairy scene in the moonlight! Then we came into tall grass, thorns, and bushes. Turn back? No, we did not want to do that. Go ahead? But we had no idea just which way to take. We raised a loud cry, but the only answer was the distant barking of a dog. Then we saw a dilapidated fellah, asleep behind a tree. Armed with a stick, with nothing but a few black rags covering his body, he looked like a demon." (Champollion called him "an ambulant mummy.") "He was frightened to death when he got to his feet, sure he was about to meet his end.... Still a good two-hour march. And finally the temple itself appeared, bathed in soft light, a picture that made us drunk with admiration. . . . On the way we had sung songs to ease our impatience, but here, in front of the propylon, flooded with a heavenly light—what a sensation! Perfect peace and mysterious magic reigned under the portico with its gigantic columns—and outside the moonlight was blinding! Strange and wonderful contrast!

"Then we built a fire of dry grass in the interior [of the temple]. Fresh delight, a new outburst of enthusiasm, like a sudden delirium. It was like a fever, a madness. Everyone was overcome by ecstasy. . . . This enchanted picture, replete with magic, was real—under the portico of Dendera."

How did Champollion report this experience? The others called him "master," and the moderate tone of his description accords with this superior status. Yet behind the sober words one can feel a pulse of excitement. "I will not try to describe," he writes, "the impression that the temple, and in particular its portico, made on us. The separate dimensions of the structure can be measured, but it is quite impossible to give an idea of the whole. To the highest imaginable degree the temple combines grace with majesty. We stayed there two hours, filled with ecstasy. Guided by our poor wretch of a fellah, we wandered through the halls and tried to read the inscriptions on the outside in the glittering moonlight."

This was the first large, well-preserved Egyptian temple Champollion had ever seen. The notes he took during this night, and at times thereafter, show how intensely this man had felt his way into ancient Egypt. In fancy, dream, and thought he had so thoroughly prepared himself for the actual scene that nothing in it came as a surprise to him. Everything he now witnessed confirmed what he had already sensed. His unexpected insights amazed his learned but less responsive companions. Most of the members of Champollion's expedition saw temple, gate, column, and inscription as so many dead stone shapes, lifeless mementos of the past. But for the leader they were part and parcel of a living scene.

All of Champollion's troop had shorn their heads and wore huge turbans, gold-embroidered jackets, and yellow boots. "We wore these well and with grave demeanor," says L'hôte. This half-joking attitude toward their outlandish costumes was not shared by Champollion, who for years had been known in Grenoble and Paris as "the Egyptian." He wore native clothes as if he had been born in the land of the Nile. All his friends testify to this.

Champollion industriously interpreted and deciphered on this trip to Egypt. He had sudden inspirations, his mind teemed with ideas. He proclaimed a triumph over the commission: This was not the Temple of Isis, as they maintained, but the Temple of Hathor, goddess of love. And was the temple "extremely ancient," as the commission said? Actually the structure had received its final form under the Ptolemies, and even after this period finishing touches had been added by the Romans. The overpowering impression made by the moonlit temple did not prevent Champollion from recognizing that though the building was "an architectural masterpiece," it was overlaid "with sculpture in the worst style." "Let us hope the commission will not be offended," he wrote, "but the bas-reliefs at Dendera are abominable, and could not be anything else, considering that they sprang from a decadent epoch. During this period sculpture was already corrupted, whereas architecture, an arithmetical art and so less susceptible to change, remained worthy of the Egyptian gods and the admiration of the ages."

Champollion died three years later, to the great loss of the new science of Egyptology. Immediately after his death his ideas were lampooned by English and German scholars. Blindly they repudiated his deciphering technique as a product of the imagination, this notwithstanding its publicly acknowledged results. Champollion was brilliantly supported, however, by

Richard Lepsius, a German, who in 1866 found the bilingual Decree of Canopus. An exhaustive study of this inscription in demotic and hieroglyphic Egyptian and in Greek generally substantiated Champollion's theories. Sir Peter le Page Renouf, in an address given before the Royal Society of London in 1896, finally paid Champollion the homage due him—sixty-four years after his death.

Champollion had solved the riddle of Egyptian writing. The long process of excavation could now begin.

| sȝ·j | ndtjj·j | Mn-ḫpr-r' | 'nḫ | dt | wbn·j | n | mr(w)t·k |
|------|---------|-----------|-----|-----|--------|----|----------|
| Son my, | avenger my, | Men-hepere-re, | may he live forever: | | I shine | with | love for you. |

| ḥnm | 'wjj·j | ḥ'w·k | m | ss | 'nḫ | ndm-wjj |
|------|--------|-------|----|-----|------|---------|
| (They) protect, | hands my, | limbs your, | with | the safeguard | of life. | How sweet |

| jrmt·k | | snbt·j | ḥmn·j | tw | m |
|--------|----|--------|-------|-----|----|
| (is) friendship your | against | breast my, | I place | you | in |

| jwmn·j | bjj·j | n·k | dj·j | bnw·k |
|--------|-------|------|------|-------|
| sanctuary my. | I marvel | at you. | Place (or plant) I | power your |

| šnḏw·k | m | trw | ndw | ḥrjjt·k | r | drw |
|--------|----|------|------|---------|----|------|
| (and) fear of you | in | lands· | all, | (and) anxiety before you at | | the limits |

| šḥnwt | nt | pt |
|-------|-----|-----|
| of the props | of | heaven. |

A modern reading of Egyptian hieroglyphs.

# 12/BELZONI, LEPSIUS, AND MARIETTE: LIFE IN ANCIENT EGYPT

This book is only a synopsis, moving from peak to peak of archæological achievement. It cannot do justice, for example, to all the scholars who, laboring like ants, have classified and catalogued, at times coming forward with some bold interpretation, a creative hypothesis, or some fruitful enthusiasm.

Throughout the decades following Champollion's decipherment of the hieroglyphs, the great Egyptological discoveries are linked with the four following names: the Italian, Belzoni, the collector; the German, Lepsius, the cataloguer; the Frenchman, Mariette, the preserver; and the Englishman, Petrie, the measurer and interpreter.

"One of the most remarkable men in the whole history of Egyptology," Howard Carter, the archæologist, called Giovanni Battista Belzoni (1778–1823), one-time strong man in a London circus. Carter was referring to the man's personality rather than to his professional accomplishments. As we know, amateurs have played important roles in the history of archæology; but of all laymen who have been attracted to the field, Belzoni is perhaps the most curious.

Belzoni was born in Padua, of a family originally Roman, and as a youth thought of entering the church. Before taking orders, however, he became entangled in political intrigues and, to escape being sent to jail, ran off to London. There, according to a newspaper account of the times, he found employment in a cheap music hall as the "Italian giant" and "strong man" who every evening carried an unbelievably large number of men around the stage. During this period, very obviously, nothing could have been farther from his mind than archæology. He seems next to have turned to the study of mechanical engineering, but his interest in this field was not entirely orthodox; for in 1815 he invented a water wheel for use in Egypt, which, he claimed, would accomplish four times as much work as native devices. He must have been a clever and persistent sort of fellow, for he finally secured permission to set up a model of his machine in the palace of Mohammed Ali.

This Mohammed Ali was a rather sinister character, and at the time had just mounted the first rung of the ladder of success. Of Albanian extraction, Mohammed Ali had been a dealer in coffee, then a general, and when Belzoni arrived had been functioning for some time as viceroy, or khedive, of Egypt for the Sublime Porte. Later he was to become absolute ruler of Egypt, and of parts of Syria and Arabia as well. Twice he had administered crushing defeats to English troops. He was also notorious for his brutal political liquidations. On one occasion he had resolved his differences with the Mamelukes by inviting four hundred and eighty beys to a banquet in Cairo and slaughtering them all. Though in many respects he was an admirer of progress, Mohammed Ali was not impressed by Belzoni's water wheel. Belzoni was not dashed. In the meantime, through the German explorer Burckhardt, he had wangled an introduction to the British consul-general in Egypt, a man named Salt. To Salt he made the audacious proposal that he be allowed to take charge of the transport, from Luxor to Alexandria, of two seated statues of King Amenophis III, or Ramses II, which today are on exhibition in the British Museum.

His next five years were spent collecting, first for Salt, later on his own. He collected everything in sight, from scarabs to obelisks. (One of Belzoni's obelisks fell off a barge into the Nile, but he fished it out again.)

He functioned during a period when Egypt, having become widely known as the greatest source of antiquities in the world, was being aimlessly plundered. Much the same exploitive methods used a couple of decades later in the California and Australian gold rushes were used in digging for golden antiquities. Either there were no laws to govern the situation, or what few there were were ignored. More than once differences of opinion were settled by gunfire.

It was inevitable that this passion for collecting objects without the least regard for their archæological significance should entail more destruction than discovery. Whatever knowledge was incidentally acquired was more than negated by the damage done. Though somewhere along the way Belzoni had picked up a smattering of archæological information, like the rest of his kind he went about his collecting hammer and tongs. He thought nothing, for example, of smashing open sealed tombs with a battering ram.

Despite Belzoni's rampageous methods—methods that would make a modern archæologist's hair stand on end—Howard Carter held him in fairly high esteem. On one occasion Carter remarked that Belzoni deserved recognition for his excavations and "the mode and method of carrying them out." This opinion is hardly intelligible unless we judge Belzoni within the rough context of his times and remember that he was, in large measure, the author of certain discoveries that gave rise to a chain of investigations not yet completed.

In October 1817, in the valley of Biban el-Muluk, near Thebes, Belzoni discovered, among other tombs, that of Sethos (Seti) I, predecessor of the great Ramses, and conqueror of Libya, Syria, and Chatti, land of the Hittites. The empty sarcophagus today is in the Soane Museum in London. The tomb actually had been empty for three thousand years. Where the mummy had disappeared to, Belzoni did not discover. The opening up of the tomb of Sethos paved the way for a long series of important finds in the Valley of the Kings. For years the whole area was intensively excavated, the greatest discovery being made in our own century.

Six months later, on March 2, 1818, the Italian opened up the second Pyramid of Gizeh, tomb of Chephren, and penetrated into the royal burial chamber. These primitive investigations by Belzoni launched the study of the pyramids, greatest structures of the ancient world. Out of the darkness of Egyptian prehistory the first human traits took shape, framed within a vast geometry.

Belzoni was not the first to burrow into the Valley of the Kings, nor the first to seek entrance to a pyramid. Yet despite his being more a seeker after gold than after knowledge, at least he was the first to disclose, in burial chamber and pyramid at two different sites, important archæological problems that were solved only in recent times.

In 1820 Belzoni returned to London, and in the Egyptian Hall that had been erected in Piccadilly some

Sethos fights the Hittites in Syria. This design comes from the temple at Thebes. At one time both sculpture and inscription were painted. Belzoni, who found the tomb of Sethos, reported that only traces of the original colors remained.

eight years before, he set up an exhibition, the chief attractions of which were the alabaster sarcophagus of

Sethos and a model of his burial chamber. A few years later Belzoni died on an exploring trip to Timbuktu. Today we can forgive him the impropriety of scratching his name into the throne of Ramses II in the Ramesseum at Thebes, an act by which he established a vandalistic precedent followed through the years by countless antiquarian Mr. Browns, Herr Schmidts, and Messieurs Leblancs, who ever since have been a thorn in the side of archæologists.

Belzoni had been the great collector; the time had come for the cataloguers and arrangers to step forth on the stage, greatest of whom was Richard Lepsius.

Alexander von Humboldt, traveler and naturalist, persuaded King Friedrich Wilhelm IV of Prussia to put up ample funds for an Egyptian expedition. Thirty-one-year-old Richard Lepsius was picked to be leader. Lepsius (born in 1810, in Naumburg, Germany) had studied philology and comparative languages. At the age of thirty-two he had become a lecturer at the University of Berlin. A year later he went on the trip to Egypt.

The three-year schedule, 1843–5, offered an advantage no other expedition had ever enjoyed: time. Quick booty was not the objective; the purpose was to catalogue and to understand; and the abundance of time permitted them to drive their spades into whatever spot seemed likely. They thus spent six months on Memphis alone, and seven on Thebes.

Lepsius's first success was the discovery of several monuments of the Old Kingdom—the early period of Egyptian history, of pyramid-building, between 3200 and 2270 B.C. He found the traces and remains of thirty hitherto unknown pyramids, thereby extending the total list to sixty-seven. He also investigated one hundred and thirty mastabas, a type of interment chamber neglected by archæologists before him. A mastaba is an oblong structure with sloping sides containing cult rooms and

connected by a shaft with a burial chamber in the rock
beneath. These mastabas were built during the period
of the Old Kingdom to serve as tombs for prominent
people. In Tell-el-Amarna Lepsius found material that
provided an initial insight into the character of the
great religious reformer Amenophis IV. He was also the
first to take measurements in the Valley of the Kings.
Under his direction casts were made of reliefs on temple walls and of countless inscriptions, and transcrip-
tions were made of cartouches containing the names of
royalty. Lepsius ransacked the ages as far back as the
fourth millennium B.C. He was the first to impress
order on what he saw, the first to see Egyptian history
as a panorama, to understand the ruins as the end
products of a process of becoming.

The treasures of the Egyptian Museum in Berlin
were fruits of this Lepsius expedition. A tremendous
array of publications, beginning with the twelve-volume
showpiece called *Monuments of Egypt and Ethiopia*
and branching out into a spate of specialized mono-
graphs on all manner of esoteric subjects, resulted from
the expedition's intensive study of Egyptological
sources.

Lepsius died in 1884, at the age of seventy-four.
His biographer, Georg Ebers, an excellent Egyptologist,
whose florid romances of Pharaonic times were avidly
read by all romantic young ladies about the turn of the
century, properly describes him as the real founder of
modern archæology. Two of the great classifier's works
assure him a permanent place in posterity: his *Egyptian Chronology*, published in 1849; and his *Book of
Egyptian Kings*, which came out a year later.

The Egyptians, like all ancient peoples, contrary to our
modern habit, did not leave us history books in the
modern sense; there were, in short, no historians, nor
did they reckon the flow of time from some fixed point
of temporal reference. Instead they dated in "king's
years," calling each year after a prominent event that

had happened in it. They compiled lists of kings divided into dynasties, beginning with the first king of the First Dynasty. The oldest annals preserved to us, the so-called Palermo Stone, date from the Old Kingdom, a tantalizingly broken fragment; the Papyrus of the Kings, also in a bad state of preservation, dates from the New Kingdom. The reconstruction of the Egyptian past was much like working out a passably accurate chronology of European history from inscriptions on public buildings, the texts of the church fathers, and the fairy tales of the brothers Grimm. This is pretty much what the pioneers in Egyptology attempted to do. We should accord this problem of constructing an Egyptian chronology at least brief notice, if only because it strikingly illustrates how the archæologists made typically keen use of every *point d'appui* at their disposal in pinning down four thousand years of human experience. The effort was so successful that today our knowledge of Egyptian dates is more exact, for example, than was Herodotus', who actually traveled in Egypt almost twenty-five hundred years ago.

Although all the old Egyptian sources had to be given due regard, a piece of writing by an Egyptian priest, as it happened, offered the first historical toehold. The priest, a certain Manetho of Sebennytus, three hundred years before Christ, or soon after the death of Alexander the Great, and sometime during the reign of the first two Ptolemaic kings, wrote a history of Egypt in Greek, called the *Egyptian Annals*, or *Egyptian History*. Manetho's work has not come down to us in complete form. We know him from epitomes found in Julius Africanus, Eusebius, and Josephus. Manetho divided the long list of Pharaohs known to him into thirty dynasties, which same division we use today.

    J. H. Breasted, the American archæologist, calls Manetho's annals a "collection of childish folk-tales." This harsh judgment ought perhaps to be qualified. We must remember that Manetho had no precedent to guide him, and three thousand years of history to account for. He was in somewhat the position of a modern Greek historian, were he to try to plot out an account of the Trojan War using only national tradition and folklore. For several decades Manetho's list was the only basic source available to archæologists. (Then, as now, *archæology* was the technical term for the general study of antiquity. Egyptian monuments and inscriptions are so numerous, however, that they require undivided attention. Since the days of Lepsius the term *Egyptology* has been used for this specialized field of archæology, as in more recent times the term *Assyriology* is used for the study of Mesopotamian antiquities.) How far the scholars of the West have departed from Manetho's chronology is shown by the following array of dates assigned, through the years, by different authorities to the unification of Egypt by King Menes, an event that marked the real beginning of Egyptian history and may be taken as the earliest happening of dynastic significance:

Champollion, 5867 B.C.; Lesueur, 5770; Bökh, 5702; Unger, 5613; Mariette, 5004; Brugsch, 4455; Lauth, 4157; Chabas, 4000; Lepsius, 3892; Bunsen, 3623; Eduard Meyer, 3180; Wilkinson, 2320; Palmer, 2224. Recently the date has been pushed back again. Breasted dates Menes at 3400, Georg Steindorff at 3200, and the newest research at 2900.

It is significant that all dates become more difficult to determine the farther back one goes into the past. As for the more recent phases of Egyptian history—and by this is meant the New Kingdom, and the Late Period, which had just drawn to a close when Cæsar was languishing with Cleopatra—it is possible to make use of comparative dates drawn from Persian, Hebrew, Greek, and Assyrian-Babylonian history.

Suddenly, in 1843, new possibilities of control for the remote past through the comparative approach appeared with the discovery of the Royal Tablet of Karnak, which was deposited in the Bibliothèque Nationale in Paris. On the tablet was inscribed a list of Egyptian rulers from the oldest times down to the Eighteenth Dynasty. Another prime source is the Royal Tablet of Sakkara, which was found in a tomb, and which now reposes in the Egyptian Museum in Cairo. On one side of the Sakkara Tablet is a hymn to Osiris, god of the underworld, on the other the prayer of the scribe, Tunri, directed to fifty-eight kings, from Miëbis to Ramses the Great, the names being arranged in two rows.

More famous, however, and even more important for Egyptology, was the Royal List of Abydos. This inscription, which was found in a gallery of the Temple of Sethos, shows Ramses II and Sethos I, the former as a crown prince. They are sculptured in the act of paying homage to their ancestors—Sethos himself swinging a censer—the ancestors listed in two rows, containing seventy-six names all told. Bread, beer, mutton, goose meat, incense, and other things used in votive offerings are all faithfully recorded on the relief. The Abydos list offered excellent opportunities for cross-checking the royal line of succession, but no help in establishing exact dates in our own calendrical fashion.

Strewn about everywhere in the ruins of ancient Egypt, however, were inscriptional and other references to the duration of this or that king's reign, to the length of such a campaign, to the length of time required to build a temple, and so on. By using the so-called "addition of minimal dates" method—that is, by adding together the regnal intervals—the skeleton of Egyptian history was gradually pieced together.

The first absolute datings, however, were made possible by recourse to something older than Egypt, older than human history, older than man himself— the movements of the stars. The Egyptians had an annual calendar correlated with the changes of the seasons, and had used it since time immemorial in forecasting the flood periods of the Nile, on which the very existence of the land depended. It was not the first calendar, as we shall see later, although, according to Eduard Meyer, it was in use at least by 4241 B.C., a date abandoned as far too early. This Egyptian calendar provided the basis for the Julian calendar, introduced in Rome in 46 B.C., the system of time-reckoning adopted by the Western World and used until replaced, A.D. 1582, by the Gregorian calendar.

The archæologists turned for help to the mathematicians and astronomers, whom they supplied with old texts, copies of inscriptions, and translations of hieroglyphic references to stellar events. By an analysis of announcements concerning the ascension of Sirius on Thout 1—that is, July 19—a date that marked the Egyptian new year, the astronomers were able to place the beginning of the Eighteenth Dynasty with some exactness at the year 1580 B.C., likewise the beginning of the Twelfth Dynasty at the year 2000 B.C., always allowing for an error of three or four years.

Henceforth there were fixed points of reference on which to build a chronology. The known reigns of a whole series of kings could now be fitted into the scheme. Presently it was discovered that the durations assigned by Manetho to some of the dynasties were fantastically exaggerated. Out of this skeletal framework of three thousand years of history a true history of Egypt gradually evolved.

Egyptian culture was a riparian culture. When the first political alliances had come about, the North Kingdom arose in the Delta region, and the South Kingdom arose between Memphis (Cairo) and the first cataract of the Nile. The real history of Egypt begins with the fusion of these two early kingdoms, an event that occurred sometime about 2900 B.C., during the reign of King Menes, of the First Dynasty.

The dynasties that followed have, for easier comprehension, been lumped together in larger groups, known as kingdoms. The dates, especially for the earliest times, are quite inaccurate and may be as much as several hundred years out of the way. The dates and divisions up to the New Kingdom used here will be those of the German Egyptologist Georg Steindorff. Thereafter an appropriate synoptical division will be used, at the same time following Steindorff's dynastic dates.

The Old Kingdom (2900–2270 B.C.) comprises the First to the Sixth Dynasties. It is the time of portentous cultural germination, a period during which the basic cultural forms, the Egyptian religions, script, and artistic idiom, took characteristic shape. It is also the time of the pyramid builders of Gizeh, of the great kings Cheops, Chephren, and Mycerinus, all of whom fall in the Fourth Dynasty.

The First Intermediate Period (2270–2100 B.C.) was introduced by the catastrophic collapse of the Old Kingdom. It may be regarded as a transitional period leading to feudalism, an interlude throughout which a factitious royalty lingered on at Memphis. The First Intermediate Period comprises the Seventh to the Tenth Dynasties, which together include more than thirty kings.

The Middle Kingdom (2100–1700 B.C.) represents a period of development dominated by the Theban princes, who threw out the Heracleopolitan kings and again united the country. This era covers the Eleventh to the Thirteenth Dynasties. We may think of it as a time of cultural efflorescence which found expression in the countless distinguished architectural works completed under the four rulers called Amenemhet and the three called Sesostris.

The Second Intermediate Period (1700–1555 B.C.) stands under the sign of the Hyksos rulers. The Hyksos were a Semitic people ("shepherd kings") who invaded the land of the Nile, conquered it, and held sway for a century. They were finally driven from the country by the Theban princes (Seventeenth Dynasty). Until most recently it had been assumed that the expulsion of the Hyksos is related to the Biblical legend of the exodus of the Children of Israel. Now this hypothesis has been completely abandoned.

The New Kingdom (1555–1090 B.C.) is the epoch of political grandeur, the time of the "Cæsaristic" Pharaohs of the Eighteenth to the Twentieth Dynasties. The conquests of Thotmes III forged relationships with the Near East. Foreign peoples were forced to pay tribute to Egypt; tremendous wealth flowed into the land of the Nile. Splendid buildings were erected. Amenophis III formed an alliance with the kings of Babylonia and Assyria. His successor, Amenophis IV (husband of Nefertiti), was the great religious reformer, who attempted to replace the old religion with a form of sun-worship and for that reason called himself Ikhnaton—"He in whom Aton (the sun-god) is satisfied." He built a new capital in the desert, which he called Tell-el-Amarna, and which became a rival of Thebes. But the new religion collapsed in civil wars and did not survive the King. Under the rule of Amenophis' stepson, Tutankhamen, the royal residence was moved back to Thebes.

Egypt, however, reached the pinnacle of political power under the rulers of the Nineteenth Dynasty. Ramses II, later called Ramses the Great, during his sixty-six-year reign, projected his omnipotence in monumental—indeed, colossal—architectural works at Abu Simbel, Karnak, Luxor, Abydos, and Memphis, and at Thebes in the mortuary temple called the Ramesseum.

After Ramses' death anarchy ensued, but Ramses III restored peace and order during a reign that lasted twenty-one years. Thereafter Egypt fell under the sway of the increasingly powerful priests of Amen (Amun, Amon).

The Third Intermediate Period (1090–712 B.C.) was a time of turbulence and changing authority. Among the kings of the Twenty-first to the Twenty-fourth Dynasties, Sheshonk I interests us as the conqueror of Jerusalem who plundered the Temple of Solomon. Under the Twenty-fourth Dynasty, Egypt came under Ethiopian rule for a short time.

The Late Period (712–525 B.C.) marks the conquest of Egypt, during the Twenty-fifth Dynasty, by the Assyrians under Esarhaddon. The Twenty-sixth Dynasty was able once again to reunite the country, though with the loss of Ethiopia. The alliance with Greece stimulated trade and cultural exchanges. The last ruler of the Twenty-sixth Dynasty, Psamtik (Psammtech) III, was defeated by the Persian King, Cambyses, at the Battle of Pelusium. Thereafter Egypt became a Persian province. The true Egyptian cultural and historical dynamic was spent by 525 B.C.

The rule of Persia (525–332 B.C.) was imposed on Egypt by Cambyses, Darius I, and Xerxes I, and collapsed under Darius II. During this period Egyptian culture lived on the past, and the land became known as the "booty of strong peoples."

The Græco-Roman Rule (332 B.C.–A.D. 638) was initiated by Alexander the Great's conquest of Egypt and the founding of the city of Alexandria, which became the focal point of the Greek-metropolitan ethos. The Alexandrian Empire began to show decline, but through Ptolemy III Egypt again rose to political autonomy and power. The two centuries preceding the birth of Christ were filled with the dynastic quarrels of the Ptolemies. Egypt drifted more and more into the Roman orbit. Under the later Roman emperors the fiction of an autonomous Egypt was preserved, but in reality the country was nothing but a Roman province, granary of the Roman Empire, a colony drastically impoverished by plundering.

Christianity took hold very early in Egypt. From A.D. 640 onward, however, the land became completely subject to the Arab caliphate, and later tributary to the Osmanli Turks. Egypt finally entered into the European historical complex through its conquest by Napoleon.

In 1850 Auguste Mariette, thirty-year-old French archæologist, climbed to the top of the citadel of Cairo. Just landed in Egypt, he was burning to have a look at the land he had heard so much about. As he slowly turned, staring raptly in all directions, an antique empire took shape before his mind's eye. He looked beyond the slender minarets of Islam to the gigantic silhouettes of the pyramids, rising out of the western rim of the desert. The past beckoned him. And though he had come on a brief assignment, what he saw from the citadel became his fate.

Born in Boulogne in 1821, Mariette had begun to study Egyptology at an early age. In 1848 he had been appointed to an assistant's post in the Louvre, and it was while there that he had been commissioned to go to Cairo to buy papyri. In Egypt he saw how its antiquities were being plundered, and soon found he was much more interested in doing something to remedy this condition than in haggling with antique dealers. How could he help? Archæologists and tourists, excavators, and everybody else who happened along seemed to be carried away by the passion for "collecting antiques" —that is, for robbing the old monuments and making off with the treasures of the land. The native Egyptians themselves assisted in this thievish process. The laborers employed by the archæologists slipped all the small objects they came across into their pockets for resale to foreigners "foolish" enough to pay money for them. This random spoliation also resulted in a great deal of irreparable physical damage. Material success was held in much higher esteem than scientific accomplishment. Despite Lepsius's orderly example, the pillaging methods of Belzoni continued to be the order of the day. Mariette, who actually was interested mainly in excavation, realized that without a conservation program the future of archæology in Egypt would be seriously jeopardized. And indeed a few years later he did organize tremendously successful controls and set up the world's largest museum of Egyptian antiquities. Yet he, too, third among the four great Egyptologists of the nineteenth century, turned to excavation and discovery first.

He had not been in Egypt very long before he noticed a most remarkable fact. Stone sphinxes of obviously identical sculptural inspiration were found on display in the private luxury gardens of Egyptian officialdom and in front of the newer temples in Alexandria, Cairo, and Gizeh. Mariette was the first to wonder where the sphinxes had come from.

Chance plays an important part in all discoveries. Walking through the ruins at Sakkara, a town near Cairo, Mariette came upon a sphinx, buried all but the head in the sand, near the great stepped pyramid that has been identified with Zoser. Mariette was by no means the first man to see this artifact, but he was definitely the first to recognize a similarity between it and those of Cairo and Alexandria. And when he found on it an inscription recording a pronouncement attributed to Apis, the sacred bull of Memphis, everything that he had read, heard, or seen about the subject fell into place in his mind; he envisioned the mysterious lost Avenue of Sphinxes, which was known to have existed, but which up to that time had never been found. Why could not the Avenue of Sphinxes be located right here at Sakkara? Mariette hired a gang of Arabs, equipped them with shovels, and set them to digging. Their labors brought to light one hundred and forty-one sphinxes! Today we call the excavational area that Mariette opened up near Sakkara the Serapeum, or Serapeion, after the god Serapis.

The Avenue of Sphinxes at one time had connected two temples. These temples Mariette also excavated, and found the artifacts traditionally identified with the site—the tombs of the Apis, the sacred bulls. This discovery provided much deeper insight than had hitherto obtained into certain Egyptian cultural forms;

that is, into a mode of religious veneration alien and sinister, a form of worship that even the ancient Greeks, in their travelogues, reported as bizarre.

The Apis bull. The white triangle on his forehead is the symbol marking him as sacred among his taurine kind.

Not until late in Egyptian history were the likenesses of the gods given human form. In the old religious consciousness of the land the gods were incarnated in the form of emblems, plants, and animals. The goddess Hathor was a cow, thought to dwell in a sycamore tree; the god Nefertem in a lotus flower; the goddess Neith was honored in the form of a shield on which two crossed arrows were nailed. Mostly, however, the Egyptian deities were represented in animal forms. The god Khnum was a ram; Horus a falcon; Thoth an ibis; Sebek a crocodile; the goddess Nut, at Bubastis, a cat; and the goddess Buto a serpent.

Not only these animal gods, as such, but actual animals, providing they met certain qualifications, were revered. The most famous of these sacred animals, the object of an elaborate cult, was the sacred bull of Memphis, Apis, whom the Egyptians conceived to be the servant of the god Ptah.

The sacred bull was worshipped as an actual animal. He was housed in a temple and tended by priests. When he died he was embalmed and buried with great ceremony, whereupon a new bull with the same markings took his place. Cemeteries worthy of the gods and kings were built for the interment of these holy beasts. At Bubastis and Beni Hasan there was a graveyard for

The god Ptah, "creator of the world."

cats, at Ombos one for crocodiles, at Ashmunein one for ibises, at Elephantine one for rams. Some of the animal cults spread throughout the whole land and in so doing developed in endless variation. Others were locally restricted, and after a sudden flare-up would fade into obscurity for centuries.

Mariette stood before the resting-place of the sacred Apis bulls. At the entrance to the subterranean chambers was a mortuary chapel comparable to those built at the entrances of the mastabas used for the interment of the Egyptian nobility. A steep shaft led down into the long burial chamber where Apis, in innumerable incarnations, had been buried in the days of Ramses the Great and for hundreds of years thereafter. Mariette found the remains disposed in separate chambers arranged along a passageway 320 feet long. Later excavations, which brought the tomb down to Ptolemaic times, increased the total length of the galleries to 1,120 feet. What a cult!

Guided by flickering torchlight, the Egyptian laborers hardly daring to raise their voices above a whisper as they slunk along fearfully behind him, Mariette went from one burial chamber to the next. The stone sarcophagi in which the bulls had been laid away were made of heavy black and red granite, each one cut from a single polished block approximately 9.6 feet high, 6.4 feet broad, and 12.8 feet long. The weight of these blocks has been estimated at about 72 tons.

The covers had been pushed off many of the sarcophagi. Mariette and his successors found only two of the stone containers absolutely intact, with all the original burial regalia inside. The rest had been rudely plundered. When? Nobody knows the answer. The robbers are nameless. Again and again Egyptologists, in dismay and helpless anger, have discovered that robbers have anticipated them. The eternally shifting sands, which drift over temples and tombs and cities, have erased all traces of the culprits.

Mariette had plunged into the dark region of lost cults. He was to be granted the privilege—after his excavations at Edfu, Karnak, and Deir el-Bahri—of having a supreme glimpse into the rich and colorful life of ancient Egypt.

Today the tourist, having emerged from the tombs of the sacred bulls, rests on the terrace of the Mariette House, to the right of the stepped pyramid and at the left of the Serapeum. There he sips Arabian coffee and lets himself be harangued by the loquacious guides in preparation for the picture world that awaits his gaze.

It was near the Serapeum that Mariette found the tomb of the courtier and great landowner Ti. The tomb of the rich man was tremendously old, in contrast with the tombs of the sacred bulls, where signs of human activity had been found dating back to the relatively recent Ptolemaic period. Indeed, work on the tombs of Apis had been terminated so abruptly that a large sarcophagus of black granite was left just inside the entrance instead of being taken down the shaft and into its allotted place. The tomb of Ti had been finished soon after the time when Cheops, Chephren, and Mycerinus were building their pyramids. This tomb was distinguished by its wealth of realistic decoration. Mariette was well acquainted with ancient Egyptian burial customs and had expected to find the usual complement of funerary gifts, the usual rich carvings and narrative friezes. All these were present in the tomb of Ti, but in unexpected abundance. The reliefs on the walls of burial chamber and corridor proved to be far superior to anything discovered up to that time in the detail used to show the daily life of the deceased. The rich man, Ti, had evidently held in high regard absolutely everything connected with his domestic and official existence. All the personalities and appurtenances of his entourage had been taken along with him, figuratively, into the realm of death. Ti himself is shown in a dominant position in all the reliefs, three or four times larger than common people and slaves. The very physical proportions of his likeness express might and meaning and a vast gap between his and the lesser lot.

The highly stylized, linear, and richly detailed wall paintings and reliefs depict the utilitarian as well as the leisure activities of the rich. We see flax being prepared, reapers mowing grain, donkeymen driving donkeys, threshers and winnowers at work on the grain. The process of building a ship 4,500 years ago is illustrated: the felling of the trees; the cutting of the planks; the use of adze, hand ram, and paring chisel. We see that saw, ax, and auger were in common use. We also see gold-smelters at work, and observe how air was blown into the ovens to produce high temperatures. We discover sculptors, stonemasons, and leatherworkers at their daily tasks.

Again and again we are impressed by the power

over his fellows invested in an official of Ti's status. Village magistrates are represented in the act of being driven like sheep to Ti's house to settle their accounts, with constables roughly hauling laggards along by the scruff of the neck. We see endless rows of peasant women bringing Ti gifts, and troops of servants, some leading up sacrificial bulls, others in the act of slaughtering them. We see Ti at the table, with his wife, with his whole family, Ti out fowling, Ti traveling with his family in the Delta, and Ti on a journey through the papyrus thickets.

In Mariette's day the reliefs were valued more for their factual than for their æsthetic qualities. Through

The great lord Ti is punted through the papyrus thickets.

them it was possible to get an idea of the most intimate particulars of the daily life of the ancient Egyptians. The reliefs showed not only what their ocupations were, but how they went about them. Other monuments came to light that greatly extended the factual type of information used as a decorative motif on the tomb of Ti. Some of these relics were found in the tomb of the vizier Ptahhotep, and the tomb of Mereruka, discovered some forty years later. All these artifacts were found at Sakkara. And these insights into the primitive yet carefully elaborated techniques developed by the Egyptians to cope with the physical problems of their time make the feat of building the pyramids all the more admirable. As for Mariette and his contemporaries, knowing what the Egyptians had to work with only increased the mystery of the pyramids. In actual fact Egyptian technology rested on an abundance of slave power. For many decades after Mariette all kinds of fantastic conjectures about the secret methods used by the Egyptians in building their Cyclopean structures continued to appear in the press, in travel books, and even in technical publications, when in truth there was no mystery at all. The principles of Egyptian engineering were revealed by a man who was born in London at the time Mariette was digging at the Serapeum.

Eight years after Mariette had his first view of ancient Egypt from the citadel of Cairo, he finally turned his mind to what from the first he had sensed to be the most essential task. In Bulak he founded the Egyptian Museum, and a little later was appointed by the viceroy to be director of the Egyptian office of antiquities and chief supervisor of all excavations.

In 1891 the Egyptian Museum was moved to Gizeh, and finally, in 1902, settled permanently at Cairo, not far from the Nile bridge built by Dourgnon in the fake antique style that was the best which could be mustered at the turn of the century. The museum became a control station as well as an Egyptological collection. Henceforth whatever was discovered in Egypt, whether found by chance or methodically disclosed, had first to be offered to the museum. By this means Mariette, Frenchman and foreigner, stopped the plunder and incontinent sale of antiquities that rightly belonged to the Egyptians. As a token of gratitude Egypt erected a statue of Mariette in the museum garden, and after his death brought his remains to Egypt, where they were laid to rest in a marble sarcophagus.

# THE TOMB OF AMENEMHET

It is astonishing how many archæologists were prodigies. While still a merchant's apprentice, Schliemann spoke half a dozen languages. At the age of twelve Champollion was able to carry on an intelligent discussion of political questions, and at the age of nine C. J. Rich caused a sensation. William Matthew Flinders Petrie, the last of the four great men who laid the foundations of Egyptology in the nineteenth century, the measurer and interpreter, was also a precocious boy. He is reported to have already shown an extraordinary interest in Egyptian excavations at the age of ten. At that tender age he evolved the principle that was to guide him throughout his lifetime: reverence and the drive for knowledge must each get its proper share, the Egyptian soil must be literally scraped, grain by grain, not only to see what was hidden in its depth, but also to recognize how things had been disposed while still in the light of day. This report on Petrie was published in a London newspaper in 1892, at the time Flinders Petrie was appointed full professor—he was then thirty-nine years old—at University College.

There is no doubt that at an early age he combined his interest in antiquities with several others that later redounded to his advantage. He experimented in the natural sciences and took more than a dilettante interest in chemistry. He also made a cult of the mathematics of measurement, on which the exact sciences have been based since Galileo. And all the while he was trotting through the London antique shops, trying out his theories on actual objects. Even as a pupil he often complained of the lack of basic work in archæology, especially in Egyptology.

What the student missed, the grown man supplied. Petrie's scientific publications number ninety volumes. His *History of Egypt*, in three volumes (1894–1905), which is packed with investigative results, is the main precursor of all his later works. His long report called *Ten Years Digging in Egypt, 1881–1891* (published 1892) still makes exciting reading. Petrie was born on June 3, 1853, in London. He did his first archæological research in England, and published a book on Stonehenge, the early bronze age stone circle. But by 1880 he was in Egypt, and there, with some interruptions, dug for forty-six years.

Petrie found the Greek colonial town and trading center of Naukratis, and dug the Temple of Ramses out of hills of debris at Nebesheh. At Kantara—the great military road between Egypt and Syria once terminated there, and there, today, planes land on the big plaza—he discovered a fort where the mercenaries of Psamtik I had once been stationed, and identified this place with the Greek town of Daphnæ and the Biblical Tahapanes. Finally he rediscovered the two colossal sandstone statues of King Amenophis III, the ones mentioned by Herodotus, and first seen by the European scholar Pater, of Erfurt, in 1672.

The Greeks had called these colossi the Columns of Memnon. When the mother, Eos, rose above the horizon, the son, Memnon, sighed and groaned in inhuman tones that stirred the hearts of all those who heard. Strabo and Pausanias recount this legend. Much later (A.D. 130) Hadrian waited with his wife, Sabina, for the cry of Memnon, and the couple were rewarded by hearing unearthly sounds that gripped them like nothing they had known before. Septimius Severus had the upper part of the statue "restored" with sandstone blocks, and the sound came no more. Even today there is no strictly scientific explanation for the tones, the existence of which, none the less, cannot be doubted.

The wind had gnawed at the stone of the colossi for centuries. Vansleb saw the lower parts of at least one of the great statues. In Petrie's day nothing but ruins remained, sufficient to enable him to estimate the height of the throne royal figures at 38.4 feet. The length of the middle finger of the southern colossus was 4.4 feet.

Petrie excavated throughout his whole lifetime, but always scattering his efforts, unlike Evans, who spent a quarter of a century exploring the one site of Knossos. Petrie actually "scraped" his way through all Egypt, and so doing traversed three millennia. It was typical of Petrie that he should become expert on the small and intimate, particularly on everything that Egypt had to offer in the way of ceramics, statuettes, and the like. In this field he was a pioneer, the first to impress temporal sequence on Egyptian miniature sculptures. At the same time he became an authority on the largest and most sublime of Egyptian artifacts, the towering pyramids, symbols of death.

In the year 1880 Petrie arrived at the Pyramids of Gizeh. After inspecting the whole site he found an abandoned mastaba that some predecessor had provided with a door, probably with the idea of using the structure as a storehouse. This queer European told his carriers that he would live in the tomb, and the following day was duly installed. A lamp smoked on a box, in the corner a kerosene cookstove made a roaring sound. William Flinders Petrie was at home. That evening, when the shadows were long and blue, a stark naked Englishman crept over the ruins to the foot of the great pyramid, found the entrance, and went in, a ghost in the chambers of the dead, where the air was as hot and close as in a henhouse filled with nesting fowl. After midnight he scrambled out of the depths. His eyes burned, his head ached, he was streaming sweat like a man escaped from a fiery oven. In this condition he squatted in front of his box and copied the notes he had made inside the pyramid, the measurements of length and cross section, of corridor slope and corner angle. He also jotted down his first hypotheses.

Hypotheses? About what? Were there any mysteries in the pyramids? They had lain open to public view for thousands of years. Herodotus marveled at them, and the ancients called them one of the seven wonders of the world. Wonders—by definition they elude explanation. Was it not inevitable that the mere existence of the pyramids should pose staggering questions for the nineteenth-century mind, for the man of technique and the reasoned approach, for an era of skepticism and but little feeling for the sublimity of immaterial goals?

The pyramids were known to be tombs, gigantic sarcophagal houses. But what under heaven had ever inspired the Pharaohs to build in a way never seen before or since? In Petrie's day the Egyptian pyramids were thought to be unique. Now, of course, Middle America has been archæologically explored, and analogues of the Egyptian pyramids discovered in the Toltec jungle, though these were temples and not tombs. What was in Egyptian minds when they made their fortresslike monuments, when they constructed artfully hidden entrances with blind doors, and culs-de-sac ending hard up against impenetrable granite blocks? What had made Cheops raise a veritable mountain of stone over his sarcophagus, a geometric heap containing 29,500,000 cubic feet of limestone? Petrie, working night after night in rubble-choked corridors, half blind and gasping for breath in the dead air, was determined to solve the riddles of the pyramids with the scientific methods of his century. Many of Petrie's results have since been verified; and many, too, have been negated by later investigations. Whenever figures are given in this text, they come from modern sources. But now as we first set out on the trail of the robbers who almost nullified the labors of the Pharaohs, we shall choose Petrie as our guide and mentor.

More than 4,500 years ago a broad stream of naked slaves, fair and dark of skin, flat of nose, swollen of lip, and shorn of skull, rolled up from the Nile. They stank of rancid oil and sweat, of onions, garlic, and radishes. The equivalent of about two million dollars was spent feeding the workers on the Pyramid of Cheops alone. They sighed and howled under the lash of the overseers as they toiled over the smooth flats of the great road of granite stretching up from the Nile to the construction site. They groaned under the ropes cutting into their collar bones as they dragged huge blocks of stone, each more than a cubic yard in size, loaded on sledges, which moved slowly along on rollers. Amid their cries, their weeping, and their dying rose the pyramid, tier on tier. For twenty long years it grew. Each time the Nile's muddy flood overran the banks of the river, bringing all field work to a halt, the complement of a hundred thousand workers was filled with replacements, so that Cheops might have his tomb, which was called *Echet Chufu*, or the Horizon of Cheops.

The pyramid's bulk waxed tremendously. Using nothing but the power of human hands and backs, 2,300,000 blocks of stone were dragged to the site and piled one atop another. Each of the four sides of the base was more than 736 feet in length. When the last block was in place, the peak of the pyramid towered 467 feet in the air. The grave of this Pharaoh is almost as tall as the tower of the cathedral of Cologne, higher than the tower of St. Stephen's in Vienna, much higher than the dome of St. Peter's at Rome, largest church of Christendom. All of St. Paul's in London could be comfortably accommodated within the pyramid. The total mass of masonry, quarried out of the cliffs and limestone beds on both sides of the Nile, contained 3,277,300 cubic yards of material, piled up on a surface covering 64,942 square feet.

Today Cairo's street car Number 14 carries the visitor almost up to the pyramid. There, at the end of the line, he is met by shrieking dragomans, donkey-drivers, camel-drivers—all looking for baksheesh. The groans of the slaves have been silenced, the Nile wind has swallowed up the whistle of the whiplash and blown away the harsh odor of human sweat. Nothing but the huge structures themselves remain. Today we can climb to the top of the Pyramid of Cheops, highest and largest of them all, and to the south see another whole group of Pharaonic monuments rising in the distance, the pyramids of Abusir, Sakkara, and Dahshur. And near by we look down upon the pyramids of Chephren and Mycerinus, second and third respectively to Cheops' in magnitude, and over to the left there is the Sphinx. Many others are visible as ruins. The upper mass of the Pyramid of Aburôash, to the north of Gizeh, has been largely removed, so that one can look down into the burial chamber, which at one time was hidden under thousands of tons of heavy stone. The Pyramid of Hawara and the Pyramid of Illahun, made of a core of stone sheathed over with unburnt bricks of Nile clay, have been weathered away. And the "false pyramid" at Medum—called by the Arabs "el Haram el-Kaddab" because it looked so different to them from the others—was most vulnerable of all to the assaults of wind and weather and flying sand, for this structure was never finished at all. Even so, it was raised to a height of 128 feet. Pyramids go back to the Oldest Kingdom, and were still built during the era of the Ethiopian rulers of Meroë. The north group at the Meroë site alone includes forty-one pyramids, housing the bodies of thirty-four kings, five queens, and two crown princes. Tombs for the chosen few who had their names written by the nameless many in stone against the sky, there to endure for an eternity! Was fame the barb that stung the Pharaohs on? Was it some urge to monumental self-manifestation? Was it only the hubris of the mighty who have lost all mortal restraint?

The meaning of the pyramids can be grasped only in terms of Egyptian religious beliefs. The urge to build pyramids was rooted in the basic Egyptian belief that after physical death the soul continues to exist through all eternity. There was a hereafter, a great beyond, a region apart from ordinary earth and sky. This beyond was peopled with the dead, who were permitted to inhabit the spirit realm provided—and this was the critical point—they were justified in the Last Judgment before the Divine Judge, knew the secret formulas, and could bring with them appurtenances proper to their earthly life. The post-mortem paraphernalia included absolutely everything used by the deceased during his daily life—for example, a substantial dwelling, food and drink, as well as servants, slaves, and officials. But above all other considerations the body itself had to be ensured against every destructive influence, to enable the freely wandering soul—*ba* in Egyptian—to find its way back where it belonged. Moreover, the body had to be safely preserved to provide a home, too, for the protective spirit, or *ka*, the innate *élan vital* of the personality. This *ka*, like the cognate *ba*, was immortal, and highly useful in providing energy for the deceased in the afterworld, where wheat grew eight ells high and had to be sown and gathered up like any other.

This conception of life after death had two related results: the practice of mummification and the construction of fortresslike pyramids. In other continents the Inca, Maori, Jivaro, and other cultures developed the art of mummification, but never to such extremes of refinement as the Egyptians. As for the pyramids, they represented a monumental device for providing the personality with double, quintuple, decuple security against all enemies who might desecrate it or disturb its rest.

Thousands of lives were sacrificed in forced labor in order to give the dead kings eternal security and eternal life. One Pharaoh, who spent ten, fifteen, twenty years on the building of his tomb, sapped the

Egyptian gods. Left: Ra, Horachti, Horus of the horizon, the morning sun. Middle: Osiris, the god of the dead. Right: Isis, his wife, the personification of the throne.

strength of the Egyptian people and weighed down his children and his children's children with enormous debts. Even after death he continued to weaken the kingdom's finances, for his *ka* demanded regular sacrifices and much priestly service. One self-providential Pharaoh signed away the revenues from twelve villages to the priests who were to celebrate the sacrifices to his *ka*.

The power of belief prevailed over any political or moral consideration. The pyramids of the Pharaohs—and only theirs, for persons of lesser degree contented themselves with mastabas, and the common man with a grave in the sand—were the fruits of a tremendously hypertrophied egocentrism, a point of view in which the interests of the community simply played no part. The pyramid-building urge was the exact opposite of the inspiration behind the great architectural monuments of Christianity. The purpose of the cathedrals of Christendom was to serve the pious community. The stepped towers, or ziggurats, of the Babylonians were sanctuaries for the gods, publicly used shrines; but the pyramids served the Pharaoh and none other; *his* dead body, *his* soul, and *his ka*.

One thing is indubitable: the size of the monuments erected by the kings of the Fourth Dynasty forty-seven centuries ago overreached the standards imposed by belief and religion and security. Later we shall see how very soon after this period pyramid building on such a gigantic scale began to wane, and eventually stopped altogether. This occurred during a time when kings like Cheops, Chephren, and Mycerinus ruled over Egypt. These monarchs were no less absolute in power than those of the Fourth Dynasty. Actually, they were more godlike than the early tyrants, and, like Sethos I and Ramses II, separated from the enslaved masses by an even greater gap.

The materialistic reason for the cessation of large-scale pyramid building was the increasing boldness of the tomb-robbers. Indeed, in certain villages for centuries on end tomb-robbing was a regular occupation; the eternally hungry many rising in reaction against the eternally well-fed few. When the safety of the dead was no longer guaranteed by the pyramids, new and different protective measures became necessary, and consequently other types of tomb construction.

But another, more compelling, non-materialistic reason for the decline in pyramid building is suggested by the historicomorphological approach. From the morphological point of view, cultures exhibit analogies in rise and fall. For example, once the cultural soul has been awakened, a tendency to heaven-storming monumentality consistently appears. Despite all differences, there is a basic relationship linking the Babylonian ziggurat, Romanesque-Gothic churches, and the pyramids of Egypt. For all these works are identified with an early cultural phase, during which colossal edifices were built with lavish outflow of barbaric energies. With a power that knows no obstacles, a power that out of the dark regions of consciousness brings forth the statics needed in the art of architectural reckoning, and that, out of a laboriously achieved understanding of nature, invents the indispensable mechanics—thus the cultural eruption finds vent.

The nineteenth century, the era of technical advance, refused to believe that this could have been possible. The Occidental technician was incapable of admitting that such gigantic structures could be built without the use of "machines," of block and tackle, windlass and crane. But the urge to monumentality had overridden all difficulties; the quantitative forces of an early culture accomplished as much in final result as the qualitative forces of later civilizations.

The pyramids were built with sheer muscle power. Holes were bored in stone in the quarries of the Mokattam Mountains, wooden sticks were driven into them, and these, swelling when soaked in water, cracked apart the rock. On sledges and rollers the resulting blocks were dragged to the site. The pyramid rose layer by layer. Candidates for a doctorate in archæology write theses on the question of whether one construction plan was used or several. Lepsius and Petrie occupy diametrically opposed positions in this controversy, but modern archæology inclines to support the Lepsian point of view. Apparently there were several plans of construction, drastic changes being necessitated by suddenly conceived additions. The Egyptians, forty-seven hundred years ago, worked with such precision that mistakes in the lengths and angles of the great pyramids can, as Petrie says, "be covered with one's thumb." They fitted the stone blocks so neatly that "neither needle nor hair" can, to this day, be inserted at the joints. The Arab writer, Abd al-Latif, remarked on this in wonder eight hundred years ago. Critics point out that the old Egyptian master builders misjudged their stresses and strains, as for example when they made five hollow spaces over the burial-chamber ceiling to reduce the downward pressure, when one would have sufficed. But these fault-finders forget, in our own day of electronically analyzed T-girders that it was not so long ago that we used to build with a safety factor of five, eight, or even twelve.

The pyramids will stand for a long time to come. The Pyramid of Cheops, for instance, is still largely intact, though most of the decorative surface of fine Mokattam limestone has slid away, baring the local yellow limestone used for the main bulk of the edifice. The tip, too, has crumbled away, making a square plateau at the top ten feet on each side. But that is the only damage inflicted by time. Cheops' monument and others as well will endure for many more millennia.

But where are the kings who sought security within them, tranquil homes for their *ka* and *ba*?

Poetic justice has been done the Pharaohs; their hubris has come to naught. Those who chose to rest in less pretentious mastabas, or in rude graves of sand, have been treated less harshly by the years than the once mighty potentates of Egypt. Many of the humbler burial chambers have survived the depredations of the tomb-robbers, but the granite sarcophagus of the great Cheops is mutilated and empty—how long since, we do not know. In 1818 Belzoni found that the lid of the sarcophagus of Chephren had been smashed and the sarcophagus itself filled with rubble. When Colonel Vyse discovered the burial chamber of Mycerinus in the thirties of the last century, the cover was gone from the basalt sarcophagus. Parts of the wooden inner coffin were lying about an upper chamber, and with them, on the floor, were strewn pieces of the royal mummy. The sarcophagus was lost when the ship carrying it to England foundered off the Spanish coast.

Millions of stone blocks were used to protect the bodies of the dead kings. Walled-up passages, all sorts of architectural tricks to keep out predatory intruders, were devised. For the burial chambers concealed almost inconceivable treasures. The King, though dead, was still a king—and if the *ka* returned into the body to reanimate it for participation in the afterworld, obviously he would need the ornaments, the luxurious ritual-

istic and personal articles of frequent daily use, the
trusted weapons of gold and other noble metals, decorated with lapis lazuli, precious stones, and rock crystal.
Did the pyramids offer any real protection? It appears
that intruders were attracted instead of being frightened
off by their vast dimensions. Only too baldly they announced: "Behold, we have something hidden here."

While the robbers—from oldest times to the present day—sought the hidden treasures, some of the respectable, learned men throughout the world theorized
on another kind of secret the ancient structures might
have held. For the past hundred years or more the so-
called "mystery of the great pyramids" has periodically
engaged the attention of Egyptologists, historians of the
world's civilization as well as laymen.

And no wonder—for wherever uncertainty exists,
there is room for conjecture, which, however, can take
the form of reasoned hypothesis or unbridled speculation. Hypothesis belongs to the working method of any
science; it is a legitimate form of speculation proceeding from established results. Though it explores possibilities, it does not presume to remove the question
mark hovering behind them. Pure speculation, on the
other hand, knows no limits. Its premises are apt to be
wishful, untested. As often as not its conclusions are
mere fancy which, dreamy-footed, treads metaphysics'
most errant paths, mysticism's darkest woods, and the
most mysterious regions of Pythagorean and cabalistic
misconstruction. Most dangerous of all, unfettered speculation can be couched in that smooth logic which the
twentieth century finds so persuasive. The finds in
Egypt, through the years, have occasioned all manner
of wild speculation. Most long-lived of these is the
message of the great pyramid.

The gist of the argument is this: The great Pyramid of
Cheops was built in order to hand down a mystical
number system known in older times. The mysticism
of numbers, of course, hardly deserves consideration.

Yet serious scientists capable of outstanding work in their own specialties have frequently become addicted to Egyptian number magic.

The great Pyramid of Cheops has often been called a Bible in stone. We know how farfetched Biblical interpretation can be; the exegesis of the Cheops Pyramid does not lag far behind. The whole history of mankind has been deduced from the ground plan of the structure, from the dimensional relationships of entrance, corridor, hall, and burial chamber. On the basis of a pyramidal theory of history one expert dated the beginning of the First World War in 1913, and believers jubilantly pointed out that he had erred "by only one year."

Still, the numerologists have some material at their disposal that can yield bewildering results if twisted out of normal context. For example, the pyramids are oriented with the four cardinal points of the compass. The northeast-southwest diagonal of the Pyramid of Cheops, if extended, coincides perfectly with the analogous diagonal of the Pyramid of Chephren.

Most claims of this nature, however, arise from faulty measurements, or from the exaggeration, or arbitrary extrapolation, of the possibilities offered by any large architectural work that has been closely measured. Meanwhile, since Flinders Petrie's initial measurements, almost exact dimensions have been assigned to the great Pyramid of Cheops. But even modern measurements are approximate, for the original form of the pyramid has been lost through the destruction of the tip. On this account any Egyptian numerology that adduces evidence in terms of centimeters or inches is *a priori* discredited.

It is not difficult to get spectacular mystical results if very small measuring units are applied to a very large piece of architecture. If the cathedrals of Chartres or Cologne were measured in inches, almost certainly all manner of unsuspected analogies with numbers of cosmic import could be derived by appropriate addition, subtraction, and multiplication. It is very probable that the claims to the effect that the pyramid builders were the first to discover the value of $\pi$ is a misconstruction of this nature.

Even if it could be proved that the Egyptians actually did project into the dimensions of the pyramids important astronomical and mathematical information of a kind not known to science until the nineteenth and twentieth centuries, still there would be no reason for reading mystical connotations into such numerical values or for deducing from them large prophecies. In 1922 the German Egyptologist Ludwig Borchardt published the findings of his intensive study of the great Pyramid of Cheops, under the title: *Gegen die Zahlenmystik an der Grossen Pyramide bei Gizeh* (Against the Mystical Interpretation of the Numbers on the Pyramid of Cheops), in which he finally cut the ground from under the mystics.

Petrie was one of those archæologists who refuse to be downed. Stubborn, unyielding, tenacious on the scent, in 1889 he dug a shaft into an unidentified brick pyramid along the Nile, unaware that he had hit on the tomb of Amenemhet III, one of the infrequent men of peace to rule over Egypt. Not being able to discover the entrance to the tomb, Petrie dug diagonally straight through the masonry.

When he had first made up his mind to attack the pyramid—it was located some twenty-three hours on donkey-back from the village of Jauwaret el-Makta—he had looked for the entrance in the usual place—that is, on the north side—and, like so many other archæologists before him, he failed to find it there. Nor did he have any better luck on the east side. He then decided to dig a tunnel slantwise into the masonry rather than fritter away any more time.

The decision was excellent, but Petrie's technical facilities were limited. Though he realized that he was faced with a formidable task, he had no idea that he would be digging for many weeks. Petrie suffered a

crushing disappointment when he finally removed the
last piece of wall shutting him off from the burial
chamber and discovered that others had got there first.
But these others had not been interested in studying
the marvels of bygone epochs; their purpose had been
plunder. Petrie's grueling labors in the heat of the
Egyptian sun, with inadequate tools and an unwilling
crew of workmen, had all gone for nothing.

Again we encounter that frustration which only too
often has been the culmination of archæological effort,
a terrific letdown that would cripple all but the strong.
(Exactly twelve years later a similar fiasco occurred,
which, in so far as it entailed the discomfiture of others,
for a change, must have given Petrie some wry satisfaction. Modern tomb-robbers broke into the burial
chamber of Amenophis II, who died about 1420 B.C.,
and, seeking royal treasure, cut open the winding cloths
about the mummy. But they, too, were disappointed—
more bitterly, no doubt, than Petrie, their purpose being what it was. Others of their thievish kind had done
their work three thousand years before so well that not
a single thing remained to reward their predatory ex-
ertions.)

The hole that Petrie had driven into the side of
the pyramid was too narrow to admit the full width of
his shoulders, but he could not wait until it had been
widened enough to let him in. He lowered an Egyptian
boy, equipped with a light, down into the vault on a
rope. The warm, flickering candlelight fell on two
sarcophagi—both plundered and empty!

There was nothing left for Petrie to do but try to
find out whose tomb it was he had invaded. New difficulties cropped up. Ground water had seeped into the
pyramid. When the first hole had been widened enough
to let Petrie in, he found the burial chamber deep in
water. Using a shovel, he cleared away the floor inch by
inch. Finally he found an alabaster vessel with the
name Amenemhet inscribed on it, and in a second
chamber innumerable funerary gifts, all bearing the

name of Princess Ptahnofru, daughter of Amenemhet III.

Amenemhet III, a king of the Twelfth Dynasty, reigned, according to Breasted, from 1849 to 1801 B.C. His family was in power for some 213 years. The period during which Amenemhet III wore the two crowns of Egypt was one of the happiest the land ever saw. For centuries the country had been periodically devastated by wars waged with barbaric borderland peoples, and by internal conflict between the central government and the chronically rebellious provincial princes. Amenemhet was a man of peace. His countless construction projects—among other things he dammed up a whole lake—served profane as well as religious ends. His social measures, from the modern standpoint, are scarcely worth mentioning, but within the context of the rigid Egyptian class division and slave economy they were actually of revolutionary import.

> He makes the Two Lands verdant more than a
>     great Nile.
> He hath filled the Two Lands with strength.
> He is life, cooling the nostrils.
> The treasures that he gives are food for those who
>     are in his following;
> He feeds those who tread his path.
> The King is food, and his mouth is increase.

Merely to have found this great King's tomb was a feather in Petrie's cap, and archæologically, at least, his results gave him some satisfaction. Still, as excavation, his work was far from being an unqualified success. How had the tomb-robbers ferreted a way into the tomb? Where was the real entrance to the pyramid? Had the robbers discovered the door, which he and other investigators had not been able to find? The robbers had evidently solved the architectural riddle built into the pyramid by the Egyptian architects; Petrie set to work retracing the robbers' trail.

This involved a major tunneling project. Ground water had risen high within the Pyramid. Dirt, brickbats, and rubble had puddled together into a tough muck. Petrie, the indefatigable, had to crawl through some of the passageways on his stomach, hardly able to breathe, mouth and nose clogged with mud. His aim was to find the real entrance, and finally he did. Contrary to all previous experience and to all Egyptian tradition, it was on the south side! Somehow the robbers had known this. Petrie was amazed. Had the robbers succeeded through pure ingenuity, or simply by sheer persistence? Petrie had an idea that he took pains to check very carefully.

Systematically he retraced the path used by the robbers. They had run into all sorts of obstacles. Every time this happened to Petrie he tried to put himself in the robbers' shoes and figure out what he would have done had he been they. Several times he was driven to admit that he would not have been able to solve the situation as the robbers had. What mysterious instinct, if instinct it was, had led the thieves safely through the innumerable pitfalls, tricks, and dodges incorporated into the pyramid by the Pharaonic architects? When stairs ended abruptly in a blind chamber, the robbers, it appeared, had quickly discovered that the way forward was up through the ceiling. One whole ceiling had been a tremendous trapdoor. Laboriously the thieves had broken their way through, much as safecrackers today force their way, little by little, through the thick steel door of a safe. And then where were they? In a corridor filled with massive blocks of stone! Petrie, the technician, could appreciate what infinite labor they had had to expend in clearing out this corridor. He could also appreciate the robbers' feeling when, having done so much, they again found themselves in a doorless chamber, and after surmounting this fresh obstacle, in still a third blind room. Petrie, who by this time had begun to admire the robbers, hardly knew whether to credit their consistent success to superior knowledge or to bull strength. Unquestionably they must have dug for weeks, months, even a year or more—and under what conditions! They must have worked in constant dread of being surprised by watchmen, priests, pilgrims who came with offerings for the great Amenemhet.

Or did they? Petrie had seen for himself how much acumen and experience were needed to overcome the obstacles deliberately planted by the ancient architects to confuse intruders and guard their kings. He doubted that the wits of those ancient Egyptian grave-robbers could have triumphed unaided over such deterrents. Was it possible—Egyptian literature offered some support for such a thesis—that the robbers had expert assistance? Could they have been tipped off and otherwise abetted by priests, guards, corrupt members of an already corrupted class of officials? This brings us to the colorful subject of the grave-robbers in Egyptian history. Its beginnings are lost in antiquity; it unfolded dramatically in the Valley of the Kings; and it came to a climax not so long ago, in a rather modern kind of criminal case.

# 14/ROBBERS IN THE VALLEY
## OF THE KINGS

Early in 1881 a well-to-do American art collector was sailing up the Nile toward Luxor, a village situated opposite the ancient royal city of Thebes, where he intended to buy antiquities. He had no use for the official traffic in museum pieces, far too strictly controlled under the influence of Mariette, and preferred to trust entirely to his own instinct. Nights he frequented the dark alleys, the backrooms of the Luxor bazaar. There he made contact with an Egyptian who offered for sale what were apparently genuine and valuable objects.

This American's method invites a brief digression. Today, every guide warns the tourist against engaging in black-market dealings in antiquities. Rightly so—most so-called antiquities are manufactured by modern Egyptian home labor, or even imported from Europe. The black marketeers have an inexhaustible bag of tricks for simulating authenticity in their wares. Even as seasoned a connoisseur as the German art historian Julius Meier-Graefe was taken in. While going about once with a professional guide who knew nothing of this, in the 1920's, he found a small figurine in the sand. That he had found it himself convinced him of its genuineness. He "bribed" the guide to keep the matter quiet and smuggled the little object into his hotel under his coat. Then, to get a pedestal for it, he took it to a dealer, whom he asked for an opinion of the work. The dealer smiled. As Julius Meier-Graefe tells it: "The dealer invited me into the back of his little shop, opened a cupboard there, and showed me four or five identical pieces, each encrusted with thousand-year-old sand. They come from Bunzlau (in Germany), but he buys them from an agent in Cairo, a Greek."

Apart from the faking of antiques as a business, scientists and scholars must look out for unpleasant surprises engineered by all kinds of practical jokers. This is illustrated by the following autobiographical story of a modern French novelist, André Malraux, one-time commissar in China, lately General de Gaulle's propaganda chief. There is no reason to doubt the anecdote, reported here only as a curiosity and certainly not to inspire imitation. In 1925 Malraux fell into conversation in a Singapore bar with a Russian collector traveling at the expense of the Boston Museum to buy antiquities. After the first exchange of courtesies, the Russian lined up on the table five little ivory elephants he had just purchased from the Hindu: "You see, my friend, I buy little elephants. When we are through with a dig, I stick them into the graves before we cover them up again. In fifty years from now, when other excavators come along and open the coffins again, they will find these inside, nicely patinaed and weathered, and they will be so mystified. . . . I rather like to give those who come after me a little headache. On one of the towers at Angkor-Vat, my friend, I engraved an extremely indecent inscription in Sanscrit; well smeared over, it looks quite old. Some know-it-all will decipher it one day. One must do one's bit toward deflating those pompous asses. . . ."

To get back to our American: while he may have been a dilettante in Egyptology, he was not lacking in expertise. Hence, when he saw the Egyptian's wares, he became rather excited and, flagrantly disregarding the oriental rituals of dickering, bought a papyrus the like of which for beauty and good preservation he had seldom seen. He hid it in his trunk and left Egypt with all speed, bypassing customs and police controls. In Europe, experts confirmed that he had got a rare treasure.

He had also, incidentally, triggered off a most remarkable chain of events in which he himself played no further part.

But before that story can be told, it is necessary to relate some of the strange history of the Valley of the Kings.

The Valley of the Kings, or the Tombs of Kings at Biban el-Muluk, lies on the west bank of the Nile, across the river from Luxor and Karnak, site of the enormous colonnades and temple buildings of the New Empire. The valley site lies near the extensive and now desert region where once the great necropolis of the city of Thebes flourished. On this west side of the Nile, during the New Empire, tombs were cut into the rocky face of the cliffs for the reception of the bodies of high personages. Here, too, temples were dedicated to the god Amen (Amun) and to various kings (see Plate IX).

The custodial care and continued construction of a gigantic necropolis required a very large personnel, which was under the direction of an official entitled the Prince of the West and Colonel of the Mercenaries of the Necropolis. The garrison assigned to guard the cemetery lived in barracks. Common laborers and construction workers were housed in clusters of huts, which in time grew into small villages. Among this working force were stonemasons and painters, artists of all kinds, and, too, the embalmers, or mummifiers, who preserved the dead and provided an eternal house for the *ka*.

This development took place, as I have said, during the period of the New Kingdom, when the mightiest potentates of Egyptian history were in power, the Sons of the Sun, the first and second Ramses. The period is identified with the Eighteenth and Nineteenth Dynasties, and ran from approximately 1350 to 1200 B.C. From the Spenglerian point of view, it was a period that bore an analogy to our own present, a time, that is, of almost pure "civilization" characterized by "Cæsarism." According to the Spenglerian concept of historical simultaneity, this Egyptian period, during which the architectural impulse ceased to find expression in pyramid building and instead produced the showy structures of Karnak, Luxor, and Abydos, corresponds with the Cæsarian era of Roman history, during which epoch the "monumental" Greek culture was absorbed into Roman "colossality." Other instances of the "colossal" historical phase are the periods when Sennacherib built up Nineveh into an Assyrian Rome, when Emperor Huang-ti ruled in China, and when the great Indian (Hindu) monuments were erected, after 1250. Moreover, the same forces at work during the Egyptian transition into colossality are at work today among us of the West who live in the skyscraper city of New York, in the ruins of Berlin, in stagnant London, or in an enervated Paris.

A remarkable change introduced by King Thotmes I (1545–1515 B.C.) signals the beginning of the era of building activity in the Valley of the Kings. Thotmes I is a definitive figure in the dynastic history of Egypt. He is also significant—though this has yet to be finally proved, and final proof will require more than a purely archæological effort—in so far as he symbolizes the evolution of Egyptian culture into civilization, a process typically involving a breakup of old traditions.

However that may be, Thotmes was the first Egyptian king to build his tomb apart from his mortuary chapel, in his particular instance distant from it by nearly a mile. And instead of having his corpse interred in a pretentious and widely visible pyramid, he left instructions to have it hidden in a rock chamber carved into the cliff face. This hardly strikes modern ears as important. But actually the decision represented an abrupt repudiation of a tradition that had lasted for some seventeen hundred years.

In making this drastic move Thotmes created immeasurable difficulties for his *ka* and seriously jeopardized his existence after death. For the viability of his *ka* depended on the giving of sacrificial gifts on certain

holy days at his mortuary chapel, which of course was
no longer intimately connected with the body around
which the *ka* putatively hovered. As compensation for
this defect, however, Thotmes hoped to gain the permanent security denied his forefathers by tomb-robbers.
The instructions he gave his master builder, Ineni, were
motivated by a consuming fear that his grave would be
desecrated. Despite the rationalistic decay and secular-
ization of religion—the Twenty-first Dynasty consisted
entirely of priest kings, and prior to that time their
power in the kingdom had been growing apace—concern about the possible destruction of his mummy was
still the dominant factor in Thotmes' mind. By the beginning of the Eighteenth Dynasty there was scarcely
a royal tomb in the vicinity of Thebes that had not
been robbed. Hardly a single mummy remained that
had not been stripped of at least a part of its "magical
armor," and so defiled for eternity. As a rule the tomb-
robbers were not apprehended, though now and again
they may have been disturbed and all forced to leave
their booty behind. Five hundred years before the reign
of Thotmes the intruder who had entered the tomb of
the wife of King Zer had been interrupted in breaking
up the Queen's mummy and had hastily hidden one of
the desiccated arms in a hole in the burial chamber.
There it was found in 1900 by an English archæologist,
intact under the wrappings, and with a valuable ame-
thyst and turquoise arm ring

The chief architect of Thotmes was called Ineni.
We can imagine the discussion that took place between
the monarch and his chief builder. After the decision to
break with tradition had been made, certainly Thotmes
must have realized that unless the site and construction of the tomb were kept absolutely secret, there
could be no final guarantee of escaping the fate of preceding kings.

The vanity of the architect has preserved for us the
story of how the project was carried out, for on the
walls of his own mortuary chapel Ineni left, as part of

a detailed biography, an account of the construction of this first cliff tomb. One pertinent sentence reads: "I alone supervised the construction of His Majesty's cliff tomb. No one saw it, no one heard it." But a modern archæologist, Howard Carter, one of the foremost authorities on the Valley of the Kings and the physical characteristics of tomb-building there, estimated the number of men who worked for Ineni. Carter writes: "It is sufficiently obvious that a hundred or more workers with a knowledge of the King's most precious secret would never be allowed at large, and we can be quite sure that Ineni found some effectual means of stopping their mouths." Conceivably the work was carried out by prisoners of war, who were slaughtered at its completion.

Did Thotmes' break with tradition fulfill its object? His cliff tomb was the first of many to be quarried in the Valley of the Kings. Into the limestone walls of a lonely, forbidding valley lying beyond the western cliffs of Thebes he had a steep passage bored according to a plan used for five subsequent centuries by Pharaonic architects. The Greeks, struck by the flutelike approach to the sepulcher, called the rock tombs *syringes*, because they called to mind a syrinx, or long shepherd's flute. Strabo, the Greek traveler who lived in the last century before Christ, described forty of these tombs as worth seeing.

We do not know how long Thotmes lay cloistered in peace. We do know, however, that it could not have been too long, in the scale of Egyptian history. The day came when his mummy, together with that of his daughter and others, was taken out of the cliff, this time not by robbers, but by the priests as a precaution against intruders. The kings had seen to it that their graves were built close together in the cliffs so that the watch over them could be concentrated, rather than scattered as hitherto, but still the robberies continued.

Thieves broke into the tomb of Tutankhamen within ten or fifteen years after his death. A very few years after the death of Thotmes IV robbers left their visiting card in his sepulcher by scratching the secret signs and slang words of their thievish kind on the walls. This tomb suffered so much that a hundred years later the pious Horemheb in the eighth year of his reign gave the official called Kej orders "to renew the burial of King Thotmes IV, justified, in the Precious Habitation in Western Thebes."

The tomb-robbers reached the peak of their activity during the Twentieth Dynasty. The rule of the autocratic Ramses I and II and of the first and second Sethos (Seti) had come to a close. The succeeding nine kings, all of whom were called Ramses, were great in name only. Their control over the kingdom was weak and chronically threatened. Bribery and corruption were rife. The cemetery guards ganged up with the priests, the supervisors of the burial area with the governors of the district. Even the mayor of Western Thebes, the highest official in the protective system of the necropolis, came to secret terms with the tomb-robbers. It seems almost uncanny to us today to find, among the papyrus collections from the period of Ramses IX (1142–1123 B.C.), a document relating to a tomb-robbery trial that took place three thousand years ago. Before this trial the tomb-robbers are anonymous; now they suddenly acquire names and come to life as real people.

Peser, the mayor of Eastern Thebes, got wind of extensive grave-robberies on the western side of the river. The mayor of Western Thebes was the publicly suspect Pewero, for whom Peser had as little use as Pewero for him. Peser, it appears, was overjoyed to have a chance to discredit his rival in mayoral office with the vizier, or governor, of the whole Theban district, a certain Khamwese. (The following is Howard Carter's report of the proceedings, based on Breasted's collection of *Ancient Records of Egypt*.)

But things turned out badly for Peser. In his denunciation of Pewero and his henchmen Peser made the tactical mistake of naming the exact number of tombs that had been rifled. According to his story, ten royal tombs, four containing the remains of priestesses, and a great many others of private persons had been desecrated. Several members of the formal investigatory commission that Khamwese now sent across the river, including the man in charge, may well have been implicated in the robberies. Even Khamwese himself might have been making a few talents on the side. As we would say today, the commission had got their cut, and their report was already framed when they rowed across the Nile. Falling back on legal formalities, they acquitted the accused, by skirting the point at hand—namely, whether tombs had been robbed—and concentrating on irrelevant issues.

The commission disputed the literal accuracy of Peser's bill of particulars. They tabled his charge on the grounds that whereas Peser said ten royal tombs had been plundered, actually this was true of only one, and instead of four priestesses' tombs, only two. That in truth nearly all the private tombs mentioned by Peser had been disturbed could not be denied, but the commission saw no reason in this to haul such a worthy official as Pewero into court. The day after the accusation had been shelved, the triumphant Pewero rounded up "the inspectors, the necropolis administrators, the workmen, the police, and all the laborers of the necropolis," and sent them as a body to the east side of the Nile for what, in modern parlance, would be called a "spontaneous demonstration." They were enjoined to parade with particular attention to the neighborhood of Peser's home.

This was too much for the mayor of Eastern Thebes. Peser could not contain his chagrin. He fell into a temper, in which unsettled condition he committed his second, and nearly fatal, mistake. Heatedly arguing with one of the leaders of the parade from the western city, in his excitement Peser swore, within the hearing of witnesses, that he was going over the vizier's head and appeal directly to the King.

This was exactly what Pewero had been waiting to

hear. As fast as he could, he rushed word to the vizier, Khamwese. Peser, he informed the governor, planned to act outside of channels, an incredible breach of bureaucratic discipline. The outraged vizier now summoned a court and forced the tactless Peser to sit with the other judges at his own trial. He found himself in the odd position of accusing himself of perjury and pronouncing himself guilty of the crime.

This strangely modern crime story, to the fully documented details of which nothing has been added here—it could have been told at far greater length, in fact—even had a "happy ending" seldom found outside fairy tales.

Two or three years after this triumph of corruption a band of eight tomb-robbers was caught. These robbers, "after being chastised with a double rod on hands and feet," gave a deposition that obviously must have come into the possession of some honest man who would not be frightened into hushing it up. Five of the names of these eight robbers have come down to us: the stonecutter Hapi, the artisan Iramen, the peasant Amenemheb, the water carrier Kemwese, and the Negro slave Thenefer. In their confession they say:

"We opened their coffins and their coverings in which they were. We found the august mummy of this King. . . . There was a numerous string of amulets and ornaments of gold at its throat; its head had a mask of gold upon it; the august mummy of this King was overlaid with gold throughout. Its coverings were wrought with gold and silver, within and without; inlaid with every costly stone. We stripped off the gold, which we found on the august mummy of this god, and its amulets and ornaments which were at its throat, and the covering wherein it rested. We found the King's wife likewise; we stripped off all that we found on her likewise. We set fire to their coverings. We stole their furniture, which we found with them, being vases of gold, silver, and bronze. We divided and made the gold that we found on these two gods, on their mummies, and the amulets, ornaments, and coverings, into eight parts."

The court found the defendants guilty, and by extension validated Peser's earlier accusations.

Yet it appears that this court action—and a number of others in which culprits were also harshly dealt with later on—could not stop the systematic plunder of the Valley of the Kings. We know that thieves broke into the tombs of Amenophis III, Seti I, and Ramses II. "Strange sights the Valley must have seen, and desperate the ventures that took place in it," writes Carter. "One can imagine the plotting for days beforehand, the secret rendezvous on the cliff by night, the bribing or drugging of the cemetery guards, and then the desperate burrowing in the dark, the scramble through a small hole into the burial chamber, the hectic search by a glimmering light for treasure that was portable, and the return home at dawn laden with booty. We can imagine these things, and at the same time we can realize how inevitable it all was. By providing his mummy with the elaborate and costly outfit which he thought essential to its dignity, the King was himself encompassing its destruction. The temptation was too great. Wealth beyond the dreams of avarice lay there at the disposal of whoever should find the means to reach it, and sooner or later the tomb-robber was bound to win through."

But the time of the Twentieth Dynasty was not peopled entirely by tomb-robbers, traitorous priests, bribed officials, corrupt magistrates, and highly organized gangs of thieves recruited from all levels of the social scale. There were honest believers, righteous men who would honor dead kings. For even as the thieves were making their nightly getaway over secret paths, little groups of the faithful were lying in wait for them. Necessity had driven these pious men to use hijacking tactics, to fight fire with fire. In the retaliatory war waged by the loyal priests and incorruptible officials against the tightly knit robber organizations, it was expedient to be even more secretive than were the outlaws.

It is exciting to picture these defenders of tradition as, with heated whisperings, they went into the tomb, holding the torch so that its light would shine into the open sarcophagus, bodies ducking in fear of being surprised. They were not afraid of the sentinels posted at the tombs themselves. Yet a single glance by a corrupt guard might be enough to let the robber gang know which king it was this night who was in protective custody and thus out of their thievish reach. And the faithful vigilantes carry away the embalmed bodies of their dead kings. They move the mummies from tomb to tomb to shield them from sacrilegious hands. They hear that new raids are planned by the robbers, and make reply with more nocturnal expeditions. And the dead kings, whose mummies should have remained at rest for all eternity, wander.

Suddenly the scene changes. The priests take protective measures in broad daylight. Police shut off the valley. Long columns of porters and beasts of burden transport the huge coffins from the threatened burial chambers to new sites, new hiding places. The military take over—and once again many eyewitnesses have to pay with their lives that the new secret may be kept.

Three times Ramses III was taken out of his tomb and reinterred. Ahmes, Amenophis I, Thotmes II, and even Ramses the Great were transferred to safer spots. Finally, for lack of any other hiding place, all were dumped into a single sepulcher.

"Year 14, third month of the second season, day 6, Osiris King Usermare-Setepnere (Ramses II) was taken to be buried again in the tomb of Osiris King Memmare Seti I, by the High Priest of Amen, Paynezem."

But even there they were not secure. Sethos (Seti) I and Ramses II were placed in the tomb of Queen Inhapi. Finally no less than thirteen royal mummies were crowded into the tomb of Amenophis II. Other kings were collected at different times and under widely varying circumstances and carried over the lonely and desolate highland path leading out of the Valley of the Kings. They were then placed in a tomb hewn in the wall of the rocky basin of Deir el-Bahri. This site was not far from the gigantic temple built by Queen Hatshepsut, sister of the third Thotmes, who was co-regent during her reign.

Here for three thousand years the mummies rested in peace. Apparently the exact location of the tomb was lost, the same contingency that protected the tomb of Tutankhamen after one superficial pillaging. It is possible that a heavy rainstorm washed away all trace of the entrance. Then an American collector's trip to Luxor in 1881 led to the disclosure that this mass grave of kings had been discovered by chance six years earlier, in 1875.

The Valley of the Kings is shrouded in darkness, a limbo without history. "We are to imagine a deserted valley," write Carter, "spirit-haunted doubtless to the Egyptian, its cavernous galleries plundered and empty, the entrances of many of them open, to become the home of the fox, the desert owl, or colonies of bats. Yet, plundered, deserted and desolate as were its tombs, the romance of it was not yet wholly gone. It still remained the sacred Valley of the Kings, and crowds of the sentimental and the curious must still have gone to visit it. Some of its tombs, indeed, were actually re-used in the time of Osorkon I (about 900 B.C.) for the burial of priestesses."

A thousand years later we find the Valley populated by the first Christian hermits who ensconced themselves in the tomb passages.

"Magnificence and royal pride have been replaced by humble poverty. The 'precious habitation' of the king has narrowed to a hermit's cell."

This also changed. Tradition had destined the Valley to be the home of kings and robbers. In 1743 the English traveler Richard Pococke gives us the first modern report of the Valley. Led by a sheikh, he was able to inspect fourteen open graves. (Strabo knew, as we have said, forty; today there are sixty-one known graves.) But it was not a safe place to visit. In the hills of Kurna a robber band was encamped. When James Bruce visited the Valley twenty-six years later, he learned of futile efforts to dislodge these gangs. "They are all outlaws, punished with death if elsewhere found.

Osman Bey, an ancient governor of Girge, unable to suffer any longer the disorders committed by these people, ordered a quantity of faggots to be brought together, and, with his soldiers, took possession of the face of the mountain, where the greatest number of these wretches were: he then ordered their caves to be filled with this dry brushwood, to which he set fire, so that most of them were destroyed; but they have since recruited their numbers without changing their manners."

When Bruce tried to stay overnight in the tomb chamber of Ramses III, while he was copying the wall reliefs in it, his native guides were overcome with terror and hurled their torches away, cursing. As the lights flickered and went out "they uttered blood-curdling prophecies of disaster that would befall soon after they had left the cavern!" Later, when Bruce rode down the Valley in the gathering darkness with the only servant left to him, trying to reach his boat on the Nile, the air was rent by shouts, and rocks came hurtling down from the side of the cliff. Bruce used his gun and his servant's blunderbuss to beat off the attack, but on reaching his boat he cast off at once, and made no attempt to repeat his visit. When Napoleon's "Egyptian Commission" arrived thirty years later, to survey the Valley and its tombs, they too were attacked and even shot at by Theban robbers.

Today the Valley attracts tourists from all over the world. One of the richest treasures ever lifted from ancient ground was discovered there only forty-odd years ago. Nowadays it is just another site where dragomans beat their donkeys; the tourists come flocking from the Cook's hostelry in Deir el-Bahri, and Arabs vociferously invite all and sundry, in magnificent English, to come view "de Kingses tombes." It is both sad and farcical, considering the immense history of the Nile Valley, its kings, and its peoples, to be told by one's guide that "The most important graves and the tomb of Tutankhamen can be seen by electric light three mornings a week."

The greatest find made in the Valley—arousing throughout the Western world a suspenseful excitement matched only by one previous archæological discovery, Schliemann's excavation of Troy—occurred in 1922.

But a few decades previously an almost equally amazing discovery was made in Deir el-Bahri, under far stranger circumstances.

When the American who had succeeded in acquiring a well-preserved papyrus in Luxor submitted it to the experts in Europe for authentication, one of them tried to draw him out. The delighted collector, feeling safe with his booty on European soil, talked freely, without hiding his light under a bushel. The expert then sent a detailed letter to Cairo, and so initiated the exposure of a most extraordinary tomb-robbery.

Upon receiving the expert's letter at the Egyptian Museum in Cairo, Professor Gaston Maspero was taken aback on two counts: first, that his museum should again have lost out on a valuable find. In the preceding six years rare treasures of great scientific value had on several occasions mysteriously appeared in the antique black market. Some of the lucky buyers, once safely out of Egypt, readily described the circumstances of the purchase, but no dealer had ever been tracked down. Usually the dealer was described as a big man. But once he was an Arab, another time a Negro, then again a dilapidated Egyptian peasant or a well-to-do sheikh. Maspero was also made thoughtful by the fact that the latest piece smuggled out of Egypt was a mortuary gift from the tomb of a Pharaoh of the Twenty-first Dynasty, the whereabouts of whose graves were unknown. Who had found those graves?

Reviewing the smuggled pieces that had been brought to his attention, Professor Maspero felt sure that they must have come from the respective graves of several kings. Could modern grave-robbers have discovered several ancient tombs all at once? Maspero was more inclined to believe that the robbers had stumbled on a large common grave.

Maspero was much impressed by the prospects that this theory opened up. Something would have to be done. The Egyptian police had failed. He would have to do his own sleuthing. After several secret consultations he dispatched one of his young assistants to Luxor.

From the moment he stepped ashore from the Nile boat, this assistant acted like anything but an archæologist. He took a room in the hotel where the American who had bought the papyrus had stayed. Day and night he roamed the bazaars, acting the part of a rich European jingling gold coins in his pocket and making occasional purchases, for which he paid top prices. After engaging the dealers in confidential conversations, he gave them good tips, but in such a way as not to arouse their suspicions. Time and again he was offered antiquities of strictly local manufacture, but the young man was not to be fooled, as both licensed concessionaries and illegal dealers soon discovered. Gradually their respect for the stranger increased, and with it their trust in him.

One day a dealer, squatting in the doorway of his store, beckoned the young man to come over. Presently the assistant from the Egyptian Museum was holding a statuette in his hand. He managed to control his emotions; he gave no sign of being deeply impressed. He sat on his haunches beside the dealer and commenced to haggle. Doing so, he turned the statuette over and over in his hand, all the while knowing from the inscription that it was a genuine piece three thousand years old, a mortuary gift from a tomb of the Twenty-first Dynasty.

The bargaining lasted a long time. Eventually the assistant bought the little piece, at the same time pretending dissatisfaction. He let it be known that he was looking for something larger and more valuable. That same day he was introduced to a tall Arab in the prime of life, who called himself Abd-el-Rasul. This Abd-el-Rasul was the head of a large family. After the young assistant had dickered for several days, during which he had been shown other mortuary objects dating from the Nineteenth and Twentieth Dynasties, he had the Arab arrested. He was convinced that he had found the tomb-robber.

But had he?

Abd-el-Rasul and several of his family were brought before the Mudir of Keneh, Da'ud Pasha, who personally conducted the hearing. An endless parade of witnesses appeared to exonerate the accused. All the inhabitants of the village where Abd-el-Rasul made his home swore to his innocence—indeed, to the innocence of the whole family, which was declared to be one of the oldest and most respectable in the community. The assistant, positively convinced of the validity of his charge against Abd-el-Rasul, had already telegraphed an optimistic message to Cairo. Now he had to stand helplessly by while Abd-el-Rasul and company were allowed to go free for lack of evidence. He appealed to the authorities; they shrugged their shoulders. He went directly to the mudir, who stared at him in astonishment, and sternly counseled patience.

The assistant waited one day, then another and another. Again he telegraphed Cairo, qualifying his first message. The gnawing of uncertainty wore him down, that and the mudir's Oriental patience. But the mudir knew his people.

Howard Carter recounts a story originally told him by one of his oldest workers who, as a youth, had been arrested for robbery and brought before this same mudir. The boy was in any case mortally afraid of the strict Da'ud Pasha, but his anxiety was doubled when instead of being taken into the regular courtroom he was brought to the pasha's private quarters. The day was very hot, and the pasha was lolling in his large earthenware bathtub.

Da'ud Pasha, so the story goes, looked at the prisoner a long time. The young prisoner was terrified by this silent scrutiny. "His eyes went right through me," he told Carter. "I could feel my knees turning to water. At last he quietly said to me: 'This is the first time you have ever been before me. You can go free. But take good care not to come here a second time.' I was so frightened that on the spot I abandoned my calling, and never got into trouble again."

Da'ud's authority—backed up, as it was, by cruelties if mere presence did not suffice—bore fruit, which came as a great surprise to the young assistant from Cairo, now lying abed prostrated by fever. A month after the original hearing one of Abd-el-Rasul's relatives and accomplices came to the pasha and made a complete confession. The mudir informed the young scientist of this development and ordered new hearings. These hearings showed that the whole village of Kurna, Abd-el-Rasul's home town, was a nest of tomb-robbers. The profession had been handed down from father to son in apparently unbroken line since the thirteenth century. A robber dynasty of such formidable lineage has never been heard of before or since.

The greatest find ever made by the Abd-el-Rasul gang was the common tomb of Deir el-Bahri. Chance and system both played a part in the finding and plundering of this tomb. Six years before, in 1875, Abd-el-Rasul, by merest chance, had discovered a hidden opening in the cliffy massif between the Valley of the Kings and Deir el-Bahri. Getting up and into the opening with great difficulty, Abd-el-Rasul found himself in a roomy mortuary chamber containing a number of mummies. A preliminary examination revealed that here was a treasure that would yield him and his family an income as long as they lived—if the secret could be kept.

None but the leading members of the Abd-el-Rasul family were let into the secret. They were solemnly sworn to leave the treasure where it had been found, that it might serve them all as a sort of mummified bank account on which to draw according to need. Incredibly enough, the secret was kept for six years, during which period the family became rich. On July 5, 1881, however, the representative of the Cairo Museum was conducted by Abd-el-Rasul to the opening in the cliff.

It was one of fate's little ironies that the museum representative was neither the young assistant who had made the apprehension of the robbers possible nor yet Professor Maspero, who had initiated the investigation. The latest telegram reporting progress had never reached Maspero, as he was away on a trip at the time. Since time was of the essence, a substitute had to go to Luxor. The man chosen was Emil Brugsch-Bey, brother of the famous Egyptologist Heinrich Brugsch, at that time conservator of the Egyptian Museum in Cairo. He arrived at Luxor to find the young assistant, who had played detective so successfully, in bed with a fever. He paid the mudir a diplomatic visit. All interested parties agreed that to prevent further robberies, the tomb should be sequestered by the government. On the morning of July 5, Emil Brugsch-Bey, accompanied by an Arab assistant and Abd-el-Rasul, set out for the tomb. What he was to see soon thereafter put him in mind of Aladdin's underground surprise, nor would he ever forget the events of the following nine days.

After a stiff climb, Abd-el-Rasul came to a halt and pointed to a hole covered unobtrusively with stones. It was an out-of-the-way spot and hidden from direct view. No wonder it had remained unnoticed for three millennia.

Abd-el-Rasul took a coil of rope from his shoulder, let the rope slide into the hole, and indicated to Brugsch that he should let himself down by it. Brugsch did not hesitate. He left the questionable guide with his trusted Arab assistant at the mouth of the shaft. Down he went, hand over hand, cautiously, not without some apprehensions about being, possibly, the victim of a clever thief's trickery. Hope of a find must have stirred in his breast, but he certainly had not the least inkling of what actually awaited him below.

The shaft proved to be some thirty-five feet deep. Safely at the bottom, he lighted his torch, moved forward a few steps and around a sharp corner—and before him saw the first gigantic sarcophagi.

One of the largest of the sarcophagi standing just beyond the outer entrance to the tunnel had an inscription showing that it contained the mummy of Sethos I, the same mummy vainly sought by Belzoni in October 1817 in the Pharaoh's original resting-place in the Valley of the Kings. The torch's wavering light revealed more coffins, and innumerable treasures of the Egyptian death cult thoughtlessly scattered about the floor and the coffins. Brugsch went farther in, clearing a way for himself as he moved along. Finally the main mortuary chamber came into view, seemingly endless in the dim light. The coffins lay any which way; some of them had been rudely pried open, others were still closed. About the mummies was a profusion of implements and decorative articles. The sight took Brugsch's breath away; for he was standing amid the bodies of the mightiest rulers of the ancient Egyptian world.

Sometimes creeping along on hands and knees, sometimes proceeding upright, Brugsch found the mummy, among many others, of Amosis I (1580–1555 B.C.), the Pharaoh who achieved fame by driving out the last of the barbaric Hyksos, the "shepherd kings." Brugsch also discovered the mummy of the first Amenophis (1555–1545 B.C.), who was later to become the guardian spirit of the Theban necropolis. Among innumerable coffins containing lesser-known Egyptian rulers he found at last the mummies of the two greatest Pharaohs, whose names had reverberated through the centuries without the aid of archæologist or historian. At this point he had to sit down, torch in hand, overwhelmed by his discovery. He had found the bodies of Thotmes III (1501–1447 B.C.) and of Ramses II (1298–

1232 B.C.), at whose court Moses, the lawgiver of the Jews and of the Western world, was then thought to have grown up. These two Pharaohs had ruled for fifty-four and sixty-six years respectively, over empires they had not only created but had known how to keep intact for a long time.

As Brugsch, still overcome and hardly knowing where to begin, scanned the inscriptions on the coffins, his eye chanced to fall immediately upon a history of these "wandering mummies." He began to visualize those countless nights when the priests labored in the Valley of the Kings to preserve the dead Pharaohs from robbery and desecration. He pictured them at work removing the coffins from their original tombs, and transporting them, often through several way-stations, to Deir el-Bahri, where they placed them in new sarcophagi, one next to another. He saw at a glance how fear and desperate haste had swung the whiplash, for some of the coffins remained rudely tipped against the chamber wall in the position where they had chanced to land. Later, in Cairo, with deep emotion he read the messages that the priests had inscribed on the coffin sides—the odysseys of dead Egyptian kings.

A count showed that the assembled rulers numbered no less than forty. Forty mummies! Forty coffins containing the mortal remains of those who once had ruled the Egyptian world like gods, and who for three thousand years had rested in peace until first a robber, then he, Emil Brugsch-Bey, had again laid eyes on them.

Despite all the care they lavished on preparations for their death and immortality, the Egyptian rulers were often pessimistic: "They who built with granite, who set a hall inside their pyramid, and wrought beauty with their fine work ... their altar stones also are empty as are those of the weary ones, the ones who die upon the embankment leaving no mourners."

Such fears did not prevent them from taking ever more precautions for the proper preservation of their bodies. Herodotus describes the rites for the dead as practiced, according to his informants, in the time of his own travels in Egypt (the quotation is from Howard Carter):

> "On the death in any house of a man of consequence, forthwith the women of the family be-plaster their heads, and sometimes even their faces, with mud; and then, leaving the body indoors, sally forth and wander through the city, with their dress fastened by a band, and their bosoms bare, beating themselves as they walk. All the female relations join them and do the same. The men too, similarly begirt, beat their breasts separately. When the ceremonies are over, the body is carried away to be embalmed."

Inseparable from the subject of royal entombment and robbery is the process of mummification. The word *mummy* has several meanings, as suggested by the observation of the twelfth-century Arab traveler Abd al-Latif that "mummies" were sold cheap for medicinal purposes. *Mumiya*, or *mumiyai*, is an Arabic word, and in the sense used by Abd al-Latif means bitumen, or "Jew's pitch." In places this pitch oozed out of the rocks, as at Mummy Mountain, at Derabgerd, in Persia. When Abd al-Latif referred to mummy he meant a mixture of pitch and myrrh. As late as the sixteenth and seventeenth centuries—indeed, even as recently as a hundred years ago—there was a lively sale of what the apothecaries called "mummy," a substance used as a remedy for fractures and wounds. Mummy also meant the hair and fingernails cut off living people. These parts, in so far as they magically stood for the whole, were useful in exorcism and hexing. Today the word *mummy* almost always means embalmed cadavers, particularly the well-preserved bodies of ancient Egyptians. A distinction is made between natural and artificial mummies. Natural mummies are those which have been kept from decomposition by virtue of favorable natural conditions rather than by special chemical treatment. The bodies in the Capuchin cloister in Palermo, in the cloister on the Great St. Bernard, in the lead cellar at the Bremen Cathedral, and in the castle of Quedlinburg are all natural mummies. The distinction between natural and artificial still holds to this day, but extensive research by Elliot Smith, and the analysis of the mummy of Tutankhamen by Douglas E. Derry, have established the qualifying fact that the unusually dry climate of the land of the Nile, and the absence of bacteria in the sand and air, account mostly for the Egyptian mummies' marvelous state of preservation, rather than the materials used in the embalming process. Mummies have been dug up intact from sandy graves, though uncoffined and uneviscerated. The cadavers from the sand, it was found, had resisted the ravages of time as well as the carefully treated corpses or even better. Some of these latter have rotted away, or jelled together into formless masses, despite lavish application of resin, bitumen, and balsamic oils, not to mention—as described in the Rhind Papyrus—"water from Elephantine, natron from Eileithyiaspolis, and milk from the city of Kim."

During the nineteenth century it was widely assumed that the Egyptians were in possession of secret chemical knowledge. Even to this day no absolutely authentic and complete account of the mummification process has been found. But now we know, at least, that the chemical treatment had about as little preservative effect as the religious and mystical adjurations. Also, we must take into consideration the fact that during the course of millennia the art of mummification underwent many changes. Mariette noticed that the mummies of Memphis, which belonged to the older period, were almost black, desiccated, and very fragile. Later specimens from Thebes, however, were yellowish in color, had a mat sheen, and were often flexible, exhibiting discrepancies that could not be explained by difference in age alone.

Herodotus reports that there were three methods

of mummification, the first being three times as expensive as the second, the third—the kind available to officials of minor rank—being cheapest. (The ordinary peasant was not embalmed at all. He simply left his dead body to the good offices of the dry Egyptian climate.)

In the oldest era the Egyptian embalmers were able to preserve only the external form of the body. Later means were found to prevent the shrinkage of the skin, which discovery made it possible for moderns to find mummies with a recognizably individual cast of features.

Corpses were usually handled in the following manner: The brain was first pulled out through the nostrils with a metal hook. The visceral cavity was then laid open with a stone knife, and the soft guts removed. An alternative method was to drag the viscera out through the anal aperture. In either method they were preserved in the so-called "canopic jars," or large vases. The heart was removed and replaced by a stone scarab. After this the remains were thoroughly washed and soaked for more than a month in brine. Finally the cadaver was dried out—a process that, some sources say, lasted for seventy days.

The pickled corpse was then interred in several nested wooden coffins, of human shape, and the coffins deposited in a stone sarcophagus. The body was placed in the innermost coffin in a reclining position. The hands were arranged in a crossed position over the chest or lap or even allowed to hang by the sides. The hair was usually cut short, though with female cadavers it was often allowed to remain at full length, after being beautifully waved. The hair about the genitals was shaved off.

To protect the cadaver from the entrance of destructive agents, the orifices of the body were plugged with lime, sand, resin, sawdust, balls of linen, and the like, with aromatic substances sometimes being added to the plugs. Sometimes, oddly enough, onions were used to perfume the stoppers. The breasts of the women were padded out. Thereafter came the tedious process of swaddling the body in linen winding cloths and bandages. These, with the passage of time, became so thoroughly impregnated with the sticky bituminous material poured over them in great quantity that the archæologist frequently has had trouble unwinding them. The robbers, whose aim was solely to get at the costly ornaments secreted within the wrappings, simply cut diagonally through the cloths, then ripped them off.

In 1898 Loret, general director for the administration of antiquities, opened the tomb of Amenophis II among others. He too found "wandering mummies," namely, the thirteen royal mummies that had also been laboriously collected for safekeeping by priests under the Twenty-first Dynasty, working during the hours of

darkness. But Loret found no treasures to compare with those that Brugsch had discovered only a few years previously. While the mummies themselves were untouched—Amenophis lay in his sarcophagus—everything else had been stolen. But only one or two years after Sir William Garstin had the tomb walled up again, to let the dead kings rest in peace, modern tomb-robbers broke in, tore Amenophis from his coffin, and severely damaged the mummy. They had probably worked in collusion with the guards, like almost all the thieves for thousands of years. It was a further proof that Brugsch had done well to clear out the common grave he had found; to have refrained from doing so out of piety would have been, and was always likely to be, a mistake as matters stood in Egypt.

To return to Emil Brugsch-Bey, when he climbed back up that narrow shaft, leaving the forty dead kings behind, he was already thinking busily about ways and means to make sure of their safety. To leave the burial place as he found it was to leave it open to further plunderings. But to clear it and transport its contents to Cairo meant taking on a great many workers—and there was nowhere to get them from but Kurna, the home of Abd-el-Rasul, the original nest of thieves! By the time Brugsch appeared for another audience at the mudir's, he had decided to do this, regardless of the risks involved. The next morning he was already back at the shaft, with three hundred fellahin. He ordered the area closed. With his Arab aide he selected a small group of men who seemed more trustworthy than the rest. While this group did heavy labor—it turned out that lifting some of the heaviest pieces took sixteen men—sending up the valuable finds one by one to the surface, Brugsch and his aide stood ready to receive each one, register it, and have it lined up with the rest at the foot of the hill. This was done in forty-eight hours. Howard Carter has commented laconically: "We do not work so fast nowadays!" This haste turned out to be excessive in more than the archæological sense, for the steamer for Cairo was several days late. Brugsch-Bey ordered the mummies to be packed up, the coffins covered, and sent to Luxor. It took until July 14 for them to be taken aboard.

But then Brugsch saw something that impressed the seasoned scientist even more than the discovery of the treasures. For the scene he witnessed as the steamer slowly made its way down the Nile affected not only the scientist but the man still capable of veneration.

The news of what kind of cargo the steamer was carrying had spread like wildfire through all the villages along the Nile and farther inland. And it became apparent that the ancient Egypt which had regarded its rulers as gods was not yet dead. Standing on deck, Brugsch saw hundreds of fellahin with their wives escorting the steamer along the banks from Luxor down, new contingents taking the place of those who dropped off as they moved along as far as Qift and Qena, at the great bend in the Nile. The men fired rifle shots in honor of their dead Pharaohs, while the women threw clay and dust upon their faces and bodies and rubbed their breasts with sand. The ship's course was accompanied by lamentations heard from afar. It was a fantastic procession, spontaneous, unadorned, deeply moving in its mournfulness.

Brugsch found the sight hard to bear and turned away. Was he doing the right thing? Could it be that in the eyes of those who were uttering their plaintive cries and beating their breasts he himself was no better than a grave-robber, one of those who had been desecrating the holy sepulchres over thousands of years? Was it enough to claim that he was serving the cause of science?

Many years afterward, Howard Carter gave a clear answer to this vexing question. Of the events around the grave of Amenophis, he remarked:

"One moral we can draw from this episode, and we commend it to the critics who call us Vandals for taking objects from the tombs. By removing antiquities to museums we are really assuring their safety: left *in situ* they would inevitably, sooner or later, became the prey of thieves, and that, for all practical purposes, would be the end of them."

When Brugsch landed in Cairo, he enriched not only one museum but the entire world with evidence of an irrecoverable greatness and splendor that had once been a part of it.

# 16/CARTER:
## THE TOMB OF TUTANKHAMEN

In 1902 Theodore Davis, an American, received permission from the Egyptian government to carry out excavations in the Valley of the Kings. There he dug for twelve long winters. Davis discovered such valuable tombs as those of the fourth Thotmes, of Siptah, and of Horemheb. He also found the mummy and coffin of the great "heretic King," Amenophis IV, whose other name, as the religious reformer who for a time introduced sun-worship as a substitute for the traditional form of Egyptian religion, was Ikhnaton. Amenophis is remembered for the phrase: "The solar disk is satisfied," and for the beautifully colored bust of his wife, Nefertiti, the most famous piece of Egyptian sculpture known (see Plate X).

In the first year of World War I Davis's concession was transferred to Lord Carnarvon and Howard Carter, and with that event began the most important of all Egyptian excavations. The story of this project, as Carnarvon's sister later wrote in a sketch of her brother's life, "starts like Aladdin's miraculous lamp and ends like a Greek saga of Nemesis."

The discovery of the tomb of Tutankhamen represents the very summit of success in archæological effort. It is likewise a critical turning point in our archæological drama, a drama in which the thematic material was supplied by Winckelmann and a long series of systematizers, methodologists, and specialists. The first rough knots in the growing net of action were tied by Champollion, Grotefend, and Rawlinson. The next archæologists substantially to advance the action and to earn plaudits for their mid-stage performance were Mariette, Lepsius, and Petrie in Egypt, Botta and Layard in Mesopotamia, and Stephens and Thompson in Yucatán. The action rose to a breathtaking dramatic pitch with the discoveries of Schliemann and Evans, the one in Troy, the other at Knossos, and those of Koldewey and Woolley in Babylon and Ur, home of Abraham. Schliemann was the last great amateur. By the time Lord Carnarvon and Carter appeared on the scene, whole staffs of experts were working steadily at Knossos and Babylon and other ancient sites. Governments, princes, rich Mæcenases, wealthy universities and archæological institutes, and private men of means from all parts of the modern world had been sending well-equipped expeditions to all corners of the antique world. But the discovery of the tomb of Tutankhamen summed up on a grandiose scale everything previously accomplished in scattered fashion throughout the whole range of archæological investigation. This triumph was one of scientific method. Layard's work had been hindered by superstitious stupidities, and Evans's by official jealousy, but all such difficulties were obviated in the Carnarvon-Carter expedition by the Egyptian government's willing support. The professional envy that injured Rawlinson's reputation and made life a hell for Schliemann was replaced by international cooperation and a readiness to help from many disparate scientific quarters. The pioneer phase of archæology was finished. Howard Carter was a disciple of Petrie and, as such, in touch with the older tradition. Under his ægis, however, Egyptology ceased once and for all to be a random striking-out into an unknown terrain and became a sort of cultural surveying process, marked by the strictest sort of adherence to method.

Yet just because he never lost his inspiration and feeling for the whole, Carter was able to make the very most of scientific exactitude and discipline. It was this combination of sweep and minute thoroughness that made Carter one of the greatest figures in the history of archæology. He definitely belongs among that select company whose primary interest was the solving of cultural mysteries.

Lord Carnarvon was a personality who could have been produced nowhere but in England, a mixture of sportsman and collector, gentleman and world traveler, a realist in action and a romantic in feeling. As a student at Trinity College in Cambridge, out of his own pocket he paid for having the wainscoting of his room, which had been disfigured by many coats of paint, restored to its original beauty. As a youth he haunted antique shops, and later became a passionate collector of old etchings and drawings. At the same time he went a great deal to the racetracks, made himself a good shot by constant practice, and also became a famous yachtsman. At the age of twenty-three, by which time he had come into a large fortune, he made a trip under sail around the world. The third automobile ever licensed in England was his, and fast driving became an obsession with him. This craze for fast driving was to give his life a new and decisive turn. About 1900 he tipped over in a speeding car on a road running into Bad Langenschwalbach and was badly hurt. All the rest of his life he suffered from difficult breathing, an infirmity that made it impossible for him to live in England during the wintertime. On this account in 1903 he went for the first time to Egypt in search of a mild climate and while there visited the excavation sites of several archæological expeditions. Immediately he saw in archæology a chance to combine his interest in collecting *objets d'art* and his delight in the sporting chance. In 1906 he began his own excavations. That same winter, realizing the deficiencies of his own knowledge, he went to Professor Maspero for advice. Maspero recommended the young Howard Carter as archæological aide.

The partnership proved to be an unusually happy one. Howard Carter was able to supply every quality that Lord Carnarvon lacked. He was the comprehensively informed scholar, who, before being made permanent supervisor of all Carnarvon's diggings, had had considerable experience with Petrie and Davis. At the same time he was anything but an unimaginative collector of facts, although some critics of his work complain about what they conceive to be his pedantry. He was ever resourceful on the practical side, and when it came to nerve—indeed, to recklessness—he could not be outdone. This was proved by an adventurous episode that happened in 1916.

At this time Carter was taking a short leave in Luxor. One day the village elders came to him in great perturbation and begged for his assistance. The war was beginning to make itself felt even in Luxor, and the official apparatus, including the police force, had been drastically reduced. As a result the bold descendants of Abd-el-Rasul were again robbing tombs.

A gang of these Egyptian tomb-robbers had made a find on the western side of the mountain beyond the Valley of the Kings. A rival gang, hearing about this, had armed themselves for an attempt to force the others to share their treasures. What now happened was like a movie.

The two gangs fought a pitched battle. The first contingent of tomb-robbers was beaten and driven from the field, but there was still great danger of further bloody altercation. Carter decided to intervene.

"It was already late in the afternoon," he wrote later, "so I hastily collected the few of my workmen who had escaped the Army Labour Levies, and with the necessary materials set out for the scene of action, an expedition involving a climb of more than 1,800 feet over the Kurna hills by moonlight. It was midnight when we arrived on the scene, and the guide pointed out to me the end of a rope which dangled sheer down the face of a cliff. Listening, we could hear the robbers actually at work, so I first severed their rope, thereby cutting off their means of escape, and then, making

secure a good stout rope of my own, I lowered myself
down the cliff. Shinning down a rope at midnight, into
a nestful of industrious tomb-robbers, is a pastime
which at least does not lack excitement. There were
eight at work, and when I reached the bottom there
was an awkward moment or two. I gave them the alternative of clearing out by means of my rope, or else
of staying where they were without a rope at all, and
eventually they saw reason and departed. The rest of
the night I spent on the spot...."

Lord Carnarvon and Howard Carter went to work. Not
until the autumn of 1917, however, were they able to
operate on a scale that promised success. And then
something often experienced in archæology came to
pass. By sheer good luck on their very first attempt the
small area in the Valley of the Kings where discovery
was possible was staked out for attack. Almost at once,
however, outside distraction put a brake on the project.
Critical deliberations, irresolutions, doubts, and, above
all, expert kibitzing delayed—indeed, almost prevented
—success.

It will be recalled in this connection that Cavaliere
Alcubierre, the Neapolitan, on April 6, 1748, by a similar stroke of blind luck, hit squarely on the middle of
Pompeii, but in his impatience to open up new and
better sites filled in the initial excavations before he had
ever begun to explore them properly. Not until years
later did he find that his first location had been the
right one all along.

Carnarvon and Carter looked down upon the Valley of the Kings. Dozens of others had dug there before
them, but not one of these many predecessors had left
behind any exact drawings or even rough plans for the
guidance of future explorers. Great heaps of rubble
towered on all sides, giving the valley floor a lunar
aspect. Among the heaps, like pit-heads, were the entrances to already exploited tombs. The only possible
mode of attack was to dig systematically down to the

rocky floor. Carter proposed to excavate in a triangular area bounded by the tombs of Ramses II, Merneptah, and Ramses VI. "At the risk of being accused of *post actum* prescience," he says, "I will state that we had definite hopes of finding the tomb of one particular king, and that king Tut.ankh.Amen."

Exactly a hundred years before, Belzoni, after opening up the tombs of Ramses I, Sethos I, and of Eje and Mentuherkhepesh, had written: "It is my firm opinion, in view of my recent discoveries, that in the Valley of Biban el-Muluk there are no more [tombs] than those which are known today. For, prior to my quitting that place, I exerted all my humble abilities in trying to find another tomb, but without success. And, still greater proof, independently of my own researches, after I left the place Mr. Salt, the British consul, resided there for four months, and labored in a like manner to find another tomb, but in vain." Twenty-seven years after Belzoni—that is, in 1844—the great Prussian expedition came into the Valley of the Kings and took detailed measurements of the whole site. When they withdrew, their leader, Richard Lepsius, was also of the opinion that everything had been discovered that was there to find. That did not prevent Loret, shortly before the turn of the century, from finding more tombs, and Davis still others shortly after Loret. But now every grain of sand in the Valley, it seemed, had been thrice sifted and turned. When Maspero, as director of the Egyptian antiquities department, signed Lord Carnarvon's concession, he said very frankly that he considered the site to be exhausted and that further investigation would be a waste of time. The Valley, in his expert opinion, simply had no more finds to offer.

What was it, then, that despite all this discouraging advice gave Carter hope of finding not merely any old tomb, but a very definite one? He was personally acquainted with the finds of Theodore Davis, and in the Davis collection was a faïence cup bearing the name of Tutankhamen. This cup Davis had found hidden under a rock. In the same area Davis had also discovered a small rock tomb, and in the tomb a badly broken wooden box containing gold leaf also bearing the name of Tutankhamen. Davis had made the mistake of rashly concluding that the rock tomb was Tutankhamen's. Carter, however, thought otherwise, and his doubts were substantiated when it was discovered that a third find by Davis had not been properly identified. This third find consisted of some apparently valueless potsherds and bundles of linen, cached away in large pottery jars, with sealed openings and hieratic inscriptions on their shoulders. A second examination, carried out at the Metropolitan Museum of Art in New York, showed that very probably the jars and contents were funerary material that had been used during the rites of Tutankhamen's interment. Moreover, Davis later found clay seals with the name of Tutankhamen in the tomb of Ikhnaton, the heretic King.

All this evidence pointed conclusively to the existence of a Tutankhamen tomb. It appeared that Carter had been justified from the first in assuming, despite the general skepticism, that the tomb must lie somewhere in the middle of the Valley, very probably near the site where Davis had made his finds. But when the effects of three thousand years of wear and tear were taken into account, the prospect did not look quite so rosy. During these three thousand years the contents of innumerable tombs had been removed by robbers and priests. Then, too, during the early days archæological research had often been crudely managed, and there was no telling what damage might have resulted from this. Carter's four pieces of evidence were some bits of gold leaf, a faïence cup, a few clay vessels, and some clay seals. To build one's hopes on such flimsy proof with an instinctively positive certainty of finding Tutankhamen's tomb was indeed playing the longest kind of shot.

Once Carnarvon and Carter had begun the actual digging, in one winter's work they cleared away from

within their triangular area of operation a large part of
the upper layers of piled rubble and reached the foot
of the tomb of Ramses VI. "Here we came on a series
of workmen's huts, built over masses of flint boulders,
the latter usually indicating in The Valley the near
proximity of a tomb.

What now unfolded was extremely exciting, viewed
within the context of the whole Tutankhamen drama.
Since further attempts to enlarge the excavation in the
projected direction would have blocked off the entrance
to the tomb of Ramses, a very popular site with tourists,
work was stopped until the work could proceed un-
hampered. Excavation was resumed in the winter of
1919–20, and at the entrance to the tomb of Ramses
VI a small, but archæologically important deposit of
funerary materials was unearthed. "This was the nearest approach to a real find that we had yet made in
The Valley," Carter remarks.

They had now "worried away," as Petrie used to
say, all of the triangle except for the one place where
the workers' huts stood. Again they left this last section untouched, for fear of inconveniencing visitors, and
moved to another spot. In a small lateral valley where
the tomb of Thotmes III was located, they dug for another two winters, finding "nothing of real value."

They now took stock and gave serious consideration to the idea of moving to a completely new site,
since several years of effort had yielded relatively little
booty. Only the place with the workmen's huts and
flint boulders had yet to be investigated, this site, as I
have said, being at the base of the tomb of Ramses VI.
After much hesitation and several reversals of plan it
was decided that the expedition would dedicate one last
winter to the Valley of the Kings.

This time Carter went to work on the one spot
where he should have concentrated six years before.
Scarcely had the workmen's huts been torn down and
the soil beneath cleared away when he was upon the
entrance to the tomb of Tutankhamen, richest in all

Egypt. "The dramatic suddenness of the initial discovery," Carter writes, "left me in a dazed condition, and the months that have followed have been so crowded with incident that I have hardly had time to think."

On November 3, 1922—Lord Carnarvon was away in England at the time—Carter began to tear down the workmen's huts. The next morning a stone step cut into the rock was discovered beneath the first hut. By the afternoon of November 5 enough rubbish had been cleared away to establish beyond doubt the fact that the entrance to the tomb had indeed been found.

But it might very well have been an unfinished tomb, one that, perhaps, had never been used. And if the tomb did contain a mummy, it might, like so many others, have already been plundered. And perhaps, to complete the list of pessimistic possibilities, the mummy was there, but might be nothing but that of some high official or of a priest.

The work was pressed feverishly, Carter's excitement mounting as the day wore on. Step after step appeared out of the rubble, and as the sudden Egyptian night closed in, the level of the twelfth step came to light, disclosing "the upper part of a doorway, blocked, plastered, and sealed. A sealed doorway—it was actually true, then! . . . It was a thrilling moment for an excavator."

Carter examined the seal and found it to be that of the royal necropolis. A royal seal was clear proof that a person of very high standing was interred within. Since the workmen's huts had lain directly above the opening, it was obvious that at least since the Twentieth Dynasty the tomb had never been plundered. And when Carter, shaking with agitation, bored a peephole in the door "just large enough to insert an electric torch," he discovered that the corridor behind the door was filled to the brim with stones and rubble—further reassurance that elaborate protective measures had been taken with the tomb.

Leaving his most reliable men to guard the tomb, Carter rode home down the Valley by moonlight, struggling against overwhelming temptation: "Anything, literally anything, might lie beyond that passage, and it needed all my self-control to keep from breaking down the doorway, and investigating then and there," he wrote, describing how he felt after he had peered through the peephole. Now again, as his donkey was trotting homeward with him, he was bedeviled by desire, by impatience, by his inner voice telling him he was on the verge of incalculable discoveries. Yet this man, having made his great find at long last after six years of laboring in vain, had the self-discipline to cover up the tomb and await the arrival of his sponsor and friend, Lord Carnarvon, before proceeding to explore it.

On the morning of November 6 Carter sent the following telegram to Lord Carnarvon: "At last have made wonderful discovery in valley; a magnificent tomb with seals intact; re-covered same for your arrival; congratulations." On November 8 two replies from Carnarvon were received: "Possibly come soon"; and "Propose arrive Alexandria 20th."

On November 23 Lord Carnarvon, accompanied by his daughter, arrived in Luxor. For more than two weeks Carter had been waiting, consumed by impatience, on guard at the carefully covered tomb entrance. Two days after the discovery of the steps he had been flooded with messages of congratulations. But congratulations for exactly what? What was in the tomb? At this time Carter could not have said. Had he dug only a few inches lower down, he would have come upon the unmistakable seal of Tutankhamen himself. "Had I but known . . . I would have cleared on," says Carter, "and had a much better night's rest in consequence, and saved myself nearly three weeks of uncertainty."

On the afternoon of November 24 the workers shoveled the last of the flight of steps free of rubbish. Carter went down the sixteen steps and stood before the sealed door. Now he could get a clear impression of the seal of Tutankhamen. And now, too, he became aware—the Egyptologist's typical experience—that others had been there before him. Here, too, robbers had done their work.

"Now that the whole door was exposed to light," Carter says, "it was possible to discern a fact that had hitherto escaped notice—that there had been two successive openings and re-closings of a part of its surface: furthermore, that the sealing originally discovered, the jackal and nine captives [the necropolis seal], had been applied to the re-closed portions, whereas the sealings of Tut.ankh.Amen covered the untouched part of the doorway, and were therefore those with which the tomb had been originally secured. The tomb then was not absolutely intact, as we had hoped. Plunderers had entered it, and entered it more than once—from the evidence of the huts above, plunderers of a date not later than the reign of Ramses IV—but that they had not rifled it completely was evident from the fact that it had been re-sealed."

But more revelations were in store for Carter. His confusion and uncertainty increased. When he had had the last of the rubbish blocking the stairs shoveled away, he found potsherds and boxes, the latter with the names of Ikhnaton, Sakeres, and Tutankhamen on them, also a scarab belonging to Thotmes III, and a piece of another, this one with the name of Amenophis III inscribed on it. Could all these names mean, against all expectation, a jointly shared rather than a single tomb?

Certainty could be achieved only by opening the door of the tomb. The next days were spent preparing for this move. Carter had seen the first time he looked through the peephole that the interior passage was clogged with rubble. This filling consisted of two clearly distinguishable kinds of stone. The shoulder-wide entrance cut by the robbers had itself been replugged with a kind of dark flint.

After several days of hard work the excavators, having penetrated thirty-two feet into the passage, found themselves hard up against a second door. The impressions of the royal seal of Tutankhamen and of the necropolis seal were also on this door, but there were signs, too, that intruders must have broken past this second obstruction.

Basing their reasoning on the resemblance of the whole layout to a cache of Ikhnaton that had been found near by, at this stage Carnarvon and Carter, with good reason, were tempted to believe that they were dealing with a common tomb, and not the original grave of an Egyptian king. And was there much to expect in a cache, especially one that had already been visited by robbers?

Their hopes, in short, for a time were dashed. The tension increased once more, however, when rubble was taken away from the second door. "The decisive moment had arrived," Carter says. "With trembling hands I made a tiny breach in the upper left hand corner."

Taking an iron testing rod, Carter poked it through the door and found an emptiness on the other side. He lit candles to ensure against poisonous gases. Then the hole was enlarged.

Everyone interested in the project now crowded about. Lord Carnarvon, his daughter, Lady Evelyn, and Callender, the Egyptologist, who had rushed to offer his help upon first receiving news of the find—all looked on. Nervously Carter lit a match, touched it to the candle, and held it toward the hole. As his head neared the opening—he was literally trembling with expectation and curiosity—the warm air escaping from the chamber beyond the door made the candle flare up. For a moment Carter, his eye fixed to the hole and the candle burning within, could make out nothing. Then, as his eyes became gradually accustomed to the flickering light, he distinguished shapes, then their shadows, then the first colors. Not a sound escaped his lips; he had been stricken dumb. The others waited for what seemed to them like an eternity. Finally Carnarvon could no longer contain his impatience. "Can you see anything?" he inquired.

Carter, slowly turning his head, said shakily: "Yes, wonderful things."

"Surely never before in the whole history of excavation had such an amazing sight been seen as the light of our torch revealed to us." So writes Carter, reporting on the sight revealed to the company as each in turn stepped up to the peephole. When the door was actually opened, on the 17th, this description proved to be not in the least exaggerated. The light of a strong electric lamp moved jerkily over golden couches, a gilded throne; and its softer reflection threw into relief two large black statues, vases of alabaster, and curious shrines. The shadows of bizarre animal heads played on the walls. A golden snake peeped out of the open door of one of the shrines. The two royal statues faced each other like sentinels, "gold kilted, gold sandalled, armed with mace and staff, the protective sacred cobra upon their foreheads."

Amid all this splendor, an abundance that the eye could not take in at a single glance, they again found traces of intruders. At the door stood a vessel still half-filled with mortar, and near by a blackened lamp. There were fingerprints on a once freshly painted surface, and on the threshold a garland of flowers left in parting.

Dumbfounded as they were by so many impressions, it was some time before Carter and Carnarvon realized with a start that neither sarcophagus nor mummy was to be seen in this museum of treasures. The question of whether they were dealing with a royal tomb or a cache again rose in their minds.

Looking over the walls more carefully, they saw that there was a third sealed door between the two sentinel figures. "Visions of chamber after chamber, each crowded with objects like the ones we had seen, passed through our minds and left us gasping for breath," writes Carter. On the 27th of the month, with the aid of powerful electric lamps installed meanwhile by Callender, they investigated the sealed door. They found that a small opening had been made in it near

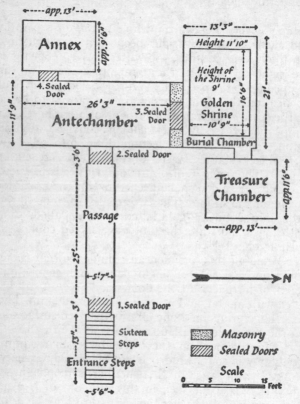

Sketch of the tomb of Tutankhamen.

the bottom, later filled up and resealed. Evidently the tomb-robbers had penetrated beyond the antechamber, as they called the first compartment of the tomb. What was there in the chamber or passage beyond? If there was a mummy beyond the door, was it all of a piece and untouched? The whole situation was shrouded in mystery. Not only was it physically unlike any of previous experience; it also posed the problem of why the robbers had gone to so much trouble to get through the third door without first making off with the wealth of valuables that lay at hand. What could they have been after to make them wade indifferently through the heaps of gold lying in the antechamber?

When Carter had got his bearings in this astounding treasure-trove, he realized that the furnishings of the antechamber were valuable in a historic and æsthetic sense, beyond the intrinsic value of the precious metal used lavishly in their construction. What information these mute things gave archæology! There was a multitude of Egyptian objects of practical and cultural use and of luxury, any single one of which would have been considered ample reward for a whole winter's hard digging. They revealed Egyptian art of a certain period in such strength and vitality that a brief survey sufficed to convince Carter that detailed study of the collection would "involve a modification, if not a complete revolution, of all our old ideas."

It was not long before still another discovery was made. Some one, peering beneath one of the three great couches, saw a small hole. He called to the others, who came crawling up to him, dragging an electric lamp with them. They now peered into a small side chamber, or annex, smaller than the antechamber, but packed full of all sorts of material, objects both of utility and of decoration. The robbers, after their visit, had not bothered to straighten out this room, as apparently they had the antechamber. The thief who had ransacked the place had "done his work just about as thoroughly as an earthquake." The intruders had turned the whole room topsy-turvy. It was obvious that they had thrown pieces taken from the annex about the antechamber, destroying some of the material. And yet in actual fact they had made off with very little, not even with the easily available articles that fell into their hands once they were beyond the second door. Had they been surprised at their work?

The discovery of the annex had a sobering effect. Up to this point the situation had been apprehended in a rush of excitement, which made for a badly confused impression of the whole. Now that the investigators were able to look more calmly, however, they became aware of the even greater treasures that might be expected behind the third sealed door. They realized, too, that a prodigious scientific task confronted them, one requiring much organization and a large labor force. The finds already made, leaving out of account those in prospect, could never be disposed of in a single winter's work.

Carter and Carnarvon decided to fill in the excavated tomb. Carter saw very clearly that under no circumstances could he plunge headlong into the task of removing the contents of ante-chamber and annex. Leaving aside the need for an exact record of the original position of all the objects—in order to determine temporal and other points of reference—Carter realized that many of the finds were in a perishable condition and would have to be given preservative treatment before, or immediately after, being removed. To this end it was necessary to lay in a large store of preservative and packing materials. Expert advice had to be sought on the best methods of procedure, and a laboratory set up for on-the-spot analysis. The cataloguing of such an immense find in itself required extensive organizational preparation. All in all, measures would have to be taken that were quite beyond the facilities then at hand. Carnarvon would have to go to England, and Carter at least to Cairo. On December 3 the entrance of the tomb was blocked with fill, a move which indicates that Carter thought tomb-robbery was still a factor to be reckoned with. Not until he had sealed up the tomb and posted Callender on guard was Carter's mind easy. And immediately upon arriving in Cairo, he ordered a heavy steel door made to cover the inner antechamber door.

From the moment of discovery generous offers of help poured in from all corners of the world. Outside experts later contributed a great deal to enhance the

thoroughness and exactitude of this most exemplary of
Egyptian excavations. Later Carter took the trouble,
rightly enough, to express his gratitude to everyone who
helped him make such a comprehensive effort. In his
book about the tomb of Tutankhamen is a letter from
Rais Ahmed Gurgar, supervisor of the Egyptian laborers, which was sent to Carter while he was off in Cairo.
It is reproduced here to illustrate that the cooperative
climate of the project extended even to nonintellectual
quarters.

KARNAK, LUXOR
5th August 1923

*Mr. Howard Carter Esq*
     *Honourable Sir,*
          *Beg to write this letter hoping that you are
enjoying good health, and ask the Almighty to
keep you & bring you back to us in Safety.*
          *Beg to inform your Excellency that Store No. 15
is alright, Treasure is Alright, the Northern Store
is alright. Wadain & House are all alright, & in all
your work order is carried on according to your
honourable instructions.*
          *Rais Hussein, Gad Hassan, Hassim Awad, Ab-
delal Ahmed and all the Gaffirs of the house beg
to send their best regards.*
          *My best regards to your respectable Self, and all
members of the Lord's family, & to all your friends
in England.*
          *Longing to your early coming—*
                         *Your Most Obedient Servant*
                         *Rais Ahmed Gurgar*

After Carter had "somewhat diffidently inquired"
about the possibility, A. M. Lythgoe, curator of the
Egyptian section of the Metropolitan Museum of Art
in New York, whose concession at Thebes was close to
Carnarvon's, placed the American photographer Harry
Burton at Carter's disposal. Lythgoe, offering his own

valuable assistance, telegraphed: "Only too delighted
to assist in any possible way. Please call on Burton and
any other members of our staff." As a result of this
offer the American draftsmen Hall and Hauser, as well
as A. C. Mace, director of the museum excavations at
the pyramids of Lisht, were also assigned to the Carnarvon-Carter project. In Cairo, A. Lucas, director of the
chemical department of the Egyptian government, then
about to leave on a three-month vacation prior to retire-
ment from the service, offered Carter his services. Dr.
Alan Gardiner undertook to handle the inscriptions,
and Professor James II. Breasted of the University of
Chicago hastened to the site to lend a hand in establishing the historical significance of the seal impressions
on the doors.

Later—on November 11, 1925—Dr. Saleh Bey
Hamdi and Douglas E. Derry, professor of anatomy at
the Egyptian University, began to examine the mummy.
A. Lucas wrote a fairly exhaustive study on "The
Chemistry of the Tomb, specifically what had happened to the metals, minerals, fats, pigments, textiles
and the like." P. E. Newberry analyzed the floral
wreaths found in the coffins of Tutankhamen and determined the kinds of flowers present nearly 3,300 years
before. He was able to state that Tutankhamen was
interred between the end of April and the middle of
May, because he knew when such flowers as the little
picris and the cornflower blossom, and when the fruit
of the bittersweet or woody nightshade ripens, as well
as that of the mandrake—the love-apple of Genesis and
the Song of Solomon. Other "Objects" and "Specimens" from the tomb were analyzed by Alexander Scott
and H. J. Plenderleith.

Such cooperation on the part of first-class specialists—including some in fields unrelated to archæology—
promised unprecedented contributions to science as a
result of clearing the tomb. Accordingly, on December
16 the tomb was reopened, on December 18 the photographer Burton took his first shots in the antecham-

ber, and on December 27 the first object was brought out of the tomb.

Thoroughness takes time. Work on the tomb of Tutankhamen lasted for several seasons. Here I will touch only on the high points of Howard Carter's colorful report. Only a few of the particularly beautiful objects will be mentioned; for example, the painted wooden casket from the antechamber, which proved to be one of the greatest treasures of Egyptian art. It was covered completely with a thin gesso, or plaster, and painted on all sides with lovely designs, wherein a sensitive use of brilliant color was combined with exquisitely refined draftsmanship. The detail of the hunting and battle scenes shown on the casket was composed with a delicacy that, as Carter says, "far surpasses anything of the kind that Egypt has yet produced." This decorative wooden casket was filled with a variety of objects. Typical of Carter's whole approach was the fact that he spent three weeks of painstaking effort emptying this box.

Equally impressive were the three great animal-sided couches, known from illustrations in tomb paintings, but hitherto never actually found. They were curious pieces of furniture, the frame being constructed with a foot panel, but none at the head. The first was lion-headed, the second cow-headed, and the third had the head of a composite animal, half hippopotamus, half crocodile. All three couches were literally buried in precious things, packed tightly together on and about them—all manner of weapons, luxury objects, and pieces of clothing. Below one of the couches stood a throne with a panel back that moved Carter to say "with no hesitation" that it was "the most beautiful thing that has yet been found in Egypt."

Finally mention must be made of the four chariots, which were so large that to get them into the tomb the axles had had to be sawn in two. The robbers, moreover, had scattered the parts all around the place. All four chariots were completely covered with gold. Every inch was decorated either with embossed designs and scenes hammered into the gold itself or with inlaid designs made of colored glass and stone.

On May 13 thirty-four heavy packing cases were loaded on little flat cars and taken, by way of a portable railroad, the five and a half miles to the waiting steam barge on the Nile. The treasures were carried away from the tomb by the same route by which they had come, borne in ceremonial procession three thousand years before. Seven days later they were in Cairo.

By the middle of February the antechamber was cleaned out. Space had been made for the one phase of the project that everyone was looking forward to with the keenest impatience: the opening up of the sealed door between the two sentinel figures. The question whether the next chamber contained a mummy would now soon be resolved. When, on a Friday, February 17, some twenty people who had been accorded the privilege of witnessing the unsealing assembled in the antechamber, excitement was running high. Yet nobody there had any idea what he would be looking at two hours later. After such prodigal finds of treasure it was hard to conceive that even more important and valuable objects would be brought to light.

The visitors—archæologists and Egyptian officials—took their places on the closely ranged chairs that had been provided for their comfort. A dead silence gripped the watchers as Carter mounted the platform built to facilitate his loosening the sealed door.

Carter used great care in picking out the uppermost layer of the stone filling. The work took a long time, and was extremely finicky, for there was always the danger that loose stones might fall inside and damage whatever lay beyond the door. He also had to try his best to preserve the seal impressions, for these had a high scientific value. He tells how, when he had made a small opening, "the temptation to stop and peer inside at every moment was irresistible."

Mace and Callender now went to Carter's assistance. A subdued murmur arose as Carter, after about ten minutes' work, took a flashlight and poked it through the hole.

He could see nothing but a shining wall. Shifting the flashlight this way and that, he was still unable to find its outer limits. Apparently it blocked off the whole entrance to the chamber beyond the door. Carter was looking at a wall of solid gold.

As fast as he dared, he removed more stones. Presently the watchers, too, could see the gold gleam. As one stone after another was taken away, "we could, as though by electric current," he says, "feel the tingle of excitement which thrilled the spectators behind the barrier." Carter, Mace, and Callender simultaneously realized what the wall really was. They were now actually face to face with the entrance to the sepulchral chamber. What appeared to them as a wall was the nearer surface of an unusually large, and of course fabulously costly, shrine. There was a delay that tried everyone's nerves while the scattered beads of a necklace were gathered up from the floor where plunderers had dropped them. With the onlookers shifting about impatiently on their hard chairs, Carter, who had all the persistence and respect of the true archæologist for seeming trifles, collected bead after bead with infinite care, though he knew he was on the brink of a tremendous discovery.

It had now become evident that the level of the burial chamber was about 3.2 feet below that of the antechamber. Carter took an electric lamp and let himself down through the hole. Yes, he was standing beside a great shrine. The structure was so large that it all but filled the room. Carter reports that the passageway between the shrine and the chamber wall was only 15.35 inches wide. This narrow corridor had to be traversed with great caution, for it was cluttered with funerary gifts.

Lord Carnarvon and M. Pierre Lacau, director general of the service of antiquities in Cairo, were the first to follow Carter inside the sepulchral chamber. They were stricken mute by the splendor of the sight. They took the measurements of the shrine, which, double-checked, proved to be 17 by 11 by 9 feet high. It was completely covered with gold, and on its sides were inlaid panels of brilliant blue faïence, showing magic symbols intended to protect the dead.

The question that now troubled everyone's mind was this: had the robbers had time to force their way into the shrine? Had they got at the mummy and injured it? Carter discovered that the folding doors at the eastern end of the shrine were bolted, but not sealed. With trembling hands he drew back the bolts and came upon another pair of folding doors, also bolted, and sealed. These doors gave ingress to a second shrine built within the first.

All three men gave an audible sigh of relief. Each chamber opened so far had shown signs of intrusion, but here, at the most critical segment of the tomb, they were definitely first. They would find the mummy untouched, exactly as it had been interred more than three thousand years before.

They closed the shrine door "as silently as possible." They had noticed the linen pall, bespangled and brown with age, drooping above the shrine. "The pall made us realize that we were in the presence of a dead king of past ages." For a moment, they felt like intruders. They went to the other end of the burial chamber. There they found a low door, which gave into another, rather small room. From the middle of this room, facing the doorway, shone a golden shrine-shaped chest, and surrounding it, unattached, were four protecting goddesses, fashioned with such grace and naturalness, with so much compassion and pleading in their faces, that "one felt it almost sacrilege to look at them. . . . I am not ashamed to confess," Carter says, "that it brought a lump to my throat."

Slowly Carter, Carnarvon, and Lacau moved back past the golden shrine and into the antechamber to enable the others to take their turn within. "It was curious, as we stood in the Antechamber, to watch their faces as, one by one, they emerged from the door. Each had a dazed, bewildered look in his eyes, and each in turn, as he came out, threw up his hands before him, an unconscious gesture of impotence to describe the wonders that he had seen."

About five o'clock that afternoon, three hours after entering the tomb, they came up to the surface. As they returned to the light of day, "the very Valley seemed to have changed for us and taken on a more personal aspect."

Further investigation of these supreme archæological treasures stretched out through several more seasons. Unfortunately, the first winter passed with very little accomplished, for Lord Carnarvon had died, and serious differences with the Egyptian government arose over whether the concession should be extended, and how the finds should be divided. Finally the case was submitted to an international commission, which eventually succeeded in arriving at a satisfactory adjustment. Thereafter work resumed. In the winter of 1926–7 the next most important steps were carried out—that is, the actual opening of the gilded shrine, the laborious separation of the various precious coffins, and the careful preliminary study of Tutankhamen's mummy as found.

This phase of the project, though it provided few surprises for a sensation-hungry public, was of great interest to the science of Egyptology, and also had its own dramatic climax. This peak of interest came when the investigators, for the first time since he had been removed from mortal purview thirty-three centuries before, looked into the features of the dead King. That this long-awaited moment should prove to be the only disappointment in the whole saga of the excavation simply goes to show that every chain of luck has its weak link.

The work began with the removal of the brick wall

between the antechamber and the sepulchral room, and thereafter the first golden shrine was disassembled. Within this shrine, they found, was a third as well as a second one.

Carter had every reason to believe that the sarcophagus itself would be inside the third shrine. "It was an exciting moment in our arduous task that cannot easily be forgotten," he writes, when he went through the opening of the third shrine. "With suppressed excitement I carefully cut the cord, removed that precious seal, drew back the bolts, and opened the doors when a fourth shrine was revealed, similar in design and even more brilliant in workmanship than the last. . . . An indescribable moment for an archæologist! What was beneath and what did that fourth shrine contain? With intense excitement I drew back the bolts of the last and unsealed doors; they slowly swung open, and there, filling the entire area within . . . stood an immense yellow quartzite sarcophagus, intact, just as the pious hands had left it." What an unforgettably splendid sight, heightened even more by the glitter of gold on the shrines! A goddess spread protecting arms and wings over the foot end of the sarcophagus, "as if to ward off an intruder." He stood in awe before this eloquent sign (see Plates XI to XVI).

The removal of the shrine from the sepulchral chamber alone took eighty-four days of heavy manual labor. The four shrines altogether consisted of about eighty-odd parts—each part being heavy, hard to handle, and very breakable.

As so often happens, a certain irony infected the prevailing mood of exaltation. Carter, the perfectionist, scolds—at a remove of three thousand years—the workmen who put the shrines together. Whereas he marvels at the masterly skill of the artisans who actually fashioned the component parts of the shrines, and praises them for carefully providing each piece with a number and location sign to facilitate assembly, he is very much annoyed with the men who had charge of the actual assembly.

"But on the other hand," he writes, "there was evidence that the obsequies had been hurriedly performed, and that the workmen in charge of those last rites were anything but careful men. They had, with little doubt, placed those parts around the sarcophagus, but in their carelessness had reversed their order in regard to the four cardinal points. They had leant them against the four walls around the sarcophagus they were to shield, contrary to the instructions written upon the different parts, with a result that, when they were erected, the doors of the shrines faced east instead of west, the foot ends west instead of east, and the side panels were likewise transposed. This may have been a pardonable fault . . . although there were other signs of slovenliness. Sections had obviously been banged together, regardless of the risk of damage to their gilt ornamentation. Deep dents from blows from a heavy hammer-like implement are visible to the present day on the gold-work, parts of the surfaces in some cases had been actually knocked off, and the workmen's refuse, such as chips of wood, had never been cleared away."

On February 3 the searchers at last were able to have a perfectly unimpeded look at the sarcophagus. It was a masterpiece, made from a single great block of the finest yellow quartzite. It measured 8.8 feet long, 4.8 feet wide, and 4.8 feet high. The lid was made of rose granite.

When the tackle for raising the heavy lid—it weighed more than twelve hundredweight—began to squeak and creak under the rising load, again an audience of prominent guests looked on. "Amid intense silence the huge slab . . . rose from its bed." The first view of the interior was disappointing: nothing to see but a bulky something bundled in linen cloths. But when these were removed, revealing the coffin itself, the revelation was so much the more impressive.

Already the King's body? No, the first thing to come to view was a golden effigy of the boy ruler on the lid of an "anthropoid coffin." The gold glittered as brightly as if it had just come from the foundry. The head and hands were cast in three dimensions, but the highly decorated remainder of the figure was rendered in low relief. Crossed hands held the royal emblems of Crook and Flail, inlaid with blue faïence. The face was of pure gold, the eyes were made of aragonite and obsidian, the brows and lids of lapis-lazuli glass. This bright visage had a rigid, masklike look, and yet seemed alive.

There was something else on the coffin that affected Carter and the others even more poignantly than the effigy. Carter describes it thus: ". . . but perhaps the most touching by its human simplicity was the tiny wreath of flowers" around the symbols on the forehead, "the last farewell offering of the widowed girl queen to her husband. . . . Among all that regal splendour, that royal magnificence—everywhere the glint of gold—there was nothing so beautiful as those few withered flowers, still retaining their tinge of colour. They told us what a short period three thousand three hundred years really was—but Yesterday and the Morrow. In fact, that little touch of nature made that ancient and our modern civilization kin." Carter writes again in much the same vein when he is describing how in the winter of 1925–6 he again descended into the tomb to open the sarcophagus: "Familiarity can never entirely dissipate the feeling of mystery—the sense of vanished but haunting forces that cling to the tomb. The conviction of the unity of past and present is constantly impressed upon the archæological adventurer, even when absorbed in the mechanical details of his work." Carter really felt these reverent sentiments. It is good to know that the scientist does not deny the claims of the spirit.

It is not really possible to linger over all the details and small incidents connected with the opening of the sar-

cophagus. The actual labor was extremely tedious, and
the working space awkwardly constricted. Any number
of mishaps—the failure of the block and tackle, the
giving way of a timber prop—might have severely damaged the treasures within, and so the greatest care was
exercised at all times. On the lid of the second coffin—
three coffins were nested one within another—was an
effigy of the young Pharaoh in ceremonial dress, richly
ornamented in the Osirian style. Nothing new of this
nature came to light, however, when the third coffin
was opened; but throughout the whole operation the
workers had been struck by the inexplicable weight of

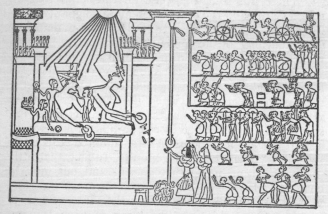

Ikhnaton and his wife. Tutankhamen's father-in-law
showers the priest, Eje, and Eje's wife, with gifts.

the nested coffins. Now came another in the seemingly
endless series of surprises afforded by the tomb.

When Burton, the photographer, had done his
work, and after Carter had removed the wreath of
flowers and the protective linen cover, the mystery of
the tremendous weight was solved. The third coffin, 6
feet 1.75 inches in length, was made of solid gold, .15
to .21 inches thick. Its intrinsic value alone was enormous.

This pleasant surprise, however, was soon tempered by concern over the discovery of some sticky stuff that had already been noted clinging to the ornamentation of the second coffin. It now appeared that the whole space between the second and third coffins had been filled with a liquid that had become a firm, hard mass. A double detachable necklace of gold and faïence beads was taken from this pitchy deposit and cleaned without too much difficulty. But now the investigators began to speculate anxiously on what injury the incontinent application of consecrated unguents might have worked on the mummy itself. When one of the workers took off the last linen shroud and the floral collarette mingled with faïence beads—all of which seemed to be in sound condition—they simply fell apart. The sacred oils and tars had completely decayed them.

At once Lucas undertook an analysis of the unguent material. Some sort of fluid, or near-fluid, substance must have been used, the basic ingredients of which were fatty matter of some sort and resin. The presence of wood-pitch, the odor of which strongly perfumed the stuff after it was warmed, could not be immediately determined. Again the tension rose; the final, decisive moment was at hand.

Some golden tenons were loosened, then the lid of the last coffin was lifted off by its golden handles, and the mummy uncovered. There lay the cadaver of Tutankhamen, after six years of preparatory labor.

"At such moments," Carter says, "the emotions evade verbal expression, complex and stirring as they are."

But who was this Pharaoh, this Tutankhamen? Curiously enough, for all the splendor of his burial, Tutankhamen was a ruler of little importance. He died at the age of eighteen. It is certain that he was the son-in-law of Ikhnaton, the "heretic King," and probably Ikhnaton's half brother as well. Tutankhamen's youth was passed during the interlude of religious reform instituted by his Aton-worshipping father-in-law. The fact that he reverted to the traditional religion of Amen is shown by his change of name, from the original Tut-ankh-Aton to Tut-ankh-Amen. We know that his reign was politically muddled. There are pictures showing Tutankhamen kicking prisoners of war, also shooting down rows of enemies. But it is not in the least certain whether he actually ever took the field in person. We do not even know the exact duration of his reign, except that it dates from somewhere about 1350 B.C. The throne came to him through his wife, Anches-en-Amen, whom he married very young, and whose portraits show her to have been a bewitching creature.

Through the numerous pictures and reliefs found in his grave, and many objects of daily personal use, we have received a pleasing impression of Tutankhamen's personality. But we know nothing of his royal deeds, the way he functioned as a ruler. It seems safe to assume that not much of significance could have been achieved by a ruler who died at eighteen. Surely Carter is justified in saying that, as far as we know, the only remarkable act of Tutankhamen's life is that he died and was buried.

However, if this eighteen-year-old Pharaoh was buried with a pomp and splendor exceeding all that our Western imagination can conceive, what must have been the tomb furnishings of Ramses the Great and Sethos I? It was to Ramses and Sethos that Derry was referring when he said that every single chamber of their tombs must have contained as much as the entire tomb of Tutankhamen. What unimaginable treasures must have passed through the hands of robbers from the royal graves in the Valley of the Kings, in the course of so many centuries!

The aspect of the Pharaoh's mummy was both splendid and terrible. A great deal of embalming unguent had been poured over the swathed cadaver, and this gluey stuff had hardened, turned black, and cemented the cerements to the body.

Contrasting with the dark, shapeless mass of the mummy was a golden mask covering the head and shoulders of the King, the gold shining with a regal gleam. The mask itself was free from the dark embalming material, as were the feet of the mummy.

After a number of unsuccessful tries, the second coffin of wood was separated from the third, golden one nested inside it, by a laborious process of heating to 932° Fahrenheit. The gold was protected with a sheathing of zinc plates after the mummy had been removed.

The next step was to examine the mummy, the only one in the Valley, so far as was known, that had remained untouched throughout thirty-three centuries. This inspection brought to light a fact on which Carter comments as follows: "Here we have a grim example of the irony which may sometimes await research. The tomb-robbers who dragged the remains of the Pharaohs from their coverings for plunder, or the pious priests who hid them to save them from further violations, at least protected those royal remains against the chemical action of the sacred unguents before there was time for corrosion." Mummies were often damaged during theft —unless the thieves were priests—but notwithstanding, they have still come down in much better state than the mummy of Tutankhamen. Indeed, the deterioration of the body was the only real disappointment in the tomb.

On November 11, about 9:45 in the morning, Dr. Derry, the anatomist, made his first incision into the outer linen cloths swaddling the mummy. Except for the face and feet, which had not been touched by the unguents, the mummy proved to be in a frightful condition. The oxidation of the resinous content of the mixture had occasioned a sort of spontaneous combustion, so intense that not only the ceremental windings, but the tissue and bones of the mummy had been carbonized. The pitchlike sheath was so hard in places, as for example under the legs and rump, that it had to be chiseled away.

An astounding discovery was the finding of an amuletic headrest under the crownlike pad bandaged with surgical skill onto the head. The amulet in itself was not at all out of the ordinary. And within the linen windings Tutankhamen had been provided with all sorts of "magical armor"—amulets, symbols, and magic signs. But the head-rest was fashioned out of pure iron, instead of the usual hematite! This amuletic head-rest, together with a number of tiny implements, evidently models, constituted one of the earliest-dated finds of pure iron known to Egyptology.

Enormous care was used in loosing the last linen wrappings from the carbonized body of the young Pharaoh. The least touch of a sable brush, and the remains of the rotten tissue fell apart. Then the countenance of the young King was laid bare to view; in Carter's words: "... a serene and placid countenance, that of a young man." "The face," we are told, "was refined and cultured, the features well-formed, especially the clearly marked lips."

One hundred and forty-three pieces of jewelry of various kinds were discovered inside the mummy's bindings. Of the thirty-three pages that Carter uses to describe the examination of the mummy, more than half are given over exclusively to listing precious articles found wrapped in the cerements. The eighteen-year-old Pharaoh was literally wrapped in several layers of gold and precious stones.

In a special monograph Dr. Derry later described the inspection of the mummy from the anatomical point of view. He claims that in all probability there was a father-son relationship between Ikhnaton and Tutankhamen, a fact of extraordinary significance in so far as it illuminates the dynastic and political conditions at the time of the moribund Eighteenth Dynasty.

Derry then goes on to record an observation, highly interesting from a cultural standpoint: namely, that the arts of representation at the beginning of the New Empire inclined strongly toward realism. "The effigy of Tut.ankh.Amen on the gold mask exhibits him as a gentle and refined-looking young man," says Derry. "Those who were privileged to see the actual face when finally exposed can bear testimony to the ability and accuracy of the Eighteenth Dynasty artist who has so faithfully represented the features, and left for all time, in imperishable metal, a beautiful portrait of the young king."

Derry was also able to arrive at a close estimate of the King's age, which history does not give. From the degree of ossification of the internal condyle of the humerus and the condition of the bony union of trochanter and femur and of the end of the tibia, he judged Tutankhamen's age to be somewhere between seventeen and eighteen years, eighteen probably being the closest approximation.

Here the story of the actual excavation of the tomb of Tutankhamen ends since the annex and the little treasure chamber yielded only mildly interesting, though important finds.

There is another aspect, however, that merits attention: the "curse of the Pharaohs." More than twenty persons connected at some time or other with the unsealing of the famous tomb died under mysterious circumstances.

During the two hundred years, more or less, of archæological history, no revelation of the lost world of antiquity received more publicity than that of Tutankhamen. Not for nothing did the incident unfold in the day of the rotary press, the camera, and the newly sprung radio industry. The world first showed its interest with a flood of congratulatory telegrams. Then reporters began to haunt the site. Presently letters from the critical and the well-meaning began to arrive. Some complained bitterly about the desecration of the dead. Others sent patented grave-digging methods. The first winter ten or fifteen crank letters arrived every day. What sort of person, Carter marvels at one point, can a man be who seriously inquires whether the discovery of the tomb will throw light on the current atrocities in the Belgian Congo?

Then visitors began to arrive in droves. In three months of the year 1926, when the publicity was at its height, 12,300 tourists visited the tomb. There were also 270 applications to examine the finds and the laboratory work.

Exactly how the legend of the "curse of the Pharaohs" arose cannot be traced. All through the 1930's, nevertheless, the theme was played up again and again in the world press. It must be admitted, however, that there is more foundation for the story than there was for the numerologies based on the Great Pyramid of Cheops, or of the "mummy wheat" taken from old Egyptian tombs, which reportedly retains its germinative power after the lapse of two or three thousand years. This wheat legend is so widely believed that even today guides often make extra tips by seeing to it that their clients find "mummy wheat" in the cracks of the masonry of the royal tombs.

The "curse of the Pharaohs" is, if nothing else, conversational material of a mildly gruesome sort, about on a par with the "curse of the Hope Diamond" and the less well-known "curse of the monks of Lacroma." If any single circumstance started the "curse of the Pharaohs" legend, very probably it was the sudden death of Lord Carnarvon. When he died, on April 6, 1923, after a three-week losing battle with the effects of a mosquito bite, people began to talk about punishments visited from the spirit realm on blasphemers.

Such headlines as "Revenge of the Pharaohs" began to appear, with subheads announcing a "New Victim of the Curse of Tutankhamen" ... "Second Victim" ... "Third Victim" ... "Nineteenth Victim," and so on. The death of this nineteenth victim was reported as follows: "Today the 78-year-old Lord Westbury jumped from the window of his seventh-story London apartment and was instantly killed. Lord Westbury's son, who was formerly the secretary of Howard Carter, the archæologist at the Tutankhamen diggings, was found last November dead in his apartment, though when he went to bed he appeared to be in the best of health. The exact cause of his death has never been determined." "A shudder is going through England . . ." another journalist wrote when Archibald Douglas Reid died as he was about to X-ray a mummy. Later the Egyptologist Arthur Weigall was catalogued as the twenty-first victim of the Pharaonic curse when he died of an "unknown fever."

Then Carter's partner, A. C. Mace, died, a man who had worked actively on the tomb. The news reports suppressed the fact, however, that Mace had been ailing for a long time and that he had assisted Carter despite the pressure of chronic ill health. Indeed, he had to give up before the project was finished.

Later, when Lord Carnarvon's half-brother, Aubrey Herbert, died of natural causes, some newspapers sought to fit his departure from life into the frame of The Curse Legend, too. When Lady Elizabeth Carnarvon died in February 1929, Howard Carter remained the only surviving co-worker.

"Death will come on swift pinions to those who disturb the rest of the Pharaoh"—such is one of the many variations of the Pharaonic curse supposedly found in an inscription in the tomb.

When it was reported that a man named Carter, living in the United States, had in some mysterious fashion become the latest victim of the Pharaohs, it seemed to clinch the argument that Tutankhamen was definitely out for revenge, and apparently working gradually toward the discoverer himself through his family. At this, serious archæologists began to feel the game had gone too far and raised a protest.

Carter himself tried to quell the tide of rumor. "The sentiment of the Egyptologist," he said ". . . is not one of fear, but of respect and awe. It is entirely opposed to the foolish superstitions which are far too prevalent among emotional people in search of 'psychic' excitement." He condemned "ridiculous stories" of Tutankhamen's revenge as a "form of literary amusement." Then he went concretely into the reports that it was physically hazardous to cross the threshold of the tomb—even if science could explain away the danger. Earnestly he pointed out the scientifically demonstrated absence of bacillary agents in the tomb. The interior had been tested for infection and given a clean bill of health. His tone became quite bitter toward the end of his protest: "... in some respects," he said, "our moral progress is less obvious than kindly people generally believe."

With a good instinct for publicity, the German Egyptologist Professor Georg Steindorff in 1933 issued a manifesto on the subject of Pharaonic curses, in which he took the trouble to track down the sources of newspaper and other reports. He established the fact that the Carter who had died in America had nothing but his name in common with the archæologist Carter. He also found out that neither of the Westburys had the least connection, direct or indirect, with the tomb, the removal of its contents, or the mummy. After piling up exhaustive evidence of irrelevance, he adduced the most telling argument of all: the "curse of the Pharaohs" simply did not exist. No such thing had been uttered or inscribed.

In this same connection Carter, who of course subscribed to Steindorff's view, writes: "So far as the living are concerned, curses of this nature have no place in the Egyptian ritual. On the contrary, we are piously desired to express our benevolent wishes for the dead."

It is a clear falsification of the intended sense to interpret as curses the few protective formulas of adjuration found inscribed on the magical manikins that were left in the burial chamber. These formulas were intended solely to "frighten away the enemy of Osiris (the deceased) in whatever form he may come."

Many expeditions have been excavating in Egypt since the discovery of Tutankhamen's tomb. In 1939, 1940, and 1946 Professor Pierre Montet found a perfect nest of royal tombs of the Twenty-first and Twenty-second Dynasty. In subterranean galleries more than three thousand feet long, hewn into solid rock, Professor Sami Gabra discovered holy places of the Ibis cult and countless tombs of sacred animals. Egypt's King Farouk equipped an expedition to seek for traces of his nation's antiquity, and burial places dating from the second and third millennium B.C. were uncovered. In 1941 Dr. Ahmad Badawi and Dr. Mustapha El-Amir stumbled upon a stele honoring Amenophis II, and an undisturbed tomb of Prince Sheshonk, with a sumptuous find of jewels.

# PART THREE

# THE BOOK OF THE TOWERS

## The Kingdoms of Assyria, Babylonia, and Sumeria

*My father, and the father of my father, pitched their tents here before me. . . . For twelve hundred years have the true believers—and, praise be to God! all true wisdom is with them alone—been settled in this country, and not one of them ever heard of a palace under ground. Neither did they who went before them. But lo! here comes a Frank from many days' journey off, and he walks up to the very place, and he takes a stick . . . and makes a line here, and makes a line there. Here, says he, is the palace; there, says he, is the gate; and he shows us what has been all our lives beneath our feet, without our having known anything about it. Wonderful! wonderful! Is it by books, is it by magic, is it by your prophets, that you have learnt these things? Speak, O Bey; tell me the secret of your wisdom.*

—Sheik Abd-er-Rahman to Austin Layard

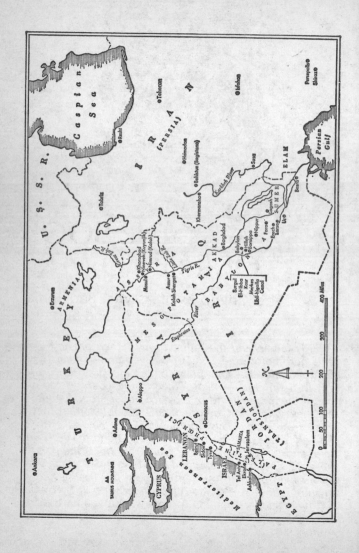

Eros frieze, showing Amor greeting the winner of a race among the gods of love.

The famous Pompeiian wall paintings.

The sacrifice of Iphigenia, from the House of the Tragic Poet. With the help of two others, Calchas is about to offer up the virgin. Agamemnon stands weeping beside the Column of Artemis.

*Photo, John H. Heffren, Courtesy Naples Museum*

PLATE I

*ABOVE:* Via Dell Abbondanza, Pompeii, much as it looked in A.D. 79. *BELOW:* The Chimera of Arezzo. From the Museo Archeologico, Florence. The bronze sculpture shows old Greek influence combined with the Etruscan. It was cast half a millennium before the destruction of Pompeii.

**PLATE II**

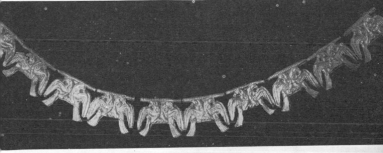

Schliemann's great find at the site of Troy, the golden treasure of one of the mightiest kings of prehistory. *ABOVE: left:* A golden mask. *Right:* A gold hairpin. *Center:* A gold necklace. *BELOW: left:* A golden bracelet. *Right:* Gold leaf-shaped ornaments.

**PLATE III**

Women of Crete, about 1600 B.C., during the golden age of the Cretan-Mycenæan culture. *ABOVE: left:* A wall painting. *Right:* Brightly colored faïence statuette from the Minoan Palace of Knossos. *BELOW:* Richly ornamented vessels still in place in the old storerooms at Knossos.

**PLATE IV**

*Photo, Ashmolean Museum*

One of the bull-paintings, similar to those found by Arthur Evans at Knossos, and before him by Schliemann at Tiryns. Are the youths dancers, acrobats, or bullfighters? Or is the painting intended to portray the legend of Theseus and the Minotaur, and of the seven youths and maidens brought to Crete to be sacrificed to the bull of Minos?

PLATE V

PLATE VI

*ABOVE:* The Step Pyramid of Sakkara, built by Imhotep for King Zoser, Third Dynasty, about 2950 B.C. *BELOW:* The Step Pyramid of Medum, built by King Snefru, Fourth Dynasty, about 2900 B.C. Orginally this pyramid had seven steps, of which only three remain.

Colonnade in the Temple of Karnak. Built during the reign of Ramses II, Nineteenth Dynasty, about 1250 B.C. The bare monumentality of the Old Kingdom, as shown in the pyramids, has now been replaced by an intricately embellished though still massive style, distinguished by much low relief, or incised sculpture.

**PLATE VII**

Noble Egyptian women. Part of a wall painting from the tomb of Weserhet at Thebes, Nineteenth Dynasty, about 1300 B.C.

**PLATE VIII**

*Photo, Ashmolean Museum*

The Valley of the Kings. The passage leading into the tomb of Tutankhamen begins behind the low stone wall. Next to it, on the left, running into the hill on which the buildings stand, is the entrance to the tomb of Ramses VI. This photograph gives a good impression of the intensity of archaeological excavation in the valley. Not a stone has been left unturned on this site.

**PLATE IX**

**PLATE X**

*Photo by David Seymour-Magnum*

Nefertiti. Found in the workshop of a sculptor named Thutmose at Tell-el-Amarna, by a German expedition headed by Ludwig Borchardt in 1912-14. It was unfinished, one of the eyes not having been painted. For some reason the Germans did not reveal its existence until 1925 when there was a world-wide Egyptological scandal about it.

**PLATE XI**

Tutankhamen's throne, made of wood covered with gold leaf, and decorated with faïence, glass, and gem inlay. The young king is shown with his wife, Anches-en-Amen. The king probably looked like this at the time of his death at the age of eighteen.

**PLATE XII**

Howard Carter opens the door of the second gilded shrine,
wherein he supposes Tutankhamen's coffin to be. He is photographed in the act of looking at a third gilded shrine.

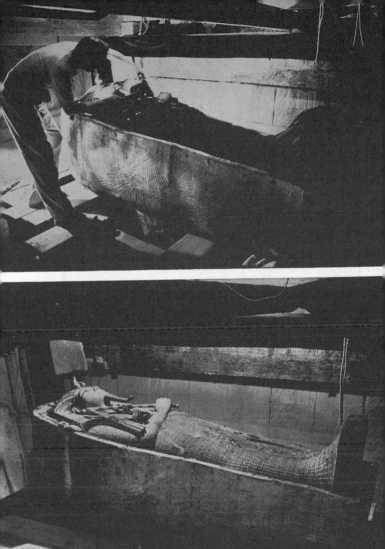

*Photos, Ashmolean Museum*

**PLATE XIII**

*ABOVE:* Howard Carter rolls back the pall covering Tutankhamen's second coffin. *BELOW:* The second coffin exposed. The photographs clearly indicate how tightly it was nested within the first (outer) coffin.

The golden mask covering Tutankhamen's head and shoulders. It s made of polished gold and is inlaid with pieces of many-colored glass, lapis lazuli, green feldspar, cornelian, alabaster, and obsidian.

**PLATE XIV**

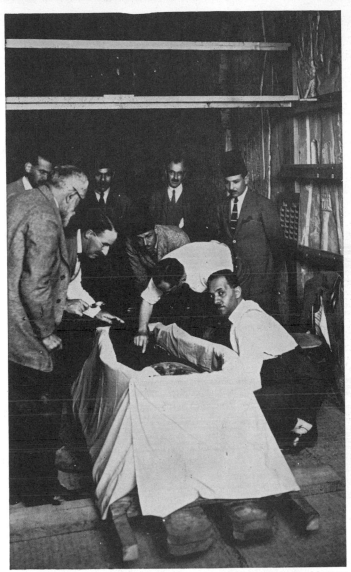

*Photo, Ashmolean Museum*

Dr. Derry, in the presence of a scientific commission, makes the first cut into the wrappings of Tutankhamen's mummy.

**PLATE XV**

The head of the mummy of Ynaa, father-in-law of King Amen-hu-det III. Found by Theodore Davis in the Valley of the Kings.

The head of Tutankhamen.

*Photo, Ashmolean Museum*

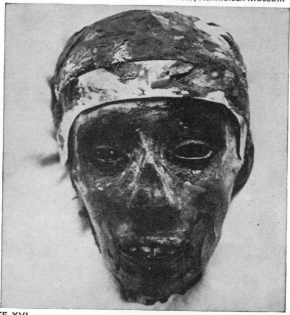

PLATE XVI

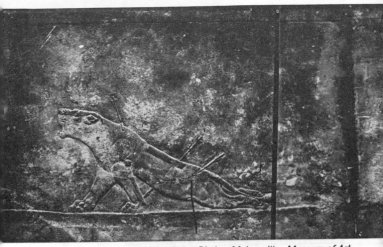

PLATE XVII

Lion hunting, the sport of Assyrian monarchs. *ABOVE:* An injured lioness raises her head in a last roar. Alabaster relief from the North Palace, Nineveh. *BELOW:* Seventh century B.C. limestone slab from the Palace of Assurbanipal, Nineveh; now in the British Museum.

PLATE XVIII

Assurnasirpal II. Statue found in his residence. Kalchu (Nimrud).

*From National Museum, Berlin*

PLATE XIX

Tablet with cuneiform text on left side. This relief is presumed, on best authority, to show the Babylonian King Baliddin (c. 700 B.C.) with the great god Marduk. On the shelf above may be seen the "dragon of Babylon," or "Sirrush."

**PLATE XX**

*From Musée Nationale du Louvre*

The stele of Naram-Sin, a Babylonian King, said to have ruled for fifty-five years. Naram-Sin belonged to the Akkad Dynasty (c. 2300 B.C.). The stele was excavated in Susa in 1899. It is approximately two yards and a little more in height. On it the King is shown victorious over the mountain people, above all over the Lulubu.

*LEFT:* Statuette of a Sumerian Queen, probably dating to the Third Millennium B.C. *RIGHT:* Statue of Gudea, the ruling prince, or king-priest, of the province of Lagash. A statue of this monarch, found by Ernest de Sarzec, now in the Louvre Museum, Paris, set archæology on the trail of the Sumerians.

**PLATE XXI**

MALCHE V DUFFELL date 1937

Reconstruction of the ziggurat (temple-tower) of Ur in Chaldea. It was here that the Englishman, Leonard Woolley, began his diggings, and found the richest evidence of what is probably the oldest culture on earth, that of the "black-headed" Sumerians.

**PLATE XXII**

Headdress of the Sumerian Queen Shub-ad, one of the oldest queens known today. She is supposed to have lived more than four thousand years ago. Leonard Woolley found the headdress in the royal tombs of Ur. Katharine Woolley modeled the head after a female skull from the same period.

**PLATE XXIII**

Ornamentation on the Temple of Quetzalcoatl in Teotihuacán. A broad flight of stairs runs from the base to the peak. The pyramid was already old—its exact age is unknown— when the Spanish conquistador Cortés climbed its steps.

**PLATE XXIV**

The same stele, drawn
by Catherwood.

Photograph of an old Mayan stele, found about a hundred
years ago in Copán (modern Honduras) by Stephens.

**PLATE XXV**

*Reconstruction drawing by Tatiana Proskouriakoff*

Copán probably looked like this before the great migration of the Mayas. The city was a huge temple complex, one comparable to anything in the Old World. Stephens bought these ruins for $50.

PLATE XXVI

Courtesy American Museum of Natural History

**PLATE XXVII**

*ABOVE:* A small, single-room structure at Chichén-Itzá, Yucatán, known as "the Iglesia." It belongs to the early or Old Empire period of the Mayas. *BELOW:* A Lacandon Indian man in front of a stele at Bonampak carved by his ancestors. He still worships at these ruins. Note the similarity of the living profile to the stone carving, which is the older by about 1,500 years.

*Photo by Giles G. Healey, Courtesy Middle America Information Bureau*

Facade of the Casa del Gobernador in Uxmal, one of the three great cities of the Maya "New Empire," founded after the sudden and mysterious abandonment of the "Old Empire." This marvelously detailed drawing was made by Frederick Catherwood more than a hundred years ago.

**PLATE XXVIII**

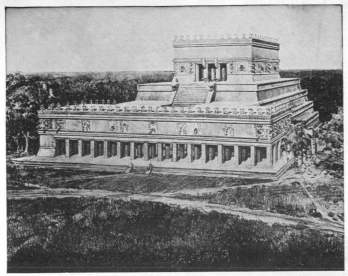

Temple of the Warriors in Chichén-Itzá. This temple is one of the most significant artifacts of the Maya "New Empire." Its sculpture and ornamentation show the Toltec influence. *ABOVE:* A reconstruction. *BELOW:* The temple as it looks today after the jungle was cleared away for the benefit of foreign visitors.

PLATE XXIX

The roof, now gone, of the Temple of the Warriors rested on the flattened crook in the erected tails of these snake columns. Only in the Maya culture do columns derive architecturally from animal motifs.

**PLATE XXX**

Thompson dredging the Sacred Well of Chichén-Itzá. *ABOVE:* View across the slimy surface through which Thompson descended and retrieved maidens' skeletons and golden ornaments. *BELOW:* The dredge at work. The top of the small ruined building behind the crane is the ancient platform from which the sacrificial victims were thrown into the pool.

PLATE XXXI

**PLATE XXXII**

Cast of the National Stone, an Aztec sculpture thought to be a small-scale model of a temple surmounted by a calendar stone. It was found in 1926 in the foundation of the south tower of the National Palace (Zócalo); it had been seen in 1831 when the foundations were dug, but no one bothered to salvage it.

The Bible tells of God's chastisement of the Jews by the Assyrians, "the rod of mine anger," of the Tower of Babel and the splendors of Nineveh, of the seventy-year captivity and the great Nebuchadnezzar, God's judgment upon the "whore of Babylon" and the chalice of His wrath to be poured by seven angels over the lands along the Euphrates. The prophets Isaiah and Jeremiah pour forth their terrifying visions of the destruction to come upon "the glory of kingdoms, the beauty of the Chaldees' excellency [that] shall be as when God overthrew Sodom and Gomorrah," so that "wild beasts of the islands shall cry in their desolate houses and dragons in their pleasant palaces" (Isaiah 13–19, 22).

During the centuries of Christian faith the word of the Bible was unassailable and the letter was sacred. Criticism came with the Enlightenment of the eighteenth century. Yet the nineteenth century, when the criticism inherent in all the materialist philosophies hardened into permanent doubt, simultaneously brought forth evidence for the historical truths so plentifully embedded in the Bible, overlaid though it was by much subsequent embroidery.

Flat was the land between the Euphrates and Tigris Rivers, but here and there mysterious mounds rose out of the plain. Dust storms swirled about these protuberances, piling the black earth into steep dunes, which grew steadily for a hundred years, only to be dispersed in the course of another five hundred. The Bedouins who rested by these mounds, letting their camels graze

241

on the meager fodder growing at the base, had no idea
what they might contain.  Believers in Allah, and in
Mohammed, his prophet, they knew nothing of the
Biblical passages describing their arid land. A question
was needed, a powerful intimation, to set in motion the
solution of the mounds' layered secrets. This and an
attack by an energetic Westerner who knew how to
make bold use of pick and shovel.

The man who was destined to drive the first spade
into that ground was born in France in 1803. Until he
was past thirty he had not the slightest intimation of
the task that was to be his life's work. For it was at
that age that he, then a physician, returned from an
Egyptian expedition. At his arrival in Cairo he had a
number of boxes among his luggage. The police demanded that they be opened. They contained, meticu-
lously stuck on rows of pins, twelve thousand insects.

Fourteen years later this physician and entomolo-
gist published a five-volume work on Assyria that
proved no less significant a stimulus to the scientific
study of Mesopotamia than the twenty-four-volume
*Description de l'Égypte* had been for Egyptology.

Not quite a century later a book appeared in Germany
(as similar works did in France and England) by Professor Bruno Meissner, entitled *Könige Babylons und
Assyriens* (Kings of Babylon and Assyria).

The importance of this work lies least of all in its
contribution to scholarship. But it was not intended as
such. Its aim was merely to report, for the general
reader, on rulers who flourished two to five thousand
years ago. The real significance of this book, and of all
books like it by scholars of other countries, for our
story of the development of archæology lies in the fact
that it could be written at all, and in a popular form
at that. For, to cite the introduction: "Such a presenta-
tion requires historical data that will contribute rich
color to the image of those great men and women, so
that they will come alive for us."

What about those historical data? Disregarding the mythicized material in the Old Testament, the fact was that "Not much more than a century ago, the history of Assyria was a sealed book, and only a few decades ago the Babylonian and Assyrian kings were hardly more than names to us. Can it be possible, so short a time afterwards, to recount the two thousand years of Mesopotamian history, including real character studies of the kings?"

Meissner's book, among others, proved that this had become possible in our own century. It shows that in a matter of a few decades a number of obsessed excavators, scholars, and amateurs were able to lift an entire culture to the light. The book even offered an appendix with a chronological table giving, with few omissions, the names and dates of the Mesopotamian rulers. This table was put together by Ernest F. Weidner, one of the most peculiar among the often very peculiar Assyriologists. For twenty years Weidner sat as an obscure second-string editor in the offices of the *Berliner Illustrierte Zeitung*. Here he edited serial stories and crossword puzzles. One day the modest man approached the managing editor most apologetically with an, for him, extraordinary request: there was some unavoidable business he had to attend to, could he have tomorrow morning off? Of course he could, said the managing editor; he was not to give it a thought. Next day Weidner was not at his desk, but a reporter came storming in waving a news item over his head. It seemed that Ernst Weidner, the nondescript colleague with whom they had been sitting desk-by-jowl for so many years without suspicion, had just won a high award at a special convocation of eminent scholars. For some time he had been quietly publishing on the side important articles about Assyrian chronology and editing an international scholarly journal with a press run of a few hundred copies that went only to universities and isolated scholars.

The office was still buzzing with the story when

the distinguished Assyriologist turned up—a bit sheep-ish, not so much because he had been unmasked, but because he had arrived for his award ceremony only to be told that he was a bit late: it had taken place the previous day. It was not long before Weidner was back in his usual dusty corner. There he stayed until 1942, when waves of Allied bomber attacks made any schol-arly work in the capital of the Third Reich impossible, and Weidner was prevailed upon to accept a professor-ship in Austria. (It was to Weidner I brought my virgin effort in writing about the history of archæology, a piece entitled "On the Decipherment of an Un-known Script." I was just twenty years old. Yet Weid-ner, the eminent expert, who was involved in the de-cipherment of Hittite cuneiform among other things, took this article from my hand without batting an eye and published it in the *Berliner Illustrierte* in 1935.)

What had made the appearance of such books as Meissner's possible was a triumph of scholarship that must be ranked above, for example, Lepsius's first Egyptian chronology. Three generations of fanatics labored indefatigably to scrape and gather together the facts compiled in them. These books were made possi-ble by innumerable hours of work in an office of the French consulate in Mosul, in a teacher's study in Göttingen, under the broiling sun between Tigris and Euphrates, as well as in a little ship's cabin in which an English naval officer sat poring over bits of cuneiform under a lamp swinging like a pendulum.

What emerged from all this hard work was one of archæology's greatest triumphs, if only because the land of mounds showed no visible traces of past greatness. There were no temples and statues to fire the archæ-ological effort, as on the classic earth of Greece and Italy. No pyramids and obelisks reared into the sky as in Egypt, and there were no sacrificial stone blocks to tell a mute story of the gory hecatombs of Mexico and the wilderness of Yucatán. The blank faces of Bedouin and Kurd failed to reflect their ancestral greatness. Local legends reached back little farther in time than the glamorous days of Harun al-Rashid. Earlier centuries swam in twilight and mist. The modern languages spoken in the land of mounds exhibited no intelligible relationship to the languages spoken thousands of years before.

Outside the mounds scattered over the dusty plain, the investigators had little to go on but some poetical descriptions from the Bible. That and some clay shards, covered with cuneiform characters which, as one early observer said, looked as if "birds had been walking over wet sand," and which many archæologists at first mistook for mere ornament. For all these reasons the archæological conquest in this arena was particularly memorable.

In the Old Testament the region between the Tigris and the Euphrates was called, simply, Aram-naharaim—Syria (land) between the two rivers—this being the Hebraic equivalent for the Greek Mesopotamia. Here were located the famous cities on which the God of the Bible visited His mighty wrath. Here, in Nineveh and Babylon, reigned terrible kings who had other gods besides Him and therefore had to be expunged from the face of the earth.

Today it is called Iraq, and Baghdad is its capital. To the north the area is bounded by Turkey, on the west by French-mandated Syria and Transjordan, on the south by Saudi Arabia and to the east by Persia, or Iran in modern usage.

The two rivers called the Tigris and the Euphrates, which made the land a cradle of culture even as the Nile gave life to Egypt, arise in Turkey. They flow from the northwest to the southeast, come together a short distance above present-day Basra—this was not so in ancient times—and empty into the Persian Gulf.

Assyria, the old land of Assur (Asshur), stretched out in the north along the rapidly flowing Tigris. Babylonia, the ancient Sumeria and Akkad, spread out in the south between the Euphrates and the Tigris as far down as the green waters of the Persian Gulf. In an encyclopedia of general information that appeared in 1867, under the heading of Mesopotamia, the following entry is found: "The land reached its peak under the Assyrian and Babylonian rule. Under the rule of the Arabs it became a possession of the Caliphate, and again bloomed. But with the Seljuk, Tartar, and Turkish incursions, it began to decline, and at present is in part an uninhabited desert."

Out of the deserts of Mesopotamia rise mysterious mounds, flat-topped, with steep, often eroded slopes, cracked open like the dried sheep-milk cheeses of the Bedouins. These curious mounds kindled the imagination of inquiring spirits to such a degree that it was in Mesopotamia that archæology as an excavational art celebrated its initial triumphs.

As a young man Paul Émile Botta had already made a trip around the world. In 1830 he entered the service of Mohammed Ali as a physician, and in this capacity also accompanied the Egyptian commission to Sennar. In 1833 the French government made him consul in Alexandria, from which point he made a trip into Yemen, the results of which he comprehensively recorded in a book. In 1840 he was appointed consular agent in Mosul, on the upper Tigris. Evenings, at twilight, when Botta had fled the suffocating heat of the bazaars to refresh himself on horseback excursions out into the countryside, he would see the strange mounds that dotted the landscape everywhere.

But it is not fair to imply that he was the first to notice these startling prominences. Older travelers—Kinneir, Rich, Ainsworth—had already suspected that ruins lay beneath them. The most interesting of these earlier explorers was C. J. Rich, a prodigy like Champollion, who commenced to study the Oriental languages at the age of nine. At fourteen he was already dipping into Chinese. At twenty-four he was counsel for the East India Company in Baghdad. From that vantage point he made trips through the whole valley of Mesopotamia, bringing home valuable booty for the science of his day. Englishmen and Frenchmen, much more often than Germans, Russians, and Italians, have combined an interest in science and the arts with practical affairs. Often, in adventurous fashion, they have been shining representatives of their nationalities in foreign parts and are remembered as men who knew how to combine a high respect for the political necessities with scientific and artistic labors. More recent examples of this type of personality are Paul Claudel and André Malraux, the French authors, and T. E. Lawrence, the English soldier.

Botta was such a man. As a physician he was interested in natural science and as a diplomat he knew how to make the most of his social connections. He was everything, it would seem, but an archæologist. What he did bring to his future task was a knowledge of native tongues, and an ability, developed during his extensive travels, to establish friendly relations with the followers of the Prophet. He also had a fine constitution and a boundless capacity for work, which even the murderous climate of Yemen and the swampy Nile flatlands could not dent.

Botta set to work without any plan or basic hypothesis to guide him. Vague hope, mingled with curiosity, carried him along. And when he was successful, no one was more surprised than he.

Evening after evening, having closed up his office, with wonderful persistence he reconnoitered the landscape about Mosul. He went from house to house, from hut to hut, always asking the same questions: Have you any antiquities for sale? Old pots? An old vase, perhaps? Where did you get the bricks for building this outhouse? Where did you get these clay fragments with the strange characters on them?

Botta bought everything he could lay hands on. But when he asked the sellers to show him the place where the pieces came from, they shrugged their shoulders, explaining that Allah was great and that such things were strewn about everywhere. One need only look to find them.

Botta saw that he was getting nowhere by quizzing the natives. He decided to try his hand with the spade at the nearest mound of any size, the one at Kuyunjik.

One must imagine what it meant to persist in such apparently fruitless activity; what it meant, particularly, when there was nothing to spur on the would-be digger but the ambiguous notion that the mound *might* contain something worth the effort of excavation; what it meant to go on day after day, week after week, month after month, without finding anything more rewarding than a few battered bricks covered with signs that nobody could read, or a few sculptured torsos, so badly broken that the original form was quite unrecognizable.

A whole year long!

Should we wonder, therefore, when Botta, after the year had run out, during which innumerable false leads had been brought to him by the natives, at first dismissed a talkative Arab who, in colorful language, reported a mound containing a rich store of all the things the Frank was looking for? The Arab gabbled on, ever more importunately, about how he came from a distant village, how he had heard about the Frank's search, how he loved the Franks and wanted to help them. Was it bricks with inscriptions that Botta wanted? There were masses of them where he lived in Khorsabad, right near his native village. He ought to know, for he had built his own stove out of these same bricks, and everybody else in his village had done the same since time immemorial.

When Botta found he could not rid himself of the Arab, he sent a couple of his workmen to look over the alleged site, some nine or ten miles away.

By sending off this little expedition Botta was eventually to immortalize his name in the history of archæology. The identity of the Arab informant is forgotten, lost in the drift of the years. But Botta is still remembered as the first to disclose the remains of a culture that had flowered for almost two thousand years, and for more than two millennia and a half had slumbered under the black earth between the two rivers, forgotten by men.

A Syrian fortress is taken. Relief on the outer side of the north wall of the Great Temple of Medinet Habu.

A week later an excited messenger came back to report to his master. Hardly had they turned the first spadeful of earth, the man said, when walls came to light. These walls, when freed of the worst of the dirt that clogged them, proved to be richly carved. There were all kinds of pictures, reliefs, terrible stone animals.

Botta rode over to the site posthaste. A few hours later he was squatting in a pit, drawing the most curious figures imaginable—bearded men, winged animals, figures unlike any that he had ever seen in Egypt, and certainly unlike any sculptures familiar to European eyes. Shortly afterwards he moved his crew from Kuyunjik to the new site, where he put them to work with pick and shovel. And soon Botta no longer doubted that he had discovered, if not all of Nineveh, certainly one of the most splendid palaces of the Assyrian kings.

The moment came when, no longer able to keep this conviction to himself, he sent the news to Paris, and so out into the world. "I believe," he wrote with pride, and the newspapers made headlines of it, "that I am the first to discover sculptures that can be truly identified with the period when Nineveh was at its height."

The discovery of the first Assyrian palace was not only a newspaper sensation. Egypt had always been thought of as the cradle of civilization, for nowhere else could the history of mankind be traced back so far. Hitherto only the Bible had had anything pertinent to say about the land between the two rivers, and for nineteenth-century science the Bible was a collection of legends. The sparse evidence found in the ancient writers was taken more seriously than the Biblical sources. The facts offered by these early writers were not entirely un-believable, yet often they contradicted one another and could not be made to agree with Biblical dates.

Botta's finds, in consequence, amounted to a dem-onstration that a culture as old as the Egyptian or even older had once flourished in Mesopotamia—older if one cared to give credence to Biblical accounts. It had risen in might and splendor, only to sink, under fire and sword, into oblivion.

France was fired by Botta's revelations. Aid was mobilized on the most generous scale to enable Botta to continue with his work. He dug for three years, from 1843 to 1846. He fought the climate, sickness, the op-position of the natives, and the interference of the pasha, the despotic Turkish governor of the country. This greedy official could think of only one explanation for Botta's tireless excavations: the Frenchman must be looking for gold.

The pasha took Botta's Arab workmen away from him and threatened them with whippings and imprisonment to get them to tell him Botta's secret. He ringed the hill of Khorsabad with guards, he wrote complaining letters to Constantinople. But Botta was not the sort to be intimidated. His diplomatic experience now came in handy: he countered intrigue with intrigue. The result was that the pasha gave the Frenchman official permission to continue with his project, but unofficially he forbade all natives, on pain of dire punishment, to have anything to do with the Frank. Botta's diggings, he said, were nothing but a pretext for building a fortress to be used in depriving the Mesopotamian peoples of their freedom.

Undeterred, Botta pressed on with his work.

Assyrian Cavalry.

The palace was laid bare, rising up from mighty terraces. Archæologists who had rushed to the site on reading Botta's original report of his find recognized the structure as the palace of King Sargon, the one mentioned in the prophecies of Isaiah. It was, in fact, a summer palace that had stood on the outskirts of Nineveh, a sort of Versailles, a gigantic Sans Souci built in the year 709 B.C., after the conquest of Babylon. Wall after wall emerged from the rubble, courtyards with richly ornamented portals took shape, public reception rooms, corridors, private apartments, a tripartite seraglio, and the remains of a terraced tower.

The number of sculptures and reliefs was staggering. At one swoop the mysterious Assyrian people were lifted out of the abyss of the past. Here were their reliefs, their household implements, their weapons; here they could be visualized in the domestic round, at war, on the hunt.

The sculptures, however, which in many cases had been made of highly destructible alabaster, fell apart under the hot desert sun after being removed from the protective covering of debris and earth. The French government then commissioned Eugène Napoléon Flandin to help Botta, and he went at once to the Middle East. Flandin was a draftsman of note, who in the past had gone with an archæological expedition that explored Persian sites, and later had written books about his experiences, containing excellent drawings of ancient sculptures. Flandin became for Botta what Vivant Denon had been for Napoleon's Egyptian commission. But whereas Denon had drawn enduring structures, Flandin had to make hurried records of material that was falling apart under his eyes.

Botta succeeded in loading a whole series of sculptures on rafts. But the Tigris, here at its upper course, was a fast-flowing and tempestuous mountain stream. The rafts whirled about, spun like tops. They tipped to one side, and the stone gods and kings of Assyria, newly resurrected from oblivion, sank once more out of sight.

Botta refused to be discouraged. He sent a new load downriver, this time taking all imaginable precautions, and the trip was a success. At the river mouth the precious pieces of sculpture were loaded aboard an ocean-going vessel, and in due course the first Assyrian carvings arrived on European shores. A few months later they were on exhibition in the Louvre.

Botta himself continued to work on a large freize, until eventually a commission of nine archæologists took the task off his hands. One member of the commission was Burnouf, soon to be known as one of the most important French archæologists—a quarter of a century later he became Heinrich Schliemann's oftcited "learned friend." Another was a young Englishman named Austen Layard, whose later fame was to eclipse Botta's.

Yet Botta ought not to be forgotten. He was the trail-breaker in Assyria, as Belzoni was in Egypt. Like Belzoni, he was a furious "digger," a determined seeker after booty for the Louvre. The role of "collector" in Nineveh, corresponding to one played by Mariette in Cairo, was filled by another French consul, Victor Place. Botta's account of Nineveh: *Monuments de Ninive découverts et décrits par Botta, mesurés et dessinés par Flandin,* is numbered among the classics of archæological literature. The first two of its five volumes contain plates of architectural and sculptural subjects, the third and fourth the collected inscriptions, and the fifth the descriptions.

# 19/GROTEFEND: A SCHOOLTEACHER DECIPHERS CUNEIFORM

The history of science shows that often discovery and practical application are widely separated in time. When Botta collected, besides his sculptures, bricks covered with strange cuneiform (wedge-shaped) characters and had them copied and sent to Paris—he himself not having the least idea how to read them—there were scattered throughout Europe and the Near East many scholars who already knew the key to the script.

Though it sounds unbelievable, for years these experts in Oriental tongues to some degree had understood the writing of a people whose actual existence, before Botta adduced evidence for it, had been purely a matter of conjecture. Indeed, at the time Botta's books were published, cuneiform script had already been known for exactly forty-seven years. All that had blocked the progress of decipherment was a lack of new, different, clearer, and more numerous inscriptions than the scholars had seen up to that time. The essential information required for the decipherment of the cuneiform system of writing had been acquired long before anything was known of Sargon's palace, or of Nineveh—the site Layard was about to explore—beyond what was related in the Bible. But after Botta's pioneer contribution, which was soon afterwards extended and enriched by the discoveries of the daring Layard—he would let himself down the wall of a cliff with block and tackle to copy an inscription—Mesopotamian material accumulated in a flood. There was an immense increase in excavational results, and rapid advances in the field of comparative linguistics led to great improvements in the art of decipherment. In the course of a single decade the heterogeneous mass of information about the history of ancient peoples of the Middle East had taken on such definitive shape that by the 1850's the archæologists were able to incorporate new information in the general scheme about as fast as it developed.

The first man to take a decisive step in the direction of deciphering cuneiform writing, however, was motivated neither by scholarly curiosity, nor by the scientific impulse. He was a German, in 1802 a young man of twenty-seven employed as assistant master in the schools of Göttingen. This schoolmaster deciphered the first ten letters of a cuneiform script simply in order to win a bet.

Knowledge of the existence of cuneiform writing goes back to the seventeenth century, when the Italian traveler Pietro della Valle brought the first inscribed brick back to Europe. In the *Philosophical Transactions* of 1693 Aston printed two lines of cuneiform writing copied by a certain Flower, agent in Persia of the East India Company. The first really exciting report on Mesopotamia—it dealt with land and people as well as with inscriptions and monuments—was by Karsten Niebuhr. This Hannoverian, who was in the service of Frederick V of Denmark, from 1760 to 1767 traveled through the Near East in the company of other scholars. Within the space of a year all members of the expedition were dead with the exception of Niebuhr. Undismayed, Niebuhr continued to explore on his own, and came back safe and sound. His *Reisebeschreibung von Arabien und anderen umliegenden Ländern* (*Description of Travels in Arabia and Adjacent Lands*) was the book that Napoleon kept with him constantly during the Egyptian expedition.

The first copies of cuneiform writing to arrive deviously in Europe were largely taken from a field of ruins seven miles to the northeast of Shiraz. Niebuhr correctly identified this gigantic heap of rubble as the remains of ancient Persepolis. The ruins at Persepolis belonged to a later culture than the one revealed at Botta in the 1840's, and largely consisted of the remains of the residence of Darius and Xerxes, a huge palace destroyed by Alexander the Great, "during a drinking bout when he was no longer in control of his wits," as Diodorus says. And Clitarchos, telling about the same banquet, says that it was the Athenian dancer Thaïs who, in the fury of her dance, snatched a burning brand from the altar and hurled it among the wooden columns of the palace, whereupon Alexander and his companions, all of whom were drunk, followed her example. Droysen, in his history of Hellenism, says that this story is a tale "spun with extraordinary talent, but at the expense of true history." Medieval princes of Islam were still occupying the palace during their heyday, but when they passed away the buildings fell completely into ruins, and the site became a grazing ground for sheep. Early travelers who visited the ruins took away with them whatever they pleased. There is scarcely a large museum anywhere in the world that does not have fragments of Persepolitan reliefs on exhibit. Flandin and Coste made drawings of the ruins. Andreas and Stolze photographed them in 1882. Like the Colosseum at Rome, the palace of Darius served as a stone quarry for later builders. Throughout the last century each decade saw further deterioration of the ruins. From 1931 to 1934 an expedition commissioned by the Oriental Institute of the University of Chicago, and led by Ernst Herzfeld, carried on the first really methodical investigation at Persepolis and, while there, took effective measures to preserve what relics were left.

In this Mesopotamian region cultures are superimposed as nowhere else in the world. The following is a quite conceivable chain of events and serves to illustrate just what this means. An Arab, let us say, brings some clay tablets covered with cuneiform writing to an archæologist at his headquarters in Baghdad. On one of the clay tablets, which has perhaps been found in the Behistun area, is written a speech by Darius, King of the Persians.

The archæologist, who has his Herodotus handy, checks the dates of Darius and finds that he was at the height of his power at about 500 B.C., at which time he had just built the capital of a mighty kingdom. By examining other tablets the archæologist finds allusions to old dynastic successions, to wars, devastations, and murderous deeds. In the course of his search he may run across a reference to Hammurabi, which will have brought him in touch with another vast kingdom, which reached its peak about 1700 B.C., or he may come upon the name of Sennacherib, which will connote a third great kingdom, this one having flourished between the eighth and seventh centuries B.C. And to round out the cycle the archæologist need only follow his Arab into the street and with him join a circle of listeners squatting spellbound about a professional teller of fairy tales, and listen while he recounts, in monotonous singsong, a story of Harun al-Rashid, the wonderful caliph who was at the height of his power about A.D. 800, at the time when Europe was under the sway of Charlemagne.

Six great and widely dominant cultures have flourished in Mesopotamia in the region between present-day Damascus and Shiraz, each of which left a powerful mark on the antique world. These cultures, all compressed in a narrow space, interlocking, mutually fructifying, yet essentially independent, together covered a span of five thousand years. Five thousand years of human history, at times fraught with horror, at times with exaltation, have unrolled in the land between the two rivers. Compared with the complexities that greeted the archæologist in Mesopotamia, Schliemann's nine-leveled Troy was a beginner's problem. For of the nine levels of Troy only one had any true historical importance, the other eight being of minor interest. As for cultural levels of minor importance in Mesopotamia,

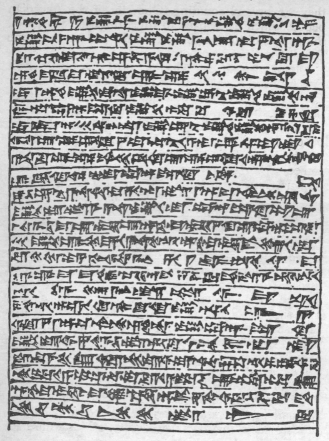

Text of a cuneiform inscription on a cylinder roll. In line 13 the king announces the founding of a temple: "Even at that time I had E-mach, temple of the Goddess of Ninmah in Babil, builded new." The last four lines are a warning directed at potential vandals: "Who with malice prepense destroys, effaces, or moves from its place this my signed attestation, may he be denounced by Ninmah before Bel, Sarrateia, his name, his seed in the land, may it be destroyed."

they are beyond counting. One city of the Akkadian period, which dates back to three thousand years B.C., shows five distinct levels of debris, and at this time Babylon was not even born.

It is obvious that during such vast stretches of time, speech and the written language, like all else, must show drastic changes. And there are even greater differences between the various types of cuneiform writings than there are between the hieroglyphs of different periods in Egypt, or between the hieratic and demotic scripts. The specimens forwarded by Botta to Paris looked quite different from those Niebuhr brought home from Persepolis. As it happened, however, the Persepolitan tablets, some two and a half thousand years old, provided the key to the variant forms of script that emerged from the debris of the Euphrates and Tigris Valley. (The first publications on the decipherment of the cuneiform writing are all concerned exclusively with the Persepolitan form, not the kind used in Assyria or Babylonia.)

The decipherment of the cuneiform script was a true work of genius. It was one of the human mind's most masterly accomplishments, and ranks with the greatest scientific inventions.

Georg Friedrich Grotefend was born on June 9, 1775, at Münden in Germany. He was trained at the Pædagogium, first in his home town, later at Ilefeld, after which he studied philology at Göttingen. In 1797 he was made an assistant teacher at the municipal school of Göttingen, and in 1803 became pro-rector, and later vice-principal, of the Frankfurt am Main grammar school. In 1817 he founded a learned society for the study of the German language, and in 1821 he became director of the Lyceum at Hannover. In 1849 he was pensioned off, according to law, and on December 15, 1853 he died.

At the age of twenty-seven, however, this man, whose life was otherwise free from the slightest hint of

divagation or extravagance, conceived the unlikely notion that he could find the key to the decipherment of
the cuneiform characters. The idea came to him while
he was drinking with some comrades, who took him
up when he offered to bet on his hunch. The only material that he had to work with was some bad copies of
the Persepolitan inscriptions. With youthful aplomb he
struck directly at the heart of the puzzle and succeeded
in cracking a problem that the best scholars of the time
had declared insoluble. In 1802 he presented the first
results of his investigations to the Academy of Sciences
in Göttingen. Amid the spate of his later philological
writings, all of which have long since fallen into oblivion, his *Beiträge zur Erläuterung der persepolitanischen Keilschrift* (*Contributions to a Commentary on
the Persepolitan Cuneiform Writing*) stands out like a
tower, untouched by time.

What Grotefend found to work upon was this:

The Persepolitan inscriptions were remarkably
diverse in character. On some of the tablets there were
three different kinds, written side by side in three different columns. Grotefend, the humanist, was thoroughly
acquainted with the history of the ancient Persian ruler
of Persepolis, through the Greek writers. It was known
that Cyrus had annihilated the Babylonians about the
year 540 B.C., sealing the fate of Babylonian civilization
and clearing the stage for the first great Persian kingdom. From this fact the inference could be drawn,
Grotefend believed, that at least one of the scripts on
the tablet represented the language of the conqueror.
It was highly probable, too, in Grotefend's opinion,

Cuneiform inscription on the masonry wall of the north
citadel of Babylon. In his day Grotefend was unable to
decipher it. It contains a proclamation by Nebuchadnezzar, which says, in effect: "The Duru of the palace,
Babylon, have I made with stones of the mountains."
A prayer follows this declaration.

that the middle column—since it is common practice to put the most important in the middle—was Old Persian writing. Moreover, one group of signs and another single sign reappeared frequently, and to Grotefend this suggested that the group stood for the word *king*; and the single character—it was a wedge slanting obliquely upward from left to right—was thought to be a word divider. These conclusions were supported by similar findings in other inscriptions.

This was Grotefend's beginning, about as slight a grip on the matter as could be imagined. As yet he had no idea even of the direction in which the inscriptions read, whether from left to right, right to left, top to bottom, or bottom to top. He was just young enough, however, not to be lured off the track by ancillary considerations and continued to press on to the roots of the problem. Champollion was not faced with nearly so complicated a problem when he deciphered the hieroglyphs twenty years later, since he had the Rosetta Stone.

Grotefend first laid down the fact that the cuneiform characters actually were a form of writing and not mere decoration. Then he reasoned that, on the evidence of a complete absence of curved lines, the characters were never meant to be "written," but rather to be impressed into some permanent medium, such as clay. Today we know that this way of recording language, though it strikes us as being exceedingly laborious, actually sufficed to regulate the whole complex of political and economic intercourse in Mesopotamia and ancient Persia up to the time of Alexander the Great. Today a typist uses carbon paper to make copies of a business communication, while the old Persian scribe inscribed the message on soft tablets of clay, keeping one copy and sending the other way. The fresh clay tablets were quickly baked hard in an oven.

Grotefend next showed that the prevailing arrangement of the characters was such that the points of the wedges headed either downwards or to the right. The angles formed by the meeting of two wedges consistently opened toward the right. This apparently simple clue gave him an idea of how the inscriptions should be read. "They must be held," he writes, "in such fashion that the tips of the vertical wedges point downwards, those of the oblique wedges to the right, and the openings of the angles also to the right. If this is done, it will be found that no cuneiform writing is written in a vertical, but always in a horizontal direction, and that moreover, the marginal figures on the seals and cylinders are no criterion for the direction of the script." Simultaneously he concluded that the script was read from left to right, which none but a European takes for granted.

All this, however, had little to do with the actual act of decipherment, which means to find the sense of a document. The critical step still lay ahead. It was at this juncture that Grotefend proved his genius. Among many other things, genius implies the ability to reduce the complicated to the simple, and to recognize inclusive structural principles. Grotefend's inspiration was astoundingly simple.

It may be assumed, he said to himself, that certain mannerisms in the writing found on monuments—the specimens of cuneiform writing he was using were inscriptions taken from monuments—must have remained unchanged throughout long periods of time. The phrase "Rest in peace" carved on the gravestones of his own district had been used by his grandparents and great-grandparents, and undoubtedly would be used by his children and his children's children. Therefore, was it not reasonable to suppose that certain introductory or salutatory words or phrases of known meaning on New Persian monuments might also be found on the Old Persian? For example, was it not possible that the Persepolitan inscriptions should begin with the familiar phrase:

X, *great King, King of Kings, King of* A *and* B, *Son of* Y, *great King, King of Kings,* etc.? In other words, was it not likely that the dynastic formula should be the same in all three columns of the tablet? This proposition was a clever extrapolation of the basic assumption that one of the frequently repeated groups of wedges stood for the word *king*. Now, from this proposition the following corollaries might conceivably be drawn: If the formula could be taken literally, the first word must be the king's name. Thereafter an oblique wedge, dividing it from the next word, must follow. Next two words would come, one of which must mean king. And this critical word, *king*, could be identified by the frequency of its repetition.

This is only the bare outline of Grotefend's complicated reasoning, but litle imagination is needed to appreciate what a feeling of exultation young Grotefend, the assistant schoolteacher, must have experienced when he finally discovered in quiet Göttingen, thousands of miles away from the land from which the original cuneiform writing came and three thousand years away in time, that his hypotheses were correct. It is perhaps too much to say that he proved the whole hypothetical interpretation. What he did do was find the genealogical salute repeated many times; also the word that must mean king. Would anyone accept his evidence? And exactly what had he gained by his discovery?

Grotefend reviewed his results and noted that in almost all the inscriptions at his disposal there were only two different versions of the same cuneiform groups at the head of the columns. However carefully he checked, the same words were at the beginning, it appeared, in either one or the other variation. These groups, according to his theory, should contain the names of kings. Now, in some inscriptions he found *both* variant cuneiform groupings in the same column heading.

Grotefend's thoughts began to race. Could this uniformity mean that all the inscriptions were identified with only two different kings? And in those cases where the name groupings appeared in close conjunction, was it not highly probable that a father-son relationship was indicated, according to the classic formula?

He noticed that when the names appeared separate, the first in the order was followed by the sign presumably standing for "king," whereas the second was not qualified in this fashion. From this, in line with his theory, he deduced the following schema:

X (King), *son of* Z,
Y (King), *son of* X (King).

Up to this point Grotefend's results had all been purely theoretical. They had depended entirely on the frequency of certain character groupings and the serial connection of these groupings. Now, when Grotefend, going over this last deduction, suddenly saw an airtight, concrete proof for his notions, his feverish excitement can be imagined. What was there to catch the eye in the formula?

The clue to the solution is plain to see. It is a lacuna, a something-left-out, which is decisive for the next step. More precisely, the lack of a word, *King,* after the name in the schema which appears as "Z."

If the formula is correct, it describes a dynastic succession of grandfather, father, and son, in which father and son were kings, but not the grandfather. Grotefend, breathing a sigh of relief, was now in a position to say: If I am able to find a royal succession among the Persian dynasties that fits this picture, I have proved my theory and deciphered the first words of the cuneiform writing.

"Fully convinced that I would have to seek for two kings from Achæmenidian dynasty . . . I began to check through the royal successions to find out which names most nearly fitted the inscriptional characters. They could not be Cyrus and Cambyses, because the two names in the inscriptions did not have the same initial letter, nor could they be Cyrus and Artaxerxes, because the first of these names, relative to the characters, was

| Characters a) | 𒀸 | 𒀸 | 𒀸 | 𒀸 | 𒀸 | 𒀸 | 𒀸 |
|---|---|---|---|---|---|---|---|
| Grotefend's Reading | D- | a- | r- | h- | e- | u- | s |
| Modern Reading | Dᵃ- | a- | rᵃ- | yᵃ- | wᵉ- | u- | š(ᵃ) |

| Characters b) | 𒀸 | 𒀸 | 𒀸 | 𒀸 | 𒀸 | 𒀸 | 𒀸 |
|---|---|---|---|---|---|---|---|
| Grotefend's Reading | Kh- | š- | h- | e- | r- | š- | e |
| Modern Reading | Hᵃ- | šᵃ- | yᵃ- | a- | rᵃ- | šᵃ- | a |

| Characters c) | 𒀸 | 𒀸 | 𒀸 | 𒀸 | 𒀸 | 𒀸 | 𒀸 |
|---|---|---|---|---|---|---|---|
| Grotefend's Reading | G- | ō- | š- | t- | a- | s- | p |
| Modern Reading | Wⁱ- | i- | šᵃ- | tᵃ- | a- | sᵃ- | pᵃ |

Grotefend read the first cuneiform text in this manner.

too short, the second too long. There were no names left to choose from but Darius and Xerxes, and they fitted so easily that I had no doubt about making the right choice. This correspondence was clinched by the fact that in the son's inscription the father's name had the sign of royalty beside it, whereas this character was lacking in the father's inscription. This observation was confirmed by all the Persepolitan inscriptions."

That was the proof. There was no denying its logic, but a final step had yet to be taken. Up to now Grotefend had been using the Greek version of the royal names, particularly that version handed down to posterity by Herodotus. Basing his interpretation on the name of the grandfather, which was known to him, he wrote as follows:

"Since a correct decipherment of the names had already given me over twelve letters, including all the letters of the royal title except one, the next move was to put names known only in Greek into their Persian form, in order to get a correct value for each character in the royal title and so divine the language in which the inscriptions were written. I now learned from the Zend-Avesta (a collective term for the sacred Persian writings) that the name Hystaspes was pronounced Goschasp, Gustasp, Kistasp, or Wistasp in Persian. This gave me the first seven letters of the name Hystaspes in the Darius inscription, and the last three I already knew from a comparison of all the royal titles."

A beginning had been made.

Improvements followed, yet, remarkably enough, more than thirty years had passed before anyone was able to make another significant advance. The next contributors to the science of cuneiform decipherment were the Frenchman Émile Burnouf, and the German Christian Lassen, the investigations of both of whom were written up in 1836.

The name of Champollion, decipherer of the hieroglyphs, is widely known, yet, paradoxically enough, hardly anyone seems to have heard of Grotefend. His theory is never taught in the classroom, and many modern encyclopedias either ignore him entirely or dismiss him with a brief reference in the bibliography. Nevertheless he, and he alone, must be accorded priority in making possible the historical interpretation of Mesopotamian excavation.

Priority, I say, for an Englishman, working independently, also succeeded in solving the riddle of the cuneiform writing. These independent discoveries, incidentally, are typical of science. The Englishman's contribution to Assyriology did not appear, however, until 1846, some time after Grotefend's interpretation had been revised and improved by Burnouf and Lassen.

None the less, the Englishman must get credit for going far beyond his predecessors. He succeeded in bringing cuneiform writing out of the specialist's study into the university classroom, in developing methods of decipherment to a point where the original language could be taught like any other. It was he who forged the tool that made it possible to handle the mass of inscriptional material that steadily accumulated throughout the nineteenth century. (On one occasion a whole library of clay tablets was found. But that is a story to be told farther along.) To give some idea of the wealth of material hidden in the Mesopotamian region, so many cuneiform tablets were collected by Volrath Hilprecht's American expedition at Nippur between 1888 and 1900 that the task of deciphering them and publishing the results has not been completed even to this day.

# 20/RAWLINSON: NEBUCHADNEZZAR'S DICTIONARY IN CLAY

In 1837 Major Henry Creswicke Rawlinson, then in the employ of the Persian War Ministry, was lowered, with the help of block and tackle, down the face of a high cliff near Behistun. His purpose was to copy some inscriptions hewn into the rock. He is the second diplomat to combine Assyriology with professional political and worldly interests.

Rawlinson's career was as adventurous as Grotefend's was conventional. The seed of his interest in Old Persian was sown by a chance acquaintance. When seventeen, Rawlinson was a cadet aboard a vessel bound around Cape Horn for India. To relieve the monotony of the long months of the voyage, he edited and published a ship's paper. One of the passengers, Sir John Malcolm, Governor of Bombay and prominent Orientalist, was much taken by the wide-awake seventeen-year-old soldier editor. He engaged the boy in long conversations, which naturally were dominated by Sir Malcolm's main interest. The Governor of Bombay was a passionate student of Persian history, language, and literature. These talks were to influence Rawlinson's avocational interest until the end of his days.

Born in 1810, Rawlinson entered the military service of the East India Company in 1826, and by 1833 was a major on duty in Persia. The year 1839 saw him employed as political agent in Kandahar, Afghanistan. By 1843 he had become British consul in Baghdad, and by 1851 consul-general with the military rank of lieutenant-colonel. In 1856 he returned to England, was elected to Parliament, and in the same year appointed to the board of the East India Company. In 1859 he became British Minister to the Persian court at Teheran. From 1865 to 1868 he was again a member of Parliament.

When he first took up the study of cuneiform writing he used the same tablets that Burnouf had worked with. An amazing thing now came to pass. In complete unawareness of Grotefend's, Burnouf's, and Lassen's contributions, he deciphered, by a method very similar to Grotefend's, the names of the three Persian kings that in English are written Darayawaush (Darius), Khshayarsha, and Vishtaspa. Beyond this he deciphered four other names, and some words as well, though he was not sure about the last. When, in 1836, he discovered Grotefend's writings, comparison revealed that in many significant respects he had improved on the schoolmaster of Göttingen. Now he needed more inscriptions, with names and still more names.

Since time immemorial a steep, double-peaked, cliffy mountain has dominated the land of Bagistana, "landscape of the gods," and the ancient road, passing by its foot, from Hamadan to Babylon by way of Khermansha. Here, about twenty-five hundred years ago, Darius, King of the Persians—Darayawaush, Dorejawosch, Dara, Darab, Dareios are variation of his name in different languages—had reliefs and inscriptions carved in the cliff face in celebration of his own person, deeds, and victories. This memorial stands some 160 feet above the valley floor.

On a great beam of stone are carved large figures that stand out boldly from the cliff. Here, poised in the glittering air, the great Darius is shown leaning on his bow, his right foot placed on the prostrate Gaumata, the magician, who had incited the kingdom to rebellion. Behind the King stand two Persian nobles, with bows, quivers, and lances. Before him, their feet bound, ropes at their necks, cower the nine "kings of lies," now brought to heel. At the sides and beneath this monument are fourteen columns of writing, recording, in three different languages, the accomplishments of Darius. Grotefend had recognized the bare fact that there were three variations of the cuneiform script at Behistun, but of course lacked the means to identify them for what they were—Old Persian, Elamite, and Babylonian. Among the records that Darius caused to be chiseled in the solid rock for the edification of posterity was an announcement that ran as follows:

> King Darayawaush gives notice thus:
> You who in future days
> Will see this inscription by order
> Writ with hammer upon the cliff,
> Who will see these human figures here—
> Efface, destroy nothing.
> Take care, so long as you have seed,
> To leave them undisturbed.

Dangling from the rope secured above, Rawlinson copied down the Old Persian version of the writing. It was only some years later that he tackled the Babylonian version, an operation that required enormous ladders, long cables, and hooks, equipment hard to come by in the Middle East. Despite these difficulties, in 1846 he laid the first exact copy of the famous inscription before the Royal Asiatic Society, and a complete translation with it. It was the first great British triumph of Assyriological decipherment.

Meanwhile other scholars had not been idle. The Franco-German Oppert and the Englishman Hincks in particular had made important advances. Comparative linguistics had proved especially effective in making use of the increasingly exact knowledge of Zend and Sanskrit—indeed, of the whole Indo-European family of languages—to clarify the grammatical structure of Old Persian. By a cooperative effort of truly international scope, sixty characters of the Old Persian cuneiform writing were gradually identified.

By this time, however, Rawlinson and others had got well into the study of the Behistun inscriptions, which provided a much greater range of material than had obtained heretofore. Rawlinson made a discovery that seemed to deal a severe blow to the hope of attaining a complete cryptology of the ancient languages of the Middle East, in particular of the inscriptional specimens collected by Botta.

As we recall, the Persepolitan and Behistun inscriptions were in three different languages. Grotefend had levered some meaning from them at a point of least resistance, where the cuneiform words were closest in time to their counterparts in known languages. The most vulnerable part of the inscription, the part, that is, on which Grotefend had concentrated, was the middle column. Even before Grotefend's time the type of cuneiform characters found in the middle column had been designated as Class I.

Most of the problems of Class I writing having been solved, the cryptologists turned to the other two types. The credit for laying the foundation of a method for deciphering the cuneiform writing of Class II belongs to the Dane Niels Westergaard, whose results were first published in Copenhagen in 1854. And the honor of deciphering Class III must be divided between Oppert and Rawlinson, the latter at this time consul-general at Baghdad.

The analysis of Class III quickly revealed a disturbing discovery. Class I was an alphabetical script in which, as in European writing, each sign equaled a sound. Not so in Class III script. Here a single sign might stand for a syllable, again for a whole word. Even worse, there were instances—and these multiplied as time went on—where the same sign, or polyphone, might represent several different syllables, or even several different words. Conversely, several signs, or homophones, could be used to express the same word. Eventually it was clearly established that changeability of meaning was the rule in the script of Class III. Total confusion reigned.

At first no one had the least idea how to go about cutting a path through this thicket of multiple meanings. And as these disenchanting revelations were published—especially by Rawlinson—there was great excitement among the scholars, and a storm of anger among the laity. The experts, of course, never entirely discounted the possibility that the characters might sometime become readable. Professionals and nonprofessionals engaged in heated arguments. Were they seriously expected to believe—authors known and unknown, specialists and laymen, asked in the scientific and literary supplements—that writing so hopelessly confused could ever have been actually used for purposes of communication? Were they expected, moreover, to swallow assurances that such a hodge-podge would sometime be read? There were loud protests; the experts were vigorously bludgeoned. Rawlinson in particular was raked over the coals for playing "unscientific jokes." Desist, he was warned.

A simple example—taken out of its context, which is too complicated to reproduce here—will serve to show just how maddening this Class III script could be. The sound *r* was expressed by six different signs, according to whether the intent was to indicate the syllables *ra, ri, ru, ar, ir,* or *ur*. But supposing one wished to reproduce the sound *ram*, or *mar*—that is, to add a consonant to *ra*, or *ar*—then an entirely new ideogram resulted from the new phonetic situation. Moreover, the pronunciation of the new ideogram could not be deduced from its component parts. In sum, the ambiguity of the script rested on the fact that when several signs were united into one ideogrammatic group to express something, the pronunciation of the whole could not be derived from the pronunciation of the constituent single signs. For example, the Class III group of char-

acters for the name of the famous King Nebuchadnezzar (Nebuchadrezzar), if pronounced according to the
discrete phonetic values, would be *An-pa-sa-du-sis*. But
in actual fact the name was pronounced *Nebukudur-
riussur*.

About this time, when to the uninformed the mud-
dle seemed complete, at Kuyunjik, where Botta had
excavated, nearly a hundred clay tablets were found in
rapid succession. These tablets, later identified as dating back to around the middle of the seventh century
B.C., might have been deliberately designed as aids to
the scholars of posterity, for they contained long listings
in which the different phonetic values and meanings of
the ideogrammatic script were correlated with those of
the alphabetical script.

This was a tremendously important find. The cryptologists now had "dictionaries" to work with! The
comparative listings had evidently served the beginner
studying cuneiform writing at a time when the older
pictographic and syllabary scripts were becoming simplified into an alphabetic version. Gradually whole

SUMERIAN · IDEOGRAM · SEMITIC

| Sumerian | Ideogram | Semitic |
|---|---|---|
| ad | 𒀖 | abu (Father) |
| gir | 𒄀 | kirr (Smelting Furnace) |
| udun | 𒌦 | utûnu (Oven, Stove) |
| gu | 𒄘 | alpu (Horned Cattle, Ox) |
| ama | 𒂼 | rimu (Wild Steer) |
| ulu | 𒅇 | ullu (Rejoicing) |
| ulu | 𒅇 | ulßu (Shout with Joy) |
| du | 𒁺 | asâmu (To be Fitting) etc |

This example gives
some idea of the
syllabaries, or sig-
naries, used by
students of cunei-
form writing in the
seventh century
B.C. These sylla-
baries were found
at Kuyunjik. A de-
vice that once
benefited the stu-
dent, more than
two thousand
years later helped
the Assyriologist
decipher cunei-
form texts.

"instruction manuals" and "dictionaries" were pieced together from the tablets. In the dictionaries the Sumerian name was given with its Semitic equivalent. Finally a prototype of the encyclopedic dictionary was discovered, containing pictures of various objects arranged in rows, these—at least the ones used in religious and legal rites—labeled with their Sumerian and Semitic names.

But important as this find was, it was still too fragmentary to provide more than a good toehold. Only the specialist can appreciate the difficulties, the roundabout paths and culs-de-sac that had to be laboriously explored before the cryptologists were able to read any cuneiform inscription, however complicated or ambiguous.

When Rawlinson issued a public claim that he could read the most difficult of the cuneiform scripts— like all great intellectual pioneers he was constantly beset and reviled—the Royal Asiatic Society in London did something seldom or never heard of in the history of scholarship.

To the four greatest cuneiform experts of the day —unknown to each of the others—the society sent a sealed envelope containing a newly discovered, lengthy Assyrian inscription, with a note urgently requesting its decipherment.

The four experts were Rawlinson, Talbot, Hincks, and Oppert. All went to work on the project about the same time, none knowing about the others, and each working according to his private methods. Finally all four returned their results in sealed envelopes, whereupon a commission examined the texts. The claims that had been so vociferously scoffed at by the public were brilliantly vindicated; it was definitely possible to read this supremely complicated syllabic writing. For all four texts agreed on essential points.

Many Assyriologists undoubtedly resented this extraordinary experiment and felt they had been grossly duped. Such a method of checking, they felt, was beneath science, however much the laity might approve.

No matter; in 1857 in London appeared *An Inscription by Tiglath-Pileser, King of Assyria, translated by Rawlinson, Talbot, Dr. Hincks, and Oppert.* There could not have been a more convincing proof of the scientific accuracy of the results, even though a diversity of approaches over paths heavily strewn with obstacles had been used.

Assyriology continued to develop apace. Ten years later the first elementary grammar of the Assyrian language appeared. Presently scholars undertook to unravel the mysteries of the spoken tongue. Today countless students are able to read cuneiform writing. Imperfectly inscribed or incomplete tablets pose the only difficulties, and of course material defects can be expected after three thousand years of wind and rain and sun beating on the ancient clay.

# 21/LAYARD:
## A DILETTANTE OUTWITS A PASHA

In 1854 the London Crystal Palace was moved from Hyde Park, where for three years it had housed the world exposition, and taken to Sydenham, where it was fitted out as a museum. With this the people of western Europe for the first time were able to form some idea of the luxury and splendor of those Biblical cities so often condemned by the prophets as sinks of sin and corruption. Two enormous Old Syrian rooms and a huge palace façade were reconstructed at this new British Museum. These exhibits offered an overwhelming impression of an architecture hitherto known only through legend, the Bible, and the fanciful travelogues written by the writers of antiquity.

A ceremonial hall and a royal chamber were also set up. Winged human-headed lions and images of the lion-killer Gilgamesh, the "conquering hero" and "master of the land," were put on display. Walls were reconstructed of Babylonian brick, a colored, glazed variety used in no other ancient architecture. There were friezes showing exciting martial and hunting scenes which happened twenty-seven centuries ago at the time of the great King Assurnasirpal (see Plates XVII and XVIII).

The man who made this exhibition possible was Austen Henry Layard. In 1839 he rode into Mosul, on the banks of the Tigris, his condition hardly better than a vagabond's; but by the time his Assyrian finds were being put on show at the British Museum at

Sydenham, Layard had become British Undersecretary for Foreign Affairs.

Layard's career is very similar to those of Botta and Rawlinson. All three were adventurers at heart, and fascinated by power; scientists of rank, yet worldly men; inclined to politics and experienced in the art of handling people, yet sensitive to the beautiful.

Layard was a member of a French family that had settled in England. He was born in Paris in 1817. After spending part of his youth in Italy with his father, in 1833 he came back to England and began the study of law. The year 1839 saw him traveling in the Orient. For a time he lived at the British Embassy in Constantinople, then in 1845 began his excavations in Mesopotamia. In 1852 and again in 1861 he was made Undersecretary for Foreign Affairs, in 1868 he became minister in charge of all public works, and in 1869 was made minister from England to Madrid with full credentials.

A longing to see the East, to visit distant Baghdad, Damascus, and Persia, colored his youthful dreams. Though at the age of twenty-two he was bent over a desk in a London solicitor's stuffy office, facing the prospect of a monotonous, confined existence, with no goal to work toward but the judicial bench, Layard shook off his bonds and followed the dream.

Layard's career was just the opposite of Heinrich Schliemann's. At the beginning both were caught up by youthful enthusiasms. Schliemann was excited by reading Homer, Layard by the *Thousand and One Nights*. Schliemann, however, first followed the paths of material success, with a unique display of self-control and method. He became a millionaire and a man with world-wide connections. Only then did he allow himself to be carried away by the long-suppressed dream. Layard, however, could not wait; he went forth as an impoverished youth into the land of fable. There he experienced even more than the fable had promised,

there he won fame and honor, there climbed the ladder
of success rung by rung.

One thing, nevertheless, he had in common with
the great German archæologist. Like Schliemann, who
in his Amsterdam garret had prepared himself for the
fulfillment of his urge by learning foreign languages,
during his youth Layard applied himself to everything
that he conceived would be needed to travel freely in
the land of his dreams. His interest inclined to practical
matters far outside the province of the law—the use of
compass and sextant, how to go about making topo-
graphical surveys, and the like. He studied first-aid
methods and ways of combating tropical diseases. Not
least, he learned some Persian and other languages
spoken in Iraq and Iran.

In 1839 he left his London office and began his
first journey into the Middle East. Very soon he
showed an ability that few of his colleagues in the
same field could match: he proved to be not only a
great excavator, but a superior writer as well, one who
could describe his accomplishments in brilliant language. Let him tell about his first Mesopotamian experience—in a somewhat abbreviated version of the
original:

"During the autumn of 1839 and winter of 1840, I
have been wandering through Asia Minor and Syria,
scarcely leaving untrod one spot hallowed by tradition,
or unvisited one ruin consecrated by history. I was accompanied by one no less curious and enthusiastic than
myself. We are both equally careless of comfort and
unmindful of danger. We rode alone; our arms were
our only protection; a valise behind our saddles was our
wardrobe, and we tended our own horses, except when
relieved from the duty by the hospitable inhabitants of
a Turcoman village or an Arab tent. Thus unembar-
rassed by needless luxuries, and uninfluenced by the
opinions and prejudices of others, we mixed amongst
the people. . . .

"I look back with feelings of grateful delight to

those happy days when, free and unheeded, we left at dawn the humble cottage or cheerful tent, and lingering as we listed, unconscious of distance and of the hour, found ourselves, as the sun went down, under some hoary ruin tenanted by the wandering Arabs, or in some crumbling village still bearing a well-known name.

". . . I now felt an irresistible desire to penetrate to the regions beyond the Euphrates, to which history and tradition point as the birthplace of the wisdom of the West. Most travellers, after a journey through the usually frequented parts of the East, have the same longing to cross the great river, and to explore those lands which are separated on the map from the confines of Syria by a vast blank stretching over Assyria, Babylonia, and Chaldea. With these names are linked great nations and great cities dimly shadowed forth in history; mighty ruins, in the midst of deserts, defying, by their very desolation and lack of definite form, the description of the traveller; the remnants of mighty races still roving over the land; the fulfilling and fulfillment of prophecies; the plains to which the Jew and the Gentile alike look as the cradle of their race.

"I left Aleppo, with my companion, on the 18th of March. We still travelled as we have been accustomed; without guide or servants. The road across the desert is at all times impracticable, except to a numerous and well-armed caravan, and offers no object of interest. . . . We entered Mosul on the 10th of April. During a short stay in this town we visited the great ruins on the east bank of the river, which have been generally believed to be the remains of Nineveh. We rode also into the desert, and explored the mound of Kalah Shergat, a vast ruin on the Tigris, about fifty miles below its junction with the Zab. As we journeyed thither we rested for the night at the small Arab village of Hammum Ali, around which are the vestiges of an ancient city. From the summit of an artificial eminence we looked down upon a broad plain, separated from us by the river. A line of lofty mounds bounded it to the east, and one of a pyramidical [sic] form rose high above the rest. Beyond it could be faintly traced the waters of the Zab. Its position rendered its identification easy. This was the pyramid which Xenophon had described, and near which the ten thousand had encamped: the ruins around it were those which the Greek general saw twenty-two centuries before, and which were even then the remains of an *ancient* city. Although Xenophon had confounded a name, spoken by a strange race, with one familiar to a Greek ear, and had called the place Larissa, tradition still points to the origin of the city, and, by attributing its foundation to Nimrod, whose name the ruins now bear, connects it with one of the first settlements of the human race."

Layard was not able at the time to investigate the history-laden mound more closely. But he was fascinated by the spectacle, he caressed the very thought of it as a miser strokes his cashbox. Again and again he returned to it in his description of his journey, always trying to find new words for the impression that it made on him.

"Kalah Shergat," he writes, "was . . . a vast, shapeless mass, now covered with grass, and showing scarcely any traces of the work of man except where the winter rains had formed ravines down its almost perpendicular sides, and had thus laid open its contents." And farther along, emphasizing the barrenness of the scene as it strikes the traveler, he says: "He is now at a loss to give any form to the rude heaps upon which he is gazing." And again: "The richly carved cornices or capitals half hidden by luxuriant herbage are [here] replaced by the stern shapeless mound rising like a hill from the scorched plain, the fragments of pottery, and the stupendous mass of brickwork occasionally laid bare by the winter rains."

Although a short time after this he had to turn back, he could not leave without at least once trying to satisfy his curiosity. "There was a tradition current amongst the Arabs," he writes, "that strange figures carved in black stone still existed among the ruins; but we searched for them in vain, during the greater part of a day in which we were engaged in exploring the heap of earth and bricks, covering a considerable extent of country on the right bank of the Tigris."

And he sums up by saying: "These huge mounds of Assyria made a deeper impression upon me, gave rise to more serious thought and more earnest reflection, than the temples of Balbec or the theatres of Ionia."

One mound most of all fettered his attention. He was held by its great size, and, too, by the name of the city that lay in ruins at its base, the city of Nimrud (Nimrod). This Biblical site, as he writes, seemed to provide him with a concrete link with the "cradle of the human race."

Cush, we are told in the tenth chapter of Genesis, was a son of Ham, whose father was Noah. This Cush, his three sons, their wives, and a host of animals began to repopulate the earth after humanity had been punished by a great deluge.

> And Cush begat Nimrod: he began to be a mighty one in the earth.
> He was a mighty hunter before the Lord: wherefore it is said, Even as Nimrod the mighty hunter before the Lord.
> And the beginning of his kingdom was Babel, and Erech, and Accad, and Calneh, in the land of Shinar.
> Out of that land went forth Asshur, and builded Nineveh, and the city Rehoboth, and Calah,
> And Resen between Nineveh and Calah: the same is a great city.

His pitifully inadequate funds having been eaten up, Layard had no choice but to turn back and go to Constantinople. There he made the acquaintance of the English Ambassador, Sir Stratford Canning. Day in, day out, Layard talked about the mysterious mounds near Mosul, and with ever more urgency, for meanwhile the world had been apprised of the finds made by Paul Émile Botta at Khorsabad. Layard's glowing descriptions and unflagging enthusiasm were not without effect on the Ambassador, though it cannot be said he was set on fire. At any rate, five years after Layard's first journey and after Botta had scaled the pinnacle of success at Khorsabad, Sir Stratford gave the twenty-eight-year-old enthusiast a present of sixty English pounds. Sixty pounds! Hardly a princely sum in view of what Layard hoped to accomplish. For his plans went far beyond anything that Botta had attempted, though the Frenchman had been helped by his government and enjoyed the income from an official sinecure in Mosul.

On November 8, 1845 Layard went down the Tigris on a river boat to begin his excavations at the mound of Nimrud. This time it was not only a lack of financial backing that jeopardized his expedition. Five years had slipped away since his last visit, and during this interval the whole region had become alive with insurrection.

The land between the two rivers at this time was under Turkish control. A new governor, or pasha, had been appointed since Layard's previous visit. It seems to have been characteristic of Oriental viceroys to regard territories in their charge as arenas of exploitation, the inhabitants as so many milch cows.

The new governor of Mosul ruled in true Asiatic style; on this point the many descriptions of his regime all agree. The pasha was a story-book villain. Even in physical appearance he fully looked the part. For example, he had only one eye, and one ear. He was small, and fat, in an insidious and Oriental way. To make matters worse, his face was covered with pockmarks. He had a terrifying voice, his gestures were uncouth and jerky, he habitually wore a mistrustful look, as if he momentarily expected to be ambushed. He was also a clever sadist, and gifted with a macabre wit. One of his first actions upon taking office was to institute a *"dish-parassi,"* or tooth-tax. This tribute went the European salt tax one better. Its purpose, the pasha announced, was to cover the attrition of his teeth and for extractions of the same occasioned by his eating the miserable diet of this benighted land.

The tooth-tax was a mere coquettish preliminary to what followed. He made the people shake in their shoes. His method was to despoil; the cities he robbed, villages he casually set on fire for the fun of watching them go up in smoke.

Despotism always breeds rumor, the news service of the weak. One day somebody in Mosul spread the story that Allah was fed up with the odious pasha and was going to take measures to take him down a peg or two. A few hours later the governor himself got wind of the story, and was inspired by it to invent a stratagem that might have been taken from an old Italian novella. For there are similar anecdotes in Boccaccio, though of less drastic consequences.

The next time the governor went out for a drive, he ostentatiously announced that he felt unwell. He was hurried back to the palace, apparently in a state of collapse. On the wings of hope eyewitness reports of this interesting development flew throughout Mosul. During the next few days the palace gates remained closed. Then the monotonous death wail of the lifeguards and eunuchs resounded from within. The people, pricking up their ears, began to shout with joy. "Allah be praised," they roared, "the pasha is dead!" Howling and hooting and screaming, wishing the supposedly defunct tyrant in the lowest depths of Gehenna, a crowd gathered in front of the palace. The gates suddenly swung open. There stood the pasha. Small, fat, loathsome. A patch over his blind eye, his face like a colander, grinning with malice. . . .

A nod, and soldiers rushed upon the terrified crowd. A cruel revenge was now carried out. Heads rolled. The pasha's sadism also took a pecuniary turn. He dispossessed all "rebels" who had anything to lose, not exempting properties previously immune from official rapacities. He did this, he said, because his victims had "spread rumors that injured the Turkish authority."

At last the country could stand this sort of thing no longer; the tribes who lived in the desert country about Mosul rebelled. They resisted in their own haphazard style. Incapable of an organized insurrection, they matched pillage with pillage. No road was safe, in consequence, no foreigner sure of his head. And it was in the midst of this hurly-burly that Layard landed in Mesopotamia, hoping to excavate the great mound of Nimrud.

Layard quickly sized up the situation. A few hours after arriving in Mosul he realized that the best policy was to keep his archæological plans to himself. As a subterfuge he bought heavy-caliber rifles and a short spear, saying that he was going down into the river bottoms to hunt wild boar.

A few days later he hired a horse and rode out alone in the direction of Nimrud, which also meant toward a village populated by thievish Bedouins.

Now the improbable came to pass. By evening he had won the friendship of Awad, the tribal sheik who ruled the roost in the territory immediately surrounding the mound of Nimrud. Indeed, by the time he lay down to sleep that night, he had hired six Arab laborers from the sheik. On the morrow, Awad promised, they would help him find what was in "the belly of the mountain"—and for delightfully modest wages at that.

The twenty-eight-year-old explorer must have spent a sleepless night. Tomorrow would prove his luck. Tomorrow? No, several months, perhaps, for had not Botta dug a whole year before getting any results? Actually, as it turned out, Layard struck into the walls of two Assyrian palaces before twenty-four hours had passed.

By early dawn he was roaming the mound. Everywhere he saw inscribed bricks. Awad, the Bedouin sheik, pointed out to his newly won friend a piece of alabaster sticking out of the ground, and this very simply decided the problem of where to dig first.

Seven men turned to and dug a long trench in the mound. The first finds, after several hours of shoveling, were some alabaster slabs that had been buried in an upright position. They proved to be parts of the frieze on the plinth of the orthostat, the decorative inside sheathing of palace walls. The richness of the decoration indicated that the walls could belong to nothing less than a royal palace.

Immediately Layard divided up his little gang of workmen. Suddenly fearing that he might be overlooking even more profitable diggings, and always hoping to

Assyrian princes on a lion hunt.

come upon walls that were perfectly intact—those he had excavated on the first attempt showed signs of having been calcined by fire—he put three of his men to work on the other side of the mound. Again their spades seemed to act like divining rods. Immediately they hit a wall covered with slabs showing carvings in relief, these separated by an inscription frieze. Layard had found the corner section of a second palace.

The better to visualize the sort of finds that Layard continued to make during this month of November 1845, listen to the archæologist's own description of an orthostat from Nimrud:

"The subject on the upper part of No. 1 was a battle scene. Two chariots, drawn by horses richly caparisoned, were each occupied by a group of three warriors; the principal person in both groups was beardless, and evidently a eunuch. He was clothed in a complete suit of mail, and wore a pointed helmet on his head, from the sides of which fell lappets covering the ears, the lower part of the face, and the neck. The left hand, the arm being extended, grasped a bow at full stretch; whilst the right, drawing the string to the ear, held an arrow ready to be discharged. A second warrior with reins and whip urged to the utmost of their speed three horses, who were galloping over the plain. A third, without helmet, and with flowing hair and beard, held a shield for the defense of the principal figure. Under the horses' feet, and scattered about the relief, were the conquered, wounded by the arrows of the conquerors. I observed with surprise the elegance and richness of the ornaments, the faithful and delicate delineation of the limbs and muscles, both in the men and horses, and the knowledge of art displayed in the grouping of the figures, and the general composition."

Bas-reliefs of this kind are found today everywhere in the museums of Europe and America. As a rule the visitor gives them a glance, then moves on. But these works of art really deserve close attention. They are so realistic in detail—at least in certain epochs—that the examination of a dozen or so of them affords a deep insight into the life of the period, particularly into the lives of the tyrants who are the object of violent Biblical stricture.

Today, in the age of photography, countless pictures give at least a superficial idea of these low reliefs, and are familiar even to schoolchildren. At the time, however, when Layard was toiling amid desert dust on the mound of Nimrud, no exemplars were available but those which Botta had shipped to Paris. And so they were a new thing, absolutely new, wonderfully exciting finds for those who were retrieving them from the debris of millennia.

Mesopotamia, one must realize, was rediscovered almost at one stroke. In 1843 Rawlinson was hard at work in Baghdad deciphering the Behistun inscriptions. That same year Botta began his excavations at Kuyunjik and Khorsabad, and in 1845 Layard was digging at Nimrud. Great advances resulted from these three years of labor. The decipherment of the Behistun inscription alone yielded more information on the Persepolitan rulers than all the authors of antiquity taken together had been able to supply. Today without exaggeration we can say that we know more about the history of Assyria and Babylonia, about the rise and decline of such cities as Babylon and Nineveh, then did the learned men of "classical" antiquity, more than all the Greek and Roman historians, who were closer in time to the subject by some two thousand years.

The Arabs who daily saw Layard's delight in chipped alabaster slabs, stained carvings, and scored bricks thought him stark, raving mad. But so long as he paid wages, they were ready and eager to dig on. Still, no pioneer in archæology, and Layard was no exception to the rule, was ever so lucky as to complete his task without interruption. Adventure has always gone hand in hand with field work, hazard with science, knavery with selfless sacrifice. Even so, Layard was a man on whom fortune smiled.

One day when the excavations were considerably advanced, when almost any hope, however vaulting, seemed justified, and the shortest breathing spells an intolerable waste of time, Awad, the Arab sheik and Layard's friend, called him to one side. In his hand he held a little figure covered with gold foil. Slyly, hinting

his willingness to play along, with much circumlocution
and many appeals to Allah, he made it clear that he
knew what the honorable Frank was really searching
for. Of course he wished Layard good luck. If there was
gold in the mound, well and good. All that he asked
was a little for himself. They—he and Layard—would
have to watch their step. These donkeys of workmen
had no idea about keeping their mouths shut. Above
all, news of Layard's successes must never get to Mohammed Pasha, in Mosul. Awad extended his arms
full length, to show just how large the pasha's ear was.

Indeed a despot has not only large ears, but ears
by the thousands. All his senses are multiplied by the
sums of the senses of all the creatures serving him
blindly as a god. It was no time at all before the pasha
began to show an interest in Layard's activities. An
officer, with soldiers, appeared on the scene. The officer
made a token inspection of Layard's trenches and
stores of excavated sculpture. He dropped hints that
he knew all about the gold that had cropped up from
time to time. Then he ceremoniously delivered an order
from the pasha, forbidding further excavation.

One can well imagine how Layard, who was inclined to be upset by the slightest delay, reacted to this
sweeping prohibition. He swung up on his horse, rode
at top speed to Mosul, and requested an immediate
audience with the pasha.

His request was granted. Thereupon Layard was
given a lesson in Oriental deviousness and chameleon
shifts of color. The pasha lifted deprecatory hands. Naturally—he would do everything, but everything, to
help Layard. He liked Franks, he admired them, honored them as a people, and he was anxious to be honored by their friendship, today, tomorrow, his whole
life long until Allah called him away. Still, digging was
really another matter. Impossible. The site, Layard
should understand, was an old Mohammedan burial
ground. The Frank really ought to look around a little
more carefully. He would find the gravestones. In the

eyes of all true believers Layard, sad to relate, was committing a sacrilege. The faithful would rise against the foreigner unless he were more careful. Also against the pasha. If that happened, it would be too bad. The pasha would no longer be able to hold a protecting hand over his friend from foreign parts.

Layard's visit was humiliating and had got him exactly nowhere. Seated one evening in front of his little hut, Layard had to admit to himself that the whole project was in danger of collapse. Having returned from his audience with the pasha, he had ridden over the mound to see whether it was true, as the tyrant had said, that Mohammedan tombstones were located there. And sure enough, there they were! The first one of these tombstones that he found—it was in an isolated spot—had aroused his suspicions. But what to do? He was still pondering what move to make next when he went to bed that night. A mistake, he thought grimly, not to have noticed the gravestones, and not to have discussed the matter more carefully with the pasha while he was at the palace.

And he was making another mistake, had he but known it, by crawling in under the bedclothes and out of sight this second night of his return to Nimrud. For this meant that he was letting slip a chance of seeing something that would have given him an excellent argument in parleying with Mohammed Pasha. This night —and the night before  had he been up and about, he would have seen ghostly shapes flitting about the mound of Nimrud, coming and going in company, with the sound of stones being softly cracked together. All night long, as Layard slept, slinking figures came and went in pairs. Were they robbers of Egyptian kidney? If so, what could they be looking for? There was nothing there to steal except some heavy stone reliefs.

Layard must have been an unusually charming man, a master in the art of dealing with people. The third morning, going up to the mound, he ran into the captain who had delivered the order to desist, and engaged him in conversation. The captain became confidential. Very privately he told Layard that he and his men, on the pasha's orders, had worked like dogs for two nights collecting gravestones from all the nearby village cemeteries to replant them on the mound of Nimrud.

"We have destroyed more real tombs of the true believers in making sham ones," said the captain, "than you could have defiled between the Zab and Selamiyah. We have killed our horses and ourselves in carrying these accursed stones."

Before Layard had devised means of coping with this astonishing development—if he had been a little more observant he would never have been caught napping in the first place—his difficulties were resolved in a quite unexpected fashion. Shortly after his elegant palaver with Layard, the pasha himself was clapped into jail. The fate which usually sees to it that despots are short-lived had worked the pasha's downfall. The Turkish government was summoning him to account for his misdeeds. Layard found him in a miserable room with the ceiling dripping rain. "Thus it is with God's creatures," the pasha complained. "Yesterday all those dogs were kissing my hands and feet." And looking up at the damp ceiling, he added: "Today everyone, and everything, falls upon me, even the rain."

With the pasha off the scene, Layard's work could proceed without hindrance. One morning the diggers, all excited and jabbering, rushed out of the pits in the northwestern sector of the mound. They waved their shovels, they shrieked and danced. Their furore was a wonderful mixture of fear and joy. "Hasten, O Bey," they yelled. "Hasten to the diggers, for they have found Nimrud himself. Wallah, it is wonderful, but it is true! We have seen him with our own eyes. There is no god but God."

Layard hurried to the spot. Hope lent speed to his steps. Not for one moment did he believe that the natives had really found an image of Nimrud. Yet, secretly remembering Botta's successes, he could not curb all high expectation. Had another one of those splendid man-headed lions been found in the rubble? Like those Botta had discovered?

Then he saw the powerfully sculptured torso, the gigantic head of a winged lion carved in alabaster. "It was in admirable preservation," he writes. "The expression was calm, yet majestic, and the outline of the features showed a freedom and knowledge of art, scarcely to be looked for in the works of so remote a period."

Today we know the figure represented one of the four astral gods that were identified with the four cardinal points of the compass. According to the Assyrian tradition, Marduk was shown as a winged bull, Nebo as a human being, Nergal as a winged lion, and Ninib as an eagle.

Layard was profoundly impressed. Later he wrote:

"I used to contemplate for hours these mysterious emblems, and muse over their intent and history. What more noble forms could have ushered the people into the temple of their gods? What more sublime images could have been borrowed from nature, by men who sought, unaided by the light of revealed religion, to embody their conception of the wisdom, power, and ubiquity of a Supreme Being? They could find no better type of intellect and knowledge than the head of the man; of strength, than the body of the lion; of rapidity of motion, than the wings of the bird. These winged humanheaded lions were not idle creations, the offspring of mere fancy; their meaning was written upon them. They had awed and instructed races which flourished 3,000 years ago. Through the portals which they guarded, kings, priests, and warriors had borne sacrifices to their altars, long before the wisdom of the East had penetrated to Greece, and had furnished its mythology with symbols long recognized by the Assyrian votaries. They may have been buried, and their existence may have been unknown, before the foundation of the eternal city. For twenty-five centuries they had been hidden from the eye of man, and they now stood forth once more in their ancient majesty. But how changed was the scene around them! The luxury and civilization of a mighty nation had given place to the wretchedness and ignorance of a few half-barbarous tribes. The wealth of temples, and the riches of great cities, had been succeeded by ruins and shapeless heaps of earth. Above the spacious hall in which they stood, the plough had passed and the corn now waved. Egypt has monuments no less ancient and no less wonderful; but they have stood forth for ages to testify her early power and renown; whilst those before me had but now appeared to bear witness in the words of the prophet [Ezekiel, xxxi, 3] that once 'the Assyrian was a cedar in Lebanon with fair branches, and with a shadowing shroud, and of an high stature; and his top was among the thick boughs.' "

Zephaniah (ii, 13–15) records the Lord's frightful promise as follows:

> And he will stretch out his hand against the north, and destroy Assyria; and will make Nineveh a desolation, and dry like a wilderness.
> And flocks shall lie down in the midst of her, all the beasts of the nations: both the cormorant and the bittern shall lodge in the upper lintels of it; their voice shall sing in the windows; desolation shall be in the thresholds; for he shall uncover the cedar work.
> This is the rejoicing city that dwelt carelessly, that said in her heart, I am, and there is none beside me: how is she become a desolation, a place for beasts to lie down in! every one that passeth by her shall hiss, and wag his hand.

Many centuries ago this prophecy had been fulfilled; and now Layard was bringing to light whatever there remained after its dire workings.

The news of the find, more or less frightening to the Arabs, spread quickly. The Bedouins came from far and near to see. The sheik appeared with half his tribe

in tow to celebrate the occasion with bursts of rifle-fire.
It was a glittering fantasy in honor of a world lost since
times primeval. The Arabs rode up to the diggings, took
one look at the gigantic image, bleached and scored by
the watery erosion of millennia, then lifted their arms
and called out to God to witness.

The sheik needed a great deal of reassuring before
he would consent to stepping down into the hole to see
for himself that the likeness was not a terrible jinni, or
god, risen out of the bowels of the earth. He stared,
and finally said: "This is not the work of men's hands,
but of those infidel giants of whom the Prophet—peace
be with him!—has said that they were higher than the
tallest date tree; this is one of the idols which Noah—
peace be with him!—cursed before the flood."

Meanwhile one of the Arab workmen, having
dropped his tools in terror, had rushed off to Mosul.
There his report that the great Nimrud had risen out
of his grave created vast excitement in the market place.

The cadi interested himself in the matter. He
called in the workmen for interrogation. What had
been found? The bones, the skeleton of Nimrud? Or
only his likeness, something made by human hands?
The cadi went into consultation with the mufti, who
reviewed the incident from the theological point of
view to determine whether Nimrud should be considered one of the faithful or a dog of an unbeliever.

The governor, successor to the tyrannical Mohammed Pasha, made a decision worthy of Solomon. He
ordered Layard to handle the "remains" with propriety
and for the time being suspend further excavation.
Layard managed to get an audience with the governor
and was able to convince him that the feelings of the
true believers would not be wounded by additional digging. Then, shortly afterwards, a firman, or official
Turkish permit, finally arrived from the Sultan in Constantinople. This relieved him permanently from all
annoyances stemming from the local authorities and
rabidly orthodox Arab tribesmen.

Scultpure after sculpture came to light. In a short

time no less than thirteen pairs of winged lions and bulls had been taken out of the ground. The imposing structure that Layard slowly revealed at the northwest side of the mound of Nimrud, a labor for which he was to be accorded fame far exceeding Botta's, was later identified as the palace of King Assurnasirpal II (reigned 884–859 B.C., according to Weidner), who had moved here to Kalah from Assur. Like his predecessors and successor, Assurnasirpal had lived in the style of Nimrud, who, as the Bible says, "was a mighty hunter before the Lord." From this palace Layard took hunting reliefs showing animals carved in a naturalistic mode that, once it had become known throughout Europe, inspired generations of modern artists. The chase was a daily occupation of the Assyrian nobility. This fact is shown in all the reliefs and sculptures, and recorded in all the inscriptions. The Assyrians had animal parks, "paradises," as they called them, precursors of our zoological gardens. Within their large confines were kept freely roaming lions and herds of gazelle. They arranged battues—that is, hunts in which the animals were driven by beaters—and hunted with nets, a sport hardly known anywhere on the face of the earth today.

Layard's most trying problem was how to send a pair of these colossal winged statues back home to London without doing them injury. The summer had ended in a bad harvest, and robber gangs were expected to be prowling about the environs of Mosul. Although by this time Layard had made many friends, it seemed advisable to expedite the work.

Accordingly the day came when a large gang of Arabs and Chaldeans shoved, tugged, and wrenched a gigantic cart over a half-rotted pontoon bridge to the site. This cart Layard had ordered to be hurriedly knocked together in Mosul. A pair of mighty water buffalo harnessed to the vehicle could hardly budge it. For the first shipment Layard had chosen a bull and a lion, two of the best-preserved specimens, also two of the smallest. Even so, the undertaking was hazardous enough, considering the limited material means at his disposal.

In order to get just one bull out of the mountain of rubble, Layard's workmen had to dig a trench 90 feet long, 16 feet wide, and up to 22 feet deep, from the place where the find was located to the rim of the mound. While Layard was becoming frantic with worry, the Arabs were having the time of their lives. They were quite different from the Egyptian fellahin, who, when they were rafting their dead kings down the Nile for Brugsch, sang mournful dirges. The Arabs dug with a merry will; they let out earsplitting roars of delight. The colossus was hauled forth on rollers amid a din of approbation.

That evening, the first step in the project being accomplished, Layard rode home with Sheik Abd-er-Rahman. He records a speech that the sheik made on this occasion:

"Wonderful, wonderful! There is surely no God but God, and Mohammed is his Prophet." And then, after a long pause, he said: "In the name of the Most High, tell me, O Bey, what you are going to do with those stones. So many thousands of purses spent upon such things! Can it be, as you say, that your people learn wisdom from them; or is it, as his reverence, the Cadi, declares, that they are to go to the palace of your Queen, who, with the rest of the unbelievers, worships these idols? As for wisdom, these figures will not teach you to make any better knives, or scissors, or chintzes; and it is in the making of those things that the English show their wisdom. But God is great! God is great! Here are stones which have been buried ever since the time of the holy Noah, peace be with him! Perhaps they were under ground before the deluge. I have lived on these lands for years. My father, and the father of my father, pitched their tents here before me: but they never heard of these figures. For twelve hundred years have the true believers—and, praise be to God! all true wisdom is with them alone—been settled in this country, and not one of them ever heard of a palace under ground. Neither did they who went before them. But lo! here comes a Frank from many days' journey off, and he walks up to the very place, and he takes a stick . . . and makes a line here, and makes a line there. Here, says he, is the palace; there, says he, is the gate; and he shows us what has been all our lives beneath our feet, without our having known anything about it. Wonderful! wonderful! Is it by books, is it by magic, is it by your prophets, that you have learnt these things? Speak, O Bey; tell me the secret of your wisdom."

Night fell, and at the mound of Nimrud the shrieks and commotion continued unabated. The success was being celebrated with music, dancing, and the crash of cymbals. Huge and pale, the winged bull looked out upon an alien world. . . .

The following morning the transport to the river began. The buffalo refused to pull such an outsize load. Layard sought help, and the sheik loaned him men, equipped with ropes, and rode on ahead with Layard to clear the way. Behind the leaders danced drummers and fifers making a hellish noise with their rude instruments.

"The cart followed, dragged by about three hundred men," Layard writes, "all screeching at the top of their voices, and urged on by the cawasses and superintendents. The procession was closed by the women, who kept up the enthusiasm of the Arabs by their shrill cries. Abd-er-Rahman's horsemen performed divers feats round the group, dashing backwards and forwards, and charging with their spears."

But even now all difficulties had not been overcome. Twice the cart bogged down. The actual loading onto the raft brought the sweat of apprehension to Layard's brow. The downriver transport of the bas-reliefs that he had already shipped home to England had not been half the problem. From Mosul the reliefs had gone to Baghdad, thence to Basra on the Persian Gulf, where the loading on board ship had been the easiest part of the job. This time, however, because of the colossal weight of the winged animals, Layard wished to avoid a transfer at Baghdad, which of course would be quite out of his control.

The Mosul shippers, who never in their lives had rafted anything as far as Basra, wrung their hands and positively refused to commit themselves to any such adventurous undertaking. Had not a certain Baghdad shipper been threatened with jail on account of his debts, the pieces might very well be there yet. Even so, Layard had to pay through the nose for special consideration. Eventually the statues were carried down to the Persian Gulf with none of the mishaps that had beset Botta's shipment down the Tigris.

And so the gigantic effigies, winged man-beasts, began their long journey downriver, after some twenty-eight centuries in oblivion. On a raft they traveled some 600 miles down the Tigris, then about 2,000 more miles over two oceans, around the length of Africa (the Suez Canal was not opened until 1869) to London, where they found a new home in the British Museum.

Before Layard temporarily left the diggings, he seems to have made one last tour of inspection, notebook in hand. This survey is recorded in the closing description of the Nimrud site found in his *Nineveh and Its Remains*:

"Let us imagine ourselves issuing from my tent near the village in the plain. On approaching the mound, not a trace of building can be perceived, except a small mud hut covered with reeds, erected for the accommodation of the Chaldean workmen. We ascend this artificial hill, but still see no ruins, not a stone protruding from the soil. There is only a broad level platform before us, perhaps covered with a luxuriant crop of barley, or may be yellow and parched, without a blade of vegetation, except here and there a scanty tuft of camel-thorn. Low, black heaps, surrounded by brushwood and dried grass, a thin column of smoke issuing from the midst of them, may be seen here and there. These are the tents of the Arabs; and a few miserable old women are groping about them, picking up camel's dung or dry twigs. One or two girls, with firm step and erect carriage, are perceived just reaching the top of the mound, with water-jars on their shoulders, or a bundle of brushwood on their heads. On all sides of us, apparently issuing from under ground, are long lines of wild-looking beings, with dishevelled hair, their limbs only half concealed by a short loose shirt, some jumping and capering, and all hurrying to and fro, shouting like madmen. Each one carries a basket, and as he reaches the edge of the mound, or some convenient spot near, empties its contents, raising at the same time a cloud of dust. He then returns at the top of his speed, dancing and yelling as before, and flourishing his basket over his head; again he suddenly disappears in the bowels of the earth, from whence he emerged. These are the workmen employed in removing the rubbish from the ruins.

"We will descend into the principal trench, by a flight of steps rudely cut into the earth. . . . We descend about twenty feet and suddenly find ourselves between a pair of colossal lions, winged and human-headed, forming a portal. . . . In the subterraneous labyrinth which we have reached, all is bustle and confusion. Arabs are running about in different directions; some bearing baskets filled with earth, others carrying the water-jars to their companions. The Chaldeans or Tiyari, in their striped dresses and curious conical caps, are digging with picks into the tenacious earth, raising a dense cloud of fine dust at every stroke. The wild strains of Kurdish music may be heard occasionally issuing from some distant part of the ruins, and if they are caught by the parties at work, the Arabs join their voices in chorus, raise the war-cry, and labor with renewed energy. . . .

"We issue from between the winged lions, and enter the remains of the principal hall. On both sides of us are sculptured gigantic, winged figures; some with the heads of eagles, others entirely human, and carrying mysterious symbols in their hands. To the left is another portal, also formed by winged lions. One of them has, however, fallen across the entrance, and there is just room to creep beneath it. Beyond this portal is a winged figure, and two slabs with bas-reliefs, but they have been so much injured that we can scarcely trace the subject upon them. Further on there are no traces of wall, although a deep trench has been opened. . . .

"We issue from between them, and find ourselves on the edge of a deep ravine, to the north of which rises, high above us, the lofty pyramid. Figures of captives bearing objects of tribute—ear-rings, bracelets, and monkeys—may be seen on walls near this ravine; and two enormous bulls, and two winged figures about fourteen feet high, are lying at the very edge.

"As the ravine bounds the ruins on this side, we must return to the yellow bulls. Passing through the entrance formed by them, we enter a large chamber surrounded by eagle-headed figures: at the one end of it is a doorway guarded by two priests or divinities, and in the centre another portal with winged bulls. Whichever way we turn, we find ourselves in the midst of a nest of rooms: and without an acquaintance with the intricacies of the place, we should soon lose ourselves in this labyrinth. The accumulated rubbish being generally left in the centre of the chambers, the whole excavation consists of a number of narrow passages, panelled on one side with slabs of alabaster; and shut in on the other by a high wall of earth, half buried, in which may here and there be seen a broken vase, or a brick painted with brilliant colors. We may wander through these galleries for an hour or two, examining the marvellous sculptures, or the numerous inscriptions that surround us. Here we meet long rows of kings, attended by their eunuchs and priests—there lines of winged figures, carrying fir cones and religious emblems, and seemingly in adoration before the mystic tree.

"Other entrances, formed by winged lions and

bulls, lead us into new chambers. In every one of them are fresh objects of curiosity and surprise. At length, wearied, we issue from the buried edifice by a trench on the opposite side to that by which we entered, and find ourselves again upon the naked platform."

This description Layard ends by writing:

"We look around in vain (having left Nimrud) for any traces of the wonderful remains we have just seen, and are half inclined to believe that we have dreamed a dream, or have been listening to some tale of Eastern romance. Some, who may hereafter tread on the spot when the grass again grows over the ruins of the Assyrian palaces, may indeed suspect that I have been relating a vision."

# 22/GEORGE SMITH:
# THE STORY OF THE FLOOD

The material that Layard took from the mound of Nimrud was both copious and excellent, and surpassed Botta's findings at Khorsabad. In the flush of success it was not surprising that he should risk his reputation with an experiment that, to outward view, seemed almost certainly doomed to misfire.

Among the many brick-strewn mounds that invited new excavations, Layard chose as the object of his next attack the mound of Kuyunjik, the same hill where Botta had dug to no avail for a whole year. Layard's decision was not so contrary as it first appears. It shows, in fact, that he had learned a lot from his excavations and did not have to depend for his collecting entirely on luck. He was now able to judge the surface promise of the mounds, drawing correct inferences from the tiniest clues.

There was poetic justice in what now happened to Layard, much as with Schliemann when the former merchant prince and millionaire, having finished digging at Troy, turned to the Lion Gate at Mycenæ. For everyone fancied that Layard's initial success had been largely a matter of luck. He would never repeat himself, it was believed, and certainly never improve on the Nimrud finds. Yet, as the situation developed, doubters were forced to admit that Layard had outdone himself. At Kuyunjik he achieved the deepest of insights into the past. From the great mound he brought forth treasures that revealed the whole spectrum, in all its richness, of the lost Assyrian culture.

It was in the fall of 1849 when Layard began to work on the mound of Kuyunjik, on the banks of the Tigris across from Mosul. There he found one of the greatest palaces of Nineveh.

He first drove a vertical shaft into the hill until he struck a stratum of bricks twenty feet down. From this level he dug horizontal tunnels in various directions and presently hit on a large hall, and on a gate, flanked by winged bulls. After four weeks' work he had opened up nine chambers of the palace of Sennacherib (704–681 B.C.), one of the mightiest and bloodiest rulers of the Assyrian kingdom.

Inscription after inscription was laid bare, also friezes, sculptures, splendid walls of glazed brick, mosaics with white cuneiform lettering on a ground of turquoise blue. The colors of the finds were strange and coldly splendid—mostly black and yellow and dark blue. The reliefs and sculptures showed an uncommonly lively and strong manner of expression and in naturalistic detail were much superior to the pieces found on the mound of Nimrud.

From Kuyunjik came the noble frieze—apparently dating from the reign of Assurbanipal—of the dying lioness. The lioness, pinned down by spears, has lost the use of her hindquarters. In her death agony she raises her head for one last roar of defiance. This relief is a carving of tremendous power, as impressive as any work of art of the same genre known to the West (see Plate XVII).

Before Layard's excavations, our knowledge of the fearsome city of Nineveh had been limited to Biblical description, in the narrow prophetic context of which it is alternately praised and cursed. By revealing the city's actual lineaments Layard dispelled the thick shroud of myth in which Nineveh had languished for so many centuries.

Nineveh was named after Nin, the great goddess of Mesopotamia. It was a city of vast antiquity. In 1700 B.C. Hammurabi, the Babylonian lawgiver, mentioned the Temple of Ishtar around which the city was built. Yet Nineveh remained a provincial community, while Assur and Kalah had become royal residences.

It was Sennacherib, who, in order to avoid Assur, his father's residence, made Nineveh the capital of a land that included all of Babylonia and extended as far as Syria and Palestine to the north, and eastward as far as the wild and chronically rebellious mountain folk.

Nineveh reached the height of its fame under Assurbanipal. It was then a city where "merchants are more numerous than the stars in the heavens." It was the political and economic hub of the Mesopotamian region, and the cultural and artistic center as well, a kind of Assyrian Rome. But during the seven-year reign of Assurbanipal's son, Sin-sharishkun, Kyaxares, King of the Medes, appeared before the walls of Nineveh with an army reinforced by Persian and Babylonian contingents. He laid siege to the city, took it, razed the walls and palaces, and left nothing behind but a heap of ruins.

This happened in 612 B.C., after Nineveh had been the capital of Assyria for only ninety years. Yet how much must have happened during this short interval to make the city a vital memory for twenty-five centuries, a lasting symbol for greatness coupled with terror and naked power, for sybaritism and civilization, for spectacular ascendancy and shattering fall, for wanton guilt and deserved punishment!

Today we know the truth. Today we know, through the combined efforts of excavator and cryptologist, enough about the lives of Sennacherib and Assurbanipal—and about those who came before and after them as well—to say that:

Nineveh was impressed on the consciousness of mankind by little else than murder, plunder, suppression, and the violation of the weak; by war and all manner of physical violence; by the deeds of a sanguinary dynasty of rulers who held down the people by terror and who often were liquidated by rivals more ferocious than themselves.

Sennacherib was the first of the half-mad Cæsars—
a forerunner of Nero, not of Julius—upon the throne of
the first metropolis. For Nineveh was the Assyrian
Rome: megalopolis, city of vast palaces, squares, ave-
nues, of unprecedented technical triumphs. The prototype of urban civilization, it was typically ruled by an
elite, whether its power was based on noble birth,
family, race, money, violence, or some combination of
these. But it was also the city of a submerged gray mass
of the disfranchised, whipped into slavish obedience for
the most part, though they were sometimes given the
illusion of freedom by slogans such as that their work
was being done for the good of all, their wars were
being fought for the people, and the like. They were a
mass in ferment, moving like a tide every twenty years
between the poles of social revolt and slavish resigna-
tion, blinded, ready to be slaughtered like sheep. In
such a city one finds, usually, a whole pantheon of
gods, many of them imported from distant places, their
primeval creative meaning and function long since lost.
Here politics is the craft of permanent mendacity.

Such a city was Nineveh.

It could be seen from far off, the façades of its
shimmering palaces reflected in the waters of the Tigris.
It was surrounded by an outer wall, then came the
Great Wall, which was named "Whose Terrifying
Glare Casts Down the Enemy." This wall rose upon a
foundation of dressed stone. It was forty bricks thick
and a hundred bricks high, 32 and 76 feet respectively.
Fifteen gates breached this wall. A moat ran around it,
77 feet wide and spanned at the "Garden Gate" by an
arched stone bridge, an architectural marvel of the
times.

On its western side stood the palace "the like of
which was never seen," Sennacherib's showplace. Like
Augustus transforming his Rome of brick into a Rome
of marble, and like Hitler laying down his "axes" diagonally traversing Berlin, he had torn down old buildings in the way of his new construction.

Sennacherib's mania for building reached on orgiastic peak at the banquet hall of the god at Assur. The temple stood on about 172,800 square feet of leveled rock. Holes were made in this rock all around the temple; they were then connected by subterranean canals, and all this covered with loam. The ruler wished to see a garden there!

He began his reign by inventing an improved ancestry for himself, beginning with Sargon, his father, whom he disowned in favor of descent from prediluvial kings, demigods such as Adapa and Gilgamesh. In this, too, he was a forerunner of the Roman Cæsars who had themselves worshipped as gods, and of the contemporary dictators whose self-deification is only a trifle less explicit.

"Sennacherib was an exceptional personality in every way. He was an extremely gifted man who loved sports, art, science, and especially its technical aspects. But all of these superior traits were canceled out by his willful, irascible temperament, which drove him to pursue his goal headlong regardless of its practicability. Because of this he was the precise opposite of a good statesman," says Meissner.

War was the essence of Sennacherib's government. He attacked Babylon, he marched against the Kassi, in 701 B.C. he took up arms against Tyre, Sidon, Ashkelon, and Ekron, against Hezekiah of Judah, whose adviser had been the prophet Isaiah. He boasted of having taken forty-six fortresses and countless villages in the land of the Jews. But at Jerusalem he met his Waterloo. In the words of Isaiah:

"Therefore thus saith the Lord concerning the king of Assyria, He shall not come into this city, nor shoot an arrow there, nor come before it with shields, nor cast a bank against it. . . . Then the angel of the Lord went forth, and smote in the camp of the Assyrians a hundred and fourscore and five thousand: and when they arose early in the morning, behold, they were all dead corpses."

As a matter of fact, it was the plague (known today as *malaria tropica*) that defeated Sennacherib's army.

After the Palestinian raid he engaged in military promenades to places as far away as Armenia. He fought again and again with Babylonia, which country would not tolerate Sennacherib's despotic satraps. Using a fleet of boats, he ventured as far as the Persian Gulf, where his men fell on the countryside like a "swarm of locusts." His chronicling of these deeds is exaggerated, and freely invented in point of numbers. Indeed, the records of Sennacherib bring to mind the typically modern picture of a dictator shouting vast lies at vast audiences, civilian or military, confident in the knowledge that they will be swallowed whole. It is hardly a consolation for us moderns when one of our archæologists finds in the ruins of Babylon a clay tablet on which this lapidary observation is inscribed: "Look thou about thee, and see that all men are fools." The recurrent parallelism between past and present is real. Analogies appear of their own accord if one has the capacity to remove cultural epochs from the temporal series and place them side by side for purposes of comparison.

Sennacherib reached the limits of despotic willfulness when, in 689 B.C., he made up his mind to erase rebellious Babylon from the face of the earth. Having forced his way into the city, he slaughtered the inhabitants one by one, until the dead clogged the streets. Private dwellings were methodically destroyed. The towered Temple of E-sagila was toppled into the Arachtu Canal. Finally water was diverted into the city, and streets, squares, and houses were drowned in the artificial flood. Even then Sennacherib's lust was not appeased. He would have the city vanish, at least symbolically, from the very sight of mankind. To this end he caused loads of Babylonian earth to be loaded on boats and carried to Tilmun, where they were scattered to the four winds.

Having now eased his ferocious spirit, he seemed to be content to occupy himself with domestic affairs. To please his favorite, Nakiya, he had Esarhaddon, one of his younger sons, named successor to the Assyrian throne, and forced the sacred oracles to approve this choice. He gathered together a sort of representative assembly, composed of Esarhaddon's older brothers, Assyrian nobles and officials, and some delegates standing for the people. Asked to approve Sennacherib's plan, they shouted a unanimous "Yea!" Nevertheless, the older brothers, secretly determined to restore the traditional mode of royal succession, at the end of 681 B.C. fell on their father as he was praying to the gods in the temple at Nineveh and killed him. So ended Sennacherib.

This was one chapter in the bloody story that Layard brought forth with his spade. He was to add to the tale when, in Sennacherib's palace, he discovered two rooms, apparently added by way of afterthought, which had functioned as a library.

The use of the term *library* to describe these rooms is not at all farfetched, even from the modern standpoint; for the treasury of information discovered there by Layard comprised nearly thirty thousand "volumes." A library of clay tablets!

Assurbanipal (688–626 B.C.), who ascended the throne through the influence of his grandmother Nakiya, one-time favorite of Sennacherib, was the exact temperamental opposite of the tyrant. His inscriptions, though as overweening in phrase as his predecessor's, voice peaceable sentiments and generally reflect Assurbanipal's inclination toward the tranquil life. From this one must not construe, however, that Assurbanipal did not engage in war. His brothers—one of whom, a high priest of the moon god, is memorable for the length of his name, Assur-etil-shameirssiti-uballitsu, otherwise Assur-ballit—caused Assurbanipal a great many headaches. Shamash-shum-ukin, the brother who had been appointed King of Babylon, was more troublesome than any of the lot. He laid waste the King of the Elamites, and after conquering Babylon—it had already been rebuilt—instead of razing it as Sennacherib would have done, he simply moved in and ruled. During the two-year siege of Babylon a black market sprang up, a symptom of economic disorder often erroneously regarded as peculiar to modern times. Three sila of grain —about two and a quarter quarts—cost one shekel, or 8.4 grams of silver. Normally this amount would have bought at least sixty times as much.

Assurbanipal received a kind of poetic eulogy such as would never have been applied to Sennacherib. It went as follows:

> *The weapons of rebellious enemies were at rest,*
> *The charioteers unharnessed their horses,*
> *Their pointed lances they stacked up,*
> *And loosened their bowstrings;*
> *Deeds of violence were suppressed,*
> *Among those who practiced war against their adversaries.*

> *Within the house and in the city*
> *None took away his comrade's goods by force;*
> *Within the whole land's circuit*
> *No man did harm unto his brother.*
> *He who went the way alone*
> *Traveled distant roads quite safe and sound.*

> *Throughout all lands a peace prevailed,*
> *Like finest oil were the world's four quarters.*

Assurbanipal made a name for himself that will endure through all time by founding his famous library, "in order that he might have that which to read." The discovery of these tablets was Layard's last great excavational triumph. After this he handed the torch to others, returned to England, and embarked on his political career.

Assurbanipal's library provided a key to the understanding of the whole Assyrio-Babylonian civilization. The collection had evidently been arranged according to a definite system. The King obtained part of the tablets from private sources, but the largest section consisted of copies he had made of originals scattered throughout all the provinces of his realm. To Babylon he sent Shadanu, one of his officials, with the following instructions:

"The day that you receive my letter, take Shuma, his brother, Bel-etir, Apla, and the artists of Borsippa whom you know, and collect the tablets, as many as there are in their houses, and as many as there are in the Temple of Ezida."

And he ended his orders like this:

"Seek out and bring to me the precious tablets for which there are no transcripts extant in Assyria. I have just now written to the temple overseer and the mayor of Borsippa that you, Shadanu, are to keep the tablets in your storehouse, and that nobody shall refuse to hand over tablets to you. If you hear of any tablet or ritualistic text that is suitable for the palace, seek it out, secure it, and send it here."

A battery of scholars and "writing-artists" were in Assurbanipal's employ. With their aid he amassed a library containing the total knowledge of his times. This fund of information was strongly colored by different kinds of magic; most of the books are made up of material having to do with the arts of exorcism, divination, and conducting rites. Yet there was also a number of medical works—tinged, to be sure, with the ubiquitous magical influence—also philosophical, astronomical, mathematical, and philological works. (On the mound of Kuyunjik Layard found the school texts that gave so much help in deciphering the Class III cuneiform writing.)

The library also contained dynastic lists, historical sketches, palace edicts of a political nature, and even a poetical literature, consisting of epic-mythical tales, songs, and hymns.

Among the purely "literary" tablets were those recording the first great epic of world history, the saga of the terrible and splendid Gilgamesh, part god, part man. This Gilgamesh Epic is the most significant work produced by the Mesopotamian civilizations.

These particular tablets were not discovered by

Layard. They were found by a man who, shortly before, had been freed from an unpleasant two-year imprisonment in Abyssinia by a rescue expedition. If, by chance, Layard had been the one to find them, he would indeed have overloaded the scales of fame. For the epic of Gilgamesh was not only fascinating from the literary standpoint; it also threw amazing light on our most primitive past, and particularly on a story that every European child is still taught in the schools, without, however, anyone having the least notion whence the tale really comes.

Hormuzd Rassam, who actually made the find, was one of Layard's assistants. When Layard gave up archæology for a diplomatic career, Rassam was appointed by the British Museum to carry on the master's work.

Rassam was a Chaldean Christian, born in 1826 in Mosul, on the Tigris. In 1847 he began his studies at Oxford and in 1854 was employed as interpreter at the British residency in Aden. A short time thereafter, though hardly thirty years old, he was made deputy resident. In 1864 he went as a diplomatic messenger to the court of King Theodore of Abyssinia. The autocratic Theodore, a black potentate who had very literal notions of the royal prerogative, had Rassam seized and held. The unfortunate messenger spent two years in Abyssinian prisons before he was freed by Napier's expedition. A little later he began his excavations at Nineveh.

Rassam was almost as successful in his projects as Layard had been, but he lacked two advantages that had redounded so strongly in Layard's favor. He was not lucky enough to be the first one on the scene, and the novelty of his finds could not be so sensational as Layard's had been. Nor did he have that budding diplomat's ability to write up his archæological experiences in a colorful, charming style studded with brilliant formulations that appealed both to the archæologists and to the public at large.

Supposing Layard had found a temple 160 feet long and 96 feet wide on the much-worked mound of Nimrud, how masterly would have been his description of it! How colorfully he would have told the story of the workmen's revolt that occurred while Rassam was digging some eight miles north of Nimrud, at Balawat, and which he put down with an iron hand. At Balawat, Rassam not only excavated a temple built by Assurnasirpal, but the remains of a terrace city as well. Among other gates he found one 22.4 feet high, furnished with double doors of bronze. This was the first evidence of the existence of doors in the modern sense in the palaces of Mesopotamia. Imagine, too, how Layard, with that brilliantly decisive and consciously reverent style of his, would have described the discovery of the Gilgamesh epic, even though, in actual fact, his competence to make a definitive evaluation of it was no greater than Rassam's.

For the full meaning of this work, which has yielded so many illuminating insights into the dawn of the human spirit, was not properly understood until many years after its discovery. Today every history of world literature mentions it somewhere at the beginning of the book. Modern literary historians however, characteristically put little stress on the Gilgamesh Epic. They cite ten or a dozen lines, call it the "wellspring of epic poetry," and let it go at that. Actually it is the whole work that leads us back to the very cradle of the human race, and pads out the bones of our remotest ancestors with living flesh. The tracking down of the Gilgamesh Epic to the ancient sources was accomplished by a man who died only four years after completing the task and whose commonplace name is most unfairly relegated to marginal comments and footnotes in the majority of archæological histories.

This man was George Smith, another archæological amateur, and a banknote engraver by profession, who was born on March 26, 1840 at Chelsea, in Lon-

don. Smith was a self-taught man who at night in his
little room gave himself over with unparalleled zeal to
the study of the first publications of Assyriology. At
the age of twenty-six he wrote a few minor commen-
taries on some cuneiform characters of debated meaning. These essays by the unknown engraver aroused a
great deal of professional notice. A couple of years later
he was made assistant in the Egyptian-Assyrian section
of the British Museum. When he died prematurely, in
1876, at the age of thirty-six, he had already published
a dozen books and linked his name with significant discoveries.

In 1872 this erstwhile banknote engraver was sitting over the tablets that Hormuzd Rassam had sent to
the museum, trying to decipher them. At this time no
one was aware that there had been an Assyrio-Babylonian literature worthy of being ranked with that of the
best of later heroic epochs. As it happened, however,
Smith was not interested particularly in the literary
quality of the tablets *per se*. Smith, basically, was a per-
severing and apparently a rather amusing man of strict
scholarly habits, not at all a poet. He was thrilled by
the bare content of the tale, by the "what" rather than
the "how" of the legend. The farther he progressed
with the decipherment, the more excited he became
and the more anxious to know how the argument
would turn out.

Bit by bit Smith unraveled the great deeds of Gilgamesh the strong. He read about the man of the
woods, Enkidu, brought into the city by a priest's whore
to subdue Gilgamesh the modest. But the violent battle of heroes ended in a draw. Gilgamesh and Enkidu
became fast friends and, working together, accomplished many noble deeds. They killed Khumbaba, terrible ruler of the cedar forest, and even challenged the
gods themselves when they had offended Ishtar, who
had offered her love to Gilgamesh.

Always laboriously translating, Smith read, farther
along, how Enkidu died of a frightful sickness, how he

was mourned by Gilgamesh, who, to avoid a similar fate, set out to find immortality. During his wanderings he met Ut-napishtim, the primeval ancestor of mankind. This Ut-napishtim and his family, when the gods visited a great punishment on the wicked human race, had been the only survivors of the debacle. Afterwards the gods had made them immortal.

Ut-napishtim then tells Gilgamesh the whole story of his miraculous escape. Smith read the Ut-napishtim legend with eager eyes. As his initial excitement began to evolve into the certainty of a remarkable discovery, bigger and bigger gaps appeared in the narrative flow of the Rassam tablets. Smith had to reconcile himself to the fact that he had only fragments of the total inscription to work with. Indeed, the most essential section of the story was entirely missing—that is, the conclusion.

What Smith had read of the Gilgamesh Epic left him no rest. Nor could he keep silent about his discoveries, though to disclose them was sure to rock the Bible-bound England of Victoria's day. Later a powerful newspaper came to George Smith's aid. The London *Daily Telegraph* announced that it was offering the sum of a thousand guineas to anyone who would go to Kuyunjik, find the missing Gilgamesh inscriptions, and bring them back to England.

George Smith himself accepted the offer. He traveled the thousands of miles separating London from Mesopotamia, and there boldly attacked the tremendous pile of rubble that was Kuyunjik—the mound, in respect of total area, had hardly been scratched—in search of the missing tablets. Smith's task was about comparable to finding one particular water-louse in the sea, or the famous needle in the haystack.

And again there occurred one of the almost unbelievable wonders that stud the history of archæological excavation. Smith actually found the missing parts of the Gilgamesh Epic.

He brought home, altogether, 384 fragmentary

clay tablets, among them the missing parts of the controversial story of Utnapishtim. This tale was a variation of the Biblical legend of the Flood. There are, of
course, flood stories in almost every folklore, but this
one was concerned with the very same deluge described,
at a later date, in Genesis. Ut-napishtim, indeed, was
none other than Noah! The following is the text of
that section of Gilgamesh concerned with Ut-napishtim.
The friendly god Ea in a dream had revealed the god's
punitive intent to Ut-napishtim, Ea's protegé, whereupon Ut-napishtim decided to build himself an ark.

> What I had I loaded thereon, the whole harvest of
>     life
> I caused to embark within the vessel; all my family
>     and my relations,
> The beasts of the field, the cattle of the field, the
>     craftsmen, I made them all embark.
> I entered the vessel and closed the door. . . .
> When the young dawn gleamed forth,
> From the foundations of heaven a black cloud
>     arose. . . .
> All that is bright is turned into darkness,
> The brother seeth his brother no more,
> The folk of the skies can no longer recognize each
>     other
> The gods feared the flood,
> They fled, they climbed into the heaven of Anu,
> The gods crouched like a dog on the wall, they lay
>     down. . . .
> For six days and nights
> Wind and flood marched on, the hurricane sub-
>     dued the land.
> When the seventh day dawned, the hurricane was
>     abated, the flood
> Which had waged war like an army;
> The sea was stilled, the ill wind was calmed, the
>     flood ceased.
> I beheld the sea, its voice was silent,

*And all mankind was turned into mud!*
*As high as the roofs reached the swamp! . . .*
*I beheld the world, the horizon of sea;*
*Twelve measures away an island emerged;*
*Unto Mount Nitsir came the vessel,*
*Mount Nitsir held the vessel and let it not*
*    budge. . . .*
*When the seventh day came,*
*I sent forth a dove, I released it;*
*It went, the dove, it came back,*
*As there was no place, it came back.*
*I sent forth a swallow, I released it;*
*It went, the swallow, it came back,*
*As there was no place, it came back.*
*I sent forth a crow, I released it;*
*It went, the crow, and beheld the subsidence of the*
*    waters;*
*It eats, it splashes about, it caws, it comes not*
*    back.*

Impossible to question the fact that the primal version of the Biblical legend of the Deluge had been found. The story of Ut-napishtim shows much more than a general analogy to the story of Noah and the ark. Specific events are duplicated, as for instance the freeing of the dove and the raven.

This text in cuneiform from the Gilgamesh Epic raised for Smith's generation the disturbing question: Was the Bible no longer the oldest historical source we had?

Once again research by spade had enabled us to take a great leap into the past. This time, new aspects presented themselves: Was the Ut-napishtim story merely the confirmation of Biblical legend by a still more ancient legend? Had not everything the Bible related of this mysterious, opulent land between the rivers been regarded as merely a legend all along? What if there was a factual basis for all these so-called legends? Could the story of the Flood, for example,

have been based on an actual historiacl event? And
how far back did the history of Mesopotamia actually
go?

What had seemed to be an impenetrable wall, a
total eclipse of history, was soon revealed as a curtain
ready to rise upon vistas of unsuspected ancient worlds.

A few years after George Smith's discovery it was
again a Frenchman, also a consular agent, Ernest de
Sarzec, who in 1880 dug out of the sands at Telloh
(Lagash) a statue of a style never yet seen in Mesopotamia. Though not unrelated in style to previous finds,
it was far more archaic and monumental, an example
of the earliest kind of art from the infancy of human
culture. It looked far older than the Egyptian art which
had been considered the most ancient till then.

The discovery of these primal peoples and cultures
was the fruit of an exceptionally bold hypothesis of
the scholars, brilliantly confirmed by de Sarzec's acci-
dental find.

Some time later, around the turn of the century,
a German archæologist began to excavate the Tower of
Babel.

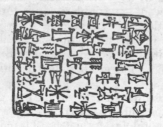

Robert Koldewey was born in 1855 in Blankenburg, in Germany. He studied architecture, archæology, and the history of art in Berlin, Munich, and Vienna. Before he was thirty years old he had dug at Assos and on the island of Lesbos. In 1887 he dug in Babylonia at Surgul and El-Hibba, later in Syria, southern Italy, and Sicily, and again in Syria in 1894.

From his fortieth to his forty-third year he was employed, most unhappily, as a teacher in the architectural school of Görlitz; then in 1898, aged forty-three, he began the excavation of Babylon.

Koldewey was an unusual man, and in the eyes of his professional colleagues a very dubious kind of scientist. His great love for archæology enabled him to overlook the fact that its findings, as a rule, were embalmed by specialists in a dead, dry style utterly foreign to his lively nature. He was ever susceptible to the charm of his surroundings and the thousand amusing incidents of everyday, and his archæological passion never hindered his looking about him long and hard at land and people wherever he went. Nothing could stopper the wellspring of his humor.

The learned archæologist, Koldewey, wrote innumerable tumbling little rhymes out of sheer joie de vivre. It was also his waggish habit to compose quirksome aphorisms in verse. At fifty-two the world-famous professor wrote this New Year's greeting:

*Dunkel sind des Schickals Wege,*
*ungewiss der Zukunft Stern,*
*eh' ich mich zu Bette lege,*
*trink ich einen Kognak gern!*

(In darkness lie the ways of fate,
The future is a mystery deep,
I like to drink a cognac straight,
Before I lay me down to sleep!)

He also wrote countless letters that more earnest scholars looked at askance, thinking them unworthy of the archæological profession. He reported on an Italian journey in this manner:

"Outside of digging, nothing much ever happens in Selinus [in Sicily]. At one time, however, the devil was on the rampage in these parts. . . . As far as the eye could see, the undulating littoral shone with the fruit of the field, orchard, and vine. And all this opulence belonged to the Greeks of Selinus, who for a couple of centuries enjoyed it all in peace and mutual understanding. This lasted until about 409, at which date, as a consequence of a quarrel with the neighboring Elymi of Segesta, the Carthaginians arrived on the scene. Hannibal Gisgon directed his battering rams against the walls of the horrified Selinusians. This was a sticky bit of business on Hannibal's part, in view of the fact that, shortly before, the Selinusians had fought on the Carthaginian side. But Hannibal forced open the neglected walls, and after a terrible nine-day street fight, in which the ladies of the town took vigorous part, 16,000 dead accumulated in the thoroughfares. The Carthaginian barbarians robbed and plundered and rousted through places profane and holy, their belts decorated with lopped-off hands and other abominable trophies. From this episode Selinus has not recovered to this day. Because of it rabbits hop freely through the streets. And because of it, too, I suppose, we have rabbit to eat of an evening now and then. These specimens are shot by Signor Gioffré, and are roasted for us as we bathe our archæologically wearied bodies in the broadly rushing surf of the ever restless sea."

When Nineveh was elevated to the rank of capital and commenced to figure prominently in Mesopotamian history, the city of Babylon had already been a capital for thirteen centuries. In fact, it had reached the peak of power and arrogance about a thousand years before, under Hammurabi, the lawgiver.

When Nineveh was destroyed, it was destroyed with a thoroughness that inspired Lucian to have his Mercury say to Charon: "My good ferryman, Nineveh is so completely destroyed that one cannot say where it stood, for not a trace of it remains." This was not so with Babylon, which was rebuilt after being razed. The general Nabopolassar created a new Babylonian Empire and made Babylon its capital. His son, Nebuchadnezzar II, again led the Babylonians to the heights of power

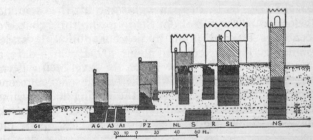

Cross section of walls fortifying north side of the south citadel of Babylon. On the middle wall of the three with battlements, a warrior has been drawn to provide a scale. A1 and A3: Nabopolassar's Walls; G1: Walls of Imgur-Bel's Tomb; SL: South Brick Wall; S: Wall of Sargon.

and splendor. The city outlasted Nineveh by seventy-three years before falling into the hands of Cyrus, the Persian.

When in 1899 Koldewey struck his spade into the east side of the mound of Kasr, the citadel of Babylon, he, unlike Botta and Layard, was acquainted in general with the history buried in the great piles of debris. The excavations at Khorsabad, Nimrud, and Kuyunjik and, above all, the huge library of Assurbanipal had yielded considerable information about the peoples and rulers of the estuary region of the two great rivers. Which Babylon would arise from the earth as Koldewey dug it free: the primeval Babylon of Hammurabi, the eleventh King of the Amurru dynasty, or a younger Babylon, reconstructed after its fearful devastation at the hands of Sennacherib?

Koldewey was aware in January 1898, though the matter had not been officially sealed, that he was going to be assigned to the supervision of the Babylonian excavations. At the time, however, he was merely reconnoitering the different mounds of rubble. During this period he sent a report on Babylon to the directors of the Royal Museum in Berlin. "In any case," he wrote to them from Baghdad, "chiefly works from the period of Nebuchadnezzar will be found there" (that is, at Kasr). Was he setting his sights too high? His jubilation when his commission finally came through allays this suspicion. And presently rich finds stilled all doubts whatsoever.

On April 5, 1899 he wrote: "I have been digging for fourteen days, and the whole business is a complete success." His first strike was the tremendous wall of Babylon. Along this wall he found innumerable fragments of reliefs—sculptured lion teeth, tails, claws, and eyes; human feet, beards, eyes; the legs of a slender-boned species of animal, probably a gazelle; and carved boar's teeth. Along one stretch of wall measuring only 25.6 feet in length he found a thousand fragments. Since he estimated the total length of the broken relief as 960 feet, he wrote in the same letter cited above: "I am counting [on finding] some 37,000 fragments."

We have Herodotus to thank for our most graphic description of Babylon, him and Ctesias, the physician-in-ordinary of Artaxerxes II. The greatest marvel of Babylon as reported by both these historians was the city wall. The dimensions which Herodotus assigned to this structure were thought for two thousand years to be the usual exaggerations of the professional traveler of olden times. According to Herodotus, the composite walls were broad enough to accommodate the passage from opposite directions of two chariots, each drawn by four horses.

Koldeway wasted no time getting at these famous walls. The digging was extremely difficult, harder by far than at any other excavation site in the world. Whereas everywhere else on the mound of Kasr the masses of rubble lay only six, nine, and up to nineteen feet deep, at the walls the litter was piled 38 feet, and sometimes as much as 77 feet or more deep. All this heavily packed cover had to be removed. For more than a decade and a half Koldewey dug steadily with a force of more than two hundred workers.

His first triumph was his demonstration that Herodotus' description of the walls of Babylon had not been greatly overdrawn. (Observe how often we encounter such confirmation. Schliemann showed that there was much truth in Homer and Pausanias; Evans

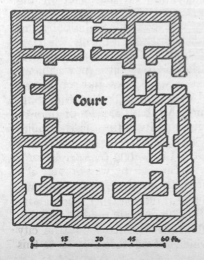

Ground plan of a Babylonian house. The notched arrangement on the front side goes back to the time when wooden beams were used, the projections then serving as end-supports. This architectural feature, though it no longer had any practical meaning, was carried over into stone construction.

demonstrated the kernel of truth in the Minotaur legend; and Layard the literal accuracy of certain Biblical descriptions.)

Koldewey laid bare a wall 22.4 feet thick, made of common brick. Next, 38.4 feet outside it, came another wall of brick, this 25 feet thick. Then there was still another wall of brick originally lining the inner side of the citadel fosse, this last wall likewise of kiln brick, and 12 feet thick. The fosse, during times of danger, had been flooded.

The space between the walls had apparently been filled with earth up to the rim of the outer bastion, so forming a path wide enough to accommodate four span of horses abreast. Guards patrolled the walls, and every 160 feet there were watchtowers. Koldewey estimated that the inner wall had 360 of these towers, and according to Ctesias there were 250 of them on the outer wall.

Koldewey had excavated the largest citadel the world had ever seen. The walls showed that Babylon had been the largest city of the Middle East, even larger than Nineveh. Indeed, if one thinks of a city in the medieval sense of being a "walled dwelling-place," Babylon, even to this day, was the largest of all cities of the type.

"I caused a mighty wall to circumscribe Babylon in the east," wrote Nebuchadnezzar. "I dug its moats; and its escarpments I built out of bitumen and kiln brick. At the edge of the moat I built a powerful wall as high as a hill. I gave it wide gates and set in doors of cedarwood sheathed with copper. So that the enemy, intending evil, would not threaten the sides of Babylon, I surrounded them with mighty waters as the billows of the sea flood the land. Their passage was as the passage of the great sea, the waters of salt. In order that no one might break through by way of the moat, I heaped up a heap of earth beside it, and surrounded it with quay walls of brick. This bastion I strengthened cunningly, and of the city of Babylon made a fortress."

The Citadel of Babylon must have been impregnable to all means of assault known at the time. And yet it is a historic fact that Babylon was taken. There is only one explanation: the enemy conquered from within, not from without. Enemies were constantly threatening, the internal politics of the city were in a state of turmoil, and there were always fifth columnists ready to let in the enemy as liberators. In this fashion the greatest fortress on earth finally fell.

Yes, Koldewey found the Babylon of Nebuchadnezzar. It was Nebuchadnezzar, he whom Daniel exhorted as "king of kings" and "head of gold," who commenced the reconstruction of the city on a monumental scale: the restoration of the Temple Emach on the fortress height, of the temples called E-sagila and Ninurta, and the older Temple of Ishtar at Merkes. He also restored the walls of the Arachtu Canal and built the first stone bridge over the Euphrates. He dug the Libil-higalla Canal, finished the construction of the South Citadel and its palaces, and decorated the Gate of Ishtar with gaily enameled animal reliefs.

Whereas Nebuchadnezzar's predecessors had used sun-baked bricks, which soon deteriorated in wind and weather, he generally used properly fired brick, particularly in his fortifications. If older Mesopotamian structures have left little trace beyond great heaps of rubble, this is due to the fact that they were made of perishable material. Nebuchadnezzar's buildings, however, which were made of much harder stuff, also met the same fate. But in this case they were demolished, through the centuries, by local inhabitants who wanted the

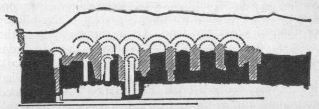

Cross section through arches which, according to Koldewey, very probably held up the "Hanging Gardens of Semiramis (or of Babylon)."

bricks for new construction, just as the temples of heathen Rome were razed during the Middle Ages for papal works. The modern city of Hilleh and several neighboring villages are built out of Nebuchadnezzar's bricks. The King's stamp is visible on them. Even a modern dam that diverts the waters of the Euphrates into the Hindiyye Canal is made largely of the same bricks that the people of ancient Babylon once trod. When at some future date the dam has fallen into desuetude, excavators may well be misled into thinking that they have hit on another of Nebuchadnezzar's works.

The Citadel of Babylon contained a whole complex of palaces, covering a considerable area. Nebuchadnezzar was forever adding new structures, for those already built, in his opinion, were "unworthy of the royal dignity." With its lavish decoration, its splendidly enameled and brightly shining brick reliefs, the Citadel could truly claim to be a wonder of the world, a miracle of cool, strange, barbaric splendor. Nebuchadnezzar, moreover, declared that he had built the whole in fifteen days, a statement that was credulously accepted as the truth for many centuries.

Of this group three works unearthed by Koldewey are of particular interest: a garden, a tower, and a street.

One day in the northeast corner of the South Citadel Koldewey found an arched structure which he at once recognized as something out of the ordinary, and which to this very day is still considered to be unique. In the first place, here were the first cellar spaces discovered at Babil, oldest part of the metropolis. Secondly, they were the first examples of vaulted construction to appear in Babylonian architecture. Thirdly, among these ruins was a well, made in the form of a triple shaft. After a great deal of thought, though not even then with absolute certainty, Koldewey identified the triple shaft as a draw-well that once, in its original state—of course the machinery had long since disappeared—had been provided with a chain pump to furnish a continuous supply of water. Fourthly, building stone had been used in the construction of the arches, as well as the customary bricks. In all Babylon there was only one other instance of stone construction; this was located at the north wall of the Kasr.

Considering all the features of this curious structure, Koldewey visualized an installation that, for the times, showed unusually fine technical and architectonic planning. Evidently the arches had served a special purpose.

In a lucky hour, Koldewey guessed what this vaulted building had been. Throughout the whole literature concerning Babylon, in Josephus, Diodorus, Ctesias, and Strabo and in all the cuneiform inscriptions relating to the "wicked city" deciphered up to that time, there were only two mentions, both emphatic, of the use of stone. One reference involved the north wall of the Kasr—where Koldewey had already found stone—the other the "Hanging Gardens of Semiramis."

Had Koldewey discovered them, those shining gardens, renowned through the ages for their beauty, numbered among the Seven Wonders of the World, and immemorially linked with the name of the legendary Semiramis?

Koldewey's instinctive belief that the Hanging Gardens of Babylon actually had been found evoked moments of feverish tension at the diggings. Everyone connected with the job debated the matter, on and off the diggings. Everybody was looking forward to the moment when the mystery of millennia would be clarified.

Koldewey again examined all the ancient sources. He weighed every sentence, every line, every word, he even ventured into the alien field of philology. Finally he felt that he was in a position to back up his claim. Yes, the arches must have held up the "Hanging Gardens." The well, a great novelty in its day, had been built to supply the plants with water.

But now the wonder of the thing shrank, the legendary trappings fell away. What did these Hanging Gardens amount to, if Koldewey's identification was correct? They had been magnificent, to be sure, an imposing arrangement on the roof of a cleverly designed building, and certainly a technical miracle for the period. Still, were they not rather insignificant in comparison with other Babylonian structures that the Greeks had not thought to include among the wonders of the world?

Moreover, all our information on the legendary Semiramis is questionable. Mostly it comes from Ctesias, who is noted for his powers of invention. According to Ctesias, the giant structure at Behistun built by Darius represents Semiramis surrounded by a hundred lifeguards. According to Diodorus, Semiramis, after being abandoned as a child, was fed by doves, grew up to marry a royal counselor, was later taken from her husband by the King, wore a garment "that did not show whether she was man or women," and finally, after handing over the royal authority to her son, flew out of the palace in the form of a dove, in which shape she entered directly into immortality.

In Genesis xi, 3–4, it is written of the Tower of Babel:

"And they said one to another, Go to, let us make brick, and burn them thoroughly. And they had brick for stone, and slime had they for mortar. And they said, Go to, let us build us a city and a tower, whose top may reach unto heaven; and let us make us a name, lest we be scattered abroad upon the face of the whole earth."

Koldewey actually excavated only the great base of the Tower, which none the less had once existed, as described in the Bible. The original structure was probably razed as early as the reign of Hammurabi, and at a later date another "tower" was built in memory of the first. Nabopolassar left these words to enlighten us: "At that time Marduk commanded me to build the Tower of Babel, which had become weakened by time

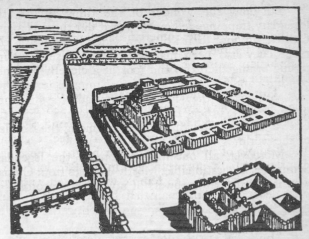

The Babylonian ziggurat of Etemenanki, the temple grounds, and the bridge over the Euphrates. A reconstruction.

and fallen into disrepair; he commanded me to ground its base securely on the breast of the underworld, whereas its pinnacles should strain upwards to the skies." Nebuchadnezzar, Nabopolassar's son, supplemented this announcement by saying: "To rise up the top of E-temen-an-ki that it might rival heaven, I laid to my hand."

The original Tower rose up in a series of enormous terraces. Herodotus describes a series of eight superimposed stages, each one somewhat smaller than the one below it. The uppermost terrace formed the base of a temple that looked out far over the land. (Actually there were seven of these terraces.)

The Tower was built in the hollow known as "Sachn," or "the pan." "Our Sachn, however," Koldewey writes, "is nothing but a contemporary simulacrum of the ancient sacred precinct where was built the ziggurat of 'Etemenanki,' the 'House of the Foundation of Heaven and Earth,' that is, the Tower of Babel. The sacred zone was surrounded by a wall, with all manner of buildings connected with the cult [of Marduk] backing up to it." (*Ziggurat, zikurat, ziggura* are variations of the name for the Sumerian-Babylonian staged pyramids, or temple towers, and come from the Assyrio-Babylonian word *ziqquratu,* meaning pinnacle, or mountain top.)

The base of the Tower was 288 feet on a side, the total height of Tower and temple also 288 feet. The first stage was 105.6 feet in height; the second, 57.6 feet; the third, fourth, fifth, and sixth, 19.2 feet each; and the Temple of Marduk 48 feet in height. The temple housed the most important god in the Babylonian pantheon. The walls of the temple were plated with gold, and decorated with enameled brickwork of a bluish hue, which glittered in the sun, greeting the traveler's eye from afar.

"But what are all these written descriptions in comparison with a first-hand impression of the ruins, however badly damaged they may be?" Koldewey writes. "The colossal massif of the Tower, which the Jew of the Old Testament considered to be the epitome of human arrogance, set amid the haughty palaces of the priests, capacious storehouses, innumerable exotic spaces —white walls, bronze gates, threatening circumambient fortifications with tall portals and a forest of a thousand towers—all this must have made a staggering impression of greatness, might, and abundance seldom seen elsewhere in the great Babylon kingdom."

Every large Babylonian city had its ziggurat, but none compared with the Tower of Babel. Fifty-eight million bricks went into the Tower's construction, and the whole landscape was dominated by its terraced mass.

The Tower of Babel was built by slaves. Here, too, overseers cracked their whips, as in the building of the Egyptian pyramids. In one respect, however, the situation was basically different. An Egyptian king built his pyramid in the course of a single lifetime, for the egocentric purpose of housing his mummy and his *ka*; the staged towers were built by generations of rulers:

what the grandfather began, the grandson was still carrying on. When the Egyptian pyramids deteriorated, or when they were desecrated and robbed, not a hand was lifted to restore them or to replenish the stolen treasures within the burial chamber; but the Babylonian ziggurats were repeatedly restored and redecorated.

For the rulers who "laid to their hands" on the construction of the ziggurats were building for everyone, not for themselves alone. The ziggurats were public shrines, the goal of processions of thousands marching to honor Marduk, greatest of the gods. What a picture it must have been when the marchers streamed through the city! The lower temple housed the god in a likeness half animal, half human, made of pure gold, seated on a throne beside a large table of pure gold and with a footstool of the same precious stuff. According to the description found in Herodotus, the total weight of statue and accoutrements amounted to 800 talents—800 talents of pure gold, worth roughly $24,000,000 at present values. In one of the priestly houses the "ur-talent" was found, a stone duck. According to the inscription chiseled on it, it was "a true talent." Its weight was 29.68 kilograms, or 66 pounds. On this scale the statue of Marduk with its accessories—if Herodotus can be credited with the truth—weighed about 23,700 kilograms, or 26.07 tons. Of pure gold!

What a spectacle, then, when the crowd in broad procession mounted the gigantic stone steps leading up to the first terrace level, 105.6 feet high! Meanwhile the priestly van of the pilgrimage would have reached the middle of the third-story flight, whence they proceeded by way of additional secret flights of stairs to the peak of the Tower, where stood the shrine of Marduk.

The glazed brickwork of the topmost temple was a deep, gleaming blue. Herodotus saw the shrine about the year 458 B.C.; that is, about one hundred and fifty years after the completion of the whole ziggurat, while it was still in a good state of repair. In contrast to the "temple below," the "temple on high" did not contain a statue of the god. There was nothing in it but a large couch, "handsomely furnished"—all highborn Mesopotamians, as well as Greeks and Romans, reclined while eating—and near the couch a gilded table. This holy of holies was not open to the common people, for within the precincts hovered Marduk himself, whose gaze could not have been endured by the ordinary mortal. No one but a chosen woman lived there, to provide pleasure for the god according to his fancy. "They say, too," Herodotus cautiously remarks, "that the god himself visits the temple and lies down upon its couch— but that does not seem believable to me."

Occupying the walled space below the Tower were the buildings where pilgrims from distant parts were housed while preparing for the procession. In this same area were also located the houses given over to the priests of Marduk. They, being the servants of a god who crowned the Babylonian kings, undoubtedly wielded great power. The courtyard precincts lying about Etemenanki may be thought of as a sort of Babylonian Vatican, though darker in aspect and of cyclopean motif.

Tukulti-Ninurta, Sargon, Sennacherib, and Assurbanipal stormed Babylon and destroyed the shrine of Marduk, Etemenanki, the Tower of Babel.

Nabopolassar and Nebuchadnezzar rebuilt the Tower. When, long after Nebuchadnezzar's death, in 539 B.C., the city was conquered by Cyrus, the Persian, he was the first to spare the great temple ziggurat. Being of younger mentality, in the historical sense, he was so fascinated by the colossality of the structure that he not only forbore from destroying the Tower, but had the monument built over his grave fashioned in the shape of a miniature ziggurat, or little Etemenanki.

Nevertheless, once more the Tower was brought crashing down. Xerxes, the Persian, reduced it to rubble, a heap of ruins that Alexander the Great inspected on his expedition into India. Alexander, like Cyrus, was entranced by the sight. For two months he put ten thousand men to work clearing away the debris, and for a time assigned his whole army to the task, expending, according to Strabo's report, some 600,000 work days on the project.

Twenty-two centuries later a Western scholar stood on the same spot. Unlike Alexander, he was seeking knowledge, not fame, and his command consisted of 250 rather than 10,000 men. Yet in eight years of unremitting labor he caused 800,000 work days to be expended on the task of reconstruction. Through Koldewey's effort Babylon was restored to a fair approximation of its original aspect—an architectural complex unparalleled.

The ancients had thought of the Hanging Gardens as one of the wonders of the world, and even today the Tower of Babel is remembered as the very symbol of human vainglory. Now Koldewey opened up another part of the city, already known through inscriptions, but as yet outside the pale of direct knowledge.

Koldewey excavated only one street in this sector, but this street turned out to be the most splendid thoroughfare of the ancient world, greater than any Roman way, greater perhaps than any avenue of modern times, if splendor is not gauged by length. The street's primary function was not to accommodate daily traffic, but to serve as a processional path dedicated to the great lord Marduk, when he was worshipped by the entire population of the city, including Nebuchadnezzar, at the Tower of Babel.

Work on the processional street must have continued without interruption during the forty-three years of Nebuchadnezzar's reign. Nebuchadnezzar described the origin and use of Procession Street in this manner: "Aibur-shabu, the street of Babylon, I filled with a high fill for the procession of the great lord Marduk, and with Turminabanda stones and Shadu stones I made this Aibur-shabu fill for the procession of his godliness, and linked it with those parts which my father had built, and made the way a shining one."

That is exactly what it was: Marduk's Procession

Street. At the same time it was integrated with the defenses of the city. For the street was constructed in the form of a tremendous trench; neither to the right nor to the left could the eye roam freely. Both sides of the deep way were hemmed in by formidable walls, 22.4 feet in height. Since the Sacred Way of Babylon ran

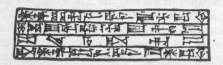

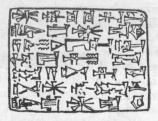

Nebuchadnezzar's brick seals. The text was repeated on each of the millions of bricks used in building the royal structures. The text reads: "Nebuchadnezzar, King of Babylon, guardian of E-Sagila and Egida, son of Nabopolassar, King of Babylon."

gullylike from the outer city walls to the Gate of Ishtar (the Ishtar-sakipatebisha of the inscriptions), which offered primary access to the interior Citadel of Babylon, any enemy aiming to storm the gate had to approach it by way of this sunken road—whereupon the road became a death trap.

The daunting effect of this stony gorge on all would-be attackers must have been heightened (especially at a time when the popular imagination teemed with monsters and daemons of all kinds) by the parade of about 120 lions, each nearly seven feet long, adorning the walls in colored glazed reliefs, and seeming to stride toward the enemy. In splendor and pride they stalked the length of the frieze—maws gaping to bare their teeth—with white or yellow pelts, yellow or red manes, against a background of light or dark blue glazes. The avenue itself was 73.6 feet wide.

In its center massive blocks of limestone more than a yard square rested on a base of brick covered with asphalt. Its sides were edged with breccia slabs about half the size of the limestone blocks, veined red and white, their angular interstices also filled in with asphalt. On its buried side each slab bore the following inscription:

> "Nebuchadnezzar, King of Babylon, Son of Nabopolassar, King of Babylon, am I. The road of Babel I have paved with Shadu slabs for the procession of the great lord Marduk. Marduk, Lord, grant eternal life."

The Gate of Ishtar resembled this kind of language. To this day the remains of its walls, some forty feet high, are the most impressive sight left of Babylon. They were once two enormous gatehouses, each with two prominent towers. Wherever one looked one was dazzled by the multicolored images of sacred beasts worked into the walls—about 575 by Koldewey's estimate. This terrifying host, in brilliant colors against a

blue background, must have fascinated and thoroughly
awed anyone approaching the might of the royal establishment behind such a gate.

It was not the lion, identified with the goddess herself, that adorned the Gate of Ishtar, but the bull, sacred to Ramman (or Adad), the weather god, and the
"Sirrush"—we really have no adequate name for the
dragon or serpent-griffon that was sacred to Marduk,
himself the ruler of the gods. Sirrush was four-footed,
long-legged, with talons on his hind paws. The long
neck of his scaly body ended in a large-eyed, flat snake-
head with straight vertical horns and a split tongue
darting forward. Such was the dragon of Babylon.

Once more a Biblical truth had been freed from
the overlays of legend. When the prophet Daniel had
been miraculously saved by Yahweh in the lion's den of
Babel, he had served to prove the impotence of the
dragon god against his own, "the living God," of future
millennia.

The "Great Lord Marduk,"
highest of the gods. At his
feet, the animal sacred to
him, the "Sirrush," or
dragon of Babylon.

"It may well be imagined," says Koldewey, "that the priests of E-sagila captured some sort of dragon-like animal, a reptile, perhaps, maybe the arval, which is found in this region, and kept him in the twilit temple room where he was exhibited as a living Sirrush. It is not surprising that the 'deity' [as described in the Apocrypha] should turn his head away from the little 'fowl' that Daniel had prepared for him out of hair and asphalt."

What a sight the great New Year procession along the street of Marduk must have been! Koldewey tries to capture the scene. "Once I saw the silver image, larger than life, of the Virgin Mary," he says, "laden with rings, precious stones, gold, and silver as votive offerings, being carried by fourteen men on a litter out through the portal of the Syracuse Cathedral. It seemed to float high over the heads of the teeming throng as it was brought forth, to the accompaniment of ecstatic music and the crowd's stormy prayers, into the Gardens of the Stonecutters. A procession in honor of Marduk, I think, must have looked the same when the god was carried in triumph out of E-sagila, perhaps through the peribolos (enclosed court) and along the great Procession Street."

Surely this analogy is inadequate. The procession of Marduk—we know the rite fairly well—must have been more violent, more forceful, more ostentatious and barbaric, entailing as it did the transport of the lesser gods from the "Chamber of Fate" in the Temple E-sabila as far as the banks of the Euphrates, where they were prayed to for three days before being triumphantly returned to their homes.

Babylon's depopulation and decline began under the rule of the Parthians. The great buildings lapsed into ruin. During the Sassanid period, A.D. 226–636, people were still living on the debris of the ancient palaces. By the Arabic Middle Ages nothing but huts were left at Babylon, a condition that continued until the twelfth century of our era.

Today one's gaze sweeps over a Babylon reawakened by Koldewey, over ruins, shining fragments, remains of former splendors. What are the words of the prophet Jeremiah?

"Therefore the wild beasts of the desert with the wild beasts of the islands shall dwell there, and the owls shall dwell therein: and it shall be no more inhabited for ever; neither shall it be dwelt in from generation to generation."

# 24/WOOLLEY:
# THE OLDEST CULTURE IN THE WORLD

How many of us realize that our superstitious impulse to turn back when a black cat crosses our path stems from the people of old Babylon? Do they come to mind when we look at the twelve divisions on our watch face, when we buy eggs by the shock (sixty), when we look up at the stars to read our fate in their movements and conjunctions?

We should be so reminded, for a part of our thinking and feeling derives from Babylon. More accurately: from Babylonia, as a geographic entity, though not necessarily from the Babylonians as such.

As we get to know more about the history of mankind, the time comes when we begin to feel the faint breath of the eternal wafted to us across the great gap of the years. We begin to see glimmerings of evidence that little human experience during five thousand years of history has actually been lost. We see, too, that often what was deemed good is now deemed bad, what once was true is now false. Regardless, the forces of the past still live on and exert their influence on us, though we may not be consciously aware of this. It is frightening to realize in full depth what it means to be a human being: that is, to realize that we are all embedded in the flux of generations, whose legacy of thought and feeling we irrevocably carry along with us. Most of us never become aware of the importance of this heritage that man alone of all mammals lugs forward through time. And seldom have we any notion how to make the most of our given burden.

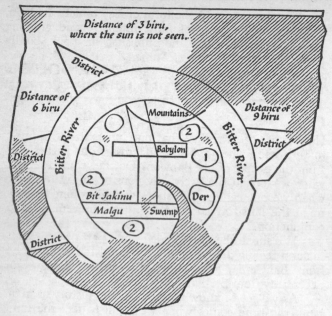

Babylonian map. 1: Assyria. 2: City. "Biru" is a linear measure giving distance between "districts." Bitter River, made up of ground water, sea, and the "heavenly ocean" (rain), flows in a circle about the land.

It was an astounding experience for the archæologists when, so to speak with every turn of their spades, they found new data showing how much in our thinking and feeling, in our conscious and unconscious, had already been thought and felt in Babylon. But the excavators were thunderstruck when evidence piled up that the lore of Babylon had been inherited from a people much older than the Semitic Babylonians, older, indeed, than the Egyptians.

In 1946 the American scholar Samuel Noah Kramer began to publish his translations of documents left behind by this people in the form of clay tablets. In 1956, after twenty-six years of most intensive and grueling labors of decipherment, he published his book, boldly entitled *History Begins at Sumer*. In this book he presented the fruit of his investigations, disencumbered of scholarly impedimenta, as a straightforward story. And he told it wittily. He established no fewer than twenty-seven historical "firsts" discovered or achieved or recorded by this people; nor did he hesitate to use the most up-to-date terms in naming them. They are as follows:

1. The First Schools.
2. The First Case of "Apple-Polishing."
3. The First Case of Juvenile Delinquency.
4. The First "War of Nerves."
5. The First Bicameral Congress.
6. The First Historian.
7. The First Case of Tax Reduction.
8. Law Codes: The First "Moses."
9. The First Legal Precedent.
10. The First Pharmacopoeia.
11. The First "Farmer's Almanac."
12. The First Experiment in Shade-tree Gardening.
13. Man's First Cosmogony and Cosmology.
14. The First Moral Ideals.
15. The First "Job."
16. The First Proverbs and Sayings.
17. The First Animal Fables.
18. The First Literary Debates.
19. The First Biblical Parallels.
20. The First "Noah."
21. The First Tale of Resurrection.
22. The First "St. George."
23. Tales of Gilgamesh: The First Case of Literary Borrowing.
24. Epic Literature: Man's First Heroic Age.
25. The First Love Song.
26. The First Library Catalogue.

27. World Peace and Harmony: Man's First
Golden Age.

In reading this list, one might be prone to the
suspicion that it is a case of an enthusiast forcing modern
terminology upon social events that took place thousands of years ago under quite different skies. But when
one reads Kramer's brilliant translations themselves,
they are truly breathtaking. The lamentations of the
father about his delinquent son, and about the youth
in general going to the bad, recorded on seventeen clay
tablets three thousand seven hundred years ago (but
many centuries older than that in their original form),
for example, read as though they might be contemporary utterances of a father and son from one's immediate neighborhood. The text begins with the father's
question: "Where did you go?" Answer: "I did not go
anywhere!"

The discovery of the existence of these older races
was one of the human intellect's most shining accomplishments. It evolved incidentally from the reflections
of the cryptologists who worked on the decipherment
of the cuneiform script. The existence of these mysterious people was, as it were, extrapolated.

One of astronomy's greatest triumphs was accurately to
predict that a certain planet, as yet unnamed and never
seen by human eye, would appear at a certain place in
the sky at a definite time, following a prescribed path,
which event actually took place.

And something of this same sort happened when
a Russian chemist, recognizing a hidden order in the
physical elements discovered up to his day, arranged
them systematically in a table, and on the basis of the
gaps in this table predicted the existence of as yet unknown elements.

It was the same, too, in the anthropological field
when, on a purely theoretical basis, Haeckel constructed
an intermediate form between the anthropoid apes and
*Homo sapiens*, which he named Pithecanthropus. This

"missing link," Pithecanthropus, was actually found by Eugene Dubois in 1892 on the island of Java, and showed a close correspondence in detail to the Haeckel construct.

When the cuneiform specialists, after the difficulties of decipherment had been solved by Rawlinson's successors, were able to concentrate on such special questions as the origin of the characters, linguistic relationships, and the like, their investigations in divers curious directions led them to the following theory:

The multiple meanings of the Babylonian and Assyrian cuneiform groups could not be explained *aus sich selber*—that is, idiocratically. Such a complicated writing system, such a mixture of alphabetical, syllabic, and pictographic scripts could not have developed spontaneously when the Babylonians suddenly appeared in the forefront of history. The written language of the Babylonians must have been handed down from an earlier age. As the results of hundreds of accumulated linguistic analyses, the idea took shape that the cuneiform script had not been invented by the Semitic Babylonians and Assyrians, but rather by another, and very probably non-Semitic, people from the eastern highlands. Up to this point, however, the actual existence of such a people had never been demonstrated by so much as a single find.

This was a very daring hypothesis. Yet as the years passed, the archæologists and language experts became so sure of its validity that they even went so far as to give their presumptive people a name, though not a single inscription had ever been found to serve as concrete evidence. Some called the precursors of the Babylonians the Akkadians; others, particularly a Franco-German, Jules Oppert, called them the Sumerians, and the latter name stuck. Both names were taken from the title of the earliest known ruler of the southern part of Mesopotamia, who had called himself "King of Sumer and Akkad."

This was the evolution of the theory, reduced to

its essentials. And as the planet, elements, and Pithecanthropus were duly found, traces of the mysterious people who had bequeathed a system of writing to the Babylonians and Assyrians were eventually brought to light. Was the legacy limited to a script? This seemed most unlikely. And it was not long before the discovery was made that the Sumerian culture adumbrated almost everything in Babylon and Nineveh.

This brings us again to Ernest de Sarzec, the French consular agent mentioned previously, another archæological "outsider." Before de Sarzec came to Mesopotamia he was completely ignorant of the problems and procedures of archæological excavation. His curiosity was aroused, however, by the ruins and mounds of the land between the two rivers, as Paul Émile Botta's had been some forty years before. But he had beginner's luck with his first hit-and-miss attempts, finding at the base of a mound at Telloh a statue of a hitherto unknown type. He continued to dig, found inscriptions, and eventually came upon the first traces of the "predicted" Sumerians.

The most precious piece that de Sarzec, together with other valuable articles, loaded aboard ship and sent to Paris and the Louvre was a statue in hard diorite of the provincial governor, or priest king, Gudea. It was carved in a style previously not known to exist in Mesopotamia. It was, to be sure, artistically related to other finds, yet at the same time it was more archaic and monumental. What excitement this find stirred up among archæologists! Even the most conservative Assyriologists had to admit that some of the newly discovered stone fragments dated back to 4000 and 3000 B.C., to a culture older than the Egyptian (see Plate XXI).

De Sarzec dug for four years, from 1877 to 1881. From 1888 to 1900 the Americans Hilprecht, Peters, Haynes, and Fisher excavated in Nippur and Fara. From 1912 to 1913 the Deutsche Orient-Gesellschaft worked at Erech, and later, in 1928, undertook new

Impression from a cylinder seal used by
Gudea of Lagash, one of the mighty provincial princes of early Babylonian times.

excavations. In 1931 an expedition sponsored by the
American School of Oriental Research dug under the
direction of Erich F. Schmidt, again at Fara.

Great buildings were uncovered, ziggurats that
were recognized as belonging as definitely to the temple
where they were found as the minaret to the mosque,
the campanile to the *chiesa*, the steeple to the church.
Inscriptions were found that made it possible to trace
the history of the Mesopotamian world back into the
very dawn of history. The discovery of this primitive
world was of the same importance for the understanding of Babylonia as the discovery of the Cretan-
Mycenæan culture had been for the understanding of
Greek antiquity.

There was one difference, however; the Sumerian
culture went much farther back in time. It seemed almost as if its beginnings coincided with the times described in Genesis. The Sumerians might well be the
same people, it was thought, who populated the earth
after the punitive deluge that wiped out all humankind but Noah and his kin.

Did not the epic of the demigod Gilgamesh, pieced
out by George Smith of the British Museum from the
million shards on the mound of Kuyunjik, record a
flood?

In the twenties of this century the English archæologist Leonard Woolley began to dig in the Biblical

Ur of Chaldea, home of Abraham. Eventually Woolley
was able to show that the great flood of the Gilgamesh
Epic and the Biblical deluge were identical, and that,
moreover, the Flood was a historic fact.

The history of Mesopotamia is not so much of a piece
as, for example, is that of Egypt. It shows a certain
similarity with the flow of the Greco-Roman culture.
In this complex a strange people came from afar and
set up bastions of their own culture in Tiryns and
Mycenæ, which in time were overrun by the barbaric
Achæans and Dorians who poured in from the north.
Out of centuries of give-and-take a true Hellenism
evolved. Similarly, Sumerian outlanders moved into the
delta of the Euphrates and Tigris, bringing with them
a mature culture, a system of writing, and a corpus of
law. They, too, were eventually extirpated by barbarians
after the passage of some centuries. Thereupon Babylonia grew up out of land richly manured with dead
and flourished where the kingdoms of Sumer and
Akkad once had stood.

Does not the Bible tell about the confusion of
tongues at the Tower of Babel? In Babylonia there
were, in fact, two official languages, the Sumerian and
the Semitic, though in the course of time the Sumerian
came to be used only in priestly and legal affairs. Then
waves of Amorites, Aramæans, Elamites, and Kassites
brought in new languages, and later the Lulubæans, the
Mitanni, and the Hittites introduced their dialects into
Assyria.

The first ruler to succeed in uniting a large part of
Mesopotamia under his scepter—the area ran from
Elam to the Taurus Mountains—was Sargon I (2360–
2305 B.C.). The legend of his birth brings to mind
Cyrus, Romulus, Krishna, Moses, and Perseus. His
mother, a virgin, put him in a container, sealed it with
pitch, and set it adrift on a stream. Akki, creator of
waters, raised the foundling to be a gardener, and later
the goddess Ishtar made him a king. For a long time it

was believed that Sharrukên ("legitimate king," Sargon) had never really existed. Today the fact has been established that Sargon did live and wield a memorable historical influence.

His dynasty lasted for one hundred years, then collapsed. Aggressive mountain people, particularly the Gutians, laid waste the land. City kingdoms competed

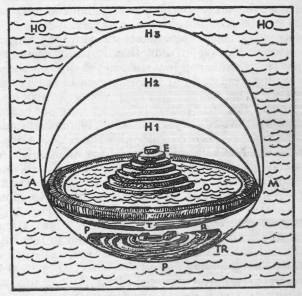

Reconstruction of the Babylonian idea of the shape of the world. E: Earth; H1, H2, H3: Heavens 1, 2, and 3; HO: Heavenly Ocean; O: Terrestrial Ocean; T: Bottom of Terrestrial Ocean; M: Morning (east), Sunrise Mountain; TR: Seven Walls and the Palace (P) of the Kingdom of the Dead.

for power. Various priest kings (*patesis, ishhakkus*) such as Ur-Bau and Gudea for a time gained wide influence in Ur and Lagash. Despite the political confusion, arts and techniques unfolded out of the Su-

merian heritage and attained a dynamic that still re-
verberates down through four thousand years of history.

It was Hammurabi of Babylon (about 1800 B.C. or
even a little later) who united the land through a series
of political and military coups into a country and culture that could claim the leadership of the Mesopotamian world. Hammurabi was much more than a simple warrior. Once seated on the throne, he had the
patience to wait for twenty-five years until his neighbor
and enemy, Rim-Sin of Larsa, had aged enough to be
easily struck down. Hammurabi was also the first great
lawgiver of history. "In order that the strong should not
oppress the weak, and that widows and orphans should
be rightly dealt with, in Babylon, even in the Temple
E-sagila . . . he had his precious words written on a
stele, and this stele placed before an image of himself
as the king of justice." (Even before Hammurabi's day
there had been other legal codifications of a sketchy
character. The kings of Isin and King Shulgi of Ur of
the Third Dynasty had all established fixed laws. And
when, in 1947, the American archæologist Francis
Steele fitted together four cuneiform fragments found
at Nippur, he found that he had discovered a section
of the legal code of King Lipit-ishtar.) King Hammurabi's great contribution, however, was to fuse local
laws and precepts into a comprehensive legal code of
nearly three hundred paragraphs. This code proved to
be an active influence on men's behavior long after the
Babylonian kingdom had fallen to pieces.

The tremendous impulsion that resulted in unifica-
tion exhausted the creative capacities of the Sumero-
Babylonian civilization for a long time thereafter. The
political power of the land became highly fragmented;
its economic hegemony, which under Kadashman-Enlil
I and Bunarbashi II had extended as far as Egypt,
began to decline. (In this latter regard the finding of
the correspondence between these two Babylonian
kings and the third and fourth Amenophis of Egypt
yielded much valuable information.) Even as the alien

rule of the Kassites was being broken, Aramæan Bedouins, and the Assyrians who poured in from the north, for the time being precluded any chance of building up a new "kingdom."

And again we see a striking developmental parallel between the Assyrio-Babylonian and the Greco-Roman cultures. The political power of Athens, its religion, art, and intellectual life, crumbled away and were absorbed into the technical and materialistic civilization of parvenu Rome. Exactly in this same fashion the culture of Babylonia and of its famous capital, Babylon, was reborn as "civilization" in newly rich Assyria and in Nineveh, a city standing in the same relation to Babylon as Rome to Athens.

Tukulti-Ninurta I (c. 1250 B.C.) was the first Assyrian to take a Babylonian king prisoner. Under Tiglath-Pileser I (c. 1100 B.C.), Assyria became a first-class power but attained such little stability that the nomadic Aramæans were able not only to take it unawares, but to settle down permanently on Assyrian territory. The new kingdom did not rise again until the reigns of Assurnasirpal (885–859 B.C.) and Salmanassar IV (781–772 B.C.), during which regnal intervals Assyrian armies forced their way to the shores of the Mediterranean, conquered all of Syria, and exacted tribute from Phœnician cities. To Assurnasirpal the Assyrian capital, Kalah, was indebted for its splendid dynastic palace, and Nineveh for its Temple of Ishtar. Semiramis (Shammuramat) reigned for four years. Her son, Adad-nirari III (810–782 B.C.), according to the principle that "Rome is worth a Mass," tried to introduce the Babylonian deities into Assyria. But it was not until the reign of Tiglath-Pileser III (known in the Bible as Pul), a remarkably resourceful usurper, that Assyria achieved the status of world power and could act accordingly. Under this same Tiglath-Pileser (745–727 B.C.) the boundaries of the Assyrian kingdom were extended from the Mediterranean to the Persian Gulf. Armenia and Persia were invaded and hitherto untamable peoples brought to heel. Damascus was also subdued, and a large section of northern Israel fell under Assyrian hegemony.

Scattered among the rulers mentioned above were many others of lesser importance. Their names and dates are known, but they do not merit being included in a brief survey.

The next King worthy of mention was Sargon II (722–705 B.C.), conqueror of the Hittites of Karkemish (Carchemish). Under his rule Assyria achieved perhaps the greatest degree of political cohesion in its history. Sargon II was the father of Sennacherib (705–681 B.C.), the mad destroyer of Babylon, and the grandfather of Esarhaddon (680–669 B.C.), who rebuilt Babylon, conquered the Cimmerians of the north, and in 671 B.C. took Egyptian Memphis, plundering it to fill the treasure chests of Nineveh. And finally there was Assurbanipal (668–626 B.C.), Sargon's great-grandson, who lost tributary parts of Egypt to the Pharaoh Psammetich (Psamtik) I, but with great energy and a keen sense for intrigue drove his brother, Saosduchin, King of Babylon, to commit suicide. In Nineveh, Assurbanipal founded the greatest library of remote antiquity, a collection not to be surpassed until Alexander's famous store of papyri had been assembled. Assurbanipal, despite his numerous military expeditions, is chiefly remembered as a man of peace.

Among the kings who followed Assurbanipal, Sinshar-ishkun (625–606 B.C.) went down in history as the ruler who lost control of the Assyrian kingdom. He was unable to cope with the ever more powerful onslaughts of the Medes and in his weakness allowed the armies to be led by Nabopolassar, the Chaldean, who proved to be a traitor. When the Medes were finally storming through the streets of Nineveh, Sin-shar-ishkun committed suicide, together with his wives, in the flames of the burning city, and destroyed his treasure. (According to Diodorus, who cites Ctesias, the treasure of Sin-shar-ishkun consisted of one hundred and fifty golden couches and as many golden tables, also ten million talents of gold, one hundred million talents of silver, and a great number of costly purple robes.)

Was this the end of Assyro-Babylonian history? In the person of the disloyal General Nabopolassar, Babylon came under a usurper's rule. Nabopolassar paved the way for his much greater son, Nebuchadnezzar II (604–562 B.C.), who became a "Cæsar" of the Mesopotamian region.

The might and splendor that now unfolded in Babylon was no longer indigenous; the tradition of the ancient city threw out roots in a new direction. The Babylonian matrix had been broken by the incursion of Assyrian Nineveh. Though the new Babylon apparently felt the influence of old cults, customs, and social forms, actually the carry-over did not completely heal the fracture of the older tradition. The New Babylonian kingdom, as we call it today, was a decadent civilization built on an old cultural base. Prolix memorials record Nebuchadnezzar's technical achievements—canals, gardens, dams, and innumerable buildings for uses both sacred and profane.

It is usual for signs of incipient decline to appear at the peak of any civilization. Six years after Nebuchadnezzar's death the dynasty was wiped out in a palace revolution. The last ruler, Nabunaid (Nabonidus) (555–539 B.C.), was a hypocritical dabbler in antiquities. He was burned to a cinder during the storming of the royal citadel by the Persians, after traitors had betrayed the city into the hands of Cyrus.

It was in the reign of Nebuchadnezzar that Mesopotamian culture drew its last great breath.

In 1911 Mrs. Winifred Fontana, wife of the British consul, had three young archæologists as guests in her home. She herself was an amateur painter, which explains her noting in her diary that ". . . all three [would make] very beautiful models." The three archæologists were David Hogarth, T. E. Lawrence, and Leonard Woolley.

Winifred Fontana, when asked in later years about

her impressions at the time, was so strongly influenced by the interim growth of Lawrence's reputation that she replied: "It was Lawrence who constantly drew my attention." A Syrian, also a guest at the consular house, was of the opposite opinion. "What an unhappy contrast *ce jeune Laurens* makes," he said of Lawrence, "with Monsieur Woolley, who is such a man of the world, and a *parfait gentilhomme*."

Much later, in 1927 and 1928, at which time he was forty-seven years old, the *"parfait gentilhomme"* began to excavate at the site of the city of Ur, legendary home of Abraham on the Euphrates. Before long he had turned up unusually rich finds identified with the people of Sumeria. There he discovered the "royal graves of Ur," and in them found valuable archæological treasures. More important than his finds of gold was the fact that he improved our fund of information on Babylonian prehistory to such a degree that this earliest segment of human culture took on real life and color (see Plate XXII).

Among the numerous finds two pieces were especially notable: the headdress of a Sumerian queen, and the so-called mosaic "standard of Ur." Most significant for our knowledge of mankind's earliest cultural experience, however, was a discovery that confirmed the historicity of one of the Bible's most famous stories. Finally, Woolley made still another find, this a particularly gruesome one, which for the first time threw light on previously unknown burial customs of five thousand years ago.

Woolley opened up the usual trenches in the mound of Ur, an operation preliminary to almost every archæological field investigation. At a depth of thirty-eight feet he came upon a layer of ashes, decayed brick, clay shards, and rubbish. The inhabitants of Ur had shoveled graves for their rulers in the layer of debris. In the grave of Queen Shub-ad he found a rich array of funerary gifts, including gold vessels and two models of Euphrates boats, one of copper, the other of silver,

The "mosaic standard of Ur," one of Leonard Woolley's most interesting finds. The drawing does not give any idea of the actual richness of detail. The original is a picture book of Sumerian life for the careful observer.

each nearly two feet in length. It was in this same grave that the headdress was found. On a thickly padded wig were arranged three wreaths made from lapis lazuli and carnelian. From the lowest of these three wreaths hung golden rings, from the middle one golden beech leaves, and to the topmost were attached willow leaves and golden flowers, these last in an erect position. Above, stuck into the wig, was a five-pointed comb, decorated with gold flowers and with lapis-lazuli inlay. Spiraled gold wires ornamented the temples of the wearer, and heavy gold earrings of half-moon shape hung down from the Queen's earlobes.

Katharine Woolley made a model of the head of Queen Shub-ad wearing the headdress. The arrangement of the Queen's hair was based on terra-cottas of a somewhat later epoch; the dimensions of the wig were gauged by measuring the gold ribbons of the headdress. This realistic model, now on exhibit at the University of Pennsylvania Museum in Philadelphia, gives a good idea how far æsthetic standards and the art of working precious metals had advanced more than four thousand years ago. Among the precious ornamental pieces found in the royal graves of Ur there were some specimens that Cartier's would not be ashamed to offer for sale.

The so-called mosaic "standard of Ur" was a highly
informative find. Woolley dates it 3500 B.C.; this standard consists of two rectangular panels about 22 inches
long by 11 inches wide, with two triangular extensions.
They were probably carried in parades and processions
atop a pole. They showed row upon row of tiny figures
fashioned of mother-of-pearl and mussel shell, inlaid
with lapis lazuli in asphalt on a wood base. Though far
from being as richly detailed as the Egyptian wall paintings in the tomb of the great landowner Ti, from which
Mariette learned so much about life in ancient Egypt,
the standard nevertheless yielded Woolley an abundance of facts about Ur and its society of 5,000 years
ago.

There is, first, a banquet scene (giving information
on dress and implements); then, servants and farmers
bringing animals (showing what domestic animals were
raised); a gang of prisoners; a line of warriors (with
weapons and the armor in use); and finally a number
of chariots, proving that it was the Sumerians who, at
the end of the fourth millennium B.C., introduced chariots into warfare—the same chariot contingents by
means of which vast empires from the Babylonian,
Assyrian, Persian to the Macedonian were all joined
and shattered in turn.

Then Woolley made a hair-raising discovery: the
royal graves of Ur contained the remains of corpses
other than those of the King and Queen, remains which
appeared to be the result of human sacrifice on a grand
scale. In one tomb chamber lay soldiers of the guard,
so identified by the copper helmets and spears found
with their bones. At the end of another chamber lay
nine ladies of the court, still wearing the elaborate gold
headdresses probably donned for the royal funeral rites.
By the entrance stood two heavy ox-carts—inside them
lay the drivers' bones, and beside the skeletons of the
bullocks lay the bones of the grooms.

In the grave of Queen Shub-ad (see Plate XXIII)
Woolley found ladies of the court lying in two parallel

rows. At the end of one of these rows lay a man's skeleton—that of the court harpist; his arm bones were still lying across his broken instrument, with its bull's head of gold and lapis lazuli, which he had evidently been holding fast even as he died. At the Queen's bier crouched the bodies of two women attendants, one at the head and one at the foot.

There could be only one explanation for all this: here the greatest possible sacrifice had been exacted of mortal men—their own lives. Woolley had discovered a scene of planned human sacrifice, probably carried out by priests intent on thus affirming the divinity of their King.

What conclusions did Woolley draw from these finds? "In no known text," he writes, "is there anything that hints at human sacrifice of this sort, nor had archæology discovered any trace of such a custom or any survival of it in a later age; if, as I have suggested above, it is to be explained by the deification of the early kings, we can say that in the historic period even the greater gods demanded no such rite: its disappearance may be an argument for the high antiquity of the Ur graves."

Woolley was anxious to get another step closer to this remote Sumerian past. He now proceeded to dig systematically at greater depths. Approximately forty feet down he came upon a layer of clay. This stratum was completely free from shards and rubbish, and not less than 8.2 feet thick.

Obviously Woolley had found an alluvial deposit, which could be best explained by the geologists. To lay down a deposit of clay 8.2 feet thick, at some time a tremendous flood must have inundated the land of Sumer. One could visualize the whole delta area being subjected to protracted rains, while exceptionally high tides and onshore winds backed up the waters of the Euphrates-Tigris estuary. In sum, as recorded in the seventh chapter of Genesis, the waters must have flowed over hill and vale, and "the same day were all the fountains of the great deep broken up, and the windows of heaven were opened. And the rain was upon the earth forty days and forty nights. . . . And the waters prevailed upon the earth an hundred and fifty days."

Woolley was on the verge of a stupendous deduction. When he took into account the correspondence between the Biblical story and the much older Gilgamesh Epic, when he consulted the lists of Sumerian kings (the flood came; and after the flood, kingship was sent down from on high), and when, moreover, he considered how often old legends and Biblical lore had been validated by Mesopotamian excavation, he could not but believe that the alluvial deposit had resulted from nothing else than the Deluge of Genesis.

Naturally, this actual flood, which gave rise to the Deluge as myth, did not destroy the whole human race with the exception of Ut-napishtim—Noah and family. It must have been an unusually severe example of the characteristic local inundations that periodically drown the Euphrates-Tigris delta region.

Woolley dated his finds in the royal graves of Ur as of the fortieth century B.C. Before his discoveries our knowledge of the period had been limited to legends and myths. Woolley brought this early epoch into the historical continuum. Later he even succeeded in documenting the existence of one of the kings of the period—one of the oldest kings, that is, among mankind.

The existence of the Sumerians was originally assumed on the basis of scientific deductions. Today their existence is no longer doubted; too many examples of their art and handicrafts are on exhibit in our museums. We still know practically nothing about their origins, however, and so once again must extrapolate as best we can.

One fact is beyond doubt: the Sumerians, a non-Semitic, dark-haired people—"black-headed" is the term for them in the inscriptions—were the last to enter the great delta of the Tigris and Euphrates. Before their arrival the land had been settled by two, probably different, Semitic tribes. But the Sumerians brought with them a superior culture, some of its basic elements already developed to their final form, which they imposed upon the barbaric Semites.

Where was the Sumerian homeland? Archæology has yet to answer this question.

The Sumerian language is somewhat similar to the ancient Turkish, or Turanian. That is all that is known

Reconstruction of a house in Ur.

about them, and everything else is pure hypothesis. People who habitually represented their gods as standing on mountains, who prayed to them from high places, and who for this purpose even built artificial hills, or ziggurats, on the plains of their adopted land, could not, it seems, have come from flat country. Could they have stemmed, perhaps, from the Iranian highlands, or from the Asiatic mountain country even farther to the east and north? This possibility is supported by the fact that the earliest Sumerian buildings excavated to date in Mesopotamia are constructed according to the principles of a wood architecture, which normally would develop only in heavily forested highlands.

And yet there can be no certainty; for this theory runs counter to some of the old Sumerian legends, which tell of a people who forced their way into Mesopotamia from the sea. And there are certain indicators to support the theory of a maritime origin.

After extensive research, Sir Arthur Keith concluded that: "One can still trace the ancient Sumerians eastwards among the inhabitants of Afghanistan and Baluchistan, until the Valley of the Indus is reached, some 1500 miles distant from Mesopotamia."

Hardly had this announcement been made when the remains of a highly developed culture were discovered in the course of excavations in the Indus Valley. Among the artifacts unearthed at this site, of particular interest were some rectangular stamp seals, identical in form, in the style of their impression, and in their inscriptions with seals found in Sumer.

Yet the question whence this mysterious "blackheaded" people came remains open. We must be patient, considering the hoary antiquity of their origin indicated by such scanty evidence of them as we have. If we consider the so-called king-lists as well, the prehistoric age from which they emerged recedes even farther.

All calendrical dating in early Babylon was related to some outstanding event that had taken place in years past. The first chronological fixing of the past occurred during the first dynasty of Isin (c. 2100 B.C.). The king-lists go back to this early period; they are schematic, yet archæologically valuable tables. There is also another, more elaborated version of the king-lists, far more recent (from the third to fourth centuries B.C.), identified with the Babylonian priest Berossos, who wrote in Greek.

According to these lists, the history of the Sumerians goes back to the creation of man. The Bible tells us that between Adam and the Deluge there were ten "mighty forefathers which were old." The Sumerians speak of their "primal kings," also ten in number. The Israelite forefathers boasted improbably long lifespans. Adam, who begot his first son at the age of a hundred and thirty years, is said to have lived for eight hundred years more. The great age of Methuselah has become a byword. Yet the life-spans of the ancient Sumerians, according to their legends, exceed these by far: according to one account, listing only eight of the ancestral kings, the total length of their reigns was 241,200 years; according to another, which lists all ten kings, it extended over 456,000 years.

Then came the Deluge. The progeny of Utnapishtim founded the human race anew. The kings of this period were listed by the Babylonian chroniclers writing about 2100 B.C. as real historical figures. However, since several of the rulers named were identified as gods or demigods in the contemporary legends, and the first dynasty after the Deluge, numbering twenty-three kings, was said to have reigned for a total of 24,510 years, three months, and three and a half days, it is not surprising that European archæologists could not take these lists seriously, especially since not a single document confirming a royal name earlier than the eighth dynasty had been found before the twentieth century.

But when Woolley saw the most ancient culture known coming to light layer by layer, he began to set a new value on the old king-lists. His situation was somewhat like that of Schliemann with respect to

Homer and Pausanias. Like that great dilettante, the professional archæologist also had his new faith confirmed by a lucky find.

At the mound of al-'Ubaid, near Ur in Chaldea, Woolley discovered a temple dedicated to the mother goddess Nin-Khursag. This structure was equipped with stairs, terraces, vestibule, and wooden columns inlaid with copper. It also contained rich mosaics, showing sculptured lions and deer. It was one of the oldest pieces of construction in the world in which notable size was coupled with artistic handling. Among other objects, some valuable, some worthless, Woolley found a golden bead.

And on this bead was an inscription that gave Leonard Woolley his first information on the builder of the temple. The name A-anni-padda was spelled out in perfectly legible characters.

Then Woolley found a limestone foundation-tablet, with an inscription on it in cuneiform writing confirming the dedication of the temple by "A-anni-padda, King of Ur, son of Mes-anni-padda, King of Ur."

Mes-anni-padda appeared in the king-lists as the founder of the third dynasty after the Flood, that is, at the head of the first dynasty of Ur. Accordingly one of the supposedly mythical kings had proved to be a real historical character.

This chapter on Sumerian excavations began by mentioning the superstition of the black cat, the "shock" (a lot or parcel of sixty pieces), and the duodecimal division of the clock face as common to the Mesopotamian ancients and ourselves. A line leads directly from the Sumerians down through the centuries to ourselves, though in places it is broken prismatically by the cultures that have lived and died in the long interim. The creative power of the Sumerian culture was extraordinary; its influence left a mark wherever it touched. The rich florescence of Babylon and Nineveh grew from Sumerian seed.

The Code of Hammurabi, inscribed on the great legal stele found at Susa, was nothing but an extension, research has disclosed, of the legal principles and customs of old Sumer. The astounding thing about this legal code from a modern point of view is the way it is governed by a clear and consistent concept of guilt. The purely juristic approach is stressed throughout, with consequent suppression of religious considerations. The vendetta, for example, which was an active feature of all later cultures and which continued to play a disruptive role in certain parts of Europe well into this century, was all but abolished by the Code of Hammurabi. The state—and this is the most modern aspect of the laws inscribed on the stele of Susa—replaced the individual as the avenger of injustice. Justice was harsh, and the many cruel physical punishments embodied in the code show all the earmarks of Oriental depotism. No matter, the objective tone of the Hammurabi Code set an example that was reflected in the codes of Justinian and Napoleon.

The Babylonian medical art, which was closely allied with magic—on this account the terms Babylonian and Chaldean have the connotation of "magician" in the Romance languages—came from Sumer. Babylonia had state-supported medical schools. In many cases the doctor's art was governed by religious prescripts. In other instances doctors were responsible to the state. Indeed, the Code of Hammurabi at times specifically regulated the physician's conduct. For instance, in paragraph 218 the penalty for a certain type of faulty practice was described in this fashion: "If a doctor operate on a man for a severe wound with a bronze lancet and cause the man's death, or open an abscess in the eye of a man with a bronze lancet and destroy the man's eye, they shall cut off his fingers." The gods and rituals of the Sumerians, who were star-worshippers, are often found under other names and in slightly altered guise in Babylonia and Assyria, and even in Athens and Rome at much later date.

A knowledge of the heavens and the movements of the stars reached the stage of an exact science in Babylonia. Babylonian astronomy provided the basis for a planetary world-picture, a calendar, and a system of time reckoning. The temple towers on the ziggurats were observatories as well as shrines. Babylonian priests reckoned the motion of the planet Mercury more accurately than Hipparchus or Ptolemy. Indeed, they succeeded in determining the lunar revolution within four seconds of the figure arrived at by the most elaborate technical means.

Babylonian mathematics derived from a fusion of the Sumerian sexagesimal and the Semitic decimal systems. The practical difficulties in calculation arising from this cross were circumvented by the use of reckoning tablets—antique slide rules. Despite their cumbersome arithmetic the Babylonians were able to express astonishingly large numerical values. In this regard it must be remembered that large numbers are of comparatively recent conception in the Western world. The Greeks, for example, to whom we accord such high mathematical-astronomical regard, still thought of the number 10,000 as a "large, uncountable aggregation." Not until the nineteenth century did the concept of a million become common in the West. By contrast, a cuneiform text found on the mound of Kuyunjik records a mathematical series the end product of which in our number system would be expressed as 195,955,- 200,000,000. This means, in other words, a number that did not again enter the realm of calculation until the days of Descartes and Leibniz.

Yet Babylonian mathematics was unquestionably infected with astrological lore and soothsaying. The least desirable part of the Sumerian and Babylonian heritage is a pervasive superstition, a tendency to invest the smallest things and happenings with a magical connotation. At times the preoccupation with magic became a kind of religious madness, which found ominous manifestation in the transports of witchcraft.

By way of late Rome and Moorish Arabia this influence found its way into the West. The *Malleus Maleficarum*, or *Witches' Hammer*, most intellectual of all such benighted works of the Western world, is a very late descendant of a cuneiform text, in eight tablets, called *The Burning*.

Leonard Woolley, whose work supplied much of our knowledge about the mysterious "blackheads," cites an architectural example to illustrate the tenacity of the Sumerian influence:

"The arch in building was unknown in Europe until the conquests of Alexander, when Greek architects fastened eagerly on this, to them, novel feature and they, and later the Romans, introduced to the western world what was to be the distinguishing element in architecture. Now, the arch was a commonplace of Babylonian construction.—Nebuchadnezzar employed it freely in the Babylon which he rebuilt in 600 B.C.; at Ur there is still standing an arch in a temple of Kuri-Galzu, king of Babylon about 1400 B.C.; in private houses of the Sumerian citizens of Ur in 2000 B.C. the doorways were arched with bricks set in true voussoir fashion; an arched drain at Nippur must be dated somewhat earlier; true arches roofing the royal tombs at Ur now carry back the knowledge of the principle another four or five hundred years. Here is a clear line of descent to the modern world from the dawn of Sumerian history."

And Woolley sums up his exposition by saying: "If human effort is to be judged merely by its attainment, then the Sumerians, with due allowance made for date and circumstance, must be accorded a very honourable though not a pre-eminent place; if by its effect on human history, they merit higher rank. Their civilization, lighting up a world still plunged in primitive barbarism, was in the nature of a first cause. We have outgrown the phase when all the arts were traced to Greece, and Greece was thought to have sprung, like Pallas, full-grown from the brain of the Olympian

Zeus; we have learnt how that flower of genius drew its sap from Lydians and Hittites, from Phœnicia and Crete, from Babylon and Egypt. But the roots go farther back; behind all these lies Sumer."

Having kept company with the archæologists in tracing our human flow back into the land between the two rivers, the land of the Deluge and the ur-kings, we begin to feel the cool breath of millennia stirring about us. And having seen the doing, the living, and the dying, in ways good and bad, more than five thousand years ago, we are driven to admit that thousands of years have been but a day in the cosmic river of time.

Up to this point we have limited our archæological explorations to a geographical area pretty much within the Mediterranean sphere. Now we shall take a great leap—geographically, if not temporally—into another land. We shall let ourselves be led by the men of the spade into a world dead for but a few centuries, yet withal stranger to us, more barbaric and in many respects more terrible and incomprehensible than any of the ancient worlds we have hitherto learned to know. With this, in sum, we shall move on into the jungles of Yucatán and the highlands of Mexico.

# PART FOUR

# THE BOOK OF THE TEMPLES

## The Empires of the Aztecs, the Mayas, and the Toltecs

*The city was desolate. . . . It lay before us like a shattered bark in the midst of the ocean, her masts gone, her name effaced, her crew perished, and none to tell whence she came, to whom she belonged, how long on her voyage, or what caused her destruction; her lost people to be traced only by some fancied resemblance in the construction of the vessel, and, perhaps, never to be known at all.*

—John L. Stephens
facing his first discovery

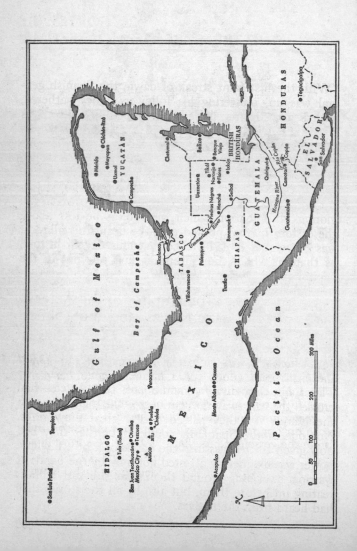

# 25/CORTÉS (I):
## THE TREASURE OF MOCTEZUMA

"With the first faint streak of dawn, the Spanish general was up, mustering his followers. They gathered, with beating hearts, under their respective banners, as the trumpet sent forth its spirit-stirring sounds across water and woodland, till they died away in distant echoes among the mountains. The sacred flames on the altars of numberless *teocallis*, dimly seen through the grey mists of morning, indicated the site of the capital, till temple, tower, and palace were fully revealed in the glorious illumination which the sun, as he rose above the eastern barrier, poured over the beautiful valley. It was November 8, 1519; a conspicuous day in history, as that on which the Europeans first set foot in the capital of the Western World."

Thus a nineteenth-century historian, W. H. Prescott, described the portentous historical moment when the Spanish adventurer Hernando Cortés, with his four hundred Spanish followers, first saw Mexico, the capital of the Aztec empire.

When Cortés's troops—there were, in addition to the Spaniards, about 6,000 native auxiliaries, mostly Tlascalans, hereditary enemies of the Aztecs—had crossed the causeway that connected the mainland with the island city, they passed over a great drawbridge. Not one of the Spaniards could doubt that they had now given themselves into the hands of a prince whose power was eloquently attested not only by the bands of warriors swarming around them, and the vast edifices rearing up before them, but also by all the stories they had heard from the natives.

The Spaniards' thundering advance moved on without hesitation.

When they reached the great main thoroughfare of the city, they saw advancing toward them a shimmering procession of men in gorgeous array. Behind three dignitaries holding golden staves of office swayed a golden palanquin borne on the shoulders of noblemen. Its canopy was fashioned of many-colored feathers bestrewn with jewels and bordered in silver. The noble bearers walked barefoot, with measured tread and eyes downcast. At the proper distance, the procession came to a halt, and from the palanquin descended a tall, slender man about forty years old. His complexion was paler than that of the ordinary natives, his black hair was smooth and not very long, his beard was sparse. He wore a cape embroidered with pearls and precious stones, tied under his chin. He was shod in golden sandals that were tied to his ankles with gold-encrusted straps. As he came forward, leaning upon the arms of two courtiers, servants spread cotton blankets before him so that he would not soil his feet. So stood Moctezuma II, Emperor of the Aztecs, before Cortés.

Cortés descended from his horse and, also leaning upon the arms of two noble companions, moved to meet the native ruler.

Fifty years later Bernal Díaz, one of the conquistador's companions, wrote of this encounter: "I shall never forget this scene; after all these years it remains as vivid to me as if it had happened yesterday."

When those two men stood eye to eye, exchanging ceremonial words of greeting, two worlds, two historical ages were meeting face to face.

For the first time in the history of great discoveries related in this book it came to pass that a man from the Christian West did not have to reconstruct an unknown rich culture from its ruins but encountered it in the flesh. Cortés before Moctezuma! It is as though Brugsch-Bey had suddenly found himself face to face with Ramses the Great in the Valley of Deir el-Bahri, or as though Koldewey had met Nebuchadnezzar strolling in the Hanging Gardens of Babylon, and they could have conversed together as Cortés did with Moctezuma.

But Cortés was a conqueror, not an archæologist. Beauty was of interest to him only when it was exchangeable for gold, and greatness only as something against which to measure his own. He was concerned with profit for himself and his Hispanic Majesty, and at most with furthering the supremacy of the Cross, but certainly not the advancement of knowledge (unless one were to consider his interest in geography a basically scientific interest). Barely a year after he had met Moctezuma for the first time, Moctezuma was dead. In less than another year, the splendor of Mexico was destroyed—and not only the city itself.

To cite a cultural historian of our own time, Oswald Spengler: "This is the only example of the violent sudden death of a culture. This culture did not wither away; it was not suppressed or inhibited. It was murdered in the full glory of its flowering, demolished like a sunflower wantonly beheaded by a passerby."

To understand what happened, it is necessary to take a glance backward across the years, now known as the Age of the Conquistadors, that formed a period in the history of the Christian West reddened by fire and blood, draped in priestly vestments, and bounded by the sword.

In 1492 the Genoese Captain Cristóbal Colón, later known as Christopher Columbus, voyaging toward India, discovered the islands of Guanahani, Cuba, and Haiti off the coast of Central America, and later Dominica, Guadeloupe, Puerto Rico, Jamaica, and finally the coast of South and Middle America. While at the same time Vasco da Gama found the true (i.e. the nearest) sea route to India, Hojeda and Vespucci and Ferdinand Magellan explored the southern coasts of the New World. After the voyage of John Cabot and Magellan's circumnavigation of the globe, the extent of the American continent was known from Labrador to Tierra del Fuego. And when Nunez de Balboa dramatically walked into the Pacific in full armor to take possession of it "for all time," and Pizarro and Almagro invaded the empire of the Incas—the Peru of our day—from the western coast, a breach had been made within a single generation for the greatest of European adventures. Discovery might be followed by exploration, but exploration had to be succeeded by conquest, for the New World was a repository of unimaginable riches, both in the sense of offering new markets and in that of being a treasure house awaiting plunder.

It was this, of course—the prospect of treasures to be had for the taking—that most inspired those daring exploits by mere handfuls of men sailing on ships of a size seen nowadays only on inland rivers. Yet it would be unjust to suppose that gold was their only objective, their only motive greed coupled with dare-devilry. Those explorers and conquerors went forth not only for themselves, for Isabella and Ferdinand and later for Charles V; they were also serving their pope, Alexander VI, the Borgia who in 1493, with one straight line across a map, divided the world neatly between Portugal and Spain. They went forth under the banner of the Virgin on behalf of his Apostolic Majesty, as missionaries against the infidels, and none of their ships lacked a priest ready to plant the Cross wherever they might land.

When the explorers and conquistadors sailed for America, a world conception was to become global for the first time in history. Ideas, religion, politics, adventurousness all played their parts. A new knowledge of the stars, of geography, and consequently of navigation, also served to implement the expansive politics of an essentially European world empire "on which the sun would never set." A creed hardened to fanaticism could send out adventurers under its sacred banners because the hearts of hidalgos had wearied of dreaming and thirsted for action.

Apart from such basic determinants of history there are also always, of course, those odd quirks of events that have so often proved decisive in the development of the science of vanished cultures. It may be amusing to note that Hernando Cortés, the great discoverer of the Aztec culture, was intended to become a lawyer. His first attempt to escape from this hated profession by joining the expedition of Nicolas de Ovando, Columbus's successor, was balked when a high wall the young man was climbing to reach the chamber of a lady love crumbled under his feet and buried Hernando under its rubble. The contusions sustained in this, the first of his known adventures, kept the young Don Juan in bed until after Ovando's fleet had sailed. We will never know what turn the history of the New World might have taken, had the wall offered less of an obstacle to young love.

Even men like Cortés, however, are replaceable when the times call for them.

The campaign in which Cortés took Mexico by storm is without parallel in history.

Sixteen years before, when he was nineteen and had just landed on Hispaniola, he arrogantly told the governor's secretary, who was offering to assign him a piece of land: "I have come to get gold, not to plow the field like a peasant." At twenty-four he took part in the conquest of Cuba under Velásquez, with distinction, but joined the party of the opposition to the new governor and was tossed into jail. He escaped, was captured, escaped again; finally managed a reconciliation with the governor. He settled on an estate, introduced European cattle to Cuba, exploited gold mines, and accumulated the impressive sum of 2,000 to 3,000 castellanos. Bishop Las Casas, one of the few friends the Indians had in the New World, commented on this: "God, who alone knows at the cost of how many Indian lives this sum was collected, will demand an accounting for it."

The acquisition of this fortune was a turning point for Cortés's career. Now that he could afford to equip every kind of fighting force he was given the command of a fleet of warships which he and Velásquez outfitted together, destined to reach at last the coast of that fabled country about which the natives had told so many galvanizing stories. At the last moment there was fresh dissension with the governor. When Cortés had reached Trinidad with the fleet into which he had put his entire fortune and that of his friends, Velásquez tried to have him arrested. But by this time Cortés was the man all his soldiers swore by. They would have rioted at any serious attempt to hold their commander. So Cortés was allowed to proceed with eleven ships, the largest of which was a hundred-tonner, into his most portentous adventure.

At this point the entire striking force—with which he had set out to conquer a country of which he had no real conception—consisted of 110 sailors, 553 soldiers (including 32 archers and 13 musketeers), 10 cannons, 4 culverins (light field guns), and 16 horses.

Under his flag of black velvet embroidered with gold thread, with a red cross and the inscription: "Friends, let us follow the Cross, for under this sign those who have faith shall conquer," he addressed his forces in words which have come down to us, ending as follows:

"You are only few in number, but strong in resolution. If you do not falter in this, have no doubt that the Almighty, who has never yet abandoned the Spaniard in his struggle against the infidel, will shield you even when you are surrounded by a swarm of enemies; for your cause is a righteous cause, and you will be fighting under the banner of the Cross. Forward then, in good spirits and confidence; let us bring the work so auspiciously begun to a glorious conclusion."

On August 16, 1519, he set out from a point on the coast near the future Vera Cruz to conquer Mexico. He had expected to fight against *tribes;* he now saw that he would have to defeat an empire. He had assumed that he would have to pit himself against savages; he now had to learn that he was at war with a highly civilized nation. He had counted on finding villages and rural settlements in his way; instead, vast cities with temples and palaces loomed up from the plain before him. That none of these confrontations and sights shook his determination to subjugate this country shows him to be one of those men who are cursed by posterity only when they fail.

The maniacal three months of conquest which swept Cortés into Moctezuma's capital city cannot be described here in detail. It is enough to say that Cortés overcame obstacle after obstacle offered by the landscape, the climate, and the unknown diseases bred by them. He waged and won battles against thirty to fifty thousand Indians. His reputation for being unconquerable preceded him from city to city. His strategy combined the most precise military science with savage butchery. Meanwhile he did a great deal of skillful political maneuvering, returning the ambassadors Moctezuma kept sending to him loaded with gifts, while playing out the Emperor's vassal peoples against each other, turning the Tlascalans, who were his enemies one day, into his friends the next. Purposefully he moved forward until Moctezuma's aimless halfway measures lost all effectiveness in arresting his advance, and the Aztec ruler, supreme lord of far over 100,000 warriors, ended by *pleading* with Cortés not to set foot in his capital.

This triumphal campaign, which is without equal in history, is almost impossible to explain. Cortés's strength lay in having a reputation of almost mythical proportions joined with the advantage of organized, disciplined military tactics. As one historian put it, it was another case of Greeks *versus* Persians. But this time the "Greeks" had—in addition to discipline—firearms, weapons unknown and terrifying to the enemy. And they had something else that threw the Indians into a panic every time: horses, thundering monsters in the eyes of the Aztec people, who saw rider and mount as one and did not lose their superstitious awe of these creatures even after they had captured one and a leader had it hacked to pieces which he dispatched to all the cities of the realm.

The day on which the capital was taken by the Spaniards, November 8, 1519, moved irresistibly closer. It could not even be called a conquest; the city was occupied by a victorious invader, without resistance. Yet Cortés's discovery, in the Mexican metropolis, of that treasure of which he had been dreaming since he was nineteen years old, and the precipitancy with which he planted the Cross upon the Aztec temples, together brought about a series of complications that came within a hair's breadth of costing him and his followers all the fruits of their victory.

On November 10, 1519, the third day after Cortés entered the capital, he asked Moctezuma for permission to set up a chapel in one of the palaces that had been turned over to him and his men. Permission was granted at once; indeed, Moctezuma sent Aztec craftsmen to lend a hand.

The Spaniards, however, did their own reconnoitering. In going over the old masonry they noticed a patch of wall where the mortar was still fresh, and with the experience gained from much requisitioning they suspected that there was a door behind it. Although they were still nominally guests in the imperial palace, they did not scruple to break into that wall. When a door was indeed revealed, they immediately opened it—and sent for Cortés.

He came, and looked through the opening they had made; then he had to shut his eyes for a moment. Before him lay a hall full of the richest, most magnificent fabrics, ornaments, precious utensils, jewels of every kind, silver and gold not only in exquisitely worked objects but stacked ingots. Bernal Díaz, the chronicler, who had seen this over Cortés's shoulder, wrote later: "I was a young man, and it seemed to me that all the riches of the world lay piled up in that room."

They were standing before the treasure of Moctezuma; that of the father, enriched by the acquisitions of the son.

Cortés proceeded with extraordinary circumspection. He ordered the door walled up again at once; for he realized that he was perched on the crater's edge of a volcano that might erupt at any moment. Considering the odds against the little troop of Spaniards inside that vast alien city, an estimated 65,000 buildings, the mere thought of their audacity is still breath-taking.

What were their chances, in fact, of bringing this adventure to a safe conclusion? Now that they had seen the treasure, how were they to get it out of that great city, under the nose of the emperor and his great host of an army? How could they suppose that they could seize power over this kingdom to secure their economic exploitation of it, as they had been able to do with the savage islands of the New World?

As Cortés proved, there was one, and only one, way to seize power within the capital, though it might occur only to such desperate adventurers as these, and be grasped only by such intrepid conquistadors. Cortés had perceived the virtually sacral status of Moctezuma; the Emperor's subjects would not dare to lift a finger against whoever had the Emperor's person in his power. After a calculated interval he invited Moctezuma to move in with him, thus combining the imperial residence with his own. His invitation included such a mixture of reasons, discreet pleadings, and covert threats (his most imposing-looking knights in full armor already posted at the doors) that Moctezuma yielded.

On the evening of the same day the Fathers Bartolomé Olmedo and Juan Díaz conducted Holy Mass in the new chapel. During this pious exercise the treasure, which each of the praying Spaniards considered his in part, lay in the adjoining chamber to the left. At the right of it sat its owner, an Emperor in the midst of his realm, and yet no more than a hostage at the mercy of a few men, letting his nobles comfort him as best they could regarding the indignity of his position. All the Spaniards, remarked Bernal Díaz, behaved with the utmost gravity and decorum during their devotions, "partly for the sake of the rite itself, and partly because of its edifying influence upon the benighted heathens."

So far Cortés had a series of unbroken successes to his credit, as though good fortune were on his side in every venture. Then three events in rapid sequence changed the picture.

The first unpleasantness arose in the ranks of the Spaniards themselves. Once Moctezuma had become his prisoner, Cortés saw no reason to leave the treasure undisturbed. (The luckless ruler tried to save face by offering the entire treasure to Cortés's distant King, his Spanish Majesty, as a gift, together with an oath of fealty—a gesture of little worth, considering his situation.) To have it properly assessed, Cortés had the treasure brought into one of the great halls. Its total value, according to the scales and weights the Spaniards had to improvise—the Aztecs, great mathematicians though they were, had never heard of such things— came to about 162,000 gold pesos, equivalent (according to a nineteenth-century estimate) to about 6.3 million dollars. It is unlikely that any sixteenth-century European ruler had ever seen the equivalent of so enormous a sum, for the time, in his treasury. No wonder the Spanish soldiers went into a frenzy when they calculated the value of an equal share for each of them.

But it turned out that Cortés had rather different plans for dividing this booty. He was, after all, the emissary of his Spanish Majesty, who was surely entitled to a proper share. And what about Cortés himself, who had furnished the ships, equipped the troops, and was still deeply in debt for all this, debts he would have to pay off one day? He therefore decreed the following division of the spoils: one fifth to the King of Spain; another to Cortés; a third part to Velásquez, the King's Governor who had to be placated, since Cortés had flouted his orders and simply gone off with all the ships; a fourth to be paid out as a premium to the noblemen, the artillerists, the arquebusiers and archers as well as the garrison left to guard the coast of Vera Cruz. This left one fifth to be distributed—100 gold pesos to a soldier!—a pittance for what they had accomplished, a wretched tip in the eyes of those who had seen the entire treasure.

Cortés's band was on the brink of mutiny. Quarrels broke out that led to duels and bloodshed. Cortés intervened, not by invoking discipline, but by resorting to eloquence. "With sweet words, of which he had a good supply for every kind of contingency," said one of his soldiers. He pacified them by feeding their imaginations with visions of a far greater reward than they had dreamed of. Meanwhile the one fifth of the treasure that was to be equally shared by the soldiers was all they received; the other four fifths remained well guarded in the palace.

A few months afterwards, something far more serious occurred. Cortés was informed by a captain from the coastal station that a fleet under the command of a certain Narváez had landed at Vera Cruz, sent by the enraged Velásquez for no other purpose than that of relieving Cortés of his command and taking him to Cuba as a prisoner charged with open rebellion and with exceeding his authority. The details were alarming: Narváez had 18 ships, holding 900 men, including 80 cavalry, 80 arquebusiers, 150 crossbowmen, and much heavy artillery. Cortés, sitting upon the powder keg of Mexico, was now facing in addition an army of his own countrymen that was not only far stronger than any force at his command, but was by far the greatest military force ever yet marshalled for battle in the New World.

What he did was extraordinary. Anyone who might have attributed Cortés's triumphs to luck, to daredevilry, to the fact that his opponents were only poorly armed Indians, must now revise his opinion. For Cortés decided to move against Narváez and crush him.

What with?

He dared to leave behind Pedro de Alvarado, one of his captains, with two thirds of his entire army, to guard Mexico and Moctezuma, still his valuable hostage. With the last third—70 soldiers in all—he was going to hurl himself against Narváez! Before setting off he painted for Moctezuma so terrifying a picture of punishment to be inflicted upon traitors from among his own people that the weak-willed ruler, fearing the worst at the Spaniard's return, turned a deaf ear to his own advisers trying to rouse him in this unexpectedly favorable hour. Moctezuma in fact did his best to mollify Cortés, accompanying him in his palanquin (well guarded by Alvarado all the way) as far as the dam, where he embraced the Spaniard and wished him good fortune!

And so Cortés and his army—or rather, his horde increased by Indian confederates to a total of 266 men —set out into the plain, the Tierra Caliente. Through heavy downpours of rain and storm his scouts brought word that Narváez had reached Cempoalla. Now only a river lay between him and his enemy.

Narváez meanwhile, far from lacking in experience and military strategy, was making toward the river to confront Cortés that very evening. But in view of the dreadful weather he inclined to heed the grumbling of his soldiers. Convinced that Cortés could not be expected on such a night, and trusting in the superiority of his weapons, he withdrew again to the town and retired for the night.

Cortés crossed the river. The enemy's sentinels were taken by surprise. On Whitsunday night, 1520, with their war-cry "Espiritu Santo!" his scanty, ill-equipped troops, with him at their van, burst into Narváez's camp which was bristling with men and weapons.

The surprise attack was a complete success. In a brief but fearful night battle, lit by torches and here and there a flash of cannon fired but once, the camp was captured. Narváez, defending himself from the top of a temple tower, caught a spear in his left eye. His scream of pain was followed by Cortés's jubilant "Victoria!"

It was said later on that the cocuyos, huge fireflies of the region, had come to the aid of Cortés and his just cause by suddenly arriving in swarms, so that the defenders believed themselves attacked by a vast army bearing lighted matchlocks. In any case the victory went unquestionably to Cortés. Its full extent showed itself when most of the vanquished offered to swear fealty to him, and when he inspected his rich booty of cannons, guns, and horses, finding that at long last, for the first time in the history of his Mexican expedition, he was in command of a really powerful striking force.

Yet this powerful force was destined to fail where the inconsiderable horde Cortés had been leading hitherto had so signally triumphed.

# 26/CORTÉS (II):
# THE BEHEADED CULTURE

The Spaniards of the age of conquest marched behind the banner of the Cross and their battle cry was "Espiritu Santo!" Wherever they carved out a foothold they planted the Cross and speedily built churches. Priests heard their confessions before they went into battle, celebrated their victories with ceremonial Masses, and at once set about converting the natives.

Before entering the Aztec kingdom, the Spaniards had been dealing with savages, whose religion was a barbaric animism in which natural forces and ghosts were revered. The rites and customs of this elemental religious complex were easily shaken. With the Aztecs, however, the situation was quite different. Their religion was of a higher order, a "culture religion." Though this was on the whole polytheistic, monotheistic tendencies showed through in the powerful cults of Huitzilopochtli and Quetzalcoatl. The whole culture, under the influence of the ubiquitously regulatory calendrical lore, acquired a stamp as distinctive as any exhibited by the universalist or redemptive religions.

The mistake of the Spanish conquistadors and their priests was that they recognized this fact too late. The outlook of sixteenth-century Europeans strongly hindered any concessions to civilizations different from their own. This narrow attitude, which recognized highs and lows only in its own scale, and on no other, was not in the least modified when the conquistadors saw in Mexico unmistakable signs of a clearly differentiated and highly developed social life. They became acquainted with educational methods in some respects superior to their own and were not impressed. Nor did the discovery that the Aztec priests were amazingly learned in astronomy have any effect on them.

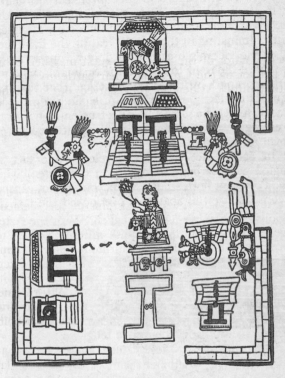

The Plan of the Great Aztec Temple, Mexico.

The purely civilizational progress made by the Aztecs, as for example in the regulation of traffic, census-registration in the cities, and the construction of buildings for sacred and profane use, had even less qualifying effect on the Spaniards' conviction that they were dealing with savages who must at all costs be converted. They saw nothing but the devil's handiwork in the rich city of Mexico, with its lagoons, dikes, streets, and floating islands of flowers.

Unfortunately the Aztec religion had one feature that repelled everyone who encountered it and inevitably fostered belief in Aztec diabolism. This was the practice of human sacrifice on an incredibly large scale, a rite culminating in the priest's tearing the living heart out of the victim's breast. And only we moderns, perhaps, have the right to remind the Spaniards, who were roused to anger by the Aztec practice, that their own Inquisition slowly roasted Spanish flesh during the autos-da-fé. At the same time it is true enough that this Aztec ritual was cruel beyond anything of the kind ever known in the world.

In actual fact a highly developed morality was mingled with barbaric amorality in the Aztec civilization. To accept both strains was beyond zealot capacity. In consequence the Spaniards overlooked the fact that

Aztec drawing showing a human sacrifice.

the Aztec people, unlike the Indians encountered by Columbus, Vespucci, and Cabral, could be humbled only up to that point at which their religion was involved. This critical point was reached when the Spaniards began to desecrate the temples and the gods. Nevertheless, they laid on with a ruthless hand. The essential incompatibility of Spaniard and Aztec set the stage for a series of violent acts that nearly destroyed the fruits of Cortés's military and political conquests.

It is worthy of remark that among the members of the Cortés expedition it was not the priests who were the worst bigots. Father Juan Díaz and Father Bartolomé Olmedo, particularly the latter, tempered the conduct of their religious office with political understanding.

According to all reports, it was Cortés himself, perhaps yielding to a subconscious impulse to justify his own deeds, who first attempted to convert Moctezuma. The Emperor politely heard out the Spaniard's harangue. When the great conquistador invidiously compared the pure and simple rite of the Catholic Mass with the hideous Aztec practice of human sacrifice, however, Moctezuma put in a word. It was much less revolting to him, he explained, to sacrifice human beings than it was to eat the flesh and blood of God himself. We do not know whether Cortés was quite able to counter this dialectic.

Cortés went even further. He asked for permission to examine one of the large temples, and after Moctezuma had consulted with his priests, this permission was reluctantly granted. At once Cortés climbed up the great stairs of the teocalli, which was located in the middle of the capital, not far from the Spanish head-

The word "Teocaltitlan" (temple people; "teo-cal-li": House of God) in Aztec hieroglyphics. according to H. Jensen's interpretation: lower left: character for lips (T-N-TLI); to the right below: a road or path as indicated by footprints (O-TLI); above left: a house (CAL-LI); above right: character for tooth (TLAN-TLI).

quarters. When he suggested to Father Olmedo that the teocalli would be the most appropriate place to house the cross, the priest advised against this. They went in to look at the jasper block on which the sacrificial victims were slaughtered with an obsidian knife. They saw the image of the god Huitzilopochtli, terrifying of visage, identical, in Spanish eyes, with the very devil himself as described by their priests. The hideous idol was embraced within the thick folds of a serpent studded with pearls and precious stones. Bernal Díaz, also present during this visit, was the first to become aware of an even more gruesome sight. The walls of the whole room were plastered thickly with dried human blood. "The evil stench," writes Díaz, "was less tolerable than that of the slaughterhouses in Castile." Then he looked closely at the altar stone. There lay three human hearts, which he fancied were still smoking and bleeding.

Having descended by way of the long teocalli stairs, the Spaniards, a little later, caught sight of a large framework building on a mound, which they were moved to explore. Within, neatly piled up to the rafters, they found the skulls of Huitzilopochtli's victims. A soldier estimated that there were 136,000 of them.

Soon after, when the phase of request had been succeeded by the phase of curt command backed by threats, Cortés moved his headquarters into one of the towers of the teocalli. After his first visit to the temple he had spoken of it rudely and sacrilegiously to Moctezuma, who was shocked but silent. This time, however, Moctezuma was sufficiently aroused to tell the Spaniard that his people would tolerate no such intrusion. Cortés, unyielding, ordered the temple to be cleaned and had an altar set up with the cross and an image of the Virgin Mary. The Aztec gold and jewels were removed and the walls decorated with flowers instead. When the *Te Deum* was heard here for the first time by the Spaniards who had gathered upon the long stairway and the platform of the teocalli, tears of joy ran down their cheeks, so moved were they by this victory of their faith.

The deed that was to exhaust the Aztecs' patience was but one step away.

The story can be told briefly. When Cortés was away
from the capital on his expedition against Narváez, a
delegation of Aztec priests asked permission of his lieu-
tenant, Alvarado, to celebrate their annual festival,
called "the incensing of Huitzilopochtli," with the customary ritual dances and songs, in the court of the great
teocalli (one tower of which now contained the Spanish
chapel).

Alvarado agreed on two conditions: that the Aztecs should offer no human sacrifice and should come
without weapons.

On the day of the festival about six hundred Aztecs appeared, mostly members of the highest nobility,
unarmed and dressed in their finest clothing and jewels.
While the religious ceremonies got under way a considerable number of Spaniards in full armor began to
mingle with the crowd. As the festivities approached
a climax the Spaniards fell on the defenseless worship-
pers at a prearranged signal and massacred every one.
An eyewitness remarked that "the pavement ran with
streams of blood like water in a heavy shower."

When Cortés re-entered the capital, with a force
greatly increased by his victory over Narváez, he found
himself in a completely changed city. Soon after the
treacherous massacre the Aztecs had risen in revolt,
chosen Cuitlahuac, a brother of Moctezuma, to lead
them on behalf of the immobilized Emperor, and since
then had been blockading the palace in which Alvarado
had barricaded himself. When Cortés appeared, Alvarado was in desperate need of relief. But to raise the
Aztec siege meant that Cortés must himself enter the
trap.

Every sortie now launched by Cortés became a
Pyrrhic victory. When he destroyed three hundred
houses, the Aztecs destroyed the bridges and dikes over
which he would have to retreat if he withdrew from the
city. When he burned down the great teocalli, the Aztecs stormed his fortifications with redoubled fury.

Moctezuma's behavior in this situation is hard to

Aztec hieroglyphics. The skull stands for
"death"; the weeping eye for
"widowed."

understand. His past military record was indisputably
good. So far as is known, he had taken active part in
nine battles. Under his rule the Aztec kingdom had
reached a peak of might and splendor. Yet after the
arrival of the Spaniards this great ruler seemed steadily
to lose his grip. He now came to the Spaniards and offered to mediate with his people. Wearing the full
insignia of his imperial office, he went onto the walls
and began to speak, but was stoned by the crowd, receiving wounds that brought about his death. On June
30, 1520, Moctezuma II died, the once great Emperor
of the Aztecs, to the last a Spanish prisoner.

Now that the Spaniards no longer held the person
of Moctezuma as a trump card in the play for Mexico,
their predicament had become serious indeed. Cortés
was to experience a most nerve-racking adventure: the
*noche triste*, as the history books call it.

As the "sad night" loomed, Cortés issued orders for a
breakout. This was a counsel of despair, in view of the
fact that a mere handful of men would have to fight
their way through ten thousand bloodthirsty Aztec warriors. Before making this final move, Cortés had the
Aztec treasure spread out, saying disdainfully: "Take
what you will of it. But beware not to overload your-
selves. He travels safest in the dark who travels lightest."
A fifth part of the treasure was reserved for the Spanish King so as to ensure royal clemency should Cortés
suffer defeat, yet live. This fifth was carried in the
middle of the retreating column.

Cortés's veterans took their leader's advice to heart
and burdened themselves with only a little gold, but
Narváez's troops loaded themselves down with valuables. They stuck gold ingots in their belts and boot-
tops, they bound jeweled implements to their bodies,

and so weighted themselves that after the first half hour they had fallen back, all out of wind, as far as the rear guard.

In this first half hour of the night of July 1, 1520, the Spaniards succeeded in withdrawing, unseen by the Aztecs, through the sleeping city and out on the causeway. At this juncture the cries of the Aztec sentinels rang out, and the priests began to sound the great drum in the temple of the war god. Hell broke loose.

By laying down a portable bridge that had been especially carpentered for this purpose, the Spaniards managed to cross the first breach cut in the causeway by the Aztecs. There was a sound like that of trees soughing in a rainy wind. Then the heavens were rent by war cries, a sound that mingled with the frantic splashing of canoe paddles. Showers of arrows and stones rained down on the Spaniards. The shrieks of their wounded were answered by the yells of the Aztecs. Warriors began to climb out of the darkness up onto the causeway, where they engaged in hand-to-hand combat with the Spaniards, using clubs furnished with iron-hard cutting edges of obsidian.

Where was the portable bridge when the Spanish van reached the second breach let into the causeway to hinder their retreat? Frantic calls to the rear elicited the alarming information that under the weight of so many men and horses the supports of the improvised bridge had sunk into the soft earth and could not be budged. What up to now had been an organized retreat degenerated quickly into a rout. The troops became a mob; each man fought aimlessly for his own life. On foot and horseback the Spaniards plunged into the waters of the lake in their frantic efforts to gain the farther shore. Packs, weapons, and finally the gold were all sloughed off and lost in the darkness of the night.

There is no point in dwelling too long on the particulars of this battle. Not one Spaniard, not even Cortés—who, according to all reports, wrought miracles of courage—came off unwounded. When the morning grayed and the remnants of the Spanish force had crossed the dike, the Aztecs meanwhile having been diverted from their harassment of the enemy by the rich spoil, the commander took stock of the situation. Contemporary accounts of the losses suffered during the *noche triste* do not agree. By conservative estimate the Spaniards lost about a third, their Tlascalan allies a fourth or fifth, of their combined forces. All the muskets and cannon had been lost, a part of the crossbows, and most of the horses. Cortés's band had been reduced to a ghostly shadow of the proud column that had entered the capital nine months earlier.

But the Spaniards Via Dolorosa was still not at an end. For eight days after the *noche triste* there was constant skirmishing as the Spaniards struggled to save themselves by retreating into Tlascalan territory. The Tlascalans, their allies, were the traditional enemies of the Aztecs. They retreated very slowly, being weakened by exhaustion and hunger. Then, on July 8, 1520, the crippled band, having toiled up the steeps enclosing the valley of Otumba, were greeted by a spectacle that seemed to seal their fate.

As far as the eye could see, the valley, the only avenue of escape, was filled with Aztec warriors arrayed in better battle order than anything the Spaniards had yet seen in Mexico. At the head of the methodically disposed battle columns the Spaniards could make out the chiefs, standing out from the rest. In their shimmering feather cloaks they looked like bright birds against the snow of the white cotton mail worn by the common warriors.

The situation was hopeless, but the Spaniards did not hang back. They had no choice but to press forward and take their chances or to become sacrificial victims for the Aztec gods. Prisoners of war taken by the Atzecs were commonly fattened in wooden cages until they were deemed acceptable to the god. The only thing to do, therefore, was face almost certain death and try to force a path through the Aztec horde. There was no other way.

And now, at the moment of complete hopelessness—the Aztecs were later estimated to have numbered 200,000 men, and the Spaniards were attacking without benefit of the firearms that had won them their initial victories—a miracle occurred.

Cortés's men broke into the sea of Aztecs in three groups: a large striking force at the center; on either wing the remaining handful of cavalry, totaling some twenty men. At once the Spaniards and their Tlascalan allies were swallowed up. The lanes that the twenty riders plowed through the enemy closed in behind as the Aztecs sprang back like grass in a plowed furrow. Cortés, who fought in the front line, lost his horse, mounted another, was wounded on the head, but hacked his way on. Still, the Aztecs were legion. Between cut and thrust he chanced to see, from a slight elevation, a cluster of strikingly ornamented warriors, and in their midst a litter. On the litter he recognized the cacique in command of the whole Aztec force, a certain Cihuacu, distinguished by his staff with a golden net for a banner, and the field-badge attached to his back. Then the miracle came to pass, not one worked by the Virgin Mary or the saints, but the miracle of Hernán Cortés, a deed worthy of being sung about any warrior's campfire. The wounded Cortés spurred his steed forward, hardly waiting for the two or three tried and trusted cavaliers who swept along in his wake. Together they pressed on, with thrust of lance and sword, riding down the Aztecs, sticking and cutting, always hammering their way diagonally through the warrior phalanx. The enemy gave way before their savage onslaught. In a few minutes Cortés's mad ride had brought him up to the Aztec cacique. Murderously he thrust him through with his lance. Tearing loose the cacique's badge, he waved it aloft over the seething battle.

Like magic the tide turned. The Aztecs, seeing their victory emblem in the hands of the conquistador, who to them seemed stronger than their gods, precipitately fled the field. This was a supreme moment.

When Hernán Cortés seized the Aztec banner, Indian Mexico was doomed and the kingdom of the last Moctezuma had died.

The historian Prescott sums up the Spanish conquest in these words:

"Whatever may be thought of the Conquest in a moral view, regarded as a military achievement it must fill us with astonishment. That a handful of adventurers, indifferently armed and equipped, should have landed on the shores of a powerful empire inhabited by a fierce and warlike race, and, in defiance of the reiterated prohibitions of its sovereign, have forced their way into the interior;—that they should have done this, without knowledge of the language or of the land, without chart or compass to guide them, without any idea of the difficulties they were to encounter, totally uncertain whether the next step might bring them on a hostile nation, or on a desert, feeling their way along in the dark, as it were; that, though nearly overwhelmed by their first encounter with the inhabitants, they should have still pressed on to the capital of the empire, and, having reached it, thrown themselves unhesitatingly into the midst of their enemies;—that, so far from being daunted by the extraordinary spectacle there exhibited of power and civilization, they should have been but the more confirmed in their original design;—that they should have seized the monarch, have executed his ministers before the eyes of his subjects, and, when driven forth with ruin from the gates, have gathered their scattered wreck together, and, after a system of operations, pursued with consummate policy and daring, have succeeded in overturning the capital, and establishing their sway over the country;—that all this should have been so effected by a mere handful of indigent adventurers, is a fact little short of the miraculous,—too startling for the probabilities demanded by fiction, and without a parallel in the pages of history."

For the sake of the record it should be mentioned

that in the months immediately following the Battle of
Otumba, prior to their final dissolution, the Aztec people rose to heights befitting their tradition as "Roman
Americans." After Cuitlahuac, who died of smallpox
after ruling for four months, came Cuauhtemoc, an
Emperor in his twenty-fifth year. So vigorously did he
defend his country's capital against Cortés, who meanwhile had added strong reinforcements to his army,
that the Spaniards suffered greater losses at his hands
than from any previous Aztec commander. Yet the end
was inevitable. Cuauhtemoc was taken prisoner, tortured, and hanged. The capital was destroyed, its houses
burned to the ground, its idols overturned, its canals
filled in.

Mexico made a new start with the Christianization
and colonization of the land by the Spaniards. During
the last siege the Spaniards from the teocalli had
watched Aztec priests in the plaza below rip the hearts

Aztec hieroglyphic writing
after Christianization. Symbols showing fourth and
fifth commandments
of the decalogue.

from the breasts of fallen compatriots. Now they built
a gleaming collegiate church on the same site and dedicated it to St. Francis. The houses of the city were rebuilt. After a few years 200 Spanish families lived in
Mexico City, and some 30,000 pure-blooded Indians.
The land round about the city was divided up according to the *repartimiento* system, which in effect imposed slavery on all the peoples who had once made up
the Aztec realm—and of course on all the tribes who
fell prey to later conquests. None but the Tlascalans, to
whose aid Cortés was so deeply indebted, were ex-
empted from the rule, and even they only for a time.

This sudden Spanish ascendancy, otherwise of such
dazzling benefit to the motherland, was marred by only

one defect: the destruction of the treasure of Moctezuma. The booty lost during the *noche triste* the Spaniards had hoped to retrieve when they retook Mexico
City, but it had all vanished and has never to this day
been recovered. Cortés had Cuauhtemoc tortured before hanging him, but he would not sing to the Spanish
tune. Cortés also had all the ditches and lagoons
searched by divers, who explored the bottom with their
feet. But nothing was gained from this effort except a
great many cut toes and a few scattered pieces that the
Aztecs had overlooked. The total value of the treasure
recovered from the lake did not amount to more than
130,000 gold castellanos, or about one fifth of the value
of the share labeled originally for delivery to the Spanish government. The conquistadors themselves must
have felt a certain grim satisfaction when the news
came to Cortés, in a letter postmarked May 15, 1522,
from the captain entrusted with the transport of the
treasure to Spain, that his vessel had been captured by
a French privateer. In the end it was not Charles I of
Spain, but Francis I of France who, to his genuine surprise, came into possession of the Aztec treasure.

Now what did this Spanish conquest mean in the
total picture of the ancient Middle American cultures?
That a true culture actually did exist in Mexico when
Cortés arrived on the scene is self-evident from the
record. But we should still like to know what sort of
impression this lost Indian world made on Cortés and
his Spanish company. Of course, the Aztec culture was
already dead and all but forgotten some eighty years
after Cortés had struck into its vitals. The 1,800,000
Aztecs, more or less, still living in Mexico today exist
like fellahin in a historical vacuum.

Cortés's reaction to Aztec culture is astonishing.
Like the majority of other contemporary eyewitnesses,
he completely ignored the might and meaning of the
people whom he brought under the Spanish heel. Had
he not done this, he would have by so much minimized
his own accomplishment in the eyes of the watching

world. The thought apparently never entered his head
that rather than destroying a barbaric kingdom of savages, he had "beheaded a culture as the passer-by
sweeps off the head of a sunflower." Strange as this may
seem, it can be explained by the spirit of an era that,
characteristically, had many chroniclers but no historians. But an even more amazing and unexampled phenomenon is the fact that the enormously detailed fund
of knowledge pertaining to Aztec life acquired at the
beginning of the sixteenth century was ignored and
finally forgotten by posterity. Even archæology itself,
until quite recent years, felt no urge to devote to the
ancient Mexican world the attention that it so richly
deserved.

The argument that this superficial treatment is due
to the circumstance that we are not bound to these
Indian cultures by the historico-developmental ties that
bind us to Babylonia, Egypt, and Greece simply will
not hold water. For we have a much more active conception of remote Chinese and Indian (Hindu) cultures than of the ancient American, though they lie
much farther outside our economic and political orbit,
the land bridges connecting them with us notwithstanding. Moreover, Mexico has been steadily hispan-
icized for more than four hundred years, and latterly
has drifted into the North American sphere of interest.
These developments, one might think, would guarantee
at least a limited interest in the Aztecs, Mayas, and the
like, but they do not. In this regard it is interesting to
note that the first real archæological institute founded
in America—in 1879—for decades concentrated its
entire efforts on the excavation of the antiquities of
Europe and Asia Minor. Even now only a small part of
the tremendous sums that American scientific institutes
allot for archæological investigations is spent in their
own back yard.

It is now time to put Aztec culture in its proper
place within the American complex. It was the first to
be discovered, but there were other far more important

Indian societies. The Aztec kingdom was really no more than the civilizational reflection of much higher and older cultures.

With this we return again to the flow of our story, and to the rediscovery of ancient Middle America. Two remarkable men are memorable in this connection. The first, without crossing the threshold of his study, resurrected the Aztecs from oblivion; the second, hacking his way through the Central American jungle with a machete, did the same for a much older people, first encountered by one of Cortés's lieutenants. This time the greatness of the Indian past evoked a spellbound recognition that simply had not been intellectually possible until the nineteenth century.

# 27/JOHN LLOYD STEPHENS
## BUYS A JUNGLE CITY

In the year 1839 early one morning a small party was riding through the valley of Camotan, along the border between Honduras and Guatemala. Two white men trotted on ahead; the rest were Indians. Their mission was peaceful, though all carried arms. But neither their weapons nor their protestations of innocence prevented them later that day from being taken in custody into the *alcaldía,* or "city hall," of a little jungle town along the way. There they were locked up, under the guard of brawling, drunken soldiers who, the night through, shot off rifles from time to time to ease their high spirits.

Such was the unfriendly reception that initiated the great archæological adventure of John Lloyd Stephens, who rediscovered the ancient Mayas.

Stephens was born in Shrewsbury, in the state of New Jersey, on November 28, 1805. He practiced law for eight years, while his private passion was antiquities, the relics of all ancient peoples. At first, for the simple reason that he was quite unaware that antiquities lay piled in heaps in Central America, Stephens concerned himself exclusively with the archæological remains of the Near East. He first traveled through Egypt, Arabia, and the Holy Land and the next year visited Greece and Turkey. Not until he was thirty-three and had already published two travel books was his attention drawn toward Central America by a report that fell into his hands by chance.

This report was a deposition concerning military

levies among the natives supervised, in 1836, by a certain Colonel Garlindo. In his report Garlindo mentioned seeing the remains of some strange and obviously extremely ancient buildings located in the wilds of Yucatán and Central America.

Stephens was tremendously excited by the dry military report. Seeking further information, he came across the work of Juarro, the historian of Guatemala, who in turn cited a certain Fuentes. This Fuentes claimed that in his day—that is, about the year 1700—an old and well-preserved architectural complex was to be found in the region about Copán, in Honduras. This complex he called the "Circus."

On the basis of this sparse information Stephens made up his mind to search for this "Circus." It is hard to believe that he went no deeper into the subject, when there was so much source material from the conquistador period available. But it should be emphasized once again that the discoveries of the Spanish conquerors, so far as their being pertinent to ancient cultures went, had all but disappeared from the public consciousness. Stephens, of course, had no way of knowing that another American with historical interests was in process of collecting all available documents on one, at least, of the old Indian peoples of Middle America. Prescott was in the middle of his great task even as Stephens was preparing for his trip to Guatemala, Honduras, and Yucatán. Without leaving his desk, Prescott could have supplied him with a great deal of valuable information, perhaps even have told him what he might expect to find. But Stephens was blissfully ignorant of this.

Looking around for a good man to accompany him on the expedition, Stephens found him in his friend Frederick Catherwood, a draftsman. Once again we come across the same sort of fruitful partnership as that between Vivant Denon and the Egyptian commission of Napoleonic days, and that between Eugène Flandin and Botta in Mesopotamia.

As Stephens and Catherwood were busy making preparations for the trip, an opportunity arose to pass on most of the financial burden of the undertaking to the government of the United States. Upon the sudden death of the Central American chargé d'affaires, Stephens succeeded in having himself appointed to the post, making good use of connections, cemented during his legal career, with Martin Van Buren, then President of the United States. Thus he was able to embark on his expedition armed not only with many private and official letters of recommendation, but also with the imposing title of *Encargado de los negocios de los Estados Unidos del Norte.*

But none of his papers seemed to be of much use to him when his party was imprisoned by drunken, ill-disciplined Guatemalan freebooters. Stephens's experience in Central America in 1839 compares with Layard's six years later on the banks of the Tigris in Mesopotamia. Both plunged into countries seething with rebellion.

During this period there were three great political parties in Central America: the party of Morazán, former President of the Republic of El Salvador; the party of Ferrera, leader of the mulattoes of Honduras; and the party of Carrera, leader of the Guatemalan Indians. This Indian, Carrera, and his followers, known contemptuously as *"cachurecos"* ("counterfeit coins"), had taken up arms. A battle had already been fought between the forces of Morazán and those of Ferrera, near San Salvador. General Morazán had been severely wounded, but had won the engagement, and the population was now expecting him to march into Guatemala. John Stephens's little caravan set out along this prospective line of march, right into the thick of things.

The countryside had been devastated. Generals of operatic aspect alternated with bandit chiefs in directing the movements of the troops, most of whom were irregulars. Both regulars and irregulars did more pillaging than fighting. The soldiers were mostly Indians and

Negroes, among them a scattering of European soldiers of fortune and deserters from Napoleon's Italian army. The villages had been stripped bare, the people were starving. When Stephens would ask where he could buy food, the answer invariably was: *"No hay!"*— "Nothing doing here!" The land had nothing but water to offer.

It so happened that Stephens's party sought shelter for the night in the "city hall" of one of the little towns along the route. The alcalde, fingering the silver-headed cane that he carried as a badge of office, received them with suspicion. That evening, leading a gang of some twenty-five men, he crashed into the room where Stephens and his party were stretched out for the night. The man in charge of the gang—they proved to be soldiers—was an officer and a Carrera partisan. In his description of the episode, Stephens calls him "the gentleman with the patent leather hat." There was a scuffle, and Stephens's servant, Augustín, received a wound on the head from a machete. Holding his head, Augustín began to shout: "Fire on them, kill them, señor!" Meanwhile, in the flickering light of a burning pine knot, Stephens was doing his best to display his credentials. He also produced the private seal of General Cascara, Cascara being an officer deserter from the Napoleonic armies who played something of a role in the country. Stephens had gone to a lot of trouble to secure this bigwig's recommendation. Catherwood, for his part, delivered an impassioned disquisition to the alcalde on international law and the niceties of diplomatic usage. Catherwood's harangue, like Stephens's credentials, made not the slightest impression. The situation suggested a scene from *Fra Diavolo;* on the other hand, with three muskets pointed at Stephens, at any moment the comedy might have taken a nasty turn.

Hopes rose when a second officer suddenly appeared. He was apparently of higher rank, for he wore an even more carefully polished patent-leather hat than the first. Again passports were examined. The officer forbade any further show of violence and made the alcalde responsible for keeping the expedition in safe custody on pain of losing his head. Stephens hastily wrote a letter to General Cascara and, to increase its impressiveness, used an American half-dollar to mark the sealing wax. "The eagle spread his wings, and the stars glittered in the torchlight," he says. "All gathered round to examine it."

Stephens's little group got no sleep that night. The soldiers had camped at the door, where they brawled, yelled, and drank large quantities of aguardiente. Finally the alcalde reappeared, bringing in his whole drunken troupe with him. In his hand he held Stephens's letter to Cascara—which of course had never been delivered. Stephens reacted vigorously. And behold, the new tone of command worked where passports and Catherwood's oratory had not. The alcalde entrusted the letter to an Indian and drove him on his way. He also took away the soldiers with him when he left. Stephens prepared for a long wait, but the situation was after all favorably resolved.

The next morning when the sun was high the alcalde, now sober, came to pay his official, and expiatory, respects. At dawn the soldiers, having received new orders, had suddenly disappeared en masse.

Copán lies in Honduras, on the river of the same name, which empties into the Motagua, which in turn flows into the Gulf of Mexico. Cortés had marched through this region when he went into Honduras, more than a thousand miles over mountains and through primeval forest, to punish a traitor.

When Stephens and Catherwood, with their Indian guides and bearers, shortly after leaving the village of their incarceration, plunged into a forested country that closed in about them like a green sea, they began to realize why so few travelers or explorers had ever ventured this way before. "The foliage," Cortés had written three hundred years before, "threw so thick a shade that the soldiers could not see where they were going." The mules sank up to their bellies in the swamps, and thorny plants tore Stephens's flesh when he dismounted to help the pack animals. The stifling heat made the white men faint, the swarms of mosquitoes rising out of the sloughs carried the ever present threat of fever. "This climate," the Spanish travelers Jorge Juan and Ulloa said a hundred years before of this tropical lowland, "this climate drains a man's strength, and kills women during their first child-bearing. The oxen lose flesh, cows their milk, and the fowl cease to lay eggs." Nature had remained exactly the same since the times of Cortés and his compatriots. It was perhaps fortunate that military disturbances precluded diplomatic activity, for had they not had a free hand to indulge their passion for discovery, they might well have given up and turned back.

Yet Stephens was the type of man who is drawn by the magic of strange places, even in adversity. The forest was not only physically enervating; it had a disastrous effect on the senses of sight, hearing, and feeling. Everything was strange. An odor of decay floated up from the low places. Mahogany, logwood, and campeachy trees hemmed in the trail. The thirty-eight-foot fronds of the corozo palm formed great overhead screens. For those with eyes for such things, many species of orchids grew along the way. The fruit of epiphytic bromeliaceæ (plants of the pineapple family) grew squatly on the branches of primeval trees like flower-pots. In the evening the forest suddenly became intensely vocal. Howling monkeys began their screeching, parrots made croaking sounds, nameless piercing cries rent the air, and desultory, hollow groanings, such as a stricken animal makes.

Stephens and Catherwood fought their way through. Scratched and bleeding, covered with mud, eyes inflamed, they battled forward. The forest seemed to have been uninhabited since the day of creation. Could it be true, after all, that large stone buildings were hidden in its depths?

Stephens was a candid man. Later he admitted that the farther he got into the green kingdom, the less faith he had in his mission. "I ought perhaps to say," he writes, "that both Mr. C. and I were somewhat skeptical, and when we arrived at Copán, it was with the hope, rather than the expectation, of finding wonders."

But the miracle did come about.

Finding old masonry built by some long-vanished people somewhere in a strange forest is interesting enough and evokes all sorts of questions, but it is hardly right, one might say, to call it a miracle. But we must picture Stephens within the context of his experience, as a man who knew half the Middle East, who had already visited almost all the archæological sites in this ancient region across the sea. This man of little hope and no great expectation was soon to be greeted by a sight that at first struck him speechless and later, when he had realized its archæological consequences, made him almost believe in the miraculous.

They had pushed on to the Río Copán, where they had spent some time in a little jungle village in order to establish friendly relations with the Christianized Indians and mestizos of the district. Moving still deeper into the jungle, they suddenly came on a wall, built out of stone blocks, closely fitted, and "in a good state of preservation." A flight of steps led up to a terrace, so overgrown that its area could not be judged.

This find was exciting, yet their jubilation was tempered by the fear that they might have found nothing but the ruins of some old Spanish fort. Meanwhile, with Stephens and Catherwood looking on, the Indian guide was using his machete to cut away a tangle of lianas from a tall object. Presently he tore the viny mass aside, as if it were a stage curtain, and he the *deus ex machina* in the drama of discovery. Expectantly

he pointed to a tall, dark object, as proudly as if he
were showing them his own work.

Stephens and Catherwood themselves now took
machetes and set about getting a clearer view. They
found themselves before a stele, a high and richly
carved slab of stone. In artistry of execution there was
nothing in Europe or Asia to compete with it. Such
sculpture had never been even remotely suspected on
the American continent.

The ornamentation on the stone likeness was magnificent beyond description. The stele—to give its mod-
ernly accepted dimensions—was 12.8 feet high, 2.85
feet wide, and 2.88 feet thick, a tall cubic column covered every inch with sculptured figures and ornamentation. High and gray it stood out against the deep, dense
green of the forest; in its grooves were vestiges of the
darkly glowing colors that at one time had been painted
on it.

A male figure was carved in powerful relief on the
front face. The visage of this figure was "solemn, stern,
and well fitted to excite terror." The sides of the stele
was covered with hieroglyphs, the obverse face was
decorated with carvings "unlike anything we had ever
seen before" (see Plate XXV).

Stephens was fascinated; but he was a genuine
archæologist, not easily tempted into hasty conclusions.
His moderate comment was: "The sight of this unexpected monument ... gave us assurance that the objects we were in search of were interesting, not only as
the remains of an unknown people, but as works of art,
proving ... that the people who once occupied the Continent of America were not savages."

As he and Catherwood worked their way deeper
into the tangle and came upon a second, third, fourth,
and finally a fourteenth stele, each more finished in
execution than the last, Stephens's enthusiasm mounted,
his judgments became less restrained. In his book telling about this experience he reminds the reader that he
has seen the monuments of the land of the Nile, and

points out that works of art like the Egyptian cannot be produced except by a highly developed culture. Yet some of the carved stone artifacts in the jungle of Copán, he adds, are executed "with more elegant designs, and some in workmanship equal to the finest monuments of the Egyptians."

For the times this was presumption indeed. The letter carrying the first news of his find evoked disbelief and laughter among his friends. Could he prove all these claims?

He himself wondered where to make a start when he began to have some idea of the extent of the ruins and of the impenetrability of the plant life in which they were buried. He remarks how for a while the undertaking looked hopeless. The ruins were scattered through the dense forest. As for carrying out interesting specimens, there was a river near by that emptied into the Atlantic, but unfortunately its course was broken by rapids. The only possibility was to transport one of the idols in pieces, he says, and to make castings of the others. "The casts of the Parthenon are regarded as precious memorials in the British Museum," he reminds his readers, tacitly assuming that his finds were equal to works which up to that day had been considered the very highest expression of creative activity.

He finally abandoned the idea of making plaster copies in favor of drawings. He urged Catherwood to get on with his drawing. But Catherwood, who had published wonderful drawings of the Egyptian monuments, was not enthusiastic. In his perfectionist way he felt out the grimacing stone faces and ran his fingers over the incomprehensible hieroglyphs and the weathered ornamentation. He repeatedly tested the light. He shook his head over the deep shadows in the heroically sculptured relief.

Accompanied by the village tailor, a mestizo named Bruno, Stephens went deeper and deeper into the jungle. He found new carved figures, new walls, stairways, and terraces. One of the monuments had been "displaced from its pedestal by enormous roots; another locked in the close embrace of branches of trees, and almost lifted out of the earth; another hurled to the ground, and bound down by huge vines and creepers; and one standing, with its altar before it, in a grove of trees which grew around it, seemingly to shade and shroud it as a sacred thing; in the solemn stillness of the woods, it seemed a divinity mourning over a fallen people."

When Stephens returned to the camp, he announced to Catherwood that he had fifty subjects to be copied. But Catherwood, the experienced draftsman, demurred. It was impossible to draw properly, he pointed out, under such poor conditions. There would have to be more light. The shadows fused together, obliterating the contours.

They knocked off work until the following morning. The village would have to supply them with a labor force. They had noticed one mestizo who seemed to be more up and coming than most of the natives. Perhaps he could advise them on getting the kind of help they needed. But when this brown man, being summoned, came strutting into the camp, he made the stunning announcement that he, Don José María, owned the land along the Río Copán where the monuments were located.

Stephens burst into laughter. The idea that the jungle ruins could "belong" to anybody struck him as absurd. When Don José María, upon further questioning, admitted that, true enough, he had only heard about the idols, never seen them, Stephens abruptly ordered him out of the camp without giving him time to finish his story.

That night, however, thinking things over in his hut, Stephens was not quite so sure of himself. Who, actually, did own the ruins? Half-asleep, he decided categorically that "they belonged of right to us, and, though we did not know how soon we might be kicked out ourselves, I resolved that ours they should be; and with visions of glory and indistinct fancies of receiving the thanks of the corporation flitting before my eyes, I drew my blanket around me, and fell asleep."

All day the sharp, neat blows of the machetes rang through the jungle. The Indians deeply ringed the boles of a dozen trees at a time, so that when one was pushed over, it would drag the rest down with it, together with the matted tangle of vines.

Stephens watched the Indians as they worked, again and again searched their faces for signs of the creative power that alone could account for such masterpieces in stone. This power Stephens sensed as utterly alien to his own nature; an urge shot through with grotesquerie and cruelty, yet expressing itself in masterly forms. The power of execution was immediately evident as the figures took shape out of the jungle green, but grew slowly on the onlooker as he stood back at a distance, seeing the figures in their wholeness. But the faces of the Indian workers seemed completely apathetic and empty to Stephens.

While Catherwood was setting up his drawing board to take advantage of the newly won light gained by cutting out clearings, Stephens again went into the jungle, and found walls on the river-bank. His first estimate of their height had to be revised upward, and he also found that they enclosed a much greater area than he had first thought. Yet they were so heavily overgrown with a kind of thorny furze that the mound looked as if someone had laid a thick green blanket over it. Monkeys howled and screamed as Stephens and his mestizos forced their way through the tangle. "It was the first time we had seen [at close hand] these mockeries of humanity, and, with the strange monuments around us, they seemed like wandering spirits of the departed race guarding the ruins of their former habitations."

Stephens presently found that he had come upon a

pyramid-like structure. He fought his way up a broad flight of stairs. The heaving action of shoots and suckers had forced the risers apart. The steps led up from the darkness of the thorny thicket into a lighter level up among the treetops, he discovered, and still higher up over the ceiba crowns to a terrace ninety-six feet above the ground. Stephens felt dizzy. What kind of people had been at work here? How long since they had died out? How many hundreds of years ago had they built this pyramid? When, and with what kind of tools, under whose mandate, and in whose honor, had they created these innumerable carved figures? One thing was clear: nothing less than the creative energies of a numerous and powerful people could account for them. And when it occurred to him that many other similar dead cities might be hidden in the jungles of Honduras, Guatemala, and Yucatán, he was dismayed by the magnitude of the archæological problem. A thousand questions crowded his thoughts, not one of which he was able to answer. He looked out over the treetops, the faintly lustrous gray of the monuments showing through gaps in the green.

"The city was desolate," he writes. "... It lay before us like a shattered bark in the midst of the ocean, her masts gone, her name effaced, her crew perished, and none to tell whence she came, to whom she belonged, how long on her voyage, or what caused her destruction; her lost people to be traced only by some fancied resemblance in the construction of the vessel, and, perhaps, never to be known at all."

When he returned to inspect Catherwood's first labors, a strange sight met his eyes. The artist was standing in front of the first stele they had discovered. Sheets of drawing paper were strewn about him on the ground. He was up to his shoetops in soft muck, covered with mud from head to foot, wearing gloves and netting over his head to protect himself from the swarms of insects, and working with the grim determination of a man resolved on conquering an unexpected difficulty, come what might. For, as it proved, Catherwood for once seemed to have bitten off more than he could chew. And yet he was one of the last great draftsmen of a tradition that, after being carried up to the turn of the last century by a handful of English etchers, died out in formalistic experimentation.

The forms he had to reproduce were utterly different from anything he had ever experienced before. They lay so completely outside any European plastic concept that for a time his crayon simply would not function. He had a great deal of trouble figuring out the essential proportions. He tried the camera lucida, the widely used drawing aid of the period, but he found it of little use to him. Was that curved thing so much ornamentation or a human limb? Was that an eye, a sun, or an abstract symbol? Was that an animal's head? If it was, what sort of beast was it supposed to be? What kind of imagination had engendered such terrifying heads? The stone had been transformed into fearsomely splendid forms without counterpart anywhere in the world. "The 'idol,' " says Stephens, "seemed to defy his art; two monkeys on a tree on one side appeared to be laughing at him."

Catherwood hammered away at the problem from early to late, and the day finally came when he had completed a drawing that he deemed up to his exacting standard. It was to be a sensation.

At this point there was a remarkable development. With the object of recruiting a larger working force, Stephens had been trying all along to make closer contact with the villagers. Like so many explorers in similar situations, he enlisted the sympathies of the natives by dispensing simple medicaments and much good counsel. For a time all went well; then suddenly a serious difference loomed. Don José María again announced himself, and this time insisted on his proprietary rights. Protracted interviews with the mestizo revealed that the field of ruins was really quite valueless to him, that he would never take any active interest in it, that the "idols," so far as he was concerned, could remain forever lost. Nothing but a feeling that Stephens had failed to give him the respect due an owner of property accounted for his importunities.

Stephens, who was fully aware that he had to tread very softly in a politically chaotic land, felt that he must keep on good terms with the local inhabitants at any cost. He now made a dramatic decision. Laying his cards on the table, he said: "What will you take for the ruins?"

"I think he was not more surprised," he writes, "than if I had asked to buy his poor old wife, our rheumatic patient, to practice medicine upon. He seemed to doubt which of us was out of his senses. The property was so utterly worthless that my wanting to buy it seemed very suspicious."

To prove the sincerity of his offer, Stephens went to all the trouble of presenting Don José with his credentials, which declared him to be a man of unexceptionable character, a traveling scientist, and a commercial attaché in the service of the great and powerful United States. A village linguist by the name of Miguel haltingly read off the papers. The brave Don José shifted from one foot to the other and finally said that he wanted to do some thinking and would be back later.

The whole comedy was repeated. Miguel read all the papers a second time. When nothing came of this, Stephens, seeing that the purchase of the old city of Copán was the only way to ensure permanent peace, concluded that more spectacular methods of persuasion were needed for the jungle mentality. A diplomatic scene now unfolded that might have been taken from a grotesque.

Stephens dragged out his trunk and got out his attaché's uniform. He had long since given up his diplomatic mission in Central America as a bad job, but at least the uniform would not be entirely lost to the moths and mold. With the astonished mestizo, José, looking on, Stephens ceremoniously put on his dress coat. Of course he was also wearing a rain-sodden Panama hat, a checked shirt, and white pantaloons stiff with yellow muck up to the knees. And of course the rain was still dripping from the trees—it had been pouring earlier in the day—and the ground all about was deeply puddled. Streaks of sunlight played on the large brass buttons of the coat, however, showing up the eagles on them. The gold braid gleamed with that air of authority which is not without effect even in more sophisticated parts of the world.

Could Don José María resist a spectacle so convincing? He could not. He gave in. And John Lloyd Stephens, looking, as he said of himself, "like the negro king who received a company of British officers on the coast of Africa in a cocked hat and military coat, without any inexpressibles," bought the ancient city of Copán.

"The reader is perhaps curious," says Stephens, "to know how old cities sell in Central America. Like other articles of trade, they are regulated by the quantity in market, and the demand; but, not being staple articles, like cotton and indigo, they were held at fancy prices, and at that time were dull of sale. I paid fifty dollars for Copán. There was never any difficulty about price. I offered that sum, for which Don José María thought me only a fool; if I had offered more, he would probably have considered me something worse" (see Plate XXVI).

Obviously such an important and wonderful event, even though nobody in the village quite understood what it was all about, had to be fittingly celebrated. Stephens gave an official levee, and the whole village showed up in gala procession, including a large contingent of old ladies. Cigars were passed around, a *cigarro* for the ladies, a *puro* for the men. Catherwood's drawings were admired, and finally the ruins and monuments themselves were inspected, whereupon Stephens was amazed to discover that not one of the villagers had ever seen the sculptures before. Not one of them had ever been moved to break trail into the feverishly steaming jungle about the site, not even the sons of Don Gregorio, the mightiest man of the village, and they, his sons, the most intrepid woodsmen. And yet the pure-blooded Indians among the villagers belonged to the same tribe and spoke exactly the same language as the long-dead sculptors in stone and the master builders of pyramids, stairways, and terraces.

When Stephens's book, *Incidents of Travel in Central America, Chiapas, and Yucatan,* appeared in New York in 1842, and, shortly thereafter, Catherwood's drawings, a storm of interest arose. There were heated public discussions of the finds. Historians saw their tightly mortised world falling to pieces. Laymen invented all manner of bold theories.

Leaving Copán, Stephens and Catherwood had gone on into Guatemala, later into Chiapas and Yucatán, in the course of which journey they encountered many vicissitudes. All along the trail they came across Mayan relics. Their description of these finds raised a cloud of questions. There was a great rush to examine the Spanish sources. The earliest mention of this remarkable Mayan people was found in accounts relating to the deeds of Hernández de Córdoba, Francisco de Montejo, and other early discoverers and conquistadors in Yucatán. Suddenly a book that had come out in Paris four years before Stephens's came into the limelight. This book dealt with the same material as that treated by Stephens, but hitherto had attracted no readers at all.

At first sight this seems strange indeed, for Stephens's work was a sensation from the start and soon ran through several editions, also being translated into several foreign languages. In sum, while everybody was talking about Stephens's work, a similar report by F. de Waldeck: *Voyage pittoresque et archéologique dans la province d'Yucatan (A Romantic Archæological*

*Journey in Yucatán*) aroused little notice and today has virtually disappeared from memory. The fact is, Stephens's account was not only more detailed, but also written in a style so sparkling that the book can still be read with real pleasure. Also, Waldeck had no man of Catherwood's ability in his party. Even photographs pale beside a Catherwood drawing, and to this day his drawings have a documentary value for archæologists.

But the main reason why Waldeck aroused such little response is something else again. At the time his book came out, France was excited about another ancient culture. There were men still living who had taken part in Napoleon's Egyptian expedition. France—indeed, all Europe, and even America—looked toward Egypt. To break the spell, traditional ideas had to be given shock after shock.

This shift of interest revolved primarily around the following question: where did these Indians come from? Did they belong to the same stock that in Stephens's day was still scattered as nomadic tribes all over the North American continent? If the Mayan and North American Indians were members of the same parent stock, how did it happen that the Mayas had developed such an advanced culture? Was it even *possible* that a unique society could have arisen on the American continent, in complete isolation from the great cultural flow of the Old World?

Now came the first bold interpretations. The possibility of an indigenous culture was out of the question, some maintained. In the remote past the Mayas must have migrated to Central America from the ancient Far East. By what route? Why, over a land bridge that had existed in the far north at the time of the Deluge. And others, stunned by the idea of having the inhabitants of an equatorial region migrate down from the Arctic Circle, claimed that the Mayas were survivors from the legendary island of Atlantis. As none of these explanations really fitted the bill, there was, of course, still another all-or-nothing school of thought, which believed that the Mayas were one of the lost tribes of Israel.

And did not some of the sculptures publicized by Catherwood's drawings bear a striking resemblance to statues of the Hindu gods? Yes, others said, but look at the pyramids; they definitely point to a connection with Egypt. Now some investigators disclosed the fact that in Spanish accounts there was mention of strong Christian elements in the Mayan mythology. The cross symbol had been found among the Mayas. The Spaniards, too, had noticed that the Mayan people seemed to have some idea of the Flood. Their god Kukulcan had seemingly played a messianic role. All this evidence pointed to the Holy Land of the Middle East.

While this argument was in full swing—and, in modified version, it is still going on—a book came out written by a man who spent his life closeted in studies and libraries, and never had the least firsthand experience of remote places. Indeed, this man was almost blind. Whatever paths he cut through the jungle perforce had to be imaginary ones, with nothing but the keen knife-edge of his intellect as tool. And whereas Stephens had located the old Mayan kingdom in Honduras, Guatemala, and Yucatán, this retiring scholar rediscovered the Aztec kingdom of Moctezuma. Now the confusion was really compounded.

William Hickling Prescott came from one of the oldest Puritan families in New England. He was born on May 4, 1796 in Salem, Massachusetts, and from 1811 to 1814 studied law at Harvard. A few years later, having meanwhile shown great legal promise, Prescott was bent over a special writing frame made for the blind and near-blind, the so-called noctograph, invented by a certain Wedgewood. The noctograph resembled a scholar's slate, with the difference that the ruled lines were replaced by horizontal brass ferrules to guide the writer's hand. To obviate the difficulty of using a quill and ink a piece of carbon paper was slipped under the ferrules, with white paper beneath, to catch the impression made by a stylus.

Prescott was almost blind, having lost his left eye in an accident while he was a student at Harvard in 1813. Intensive study weakened the remaining eye so seriously that he went to Europe for two years to be treated, unsuccessfully, by a series of ophthalmologists.

A legal career being virtually impossible, Prescott, with an incredible display of self-discipline, turned his energies to writing histories. With the help of the noctograph he wrote *The Conquest of Mexico*, a breathtaking description of the conquests of Cortés and something more besides. In this book the smallest details left by Spanish contemporaries of the great conquistador were woven with superhuman industry into a panorama of the Aztec kingdom before and after its conquest. When the work appeared, in 1843, the newly discovered Mayan culture had a rival in the hardly less mysterious Aztec civilization.

What had come to light through Prescott's efforts? Very plainly there was a connection between the Aztecs and the Mayas. Their religions, for example, obviously showed large areas of correspondence. Their buildings, temples, and palaces seemed to have been produced by the same sort of mentality. But how about the Mayan and Aztec languages? Even superficial examination revealed that the roots of the Aztec language differed from the Mayan. And whereas the Aztecs manifestly had been "beheaded" by Cortés at the peak of their cultural efflorescence, the Mayas had reached their cultural and political climax centuries before and were a people in the last throes when the Spaniards landed on their shores.

That school of thought which felt no qualms about identifying the prehistoric inhabitants of Central America with the lost tribes of Israel would no doubt have explained away these contradictions had not Prescott permitted himself the liberty of some marginal notes that posed a dozen new riddles in the Middle American scene.

At one point, for example, Prescott breaks the flow of his narrative of Cortés's *noche triste* to describe a field of ruins along the route of the Spanish flight. Out of these ruins rose the pyramids of Teotihuacán, most prominently the pyramids of the sun and the moon, structures large enough to stand comparison with the great tombs of the Pharaohs. The Pyramid of the Sun is more than 190 feet high, and covers an area more than 640 feet on each side of its perimeter (see Plate XXIV).

This gigantic temple site located in the heart of the Aztec kingdom is hardly one day's march out of Mexico City, and today only an hour's ride by railroad. Prescott, however, refused to be misled by the pyramids' proximity to the Aztec capital. Basing his argument on Indian tradition, he theorized that the pyramids must have already been in existence when the Aztecs invaded the region and conquered it. He believed that another and very much older culture had antedated both the Mayan and the Aztec cultures in Central America.

"What thoughts must crowd on the mind of the traveller," he writes, ". . . as he treads over the ashes of the generations who reared these colossal fabrics, which take us . . . into the very depths of time! But who were their builders? Was it the shadowy Olmecs, whose history, like that of the ancient Titans, is lost in the mists of fable? or, as commonly reported, the peaceful and industrious Toltecs, of whom all that we can glean rests on traditions hardly more secure? What has become of the races who built them? Did they remain on the soil, and mingle and become incorporated with the fierce Aztecs who succeeded them? Or did they pass on to the South, and find a wider field for the expansion of their civilization, as shown by the higher character of the architectural remains in the distant regions of Central America and Yucatan?"

Speculation of this sort poured in from all sides. Prescott is quoted in this connection merely for the sake of simplicity. In any event, the waters became so badly muddied that no one could see. When Prescott says, however, that "it is all a mystery,—over which Time has thrown an impenetrable veil," a veil "that no mortal hand may raise," he is taking altogether too dim a view. Mortal hands are still digging away to this very day and have already illuminated what only a century ago was a seemingly hopeless puzzle. There is every reason to believe that archæology will eventually solve many more problems that up to now have proved insoluble.

In 1863, just twenty years after the appearance of Prescott's *The Conquest of Mexico,* a visitor at the Royal Library in Madrid rummaging in the state archives found a manuscript sere with age that had evidently never been read by anyone. It bore the date 1566. Entitled *Relación de las cosas de Yucatán,* it was illustrated with a number of strange, incomprehensible sketches. The author was one Diego de Landa.

Anyone else would probably have put this manuscript back unopened, as a great number of people had apparently done already. But the man who was now looking at it had been the almoner of the French embassy in Mexico for ten years, and was the priest of the Indian village of Rabinal in the district of Salama in Guatemala since 1855. Much of his time had been devoted to the study of Indian languages and the relics of the ancient cultures. That this priest, missionary to the Indians, and scholar had also published a series of stories and historical novels under the pseudonym Étienne Charles de Ravensberg is worthy of mention in order to indicate the range of his interests.

When Charles Étienne Brasseur de Bourbourg (1814–74) kept the yellowed little book by Diego de Landa and studied it attentively, a most important discovery in the field of Central American studies was about to be made.

William Prescott had been nine years older than Stephens. Brasseur de Bourbourg was nine years younger. Though he made his significant find as late as 1863, the work of these three men belongs together. Stephens had unearthed the monuments of the Mayas; Prescott had put together and for the first time described a continuous phase, even if it was the final phase, of Aztec history. And Brasseur de Bourbourg provided the first key, albeit a small one and one that was far from fitting all the locks, to the understanding of a whole series of hitherto incomprehensible ornaments and hieroglyphs. But before we can proceed to explain the importance of this discovery, it is necessary to make clear the difficulties facing the archæologists in the solution of the American problem, which differed radically from any of the problems set by the Old World.

When the Chinese began to form their empire in the third millennium before Christ—after their equivalent of the Biblical Flood—they did it along their two great rivers, the Hwang Ho and the Yangtze Kiang. In India the earliest settlements were formed along the banks of the Indus and the Ganges rivers. After the Sumerians had invaded Mesopotamia, a Babylonian-Assyrian culture arose from their early settlements between the Tigris and the Euphrates. The culture of the Egyptians flourished not only along the Nile but with the Nile. What these rivers meant to these peoples, the narrow Aegean Sea meant to the ancient Greeks. In short, the great cultures of the past were riparian cultures; scholars are accustomed to consider the presence of such a river as the presupposition for the rise of a culture. Yet the American cultures were not river-based. This is also true of the Inca culture on the high plateau of Peru, between which and the ancient Central American cultures there is no direct connection.

Another premise for the rise of a culture was always thought to be the inclination and capacity of a people for agriculture and animal husbandry. The Mayas did practice agriculture—though with a difference, as we shall see. But as for animal husbandry, theirs is the only known culture to have had no domestic animals, no beasts of burden, no carts or wagons of any kind!

This is not the only peculiarity in the case of the Mayas. Most of the peoples who created cultures in the Old World are dead, vanished without a trace, and their languages died with them. We have to relearn their "dead" languages most laboriously, by the long, weary processes of decipherment. But the Mayas are still living, more than a million strong, nor have they changed physically, and only slightly in their way of life, in their clothing. The contemporary explorer turning to his Indian servant is likely to see the same face he has just finished copying from an ancient Maya relief carving. When *Life* and the *Illustrated London News* in 1947 published photographs of a new excavation, they showed a Maya man and a girl in profile against two ancient relief carvings of faces, and it looked as though they had been the models for the carvings! And if the stone heads could have given utterance, they would have spoken in the same language in which the modern Maya servant asks the explorer for his pay.

All this might seem to be extremely helpful to the scholars—but it is not much use at all. For even though the Maya culture—again, in contrast with all the Old World cultures—perished not 2,000 or 3,000, but only 450 years ago, we have fewer starting points for a thorough study of it than in any other case.

Our knowledge of Babylon and Egypt, of the ancient peoples of Asia, Asia Minor, Greece, has come to us continuously over the centuries and from the beginning. Much has indeed been lost, but a great deal of the written or oral tradition has been preserved. While they died a long time ago, even in dying they passed on what they had created to posterity, and they took a long time dying. But the Central American cultures were, as we have said, "beheaded." Hard upon the Spanish soldiers, high on their horses and swords in hand, followed the priests upon whose pyres the records and pictures that might have told us so much were incinerated. Don Juan de Zumárraga, first bishop of Mexico, destroyed every scrap of writing he could find in a gigantic auto-de-fé; the other bishops and priests followed his example; the soldiers, with no less zeal, demolished everything that was left. When Lord Kingsborough in 1848 completed his collection of what remained of the ancient Aztec records, not a single piece of Spanish provenance had been found. And of Mayan documents from pre-conquistador times exactly three manuscripts are left to us.

One is in Dresden, one in Paris, and two that belong together are deposited in two different places in Spain: the "Codex Dresdensis" (the oldest), the "Codex Persianus," and the codices "Troano" and "Cortesianus."

Another obstacle to knowledge in this case is the extraordinary hardship of first hand exploration. While archæologists in Italy and Greece find themselves traveling in civilized countries, and the explorer in Egypt is at least working in the most healthful climate within those latitudes, the man setting out on a search for new traces of the Mayas and Aztecs in the last century was removing himself to an infernal climate, far from all civilized comforts and facilities. To this day, as the 1960's are drawing to a close, there is no land route for tourists to one of the most important sites, Tikál in Guatemala, where teams from the University of Pennsylvania under the direction of William Coe have been excavating and studying more than 300 gigantic edifices for over a decade. Nowadays, however, they can fly there in an hour from Guatemala City and stay in the comfortable Jungle Lodge, an "American plan" hostelry.

Exploration in Central America was accordingly beset with three difficulties: first, the unique problems posed by the peculiar character of these cultures; second, the paucity of data as a basis for the necessary comparisons and conclusions; and third, the physical resistance of the terrain to rapid penetration and excavation.

It is not too surprising, therefore, that the Mayas and Aztecs, soon after being so gloriously rediscovered by Stephens and Prescott, again dropped from public awareness; nor that what knowledge there was remained the preserve of only a very few scholars throughout four decades. While there had been numerous minor accretions to this knowledge, no really significant discovery occurred between 1840 and 1880. Even Brasseur de Bourbourg's find in Madrid stirred the interest of none but a few specialists.

Diego de Landa's book, disregarded for 300 years though quite accessible, held the Open Sesame to at least a part of the meaning of the few Mayan documents and monuments extant. But there were too few documents, stones, carvings, or sculptures to which to apply this key and test its worth.

# 29/THE MYSTERY OF THE ABANDONED MAYAN CITIES

Lines drawn from Chichén-Itzá, in northern Yucatán, south to Copán in Honduras, and from Tikál and Ixkún, in Guatemala, west to Palenque in Chiapas, bound the area covered by the Mayan culture. It was this territory that the Englishman Alfred Percival Maudslay explored between 1881 and 1894, some forty years after Stephens.

Maudslay accomplished more than Stephens. His function was to pave the way for a program of exploration systematically pursued. In the course of seven expeditions into the jungle he gathered a vast amount of data. He brought out many drawings of Mayan architecture, original pieces of sculpture, and many expert plaster-of-paris castings and paper stereotypes of reliefs and inscriptions. His collection went to England, and was eventually moved from the Victoria and Albert Museum into the British Museum. Once the Maudslay Collection became available for general study, scholars enjoyed the advantage of having a variety of original material to work with in determining cultural age and origin.

This phase of Middle American archæology brings us back to the manuscript entitled *Relación de las cosas de Yucatán,* written in 1566 by Diego de Landa (1524–79), Bishop of Yucatán, and discovered in the Royal Library of Madrid in 1863. The bishop must have been a man in whom religious and intellectual impulses conflicted. The zealot in him won out. Diego de Landa, faithfully playing his part as man of God, had all

Mayan hieroglyphics of months of
the year.

Mayan documents within his reach collected and
burned as the devil's work. But the other Diego de
Landa could not resist the temptation of cultivating the
acquaintance of one of the surviving Mayan princes
and recording the strange tales he and others had heard
of Mayan gods and battles. Nnot only did Diego de
Landa act as amanuensis for the Mayan Scheherazade;
he also made sketches of the hieroglyphs used to desig-
nate the days and months.

Interesting enough, one might say, but what particular value did such information have? Thanks to these few sketches from the hand of Diego de Landa, the weird hieroglyphic ornamentation of the Mayan monuments suddenly acquired life and meaning for archæologists of later generations.

With Bishop de Landa's drawings as reference material, and armed with the newly won understanding of Mayan hieroglyphics to which these drawings had already signally contributed, the archæologists stood before temple, stairway, column, and frieze and saw:

That everywhere in this Mayan art, in buildings that had been raised tier on tier in the jungle without the aid of draft animals or carts, in sculptures executed in stone with stone tools, there was not a single ornament or relief, animal frieze or sculptured figure, that was not directly related to some specific date. Every piece of Mayan construction was part of a great calendar in stone. There was no such thing as random arrangement; the Mayan æsthetic had a mathematical basis. Apparently meaningless repetitions and abrupt breaks in the conformation of the gruesome stone visages were, it appeared, occasioned by the need for expressing a certain number or some particular calendrical intercalation. When the ornamentation on the ramp of the Hieroglyphic Stairway at Copán was repeated some fifteen times, this was in order to express that number of elapsed leap years. The seventy-five steps in the stairway, it was discovered, stood for that number of elapsed intercalary days. This calendrical correlation of Mayan art and architecture was unique. And as research pried ever more deeply into calendrical mysteries—scholars dedicated whole lifetimes to the Mayan calendar alone —a further surprise was in store: the Mayan calendar was the best in the world.

It was differently constructed from any calendar familiar to us; and at the same time it was more accurate. Leaving out of account various fine points that even today are far from being explained, the structure of the Mayan calendar is roughly as follows. It consists of a series of twenty different day-glyphs, or pictographs, to which may be prefixed any of the numbers 1 to 13. The numbers and day-names together provide for a series of 260 in the *tzolkin*, or count of days (in Aztec, *tonolamatl*). This *tzolkin* is the sacred, as distinguished from the true, calendar year. The true calendar year—that is, the one corresponding to solar movements—is made up of 18 months, each with its glyph, and each consisting of 20 days, pieced out with a 19th month, this one of 5 days. In Mayan this calendrical year of 365 days is called the *haab*. The enmeshment of sacred

Mayan hieroglyphics for days.

year and calendar year—that is, of *tzolkin* and *haab*—yields what has been called in English the calendar round. This calendar round is the period required for the coincidence of a particular date in one system and a particular date in the other system to recur. This period covers 18,980 days, or 52 years of 365 days each. The calendar round, as we shall see, was of critical importance in Mayan life. Finally, the Mayas also used an "initial series," or long-count, calendrical system, based on a date arbitrarily selected as a calendrical point of departure. The starting point of Mayan chronology was "4 Ahau, 8 Cumhu," which corresponds, if we dare venture a cautious comparison, with our own way of using the base date of the birth of Jesus Christ. It must always be borne in mind that the similarity here is purely functional and does *not* imply correspondence in time.

By means of these interlocking systems of reckoning time, methods so complicated and highly developed that their detailed description would require a whole book in itself, the Mayas achieved greater calendrical precision by far than any other people in the world. It is a mistake to assume that our own calendar, the one in common use today, is the best possible solution for keeping track of time. All that can be said for it is that it represents an improvement over its lineal predecessors. In the year 238 B.C., Ptolemy III corrected the old Egyptian time count; Julius Cæsar adopted the corrected system, which until 1582 was known as the Julian calendar; after which it was replaced by the Gregorian calendar, the further correction of Pope Gregory XIII. If we compare the length of a year in these various calendars with an absolute year as sidereally determined, we see that the Mayan calendar offers the best approximation. For the year according to the

| | |
|---|---|
| Julian calendar is | 365.250,000 days |
| Gregorian calendar is | 365.242,500 days |
| Mayan calendar is | 365.242,129 days |
| Sidereal reckoning is | 365.242,198 days. |

And yet the Mayan people, though able to make quite exact astronomical observations and handle a fairly complex mathematics, in other respects were in thrall to the worst form of mysticism. Having produced the world's best calendar, these otherwise rationalistic Mayas became its slaves.

Three generations of archæologists have labored to unravel the mysteries of the Mayan calendrical systems. This effort dates back to the first attempts to explain de Landa's material on the Mayas. Initial successes

Mayan hieroglyphics for numbers of the Mayan vigesimal system.

were achieved by using the Maudslay collection, and the work continues into the present. Many names are prominently identified with the translation of the Mayan hieroglyphs, including those of calendrical import. Among these names are those of E. W. Förstemann, a Germanist to the core, who was the first to write a commentary on the Codex Dresdensis; and Eduard Seler, at one time a teacher, later head of the Berlin Völkerkunde Museum, whose *Abhandlungen*, or *Treatises*, is one of the richest sources of Mayan and Aztec material. Other important figures in the field of Middle American archæology and cryptology are E. H. Thompson, F. T. Goodman, Franz Boas, P. Preuss, Oliver G. Ricketson, Jr., Walter Lehmann, Charles P. Bowditch, and Sylvanus Griswold Morley, Alberto Ruz, and William Coe. Yet any selection of names is bound to slight the memory of countless others who also ventured into the jungle to copy inscriptions or who labored in their studies deciphering and impressing order on loose detail. The science of American cultures is a cooperative achievement. The supremely difficult step from calendar to chronology was accomplished by a community of effort.

The calendrical lore of the Mayas was more than an end in itself. It had social utility, and it served an æsthetic purpose. The hideous faces that were the hieroglyphic signs for the names of the month, day, and period were scattered everywhere on the façades, columns, friezes, and stairway ramps of temple and palace. Every building, as it were, had its birth-date stamped on its forehead. The archæologists had to understand these hieroglyphs in order to group Mayan works in proper chronological order and define stylistic changes from group to group—in short, in order to reconstruct Mayan history.

Reconstruct what history?

The history, to be sure, of the Mayan people. The answer appears to be self-evident, and yet the question is not quite so pedantic as might appear at first sight. For all the data at the archæologists' disposal lay within the Mayan historical frame and no other. Mayan dates, in other words, showed no correlation whatsoever with our own reckoning of time. In view of this, it was no easy matter to reconstruct a true history of the Mayas, since history unrelated to other history is meaningless.

Archæology was faced with a problem unknown in Old World cultures in such difficult form. To make the essential difficulty easier to understand, let us imagine a European analogy to the Mayan situation. Let us assume England had never been historically linked with the Continent, and that English calendrical reckoning was not based on the birth of Christ, but on some unknown arbitrary point. Everything in English chronological records is dated in terms of this unknown point of temporal reference. Then Continental historians suddenly discover England. They clearly recognize the historical relationship between Richard the Lion-hearted and Queen Victoria. Lacking a fixed point of reference common to both Continental and English reckoning of time, however, they still have no idea whether Richard the Lion-hearted was a contemporary of Charlemagne, or Queen Victoria of Lucrezia Borgia.

This analogy exactly sums up the Mayan problem. In fairly short order the archæologists were able to tell, for example, how many years older the buildings of Copán were than those of Quiriguá. But as for determining in which century according to Christian reckoning these two cities were built, they were completely lost.

Clearly the next task was to establish a correlation between the Mayan chronology and our own. But as progress was made in this direction, increasingly precise datings brought another problem to light, this entailing one of the most mysterious happenings in the history of a great people—the mystery of the abandoned cities.

During the past century the *Books of Chilám Balám* were found in various places in Yucatán. These books were Mayan chronicles from the post-conquistador period, colorful and filled with stories of political intrigue, and valuable in that they derived, at least in part, from much earlier Mayan documents.

The most important manuscript in this collection was found in the 1860's at Chumayel, and came into the hands of Bishop Crescencio Carillo y Ancona, the historian. Later the University of Pennsylvania issued a photostat of the manuscript. Upon the bishop's death the manuscript landed in the Cepeda Library, in Mérida. And there, in 1916, it vanished without a trace. Quite apart from its checkered career—it was, of course, still preserved in photostat—the book was a curiosity. It was written in the Mayan language as transposed, under Spanish influence, into Latin script. But unfortunately the Mayan priests, when they used Latin letters to express Mayan sounds, had paid no attention to Latin punctuation and word division. Some of the Mayan words were broken up, others were fused together, minus the proper affixes or suffixes, into monster words. Again, certain Mayan sounds that had no analogues in Spanish had been represented by arbitrary combinations of Latin letters whose exact phonetic value had been lost. The decipherment of the *Books of Chilám Balám*, it is plain, was an arduous task, additionally complicated by the cabalistic nature of much of the content.

The discovery of these books, however much appreciated in view of the paucity of correlative material, occasioned further difficulties when it was found that a method of reckoning time was used in them that had been quite unknown in the old Mayan kingdom. This was the "count of the katuns," called by students of Mayan the "short count," in contradistinction to the "initial series," or "long count." Although research rather quickly established the fact that the "count of the katuns" was merely a simplification of the "long count," it was obvious that a correlation would have to be worked out not only between the "long count" and Christian chronology, but also between both and the "count of the katuns."

This distasteful prospect was mitigated, to some

degree, however, by the gradual realization that the labor of achieving a three-way correlation yielded a great deal of information on the last period of Mayan history. Slowly a picture took shape, came to life, and became actually datable. Whereas previously everything that we had known about the old Mayas had been alien and remote, frozen in architectural monuments, at least this last piece of history was like any other—that is, a succession of raids, wars, betrayals, and revolutions. In other words, it was typically human.

We hear about the families of Xiu and Itzá, who warred to see who would have dominion over the common people. In the *Books of Chilám Balám* we learn about the splendors of Chichén-Itzá, the metropolis, and about its public buildings, which, when compared as to size and style with those of the older cities of southern Yucatán, show a strangely alien influence. We learn, too, about Uxmal, where the buildings have a monumental simplicity characteristic of what may be called the Mayan architectural renaissance (see Plate XXVIII), and of Mayapan, in which both early and late styles were found. We are told of a league of cities, comprising Mayapan, Chichén-Itzá, and Uxmal, called the League of Mayapan, which was betrayed into ruin. The armies of Chichén-Itzá assembled to do battle against the forces of Mayapan. The leader of the army of Mayapan, Hunac Ceel, or Ah Nacxit Kukulcan, as he is less commonly known, made use of Toltec mercenaries from Mexican garrisons kept at Xicalanco. Chichén-Itzá was conquered. Its princes were brought to the court of Mayapan as hostages and later set up as vice-regents. But the driving force of the League meanwhile had been permanently weakened. In 1441 there was an uprising of the oppressed elements, led by the Xiu Dynasty of Uxmal. Mayapan was taken, and the League completely collapsed, and with it the kingdom of the Mayas. The Xius, however, founded another city, called Mani, which meant "it is passed" in the Mayan language. When the Spaniards arrived, Mani fell more easily than Mexico City had fallen to Cortés.

These new insights into the Mayan past—that is, into the New Empire phase of Mayan history—greatly stimulated research. We must not imagine, however, that the results gained from the *Books of Chilám Balám* unfolded in an orderly, chronological fashion. A great deal of labor had to be expended before the historical events could be arranged in their actual relationship according to thesis and antithesis. Brooding over the *Books of Chilám Balám*, the archæologist made use of some odd fact brought to light by a colleague's excavations thirty years before, tied in this fact with another discovered ten years before by an expert in the Mayan language, and correlated the two facts with results gained by some calendrical hieroglyphist. Never in actual research did revelations of this lost culture proceed in an orderly, step-by-step fashion. Rather the picture was gradually filled in by supplying details here and there according to archæological circumstance.

It was in a piecemeal manner, then, that the total picture of this unique cultural interlude achieved its ultimate richness. But even today Mayan history remains to be explained with a clarity beyond challenge.

The term "New Empire," as opposed to "Old Empire," has just been used, and here I have anticipated a little. But now that we have learned a little about Mayapan, Chichén-Itzá, and Uxmal, the most important cities of the New Empire, I shall take the liberty of playing a little question-and-answer game with the authorities on Mayan chronology.

Why do you call these settlements in northern Yucatán the "New Empire"?

They reply: Because these settlements were founded very late in Mayan history, some time between the seventh and tenth centuries; and because this New Empire in all its typical modes of expression—in architecture, sculpture, and calendrical reckoning—is clearly differentiated from the Old Empire.

But what do "settlements" mean in this case? Normally a new imperial form grows out of an older form, does it not?

They reply: This case departs from the norm in so far as the New Empire was actually settled in virgin jungle territory. That is, absolutely new cities were established. The Old Empire was located in the southern part of the Yucatán peninsula, in present-day Honduras, Guatemala, and the Mexican states of Chiapas and Tabasco.

Then are we to understand that the New Empire was colonized by pioneers from the Old Empire?

They reply: No, not at all. The whole Mayan people had a hand in building the New Empire.

Do you mean to say that one day the whole Mayan people abandoned its nicely arranged empire, including all its solidly established cities, and built a new empire in the north, in the midst of virgin jungle?

And the archæologists smile this time as they reply: That is exactly what we mean. We realize that it sounds improbable, but none the less it is a fact. For example...

Now they present us with a series of dates. And we must remember, in this connection, that the Mayas had developed the world's best calendar and become slaves of their time-reckoning system. The Mayas, in brief, did not raise their great structures solely for reasons of utility or art, but in part because their calendar itself dictated the construction. Every five, ten, or twenty years they erected a new edifice, which they supplied with an appropriate birth-date. Often they built another pyramid around one already standing if a new intercalation had to be memorialized. They did this for hundreds of years with impeccable regularity, as shown by the dates chiseled into the stone. Only during times of catastrophe or migration was this calendrically governed activity interrupted.

Accordingly, when we see building activity in one city broken off at a definite date, to be resumed at approximately the same date in another city, the only possible inference is that the population of the first city suddenly quit the place and settled elsewhere.

A local event of this sort, although it may raise a whole series of difficult questions, at any rate can be explained. About A.D. 610, however, something happened in the Mayan kingdom that seems to defy reasonable interpretation. For at this time a whole people, city-dwellers, packed up and abandoned their comfortable homes, their familiar streets and squares, their temples, and palaces, and migrated into the wild country farther to the north. Not a single one of these pilgrims ever returned. The forsaken cities crumbled, the jungle crept into the streets, plants grew over stairs and sills, forest seeds sprouted in the cracks of the masonry in wind-packed bits of earth, and the vines, as they grew larger, split apart the stone blocks. No man ever again trod the courtyard pavement or climbed the pyramid steps.

Suppose a modern nation like the French, let us say, with a thousand years of history behind it, suddenly moved in a body to Morocco: one must imagine the people streaming *en masse* out of Paris, Marseilles, Toulouse, Bordeaux, Lyons, Nantes, taking to the long, weary road, finally reaching the distant coastland—only to set to work putting up replicas of their abandoned cities, with the cathedrals and palaces, in their new home. We would surely find such behavior extremely puzzling. When the historical fact of its occurrence among the Mayas was established, explanations came thick and fast. The most natural one was to assume that invaders had driven out the Mayas. But who could these invaders have been? The Mayas were at the peak of their social development and were militarily superior to any of their neighbors. This explanation is also inadequate on another ground. There is not a trace of foreign intrusion in the abandoned cities.

Was the migration caused by some natural catastrophe? But here again we must ask where are the marks that it surely would have left, and moreover, what kind of catastrophe it could have been that would have made a whole people set to work building a new

kingdom instead of returning home once the danger
had passed.

Could there have been a severe epidemic? There is
no indication that the Mayan population suffered any
heavy losses before the exodus began; on the contrary,
the people who built up such new cities as Chichén-
Itzá were extremely numerous.

Did the climate, perhaps, suddenly change, making
further existence impossible? No, the distance as the
crow flies between the center of the Old Empire and
the center of the New Empire was only 240 miles. Any
climatic change—and there are in any case no vestigial
signs of such an event—drastic enough to bring about
the complete collapse of a whole society would surely
have also been effective 240 miles away.

What other explanations are there left?

The right answer, it would appear, has been found
only in recent years. It must have more cogency than
any other, in view of the fact that more and more archæologists are acknowledging its pertinence. The theory was formulated by Sylvanus Griswold Morley, an
American, and by him impressively defended. To get
at the roots of this interpretation we must take a look
at the history and social structure of the Mayan people.

We shall assume, for synoptic expediency, and also because the actual dates suggest a division of this sort,
that the so-called Old Empire of the Mayas consisted
of three temporal segments.

## OLD EMPIRE

The Old Empire, according to correspondences assumed
by S. G. Morley between Mayan building dates and
Christian dates, lasted from some undatable time to
A.D. 610. (See the Mayan chronology for other interpretations.)

*THE EARLY PERIOD* is undated until A.D. 374. The
oldest city appears to be Uaxactún (none older has

been found), which lies on the northern border of present-day Guatemala. Tikál and Naranjo arose not far from Uaxactún. Meanwhile, in present-day Honduras, Copán was founded, later Piedras Négras on the Usumacinta River.

THE MIDDLE PERIOD lasted from A.D. 374 to A.D. 472. During this century Palenque was founded. This city lay on the boundary between Chiapas and Tabasco, and also on the temporal boundary, so to speak, between the Early and Middle Periods. Often it has been identified with the Early Period. Later Menché was built in Chiapas, and finally Quiriguá in Guatemala.

THE GREAT PERIOD lasted from A.D. 472 to A.D. 610. During these years the cities of Seibal, Ixkún, Flores, and Benque Viejo were constructed. At the end of the Great Period the exodus began.

If we examine the geographical area where the cities of the Old Empire were settled, we see that it forms a triangle, the three points of which are Uaxactún, Palenque, and Copán. We see, too, that the cities of Tikál, Naranjo, and Piedras Négras lie either along the sides of or just within the triangle. And now we see that the cities that were founded last, and that had the shortest lives (with the single exception of Benque Viejo) all lie well inside the triangle, these cities being Seibal, Ixkún, and Flores.

These locations bring to light one of the most amazing historical phenomena on record. The Mayas may be the only people in the world whose kingdom, or living space, developed centripetally rather than centrifugally.

The Mayan complex was an imperialism growing toward its own center, a process of growth beginning with the limbs and ending at the heart. For actual growth and expansion were involved. The Empire was not compressed by foreign powers, as there was no political power superior to the Mayas. The process reversed all logic and historical experience, and this without the action of outside forces.

The Mayas were an urban people in the limited sense that all European peoples have been town dwellers for the past five hundred years. In essence, all sovereignty, all culture, all spiritual activity, and all good breeding have come out of the towns. Yet the cities, Mayan or European, would not have been viable without the farmers to support them with the fruits of the land, and especially with a staple grain supply, which in the case of the Mayas meant Indian corn, or maize. Maize provided nourishment for the ruling classes in the Mayan cities. The whole culture was kept alive by this wonderful grain. Maize-growing even created the cleared spaces where the Mayan culture was deployed, for the cities were built on land that had been burned off to make cornfields.

But the Mayan social structure was fraught with harsher contrasts than any we know of, despite the seeming leveling tendency of urban dependence on agriculture. A good idea of the Mayan social pattern can be gained by comparing a Mayan city with one in modern Europe. The modern city is a structure in which the social contrasts, to considerable degree, are not visible to outward view. And though there are striking peripheral contrasts, these are softened by a dozen intermediary stages and by innumerable interrelationships and transitions linking the harsh contrasting situations. Extremes of social status in a Mayan city, on the other hand, stand out vividly. The palaces of the nobility and the temples of the priests were built mostly on high ground, and formed enclosed areas of almost fortresslike character. In fact, they must have often been used for military purposes. About the stone city were clustered the thatched wooden huts of the common people. There were no intermediate social estates. The Mayas were divided into a steadily dwindling ruling class and a correspondingly increasing mass of ruled.

The gap separating the two classes was almost inconceivably great. A median bourgeois class appears to have been completely absent from the Mayan pattern. The nobility was extremely exclusive. The nobles called themselves the *almehenob*—that is, "those who have fathers and mothers," meaning those who could boast of a genealogy. This noble class included the *halac uinicil*, or independent native Mayan rulers or hereditary princes. The words *halac uinicil* mean "the true man," "the real thing." The priesthood was also part of the ruling class, and its members were recruited from the nobility. The common folk labored for the few "who had fathers and mothers." The farmer gave a third of his harvest to the nobility, a third to the priest, and kept only the other third for himself. (It will be recalled in this connection that the medieval tenth, or tithe, was felt to be an intolerably excessive tribute and ultimately led to social revolution.) Between sowing and harvest the farmer appeared with all his slaves to engage in building-construction. The blocks of stone were hauled to the site without use of carts or draft animals. The wonderful sculpture and reliefs were chiseled with nothing but stone implements; iron, copper, and bronze were not yet used. Yet the results attained by these Mayan craftsmen were not inferior to those achieved by the Egyptian pyramid builders; indeed, they may have been superior.

A social organization of such oppressive inspiration—the tyrannical arrangement apparently did not change for a full thousand years—carries within itself the seeds of decline. Of necessity the high culture and superior knowledge of the priesthood became increasingly esoteric. No leavening came into the ruling class from below; there was no exchange of experience. The keen minds of the Mayan savants were preoccupied ever more exclusively with the stars. The priests forgot to lower their eyes to the farm lands from which, over the long run, they drew their strength. The Mayan leaders neglected to invent means of averting impending social catastrophe. Despite their impressive technical and artistic achievements, the Mayas were unable to invent the most important, yet one of the simplest, of artifacts: the plow. This default can be explained only by the incredible intellectual arrogance of the nobles and the priesthood.

Throughout their whole history, agriculture among the Mayas remained on a level of unexampled primitivity. The system, still practiced in much the same form today, is known as *milpa* agriculture. The jungle trees and bush are cut down, allowed to dry out, then burned shortly before the onset of the rainy season. The corn is planted with the use of pointed planting sticks, several seeds being dropped in each hole. After the fields are worn out, the farmer moves to another clearing. No fertilizer is used except the natural manures available near settled places, and worn-out land must remain fallow for a long time before it can be replanted.

And now we approach what may be the real reason why the Mayas were forced to abandon their cities after such short stays.

The available land supply simply became exhausted. The fallow period needed for a field to become once more overgrown with trees and bushes, after which it could be recleared by burning, steadily increased. A necessary consequence was that the Mayan farmer had to go farther and farther into the jungle to find suitable woodland to clear for cultivation, and so farther and farther away from the cities it was his duty to nourish, which could not live without him. A wide belt of burned and worn-out steppe appeared between the arable farm lands and the cities. The great culture of the Old Empire of the Mayas collapsed as the agricultural fundament slowly proved inadequate. Though it is possible to have culture without techniques, there are no viable cultures without the plow. The pangs of hunger finally drove the Mayas to migrate, after the cities were completely surrounded and ultimately linked together by areas of dry, grassy steppe.

And so the people departed, leaving cities and

ruined land behind. While the New Empire was gradually taking shape in the north, the jungle slowly crept into the forsaken temples and palaces. Fallow wasteland again became forest, and green things grew over the buildings, hiding them from view for a thousand years. Such may well be the explanation of the mystery of the abandoned cities.

# 30/EDWARD HERBERT THOMPSON: CHICHÉN-ITZÁ AND THE SACRED WELL

A full moon was shining down on the jungle. Accompanied only by an Indian guide, the American explorer and archæologist Edward Herbert Thompson—thirteen hundred years after the Mayas had left their cities and made a break for the country farther north—was riding through the New Empire that they had built for themselves, which had collapsed after the arrival of the Spaniards. He was searching for Chichén-Itzá, the largest, most beautiful, mightiest, and most splendid of all Mayan cities. Horses and men had been suffering intense hardships on the trail. Thompson's head sagged on his breast from fatigue, and each time his horse stumbled he all but fell out of the saddle. Suddenly his guide shouted to him. Thompson woke up with a start. He looked ahead and saw a fairyland.

Above the dark treetops rose a mound, high and steep, and on top of the mound was a temple, bathed in cool moonlight. In the hush of the night it towered over the treetops like the Parthenon of some Mayan acropolis. It seemed to grow in size as they approached. The Indian guide dismounted, unsaddled his horse, and rolled out his blanket for the night's sleep. Thompson could not tear his fascinated gaze from the great structure. While the guide prepared his bed, he sprang from his horse and continued on foot. Steep stairs overgrown with grass and bushes, and in part fallen into ruins, led from the base of the mound up to the temple. Thompson was acquainted with this architectural form, which was obviously some kind of pyramid. He was familiar, too, with the function of pyramids as known in Egypt. But this Mayan version was not a tomb, like the Pyramids of Gizeh. Externally it rather brought to mind a ziggurat, but to much greater degree than the Babylonian ziggurats it seemed to consist mostly of a stony fill providing support for the enormous stairs rising higher and higher, toward the gods of the sun and moon.

Thompson climbed up the steps. He looked at the ornamentation, the rich reliefs. On top, almost 96 feet above the jungle, he surveyed the scene. He counted one—two—three—a half-dozen scattered buildings, half-hidden in shadow, often revealed by nothing more than a gleam of moonlight on stone.

This, then, was Chichén-Itzá. From its original status as advance outpost at the beginning of the great trek to the north, it had grown into a shining metropolis, the heart of the New Empire. Again and again during the next few days Thompson climbed onto the old ruins. "I stood upon the roof of this temple one morning," he writes, "just as the first rays of the sun reddened the distant horizon. The morning stillness was profound. The noises of the night had ceased, and those of the day were not yet begun. All the sky above and the earth below seemed to be breathlessly waiting for something. Then the great round sun came up, flaming splendidly, and instantly the whole world sang and hummed. The birds in the trees and the insects on the ground sang a grand *Te Deum*. Nature herself taught primal man to be a sun-worshipper and man in his heart of hearts still follows the ancient teaching."

Thompson stood where he was, immobile and enchanted. The jungle melted away before his gaze. Wide spaces opened up, processions crept up to the temple site, music sounded, palaces became filled with reveling, the temples hummed with religious adjuration. He tried to recognize detail in the billowing forest. Then suddenly he was no longer bemused. The curtain of fancy dropped with a crash, the vision of the past vanished. The archæologist had recognized his task. For out there in the jungle green he could distinguish a narrow path, barely traced out in the weak light, a path that might lead to Chichén-Itzá's most exciting mystery: the Sacred Well.

In the record of archæological discovery in Mexico and Yucatán, up to this point there has been no personality of Schliemann's, Layard's or Petrie's stripe. There has been a lack, too, except in the trail-breaking explorations of John L. Stephens, of that piquant combination of research and adventure, of scientific success and treasure-hunting, of that romantic éclat which comes when the excavator's spade suddenly strikes on a find of great material and intellectual value.

In one respect at least, Edward Herbert Thompson was very much the Schliemann of Yucatán, for when he pushed forward to Chichén-Itzá he was staking everything on a book that no one but himself took at all seriously. Schliemann himself could not have acted more credulously. Thompson also brings Layard to mind, for like Layard, who set out on his first expedition with only sixty pounds in his purse and one companion to guide him, he plunged into the depths of the jungle with hardly a penny of backing. And when he ran into difficulties that would have cowed any other man, he reacted with all of Petrie's stubbornness.

When the world was excited by Stephens's first discoveries, the question was hotly debated whether the Mayas were the descendants of the people of the lost Atlantis, one of the lost tribes of Israel, an offshoot of the primordial American Indian stock, or what not.

As a budding archæologist, Thompson defended the Atlantean theory of Mayan descent in an article published in 1879 in a popular periodical. This was one of his very first ventures into print. The special problem of origins slipped into the background of his critical consciousness, however, when he actually went to Yucatán in 1885. At this time he was twenty-five years old, the youngest man in the American consular service. Once on the spot, he had no time for theory.

It was a hunch, a mere belief, rather than a considered judgment that drew Thompson to Yucatán. Thompson took a long chance on the validity of Diego de Landa's reports. In one of the volumes written by the bishop he discovered the story of the Sacred Well, the "Cenote" of Chichén-Itzá. Basing his account on old Mayan stories, de Landa described how, in times of drought or disaster, processions of priests and common people went to the Sacred Well of Sacrifice to propitiate the angry gods who lived in the depths. The marchers brought offerings with them to appease the deity, including beautiful maidens and captive warrior youths. After solemn ceremonies the maidens, de Landa said, were cast into the well, which was so deep that no victim ever rose to the surface.

The way of the young Mayan maidens was a path leading only to death in the terrible Cenote. They approached the brink of the pool in all their finery; then their muffled cries echoed from the walls as they struck the stagnant water.

But what else was there to Diego de Landa's story? It was a custom, he said, to throw in rich offerings after the sacrificial victims—household utensils, ornaments, gold. Thompson had read that "if this land once contained gold, the largest part of it must be in the Well." Generally this description had been dismissed as a quaint old tale with a great deal of rhetorical flourish and little factual basis. But Thompson accepted it as the gospel truth. He believed, and became grimly determined to prove the validity of his belief. When he looked down on the Way to the Well of Sacrifice from the pyramid platform, little did he know what toil was to be his before arriving at the goal.

When Thompson went to the well a second time many years later, he was an experienced jungle-man. He had roamed the length of Yucatán from north to south, his eyes had been sharpened for the task of penetrating ancient mysteries. All about him were magnificent structures, begging to be explored, offering a wonderful challenge to any archæologist. But Thompson instead turned to the well, a dark pit filled with slimy water, stones, and the woody debris of generations. Even if Diego de Landa's story were based on fact, was there the least prospect of finding in this stinking, inky hole the treasure that the priests had allegedly thrown in after their victims?

How go about exploring the depths of the well? Thompson had an adventurous answer: by the use of diving apparatus.

Having returned to the United States to attend a scientific congress, Thompson set about trying to raise money for his project. He finally got what he wanted, though everyone who listened to his plan thought him mad. "No person," he reports them as saying, "can go down into the unknown depths of that great water pit and expect to come out alive. If you want to commit suicide, why not seek a less shocking way of doing it?" But Thompson had weighed the pros and cons, and made up his mind.

"My next step was to go to Boston and take lessons in deep-sea diving," he writes. "My tutor was Captain Ephraim Nickerson, who passed to his reward a score of years ago. Under his expert and patient teaching, I became in time a fairly good diver, but by no means a perfect one, as I was to learn some time later. My next move was to adapt to my purpose an 'orange-peel bucket' dredge with the winch, tackles, steel cables, and ropes of a stiff-legged derrick and a thirty-foot swinging boom. All this material was crated and ready for immediate shipment when ordered by either letter or wire."

At last he was back at the well. The hole, at its widest point, was some 187 feet across. With the sounding lead he determined the depth of the slimy waters as approximately eighty feet. He shaped wooden logs like human beings, attached ropes to them, and threw them into the water about as far as the sacrificial maidens, in his judgment, could have been hurled by the priests when they were providing brides for the gruesome god down below. By measuring the rope after it had been hauled in, he was able to establish the greatest distance that the girls could have been tossed. The idea was simple: to localize the search at the bottom of the well. Once this had been done, Thompson set to work with his dredge.

"I doubt," he writes, "if anybody can realize the thrill I felt when, with four men at the winch handles and one at the brake, the dredge, with its steel jaw agape, swung from the platform, hung poised for a brief moment in mid-air over the dark pit and then, with a long swift glide downward, entered the still, dark waters and sank smoothly on its quest. A few moments of waiting to allow the sharp-pointed teeth to bite into the deposit, and then the forms of the workmen bent over the winch handles and muscles under the dark brown skin began to play like quicksilver as the steel cables tautened under the strain of the upcoming burden.

"The water, until then still as an obsidian mirror, began to surge and boil around the cable and continued to do so long after the bucket, its tightly closed jaws, dripping clear water, had risen, slowly but steadily, up to the rim of the pit. Swinging around by the boom, the dredge deposited on the planked receiving platform, a cartload of dark brown material, wood punk, dead leaves, broken branches, and other debris; then it swung back and hung, poised ready to seek another load. . . . Once it brought up, gripped lightly in its jaws, the trunk of a tree apparently as sound as if toppled into the pit by a storm of yesterday. This was on a Saturday. By Monday the tree had vanished and on the pile of rocks where the dredge had deposited it only a few lines of wood fiber remained, surrounded by a dark stain of a pyroligneous character. Another time the dredge brought up the bones of a jaguar and those of a deer, mute evidence of a forest tragedy."

And so the work went on, day after day. The dredge would breech the surface of the pool with a load of mud and slime, with stones and branches, with the skeleton of an animal that in some time of drought, smelling the waters of the Well of Sacrifice, had come to drink and drowned. The sun burned down on the men, the stench of decay rose from the water and came in billows from the piles of muck that towered higher and higher about the rim of the pool (see Plate XXXI).

"I began to get nervous by day and sleepless by night," says Thompson. " 'Is it possible,' I asked myself, 'that I have let my friends into all this expense and exposed myself to a world of ridicule only to prove, what many have contended, that these traditions are simply old tales, tales without any foundation in fact?' "

Then came the day when Thompson dredged up strange, yellowish-white, resinous lumps, which he retrieved from the muck. He smelled them, he even tasted them. Happily he thought of holding the resinous substance over the fire; a stupefying perfume spread on the air. Thompson had found Mayan incense at the bottom of the well, perfumed resin burned during sacrifice.

Did this prove that Thompson was on the right track? Two small pieces of sacred resin—could they discount mountains of muck and slime? For most people they would have proved exactly nothing, but their effect on Thompson was electric. His fancy took wing. "That night for the first time in weeks," he writes, "I slept soundly and long."

And Thompson carried the day. Piece after piece of the long-awaited treasure came to light, one object after another. Implements and ornaments, vases and lanceheads, obsidian knives and bowls of jadeite were lifted from the depths. Presently the first human skeleton was found. Diego de Landa had told the truth.

Before Thompson came to "the weirdest part of the weird undertaking," by chance he discovered the meaning of an old Mayan tradition. Diego de Landa, the bishop, had shown him the Way to the Well, but it was Don Diego Sarmiento de Figueroa, alcalde of Madrid in 1579, who turned Thompson's attention to the sacrificial rites connected with the Well of Sacrifice. According to Figueroa's account, which at first Thompson thought obscure to the point of being incomprehensible:

"The lords and principal personages of the land had the custom, after sixty days of abstinence and fasting, of arriving by daybreak at the mouth of the *Cenote* and throwing into it Indian women belonging to each of these lords and personages, at the same time telling these women to ask for their masters a year favorable to his particular needs and desires.

"The women, being thrown in unbound, fell into the water with great force and noise. At high noon those that could cried out loudly and ropes were let down to them. After the women came up, half dead, fires were built around them and copal incense was burned before them. When they recovered their senses, they said that below there were many people of their nation, men and women, and that they received them. When they tried to raise their heads to look at them, heavy blows were given them on the head, and when their heads were inclined downward beneath the water they seemed to see many deeps and hollows, and they, the people, responded to their queries concerning the good or the bad year that was in store for their masters."

This story, on the surface mere fable, gave Thompson, who was always on the alert for historical nuclei, many a puzzling hour. One day, however, he was sitting on the flat scow that had been lowered into the pool for use in diving operations. The scow was moored sixty or more feet below the overhang of the cliff, beneath the spot where the derrick had been set up. Looking over the low gunwale of the scow, Thompson saw something that gave him a start. "It was the key," he says, "to the story of the women messengers in the old tradition."

"The water . . . of the Well of Sacrifice," he goes on to explain, "is . . . dark-colored and turbid, changing in hue at times from brown to jade green and even to a blood red, as I shall later describe, but it is always so turbid that it reflects the light like a mirror rather than deflecting it like a crystal.

"Looking over the gunwale of the pontoon and downward to the water surface, I could see, as if looking down through great depths, 'many deeps and hollows.' They were in reality the reflections of the cavities and hollow places in the side of the cliff directly above me.

"When they recovered their senses, the women had said: 'Below, there were many people of their nation and they . . . responded to our queries.' As I continued to gaze into those deeps and hollows, I saw below many people of their nation, and they, too, responded. They were the heads and parts of the bodies of my workmen, leaning over the brink of the well to catch a glimpse of the pontoon. Meanwhile they conversed in low tones and the sound of their voices, directed downward, struck the water surface and was deflected upward to my ears in words softly sounding in native accent, yet intelligible. The whole episode gave me an explanation of the old tradition that developed as clearly as the details of a photographic negative.

"The natives of the region have long asserted that at times the waters of the Sacred Well turn to blood. We found that the green color the water sometimes shows was caused by the growth of a microscopic algæ; its occasional brown hue was caused by decaying leaves; and certain flowers and seed capsules, blood-red in color, at times gave the surface of the water an appearance like that of clotted blood.

"I mention these discoveries to show why I have come to believe that all authentic traditions have a basis of fact and can always be explained by a sufficiently close observation of the conditions."

The most difficult part of the project was yet to come, but Thompson was now to achieve a success that put all his previous ones in the shade. As the dredge went down again and again, never bringing up much besides a few stones, Thompson saw that the time had come to search with his own hands for the objects that the jaws of the dredge were letting slip through.

"Nicolas, a Greek diver with whom I had previously made arrangements," Thompson writes, "arrived from the Bahamas where he had been gathering sponges. He brought an assistant, also a Greek, and we prepared at once for under-water exploration.

"We first rigged the air pump in the boat, no longer a scow but once more a dignified pontoon, and then the two Greeks, turned instructors, taught a chosen gang of natives how to manage the pumps and send through the tube, in a steady current, the air upon which our lives depended, and how to read and answer signals sent up from below. When they considered that the men were letter perfect, we were ready to dive.

"We rode down to the pontoon in the basin of the dredge, and, while the assistant took his place by the men at the pump to direct them, we put on our suits, outfits of waterproof canvas with big copper helmets weighing more than thirty pounds and equipped with plate-glass goggle-eyes and air valves near the ears, lead necklaces nearly half as heavy as the helmets and canvas shoes with thick wrought-iron soles. With the speaking tube, air hose, and life-line carefully adjusted, I toddled, aided by the assistant, to where a short, wide ladder fastened to the gunwale led down into the water.

"As I stepped on the first rung of the ladder, each of the pumping gang, my faithful native boys, left his place in turn and with a very solemn face shook hands with me and then went back again to wait for the signal. It was not hard to read their thoughts. They were bidding me a last farewell, never expecting to see me again. Then, releasing my hold on the ladder, I sank like a bag of lead, leaving behind me a silvery chain of bubbles.

"During the first ten feet of descent, the light rays changes from yellow to green and then to purplish black. After that I was in utter darkness. Sharp pains shot through my ears, because of the increasing air pressure. When I gulped and opened the air valves in my helmet a sound like 'pht! pht!' came from each ear and then the pain ceased. Several times this process had to be repeated before I stood on the bottom. I noted another curious sensation on my way down. I felt as if I were rapidly losing weight until, as I stood on the flat end of a big stone column that had fallen from the old ruined shrine above, I seemed to have almost no weight at all. I fancied that I was more like a bubble than a man clogged by heavy weights.

"But I felt as well a strange thrill when I realized that I was the only living being who had ever reached this place alive and expected to leave it again still living. Then the Greek diver came down beside me and we shook hands.

"I had brought with me a submarine flashlight and a submarine telephone, both of which I discarded after the first descent. The submarine flashlight was serviceable in clear water or water merely turbid. The medium in which we had to work was neither water nor mud, but a combination of both, stirred up by the workings of the dredge. It was a thick mixture like gruel and no ray as feeble as that of a flashlight could ever penetrate it. So we had to work in utter darkness; yet, after a short time, we hardly felt the fact to be a serious inconvenience; for the palpic whorls of our finger-ends seemed not only to distinguish objects by the sense of touch, but actually to aid in distinguishing color.

"The submarine telephone was of very little use and was soon laid aside. Communication by the speaking-tube and the life-line was easier and even quicker than by telephone. There was another strange thing that I have never heard mentioned by other divers. Nicolas and I found that at the depth we were working, from sixty to eighty feet, we could sit down and put our noses together—the noses of our helmets, be it understood—and could then talk to each other quite intelligibly. Our voices sounded flat and lifeless as if coming from a great distance, but I could give him my instructions and I could hear his replies quite clearly.

"The curious loss of weight under water led me into several ludicrous mishaps before I became accustomed to it. In order to go from place to place on the bottom, I had only to stand up and push with my foot on the rock bottom. At once I would rise like a rocket, sail majestically through the mud gruel and often land several feet beyond where I wanted to go.

"The well itself is, roughly speaking, an oval with one hundred and eighty-seven feet as its longer diameter. From the jungle surface above to the water surface varied from sixty-seven to eighty feet. Where the water surface commenced could be ascertained easily, but where it left off and the mud of the bottom began was not so easy to determine, for the lines of demarcation did not exist. However, I can roughly estimate that of the total depth of mud and water, about sixty-five feet, thirty feet was a mud deposit sufficiently consistent to sustain tree-branches and even tree-roots of considerable size. About eighteen feet of this deposit was so compact that it held large rocks, fallen columns, and wall stones. Into this mud and silt deposit the dredge had bitten until it had left what I called the 'fertile zone' with a vertical wall of mud almost as hard as rock at the bottom and fully eighteen feet high. In this were embedded rocks of varied shapes and sizes, as raisins are embedded in plum puddings.

"Imagine us, then, searching in the darkness, with these mud walls all about us, exploring the cracks and the crevices of the rough limestone bottom for the objects that the dredge had failed to bring up to the light of day. Imagine also that every little while one of the stone blocks, loosened from its place in the wall by the infiltration of the water, would come plunging down upon us in the worse than Stygian darkness that was all about us. After all, it was not so bad as it sounds. It is true that the big blocks fell when and where they would and we were powerless to direct or even to see them, but so long as we kept our speaking-tubes, air hose and life-line and ourselves well away from the wall surface we were in no special danger. As the rock masses fell, the push of the water before and around them reached us before the rock did and even if we did not get away of our own accord, it struck us like a huge, soft cushion and sent us caroming, often head down and feet upward, balancing and tremulous like the white of an egg in a glassful of water, until the commotion had subsided and we could get on our feet again. Had we incautiously been standing with our backs to the wall, we should have been sheared in two as cleanly as if by a pair of gigantic shears and two more victims would have been sacrificed to the Rain God.

"The present natives of the region believe that big snakes and strange monsters live in the dark depths of the Sacred Well. Whether this belief is due to some faint remembrance of the old serpent worship, or is based upon something seen by some of the natives, can only be guessed at. I have seen big snakes and lizards swimming in these waters, but they were only snakes and lizards that in chasing their prey through the trees above had fallen into the pool and were trying to get out. We saw no traces of any reptiles or monsters of unusual size anywhere in the pool.

"No strange reptile ever got me in its clutches, but I had one experience that is worth repeating. Both of us, the Greek diver and I, were busily digging with our fingers in a narrow crevice of the floor and it was yielding such rich returns that we neglected some of our usual precautions. Suddenly I felt something over us, an enormous something that with a stealthy gliding movement was pressing down on me. Something smooth and slimy was pushing me irresistibly into the mud. For a moment my blood ran cold. Then I felt the Greek beside me pushing at the object and I aided him until we had worked ourselves free. It was the decaying trunk of a tree that had drifted off the bank of mud and in sinking had encountered my stooping body.

"One day I was seated on a rock gloating over a remarkable find, a moulded bell of metal, and I quite forgot to open the air valves as I should have done. I put the find in my pouch and rose to change my position, when suddenly I began to float upward like an inflated bladder. It was ludicrous, but also dangerous, for at this depth the blood is charged with bubbles like champagne and unless one rises slowly and gives the blood time to become normal, a terrible disease called the 'bends' results, from which one can die in terrible agony. Luckily I had enough presence of mind to open the valves before going up very far and so escaped the extreme penalty, but I suffer the effects of my carelessness today in a pair of injured ear drums and greatly impaired hearing.

"Even after I had opened the valves and was rising more and more slowly, I struck the bottom of the pontoon topsy-turvy, half dazed by the concussion. Then, realizing what had happened and laughing at the thought of the fright my boys must have had when they heard me thump on the bottom of the boat, I scrambled from under it and threw my arm over the gunwale. As my helmet appeared over the side I felt a pair of arms thrown around my neck and startled eyes looked into the plate-glass goggles of my helmet. As they took off my diving-suit and I rested on a seat, getting back into normal condition and enjoying a cup of hot black coffee and the sunlight, the young Greek told me the story.

" 'The men,' he said, 'turned a pale yellow with terror when they heard the knock on the bottom that announced your unexpected arrival. When I told them what it was, they shook their heads mournfully and one of them, faithful old Juan Mis, said: 'It's no use, *El Amo* the master is dead. He was swallowed by the Serpent God and spewed up again. We shall never hear him speak to us again'; and his eyes filled with tears. When your helmet came over the gunwale and he looked into its window, he raised both arms high above his head and said with great thankfulness, 'Thank God, he is still alive, and laughing.'

"As for the results of our dredging and diving into the great water pit, the first and most important is that we proved that in all essential details the traditions about the Sacred Well are true. Then we found a great store of symbolical figures carved on jade stone and beaten on gold and copper disks, copal masses and nodules of resin incense, many skeletal remains, a number of *hul chés,* or dart-throwers, and many darts with finely worked points of flint, calcite, and obsidian; and some bits of ancient fabric. All these had real archæ-ological value. Objects of nearly pure gold were encountered, both cast, beaten, and engraved in *repoussé,* but they were few in number and relatively unimportant. Most of the so-called gold objects were of low-grade alloy, with more copper than gold in them. That which gave them their chief value were the symbolical and other figures cast or carved upon them.

"Most of the objects brought up were in fragments. Probably they were votive offerings broken before being thrown into the well, as a ritualistic act performed by the priests. The breaking was always in such a way that the head and features of the personages represented on jade plaque or gold disk were left intact. We have reason to believe that these jade pendants, gold disks, and other ornaments of metal or stone when broken were considered to have been killed. It is known that these ancient civilized races of America believed, as did their still more ancient forbears of northern Asia and as the Mongols to this day believe, that jade and other sacred objects have life. Accordingly these ornaments were broken or 'killed' that their spirits might serve as ornaments to the messenger, whose spirit would be appropriately adorned when it finally appeared before the *Hunal Ku,* the One Supreme God in the Heavens."

When Thompson's report of his finds in the Sacred Well reached the public, the world pricked up its ears. The circumstances of the finds were so unusual, the treasure brought to safety out of the soupy silt of the pool so rich, that the whole affair was bound to attract notice. Yet in truth the material value was of secondary consideration.

"The value in money of the objects recovered from the Sacred Well with so much labor and at such expense is, to be sure, insignificant," Thompson writes. "But the value of all things is relative. The historian delves into the past as the engineer digs into the ground, and for the same reason, to make the future secure. It is conceivable that some of these objects have graved upon their surfaces, embodied in symbols, ideas and beliefs that reach back through the ages to the primal homes of these peoples in that land beyond the seas. To help prove that is well worth the labor of a lifetime."

Even so, the value of the treasure of Chichén-Itzá has been surpassed in our time only by the treasure of Tutankhamen. The gold of the Pharaoh had been found interred with a mummy, laid to rest in a stately tomb. But the gold of the Cenote was fished out from among the bones of young maidens who had been hurled, screaming, into eternity by cruel priests as offerings to cruel gods. Had ever one of the girls pulled a priest into the water with her? Among the many female skulls Thompson found one of a man, a skull with the protuberant glabellæ of an old man. A priest's?

When Thompson died, in 1935, he had no cause for regretting the way he had spent his life, though he himself says that he squandered most of his substance investigating the ancient Mayas. During the twenty-four years that he served as United States consul in Yucatán, and in nearly fifty years of archæological digging, he had seldom seen the inside of an office. He roamed the jungle and lived with the Indians, literally sharing their lot, eating their food, sleeping in their huts, speaking their languages. An infection left him with a lame leg, and diving into the Sacred Well resulted in a chronic disturbance of his hearing. His work shows all the signs of excessive enthusiasm. His first reports often overshot the mark by far. Once, when he found several superimposed graves in a pyramid, and later the main grave in the rock beneath the base of the pyramid, it seemed to him that he had discovered the last resting place of Kukulcan, the fabled primeval teacher of the Mayan people. Finding precious ornaments of jadeite that had been quarried at considerable distance from Yucatán, he immediately revived his old Atlantean theory of Mayan origin, though by this time he was an experienced archæologist. And yet is not enthusiasm a necessary thing? How else still crippling doubts if not with the exuberance of the ever hopeful?

Meanwhile extensive excavations have been carried out in Yucatán, Chiapas, and Guatemala. More recently airplanes have proved useful in archæological exploration of this difficult terrain. Colonel Charles Lindbergh was the first to photograph bird's-eye views of a civilization that was already hoary with age when Cortés discovered the New World. In 1930 P. C. Madeira, Jr., and J. A. Mason flew over the virgin forest of Middle America, and from the air photographed and mapped hitherto unknown Mayan islands of settlement in the jungle.

Most recently, in 1947, an expedition was sent to Bonampak in Chiapas. Discoveries were made that appear to have added significantly to the already rich finds of the past. The expedition was financed by the United Fruit Company and scientifically sponsored by the Carnegie Institute of Washington. The United Fruit Company expedition was led by Giles Greville Healey. In a short time eleven fine temples of the Old Empire period were found, dating back to the years immediately preceding the great migration, and also some magnificent stelæ, one of them twice as large as any previously discovered. This stele is 19.2 feet high and covered with carvings. But the most wonderful thing brought to light by Healey in the jungle was the wall paintings. The once brilliant red, yellow, ocher, green, and blue colors were revealed by technical means, and showed warriors, kings, and priests in full ceremonial costume. Pictures of this sort had been found before only at Chichén-Itzá in the Temple of the Warriors.

The most intensively excavated Mayan site has been Chichén-Itzá, the Mayan metropolis. The contemporary visitor is greeted by an altogether different sight from the one that met the eyes of Thompson on that memorable moonlit night. The jungle has now been cleared away from the ruins, allowing them to rise free and well-kept out of open spaces. The tourists come in buses over roads originally hacked out of the forest with machetes. They look at the Temple of the Warriors, with its northwest colonnade, just inside of which begin the steep stairs leading to the platform top of the pyramid. They see the great observatory, a circular structure with windows so placed as to focus the eye on certain astronomical lines of sight. They wander through the ball courts, the largest of which, in the northern part of the city, is 545 feet long and 225 feet wide on the outside. Here the Mayan *jeunesse dorée* played a game somewhat resembling basketball. And they come at last to the "Castillo," the biggest of the pyramids. The steps mount the eight terraces of the edifice, which on its upper platform bears the Temple of Kukulcan, the Plumed Serpent (see Plate XXIX).

The onlooker is overwhelmed when he looks into the terrible stone visages at close range, the monstrous snake-heads, the gargoyle gods, the screaming jaguars. And he is taken aback again when he discovers that every symbol, picture, and relief is related to some astronomical number. The two crosses on the eyebrows of a serpent-head; a jaguar claw at the ear of the god Kukulcan; a gate-like shape; a series of "shells"; a recurrent step form—all these glyphs expressed number and time. Nowhere in the world have these categories been coupled with such terrifying forms of artistic expression. (Graham Greene, the English novelist, who hates all ruins, and who took a trip some ten years ago through Mexico and Yucatán, remarks that: "Here heresy was not a confusion of human feeling—as for example Manichæism—but a mistake in reckoning! ... One expects to see a *quod erat demonstrandum* [he is referring to pyramids in general and that of Teotihuacán in particular]—the pyramids correctly added, the number of the terraces multiplied by the number of steps and divided by the total area—and a result as inhuman as an algebraic problem!") Realizing that frozen mathematics can be a hell, the thoughtful visitor looks around for some signs of life in the ornamentation, at least for a plant motif. And, behold, he discovers that the whole magnificent body of plastic works produced by the Mayas, though they literally depended for their lives on the maize plant and were surrounded by the rankest, lushest sort of vegetation, is remarkable for a scarcity of plant forms. Of the eight hundred species of cactus in the region, not one has given rise to a decorative device, and only a few of the innumerable kinds of flowers were ever reproduced in stone. Recently a five-sectioned ornamental figure has been identified as the blossom of the *Bombax aquaticum*, a tree that grows half in water, and is considered a rarity in Mayan art. Even the columns of Mayan architecture represent the erect bodies of hideous snakes with darting tongues (see Plate XXX), whereas in architecture elsewhere in the world the upward-thrusting tree trunk is the usual inspiration.

Two of these serpent columns are found in front of the Temple of Warriors. The snake's horned head is pressed to the ground, the mouth gapes wide, with the body stretching a short distance flat on the ground, then rising vertically to support the temple roof. The feathered serpent columns and the whole Temple of the Warriors—indeed, almost all the structures in Chichén-Itzá—convinced the archæologists that here they were dealing with a special architectural style. The general motif of Chichén-Itzá did not accord completely with the New Empire style, as distinguished from that of the Old Empire. Certain features set it apart from the architecture of Copán and Palenque, Piedras Négras and Uaxactún. An intensive study was made of Chichén-Itzá artifacts. The archæologists tested and compared, here a line, there an ornamental figure, here a ceremonial mask, there an intercalary glyph. They concluded that alien hands had been at work in Chichén-Itzá. There were definite signs of foreign thinking and foreign techniques.

But where did this intrusive influence come from? The archæologists turned their attention to central Mexico, though not to the architecture of the Aztec empire, which was much younger than the Mayas, but to those buildings which were already ancient when the Aztecs invaded Mexico.

Was there no historical evidence, no guide like Diego de Landa, who might lead to the understanding of the astounding fact that the mighty Mayan culture had once yielded to a foreign influence? Was there no one who at least might give a hint as to the origins of these great "architects" from outside the Mayan kingdom?

There was a man whose allusions to this paradox had been known for a long time, but who never before had been accorded serious attention. He was an Aztec prince, Ixtlilxochitl—a perfectly amazing man.

# 31/AZTECS, MAYAS, AND TOLTECS: WHENCE DID THEY COME?

"Fernando de Alva Ixtlilxochitl, who flourished in the beginning of the sixteenth century," wrote Prescott, "was a native of Tezcuco, and descended in a direct line from the sovereigns of that kingdom. . . . He filled the office of interpreter to the viceroy, to which he was recommended by his acquaintance with the ancient hieroglyphics, and his knowledge of the Mexican and Spanish languages. . . . He has often lent a too willing ear to traditions and reports which would startle the more skeptical criticism of the present time. Yet there is an appearance of good faith and simplicity in his writings, which may convince the reader, that, when he errs, it is from no worse cause than national partiality. And surely such partiality is excusable in the descendant of a proud line, shorn of its ancient splendors, which it was soothing to his own feelings to revive again,— though with something more than their legitimate lustre,—on the canvas of history. . . . His earlier annals— though no one of his manuscripts has been printed— have been diligently studied by the Spanish writers in Mexico . . . and his reputation, like Sahagun's, has doubtless suffered by the process."

Others have expressed a much less tolerant opinion of this prince among scholars. The "century of source criticism" considered him to be nothing more nor less than a romantic teller of tales, a kind of Indian bard. They gave no credence at all to his colorful account of his people's past. And it is very true that some of Ixtlilxochitl's statements are hard to swallow—indeed, virtually unbelievable. The two most important German students of Mexican archæology, Eduard Seler and Walter Lehmann, were the first to give the Tezcucan chronicler belated credit for having told far more truth than anyone had ever suspected.

Repeatedly in our history of archæology we have encountered situations where some new collection of data has threatened to knock the accepted and hard-won historical picture into a cocked hat. We have seen, too, how often this danger, for a time, has been met either by ignoring the new facts or by carefully skirting them. For there is a self-protective, conservative tendency at work in science as well as everywhere else.

The know-nothing spirit has had its day in Mexican archæology. For example, certain Mexican ruins are half-buried in lava, which suggests that they are very old. These prehistoric artifacts, which were found in the shadow of much younger monuments, could not be fitted into the cultural picture developed through the study of the later Mexican and the Mayan societies. Whenever during the nineteenth century the archæologists ran into one of these antique structures—no one made it his business to seek them out—they turned their eyes the other way. Prescott's interesting remarks on Teotihuacán, the city of ruins past which Cortés marched on his flight from Mexico City after the *noche triste*, could not be entirely ignored, one might think. Nevertheless they were, and almost all archæologists can be charged with this obvious oversight until the turn of the last century.

Cautious intimations and many question marks—that was about all the commentary on these very old ruins amounted to. Then, in rapid succession, the ruins were laid bare. An excavation program that could have been undertaken long before was abruptly condensed in three decades. The most surprising feature of this persistent neglect is the fact that no expeditions had to be outfitted to get at these particular pyramids. There was no need here for risking fevers, encounters with jungle animals, fighting one's way through swamp and forest with the machete, and the like. All the archæologist

had to do, believe it or not, was board a train and ride
to the sites. He could even see them on a Sunday afternoon walk. For several of these largest and most impressive monuments of Middle American culture lay
within an hour's ride by train from the center of Mexico City—indeed, actually on the municipal boundary
lines.

Ixtlilxochitl was a baptized native prince, a well-edu-
cated man, thoroughly versed in the religious practices
of the Mexican Indians. When the wars of the period
of conquest were over, he began to sketch out the history of his people. He kept his ear pressed close to the
lips of tradition. His history (which later generations
refused to trust) went back to gray primeval times
when the city of Tula (Tollan in the present Mexican
state of Hidalgo) was founded by the Toltec people.
Ixtlilxochitl told great tales about these Toltecs. They
had known how to write, he maintained, and how to
reckon, make calendars, build palaces and temples. The
rulers of Tula also had a great reputation for wisdom.
Their laws were just, their religion was mild and free
from the cruelties of later epochs. Their empire, according to Ixtlilxochitl, lasted five hundred years. Then
came famine, civil war, and dynastic quarrels. Another
people, the Chichimecs, got control of the land. The
Toltec survivors migrated first to Tabasco, later to
Yucatán.

It is notable that the first man—he was a Frenchman—to validate Ixtlilxochitl's chronicles by an actual
find did not even then succeed in establishing the Indian historian's credibility among archæologists as a
whole. In the first place, no reputable archæologist believed in the existence of the city of Tula, which figured so prominently in the Indian Prince's writings.
Ixtlilxochitl wrote factually enough about his Tula, but
no matter, he was blandly ignored. Some commentators
suggested that Tula and the mythical Thule were somehow connected. Even the very physical existence of a
little town called Tula to the north of Mexico City

made no impression, for nowhere in the vicinity of Tula were to be seen any of the ruins mentioned in the legends recorded in the works of Ixtlilxochitl. Even when the Frenchman Désiré Charnay in the course of a treasure hunt in the 1880's found vestiges of a pyramid at Tula de Allende, the archæologists paid no attention to his report.

Not until World War II, at a time when almost all the rest of the world was busy making ruins of contemporary artifacts, did Mexican archæologists begin to excavate the ancient Toltec sites.

And behold!

In 1940 the whole archæological world had to bow before Prince Ixtlilxochitl! Had not similar submissions been exacted for Homer by Schliemann, and for the Bible by Layard? The amazed archæologists found ancient Tula, first city of the Toltecs! Previously they had found the Pyramids of the Sun and the Moon. They discovered well-preserved relics and fine sculptures under three feet of rubbish and earth.

Thus in rapid succession artifacts of the Toltec "culture beneath the cultures" was brought into the light of day. Actually the inhabitants of Mexico City had lived for several hundred years in the very midst of these pyramids without knowing about them. They had walked by them on the way to work in the fields. They had lain at their feet when they took time out for a drink of pulque, that man-murdering agave schnapps which the Toltecs themselves used to ferment. One might say that all the people of Mexico City and environs had to do was follow their noses and bump into a pyramid.

The exploration of the Toltec pyramids proceeded with the typically swift pace of an archæological investigation once fairly launched. Within three decades excavations of the most sensational import were carried out. In 1925 the archæologists digging out the Pyramid of the Serpent at the northwest boundary of Mexico City found that they were working not on one pyramid, but on eight of them—an onion in stone, so to

speak, one shell nested within another. Calendrical data
revealed that probably every fifty-two years another
shell had been added to the pyramid. A little arithmetic
shows that this structure alone had been worked on
for over four hundred years. Except for the cathedral
building of the West, there is no single architectural
project anywhere that continued so long. In the middle
of Mexico City archæologists dug for the remains of the
great teocalli, the one destroyed by Cortés, and actually
found the foundation walls. The excavators then betook
themselves out of the city, to the present-day San Juan
Teotihuacán, some thirty-one miles away. Here was located the largest of all the pyramid fields, the most
splendid relic of the ancient Toltec culture, the city
"where god was offered prayers." (Such is the meaning
of the name Teotihuacán. Note the peculiarity that the
Mexican word *teo* is the same as the Old Greek word
for "god." It is only proper to add, however, that no
inferences of any kind may be drawn from this phonetic
coincidence.) The already exposed section of this field
of ruins now covers 7.6 square miles—and but a fraction
of the whole field has been opened up. This is the city
that the Toltecs, before their flight southward, seemingly covered with a layer of earth a yard deep—a su-
pererogatory measure hardly less astonishing than the
structures themselves. The larger of the pyramids—they
are stepped pyramids with the characteristic stairways—
is 128 feet in height.

Eventually the archæologists struck out into the
provinces. Eduard Seler was the first to describe the
fortress pyramid of Xochicalco, fifty miles south of the
Mexican capital. Diggings were carried out at Cholula,
where Cortés committed one of his worst acts of be-
trayal. Working inside the largest pyramid—which once
covered a larger area than the Pyramid of Cheops—the
excavators disclosed labyrinthine passages five eighths
of a mile long. The search then moved farther south.
In 1931 Alfonso Caso, a Mexican, on government commission, dug into Monte Albán at Oaxaca—and what
every excavator almost certainly secretly hopes for came

to pass. Alfonso Caso found a treasure—the treasure of Monte Albán.

"Is there any other spot on earth," asks Egon Erwin Kisch, a noted journalist of our time, "so completely shrouded in darkness and so mute in the face of all our questions? Which feeling is paramount in us, enchantment or bewilderment?" And then he inquires into the reasons for this conflict of feeling. "Is it the spatial complex, the outlines of which suggest a prospect of infinity? Or is it the pyramids, which look like stately stairways leading on and up into the inner reaches of heaven? Or is it the temple court which— thanks to our powers of imagination—is filled with many thousands of Indians in impetuous prayer? Or is it the observatory, with peepholes let into the masonry walls which provide a line of sight along the azimuth of the meridian? Or is it the spectacle of a stadium such as Europe has never built from ancient Roman days to the twentieth century, one hundred and twenty steeply rising tiers of stone seats?

"Or is it the system," he goes on, "of arranging hundreds of tombs so that no grave disturbs its neighbor, with consequent avoidance of a cemetery effect? Could it be the gay mosaics, the frescoes with their figures, scenes, symbols, and hieroglyphs? Or the vessels of clay, sacrificial bowls of noble sweep, urns of geometric rectilinearity, four-footed, and within each of the feet a little bell that tinkles for help if an intruder threatens to make off with it?

"Or is it the ornamentation? . . .

"Who would have ever imagined 'savages' could polish rock-crystal with such precision technique, or assemble necklaces in twenty rows made of 854 chiseled and mathematically equal constituent parts of gold and precious stones? A brooch shows a knight of death that Lucas Cranach himself could not have made more apocalyptic. Garters that are like the ones worn by the Knights of the Garter. Ear-rings seemingly woven from tears and thorns. Headdresses—tiaras worthy of a pope of popes. Plaited rings to set off the fingernails. Brace-

464     The Aztecs, the Mayas, and the Toltecs

lets and arm-bands with fat embossments, cloak-pins, and clasps made of jade, turquoise, pearls, amber, coral, obsidian, jaguar-teeth, bones, and mussel shells. A gold mask over the cheeks and nose of which is sculptured a trophy made of human skin. Fans fashioned from the feathers of the quetzal bird—what Byzantine empress, what Hindu maharani, what American multimillionairess ever in her whole life owned such a lovely trinket as many of these Indians keep beside them even in the grave?"

"Questions, nothing but questions on Monte Albán," is the Kisch chapter heading for this piece on Mexico. But is it only Monte Albán that invites interrogation?

We must admit that up to the present we know less than nothing about the master builders of pre-Aztec times. Less than nothing also implies, in this case, that we are burdened with a great deal of false information. Mexico and Yucatán are jungle-lands; and when the archæologist begins to interpret the Toltecs, he loses himself in these jungles. How much is actually known?

This much has been confirmed: the Aztec, Mayan, and Toltec cultures are all closely related. All three societies built pyramids, with steps leading up to the gods of sun or moon. All these pyramids, we know today, were located according to astronomical lines of sight and erected under calendrical dictate. Oliver G. Rickertson, Jr., an American, was the first to prove this, in 1928, using evidence found on a Mayan pyramid in Uaxactún. Today we have further proof of this practice in later times from Chichén-Itzá, and for more ancient times from Monte Albán. All these peoples lived under the Damoclean sword of their great calendrical cycles, as for example when they believed that the world came to an end every fifty-two years. The power of the priesthood depended on the universal acceptance of such ideas. The priests alone were able to avert the threat of disaster. The means that they used to do this became with the passage of time more drastic—that is,

The sky god Quetzalcoatl as a feathered serpent, from a relief at Xochicalco. Drawing by Miguel Covarrubias from his "Mexico South" (copyright 1946 by Alfred A. Knopf, Inc.).

more cruel—and finally degenerated into frightful human offerings and the feast of Xipec Totec, the god of earth and spring, in whose honor the priests flayed human beings, drawing the bloody skin off the quivering victim while he was still alive.

The close relationship of Aztecs, Mayas, and Toltecs appears again in their gods, which in this respect are comparable to the Greek and Roman pantheons. One of the principal Aztec-Toltec gods was the great and wise Quetzalcoatl, who was called Kukumatz in Guatemala, and Kukulcan in Yucatán. His image, the plumed serpent, is found on both the oldest and the most recent Indian edifices. Even the mode of life was —and still is—much the same among all the Middle American Indians. And although their languages are numerous, they all belong—if we take into account only the civilized tribes—to one or the other of two large linguistic groups.

Once these basic kinships have been established (recently an almost incalculable amount of detail has been collected on the subject) the question of external relationships arises, of the wavelike contacts among these peoples as they flowed against and over one another—in short, the question of their history. Here, so far as the very oldest phase goes, we are groping in the dark. In spite of outstanding research, which has yielded a highly accurate correlation of the Mayan calendar with our own, we still lack fixed points of reference. The jungle we are clearing away from the pyramids and palaces of prehistoric America gives up abundant architectural remains, but as yet no panoramic vision of the past. We find dates, but no history. We can spin theories, but the supporting facts are inadequate.

Some investigators, basing their opinion on a variety of signs, believe that the great pyramid in Mexico City was built by the Toltecs in the fourth century of our era.

Now, several of these pyramids located at different sites from Tula to Monte Albán have been discussed, yet one of the most important has yet to be mentioned. This is the Pyramid of Cuicuilco, which stands on a mound 22.4 feet high, situated at the southern limits of Mexico City. The Pyramid of Cuicuilco rises up out of a weird landscape of darkly stony aspect. At one time the volcanoes Ajusco and Xitli (perhaps only the latter) erupted. The god within the pyramid was apparently remiss in diverting the glowing flood of lava that flowed about the pyramid, for half the structure was drowned in bubbling muck. The archæologists investigating this phenomenon called on colleagues from another faculty, the geologists, for help. How old is the lava, they inquired. The geologists, not realizing that their answer was knocking a world picture awry, answered: "Eight thousand years." We have learned since then that this answer was wrong, because the geologists' methods of dating are inadequate for relatively brief time spans.

We now assume, though without absolute proof, that the early American Indians were descendants of Mongolian tribesmen who came either by boat or by way of a land bridge from Siberia to Alaska and so down the coast to the lower latitudes of the continent. Where the Toltecs in particular came from, assuming the existence of a migratory parent group, and why the Toltecs should have been the only people from Alaska to Panama capable of inventing the ingenious devices that mark their culture, we do not know.

Indeed, we do not even know exactly whether it really was the Toltecs who set the cultural stage in Middle America. What prehistoric role, we might ask, was played by the Zapotecs, or the Olmecs, vestiges of which societies can be found all over Mexico? If we name the Toltecs as the precursors of the Mayan and Aztec cultures, we are using the word Toltec as a collective label for all the creators of Middle American culture. The term Toltec may mean nothing but "master builder."

We may be justified, in order to clarify the interaction of the three great Indian empires, in taking the liberty of quoting an analogy between Middle American and Old World cultures mentioned in one of the works on Mexico by the German archæologist Theodor-Wilhelm Danzel: "Occasionally in order to characterize the Aztec, as distinguished from the Mayan, culture," he says, "analogies with the Old World have been adduced, in which the Aztecs have been compared to the Romans, and the Mayas to the Greeks. These parallels, on the whole, are apt. The Mayas were indeed a people who (like the Greeks) split up into many communities, who quarreled among themselves, and who formed temporary alliances only when it became necessary to resist a common enemy. But even though the Mayas did not distinguish themselves as a political power, they have to their credit remarkable achievements in sculpture, architecture, astronomy, and mathematics.

"The Aztecs, on the other hand," he goes on to say, "were a warlike folk, who built their empire on the ruins of another people (the Toltecs) unable to resist the power of their onslaught. The Toltecs, if we carry our analogy still further, would parallel the Etruscans."

We might draw still another analogy. In respect of historical function the Toltecs are similar to the inventive Sumerians. The Mayas, in this analogy, then become the Babylonians, who as the usufructuaries of the

Sumerians' superior inventions built a cultural empire of their own. And the Aztecs, in this context, then bring to mind the bellicose Assyrians, who used their superior mentality for pure power ends. Carrying out the parallel still further, Mexico City, "beheaded" at the height of its fame by the Spaniards, compares with proud Nineveh, capital of the Assyrians, which suffered a like fate at the hands of the Medes.

Both analogies, however, fail to hit the mark in one respect. They give no clue to why the Toltecs, long after their own empire had collapsed, should suddenly decamp and penetrate the New Empire of the Mayas, where they left their stamp on the city of Chichén-Itzá. There is no parallel for this in ancient history. But did such a thing actually happen? Everything in fact could have been quite different. There is a Mexican legend that suggests a different historical sequence, a legend in which even the coming of the Spaniards is prefigured in mythical language.

The legend tells how the Indian deity Quetzalcoatl came from the "Land of the Rising Sun." He wore a long white robe and had a beard; he taught the people crafts and customs and laid down wise laws. He created an empire in which the ears of corn were as long as men are tall, and caused bolls of colored cotton to grow on cotton plants. But for some reason or other he had

The Aztecs attack Tehuantepec (Durán). Drawing by Miguel Covarrubias from his "Mexico South" (copyright 1946 by Alfred A. Knopf, Inc.).

One of the greatest Mayan and Aztec gods, Quetzalcoatl, known in Guatemala under the name of Kukumatz, and in Yucatán as Kukulcan. All these names mean "Feathered Serpent." The drawing is after a relief found in Chichén-Itzá, and illustrates the Toltec influence on Mayan art of the New Empire.

to leave his empire. He took his laws, his writings, his songs, and went away down the same road he had come. In Cholula he tarried, and there once more gave the people the benefits of his wisdom. Then he betook himself to the seashore, where he began to weep, and ended by immolating himself in fire, whereupon his heart became the morning star. Others say that he went aboard his ship and journeyed back to the land whence he came, across the sea. But all the legends of Quetzalcoatl unanimously agree that he promised to come again.

So often throughout our story have we seen the kernel of a legend historically validated that we must not make the mistake of dismissing this story as mere poetic invention, however fictitious it may appear at first sight. May we not think of the white robe as connoting a white skin? Especially in view of the fact that Quetzalcoatl is supposed to have worn a beard, whereas beards are extremely rare among Indians.

It has been suggested that Quetzalcoatl was actually a missionary from some distant, unknown country. The theory that he may have been an early Catholic missionary of the sixth century may safely be dismissed. Nor need we spend much time on the supposition that he was the Apostle Thomas himself. Those who seek to use the legend of Quetzalcoatl as a possible support for the notion that Mayan culture was founded by Atlanteans—a theory that once appealed to the young Thompson—can hardly expect to prevail. The Atlantis theory enjoys absolutely no scientific probability.

There is simply a great deal we do not yet know.

We know only this: the Spaniards, who appeared to the Aztecs as "the white gods from the east" when they first arrived in Mexico, because the Aztecs remembered the bearded white god and his promise to return —these representatives of European civilization surely did not behave like descendants of Quetzalcoatl, who had preached morality and justice.

# PART FIVE

# BOOKS THAT CANNOT YET BE WRITTEN

*If we human beings want to feel humility, there is no need to look at the starred infinity above. It suffices to turn our gaze upon the world cultures that existed thousands of years before us, achieved greatness before us, and perished before us.*

We are at the end of the panorama of great archæological discoveries, at the end of a promenade that has led us through five millennia. Yet the theme is by no means exhausted. At the same time the choice we have made among the multiplicity of archæological discoveries was guided all along the route by a definite intention. By arranging excavations according to the cultural arena where they occurred, rather than in chronological order, we have achieved in our four "books" an almost spontaneously created picture of four closed cultural provinces, four of the most important advanced cultures known to mankind. It must be remembered in this connection that between the few great cultures and the myriad primitive societies throughout the world a difference obtains that suggests the difference between "history" and vegetation, between apperception and instinct, between a creative molding of the environment and passive subsistence.

By "books that cannot yet be written" it is implied that there are three cultures that rank almost as high in the developmental scale as those already explored. These three are the Hittite, the Indus, and the Inca cultures. The archæological literature given over to them has yet, however, to reach a stage definitive enough to allow its condensation into the sort of "books" of which our story is constructed.[1]

[1] This was written in 1949. In 1951 and 1953 the author participated in two digs in the southeast of present-day Turkey. *See* C. W. Ceram: *The Secret of the Hittites: The Discovery of an Ancient Empire* (New York: Alfred A. Knopf; 1958).

I have deliberately chosen for portrayal those cultures whose exploration has been richly fraught with romantic adventure. Actually we know almost as much about the Incas as about the Mayas; but there is neither a Stephens nor a Thompson among the archæologists who have worked in the Andes. On the other hand, we also know a great deal about the history of Chinese culture. Here, however, our knowledge derives only negligibly from excavational activity; and so it is plain why both these cultures have been left out of account.

For some decades the Hittite and Indus Valley regions have been thoroughly investigated, and with much success. "Books" about them, accordingly, will some day have to be written. Yet one fact we must bear clearly in mind. Even were we to extend our four books by three more, even then we should by no means have covered all cultures of advanced status. For the ordinary educated man of our time, the Greco-Roman culture, outside the Christian-European heritage, is the only spiritual influence of which he is actively conscious. Yet even when we were treating the mysterious Sumerian people, we were beginning to realize that many much more remote and older cultural forces still lurk in the hinterland of our being. The modern English historian Arnold J. Toynbee sees the history of mankind as a contiguity and succession—mostly in a father-son relationship—of *twenty-one* cultures.

Toynbee arrives at this high count because he understands culture to mean a "civilized society," unlike Spengler, who thinks in terms of "cultural spheres" of much wider scope. For example, Toynbee separates the Christian-Orthodox society into two different aspects: the Byzantine-Orthodox and the Russian-Orthodox. He also considers the Japanese-Korean culture apart from the Chinese.

Toynbee's modestly titled *A Study of History* in twelve volumes (a two-volume condensation of Volumes I–X has also been published for popular consumption by D. C. Somervell) may well prove to be the most significant cultural history of recent decades. Among other things, it finally buries a concept already shaken by Spengler: namely, the idea of "progressive development" that is still taught in our schools. This notion has really become untenable—for example, as in the traditional schema of "Antiquity—Middle Ages—Renaissance—Modern Times."

To give a proper picture of the cultures that the modern historian must reckon with—including those which I have tried to bring to life—let us count them off after Toynbee:

| | |
|---|---|
| the Western | the Japanese-Korean |
| the Byzantine-Orthodox | the Minoan |
| the Russian-Orthodox | the Sumerian |
| the Persian | the Hittite |
| the Arabic | the Babylonian |
| the Hindu | the Egyptian |
| the Far Eastern | the Andean |
| the Hellenic | the Mexican |
| the Syrian | the Yucatán |
| the East Indian | the Mayan |
| the Chinese | |

Actually this listing, if we cared to follow other authorities, would have to be increased to at least twenty-two. It is Plato who tells us about the lost culture of Atlantis. Since Plato's day approximately twenty thousand volumes have been written on the Atlantis theme, though as yet no one has been able to prove the existence of the mythical continent. In this literature are countless works that treat Atlantis as an integral part of the world picture. And the great German cultural historian and African explorer Leo Frobenius would have insisted on adding some "black cultures" to Toynbee's list. Frobenius, too, consistently used the concept of an "Atlantean culture."

Who dares claim that the archæologists have dug up all possible cultural vestiges? Throughout the world are scattered monuments which, standing alone and mysterious, have yet to yield the secret of the culture that gave them being. The most discussed artifacts of this category are the more than 260 statues of black volcanic rock on Easter Island, which at one time were decked with broad hats of the same kind of stone, only of reddish hue. These likenesses are silent, but there are some twenty wooden tablets covered with what appears to be a hieroglyphic form of writing, and these might solve the riddle of the statues were we able to decipher them.

A promising step in this direction has been made by Thor Heyerdahl of *Kon-Tiki* fame. As the world knows, the young Norwegian explorer crossed the Pacific from the Peruvian port of Callao to one of the Tuamotu islands on a raft built in Inca style and named after the Inca sun-god, in the spring of 1947, to prove a connection between the Inca culture and that of the South Sea islands. Less than ten years later he paid a visit to Easter Island. Even his early, popular account of his findings in 1957 aroused widespread interest. Then, in 1958, Thomas Barthel, a German anthropologist, published his extraordinarily acute *Grundlagen zur Entzifferung der Osterinselschrift* (Principles of Deciphering the Easter Island Script), with his interpretations of many hieroglyphs. These interpretations have now been challenged, however, by the publication in 1965 of the full scientific analysis of Heyerdahl's data, including more inscriptions. It seems that the Easter Island script is more mysterious than ever.

But the philological axiom that texts in an unknown tongue *and* an unknown script cannot be deciphered without a *bilingue* has now been disproved. Back in 1930 the German Hans Bauer managed to decipher Ugaritic in one bold sweep—he correctly interpreted seventeen out of thirty signs in only a few weeks. The rare good fortune of finding another *bilingue* fell to Helmuth Bossert in 1947, when he discovered a tablet covered with Phoenician and Hittite hieroglyphics on the Karatepe in southeastern Turkey. The task of decipherment that had baffled three generations of scholars could now be accomplished.

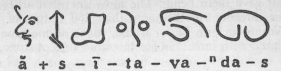

ă + s – ī – ta – va –ⁿda – s

Signature of Asitawandas, king of a Hittite grand
duchy on Karatepe ("Black Mountain") in
southeastern Turkey.

But the greatest feat of decipherment in our century was achieved by a "dilettante": the young English
architect Michael Ventris managed, in 1953, where
scholars all over the world had struggled in vain for
fifty years, to decipher the Cretan so-called "Linear-B"
—finding it to be an ancient Greek dialect (see page
80).

Recent efforts to develop electronic translation
machines have led not so much to translation by com-
puter as to new approaches in the study of language as
such. It is possible, however, that the new electronic
data-processing devices may come to be of some use in
the decipherment of ancient scripts as well.

In our own century the number of archæological
excavations has increased from decade to decade, interrupted only by our senseless wars. Some researchers
have given their entire lives to a single complex of problems. Thus the Frenchman Claude F. A. Schaeffer concentrated on the ancient Syrian harbor town, Ugarit;
the Italian Amedeo Maiuri burrowed in Pompeii for
over forty years, until 1962—yet only three fifths of that
city has been unearthed so far. The German Kurt Bittel
has been digging since 1931 in the ancient Hittite capital, Hattusas (modern Bogazköy). Sir John Marshall
made the excavation of the Indus culture his life's
work. In 1922 the first finds were made at Harappa,
in the southwestern Punjab. In 1924 excavations at
Mohenjo-Daro disclosed evidence of a rich culture
reaching back into the second millennium B.C. Sir
Mortimer Wheeler's excavations at Harappa brought to
light, in 1946, ancient fortifications showing an aston-

ishing similarity to old Mesopotamian military works. A joint reopening of the Mohenjo-Daro site by the University of Pennsylvania and the Pakistan government department of archæology—initiated during the winter of 1964-5 as part of the three-year program— has already found much evidence that the Harappan civilization, far more extensive than originally supposed, was destroyed by flood rather than invasion.

A number of extraordinary finds made headlines either because of their actual significance or the sensational circumstances surrounding them. Leonard Woolley, the great excavator of Ur, had been working at Alalakh, now called Atchana, in Turkey, from 1937 to 1939, and again from 1946 on. In 1947 he announced that he had come upon the grave of King Yarim-Lim, almost four thousand years old. The American Nelson Glueck crowned a successful archæological career by uncovering "King Solomon's Mines." The Mexican Alberto Ruz demolished the seemingly sacrosanct thesis that, while the Egyptian pyramids were royal graves, the Mexican pyramids were only temple pediments: in 1949 he found the grave of a ruler in the Maya pyramid of Palenque. And in one of the sacred wells of sacrifice, a Cenote of the Mayas in Yucatán, into which Edward Herbert Thompson descended as an amateur diver a generation ago to bring up golden treasure, modern aqualung divers in our own decade brought to light four thousand more cult and art objects within four months. In 1954, the Egyptian Zakaria Goneim defied improbability by unearthing, near Sakkara, a totally unknown step pyramid.

Another momentous feat was the exemplary excavation of a neolithic town near Çatal Hüyük in Turkey (probably an actual town as early as 6000 B.C.) begun in 1958 by an Englishman, James Mellaart—after another surprisingly ancient town had been dug up under the ruins of Jericho by Kathleen Kenyon and others. Final dating, as well as whether it can be called a town or a city, is still under discussion, being a question for the sociologists among cultural historians rather than for the archæologists as such. Perhaps the most spectacular of recent excavations is the one undertaken in 1963–5 by Yigael Yadin, former chief of staff of the Israeli army and archæologist, who exposed the rock fortress of Masada in the Judaean desert, where, according to the great Jewish historian Josephus, 960 Zealots committed suicide rather than surrender to the Roman besiegers.

It was, however, a stroke of pure luck that led to what is probably the most interesting and significant find in all Christian-Occidental archæology, and one that is keeping scholars all over the world glued to their desks even now: Bedouin goatherds in 1947 found ancient Hebrew scrolls in a cave near Qumran, north of the Dead Sea, including a complete text of the Book of Isaiah. More discoveries in other caves nearby were added. The now world-famous Dead Sea scrolls cast an entirely new light on what was happening in the sphere of religion before the birth of Christ. Each new find means that we have extended our knowledge by so much. Occasionally it means, too, that we have to revise our seemingly secure opinions. Some years ago a new argument about Troy broke out. Neither the Schliemann nor the Dörpfeld interpretation of Trojan archæology was correct, it was asserted. The American Professor Carl William Blegen in 1932 re-examined the diggings on the mound of Hissarlik. As a result of this search he maintains that it was not level VI—as Dörpfeld, in later years, vigorously claimed—that contained the ruins of Homeric Troy, but level VIIa, the level identified, according to Blegen, with the period between 1200 and 1190 B.C.

For archæology in general, the most important development since World War II is the sweeping methodological effect of certain advances in the natural sciences and technology. Two new branches of investigation, aerial and marine archæology, barely attempted heretofore, leaped to maturity almost overnight. Since

Paul Kosock used aerial photography over the Andes, it has been taken for granted as a preparatory measure in planning an excavation, especially the kind of large-scale dig that aerial survey has helped to make possible today by taking in enormous areas impenetrable to the antlike surface traveler. Among other things the aerial photograph reveals traces of ancient structures *beneath* the surface, by registering subtle variations in the ground cover and in the coloring of the soil.

Something started by isolated sponge divers on the coasts of Greece at the turn of the century, when they rescued an occasional amphora from the "Blue Museum," has been transformed into systematic underwater archæology by the daring Frenchman Jacques-Yves Cousteau, the inventor of the aqualung. What may be hidden in those hundreds of ancient shipwrecks lining the Mediterranean coastal shelf is still beyond surmise.

Once more it was an outsider who revolutionized modern archæology, this time by means of technology and physics. The Italian engineer and industrialist Carlo Maurilio Lerici applied geophysical methods, hitherto used only for finding oil or water in deserts and mountains, to archæological exploration. He began with the vast old Etruscan burial grounds north of Rome, locating hundreds of grave chambers underground in the briefest possible time with his highly sensitive instruments. One of these was a special drill for cutting through surface layers above a grave chamber, so that a "periscope" could be lowered into the chamber. By this means it was possible to explore the inside photographically before opening it up—thus saving a great deal of time and effort that might otherwise have been expended on excavating an empty cavity. Lerici might be called another Schliemann; like the excavator of Troy, he first made his fortune in industry, then at the height of his career turned entirely to archæology and spent a fortune on it. In 1964, after barely a decade of work, he announced the discovery of 5,250 new Etruscan graves in Cerveteri and Tarquinia alone!

It was from America, however, that the two most significant scientific aids to modern archæology came: contributions from atomic physics and biology respectively. They brought the fulfillment of archæology's oldest dream, the possibility of exact dating.

In 1948 the American Willard F. Libby worked out his method of radiocarbon dating. It was based on the fact that the rate of decomposition of an isotope found in all organic matter, carbon 14, is known. Relics from graves before the periods for which we have written records can now be accurately dated by Libby's "timeclock."

But such physicochemical dating could not be exact to the *year*; it had always to be stated with a plus-or-minus differential that increased with the age of the object. Another American, Andrew E. Douglass, physicist and astronomer by profession, had for some decades been developing a different method which was now within a few years brought to a high degree of accuracy by a team at the University of Arizona: the method of tree-ring dating or dendrochronology. The number and character of the annual growth-rings in trees, tree stumps, even carbonized remains of trees, provided a sort of natural calendar from which exact annual dates could be read. Since there was found to be a certain overlapping when the annual rings of trees of various ages were compared, one could work his way backward into the past from tree to tree, as it were, wherever tree remains were found in ruins and graves.

Thus it became possible to move forward—or rather, backward—into the early centuries of our era in studying pre-Columbian ruins in North America. So-called "flowing" chronologies—without linkage to any fixed date of our own chronology—such as the decision whether a certain object is a year older or younger than another, can be worked out by this method in all millennia and will be invaluable aids in either confirming or refuting corresponding dates already established in our old world.

All these new techniques have not only refined the quality of archæological research but also quite considerably increased the *quantity* of its results. Formerly the expeditions in the field at any one time could be counted on two hands. Today the University of Pennsylvania alone is supervising more than twenty expeditions annually. Indeed, the accumulation of materials in some areas is *too* great—the purely scientific labor of classification and interpretation cannot keep up with it. Too often the newly excavated materials—and this is a new danger—tend to wander into the museums, there to be reburied at once.

But the light of publicity poured on the originally esoteric pursuits of the archæologists has had at least one welcome result. Humanity, which used to be so entirely absorbed in the daily assaults of contemporary events and future threats, has learned to be curious about its past and even fascinated by it. This new appreciation manifested itself with a violence no one would have suspected when the technicians announced that they were planning to build a dam in Egypt that would result—unfortunately!—in the total immersion of a few old monuments. Involved primarily were the monumental rock sculptures of Abu Simbel and about a hundred others; they merely happened to be among the oldest and most significant works of art in human history. An outcry arose throughout the civilized world. From the largest organizations to the smallest classes of schoolchildren fund-raising campaigns were set up. UNESCO intervened, and more than twenty countries united to save Abu Simbel.

What more remains to be said?

Digs are in progress all over the world. For we need to understand the past five thousand years in order to master the next hundred years.

# CHRONOLOGICAL TABLES, BIBLIOGRAPHY, AND INDEX

## TABLE I.  THE NEAR EAST

| B.C. | Crete and Greece | Egypt |
|---|---|---|
| 3000 | | DYNASTIES I–II |
| 2900 | NEOLITHIC | Menes, founder, unites Upper and Lower |
| 2800 | | Egypt |
| 2700 | I | OLD KINGDOM |
| | | DYNASTY III, Zoser |
| 2600 | | DYNASTY IV, Khufu (Cheops) |
| | | (pyramids) Chephren, Mycerinus |
| 2500 | | DYNASTY V–VI |
| 2400 | EARLY        EARLY | |
| | MINOAN  II · HELLADIC | |
| 2300 | | FIRST INTERLUDE |
| | | DYNASTIES VII–X |
| 2200 | | |
| 2100 | III | MIDDLE KINGDOM |
| | | DYNASTY XI |
| 2000 | I | Amenemhet I |
| | MIDDLE      MIDDLE | DYNASTY XII { Sesostris I |
| 1900 | MINOAN  II  HELLADIC | Sesostris III |
| | | Amenemhet III |
| 1800 | | SECOND INTERLUDE |
| 1700 | III } | DYNASTIES XIII–XVII, including |
| | LATE | HYKSOS |
| 1600 | LATE  I } HELLADIC I | |
| | MINOAN III } (EARLY MYCENÆAN) | NEW KINGDOM |
| 1500 | LATE HELLADIC (MIDDLE MYCENÆAN) | Hatshepsut |
| | | Thotmes III |
| 1400 | LATE HELLADIC III | DYNASTY XVIII { Amenhotep III |
| | (LATE MYCENÆAN) | c. 1555–1335 Amenhotep IV |
| 1300 | | Tutankhamen |
| | | DYNASTY XIX, Ramses II |
| 1200 | GREEK MIGRATIONS | c. 1335–1205 |
| | c. 1100, Doric Migrations | DYNASTY XX, Ramses III |
| 1100 | | c. 1200–1090 |
| 1000 | GREEK ANTIQUITY | THIRD INTERLUDE |
| | c. 800, Homer | DYNASTY XXI, c. 1090–945 |
| 900 | | DYNASTY XXII, c. 945–745 |
| | GREEK MIDDLE PERIOD | DYNASTY XXIII, c. 745–718 |
| 800 | (Period of colonization and rise of the | DYNASTY XXIV, c. 718–712 |
| | city states) | |
| 700 | 776–traditional date for 1st Olympiad | LATE PERIOD, DYNASTY XXV, 712–670 |
| | c. 750, Hesiod; c. 621, Draco; c. 594, Solon | |
| 600 | PERSIAN WARS | ASSYRIAN RULE |
| | 480, Battles of Thermopylæ, Salamis | DYNASTY XXVI, 663–625 |
| 500 | GREAT AGE OF ATHENS, 480–431 | |
| 400 | DISINTEGRATION OF CITY STATES | PERSIAN RULE |
| | 431–404, Peloponnesian War | |
| 300 | | |
| 200 | HELLENISTIC AGE | HELLENISTIC AGE |
| | 336–323, Alexander the Great | 332, Alexander conquers Egypt |
| 100 | | |

All dates are B.C.

## TABLE I. THE NEAR EAST

*Mesopotamia (Sumeria, Babylonia, Assyria)*                    B.C.

| Mesopotamia (Sumeria, Babylonia) | Assyria | B.C. |
|---|---|---|
| JEMDET NASR (PRE-DYNASTIC) | | 3000 |
| | | 2900 |
| | | 2800 |
| EARLY DYNASTIC DYNASTIES OF KISH, ERECH, UR c. 2500, Entemna after 2500, Urukagina c. 2360, Lugal Zaggisi | | 2700 |
| | | 2600 |
| | | 2500 |
| DYNASTY OF AKKAD, c. 2360–2300—Sargon I, c. 2360–2305 | | 2400 |
| DYNASTY OF GUTIUM Gudea, after 2300 | ASSYRIA* c. 2225, Zariku of Assur—oldest known inscription of an Assyrian prince | 2300 |
| SUPREMACY OF UR THIRD DYNASTY OF UR—Ur-Nammu Shulgi | | 2200 |
| | c. 2050, Ilu-Shuma of Assur | 2100 |
| DYNASTY I OF BABYLON c. 1700 Hammurabi | | 2000 |
| | c. 1800, Samsi-Adad I | 1900 |
| | *Independent historical events now begin to appear farther to the north, in Assyria; from here on, the table is divided into separate Babylonian and Assyrian columns. | 1800 |
| KASSITE DYNASTY Ulamburiash c. 1400, Kuri-Galzu III | | 1700 |
| | | 1600 |
| | | 1500 |
| | EARLY ASSYRIAN EMPIRE c. 1400–885 | 1400 |
| SECOND DYNASTY OF UR, c. 1170–1039 Nebuchadnezzar I, c: 1146–1123 | c. 1380–1340, Assur-uballit I c. 1310–1281, Adad-narari I | 1300 |
| | c. 1280–1261, Salmanassar I | 1200 |
| SECOND DYNASTY OF THE SEA COUNTRY; DYNASTY OF BASSU; ELAMITE DYNASTY | c. 1115–1093, Tiglath-Pileser I | 1100 |
| ASSYRIAN/ELAMITE/CHALDEAN RULE, 990–625 | | 1000 |
| 728–727, Tiglath-Pileser III 709–705, Sargon II 701 703 & 688 681, Sennacherib 680–669, Esarhaddon 647–626, Assurbanipal (Kandalanu) | LATE ASSYRIAN EMPIRE (GREAT AGE) 885–859, Assurnasirpal II 745–727, Tiglath-Pileser III 722–705, Sargon II; 705–681, Sennacherib 680–669, Esarhaddon | 900 |
| | | 800 |
| CHALDEAN DYNASTY—625–605, Nabopolassar; 604–539, Nebuchadnezzar II | 668–626, Assurbanipal | 700 |
| NABUNAID, LAST BABYLONIAN KING, 555–539 | PERSIAN EMPIRE 555–529, Cyrus; 529–522, Cambyses | 600 |
| | 521–485, Darius I; 485–464, Xerxes 424–404, Darius II | 500 |
| PERSIAN RULE 559–330 | 333–330, Darius III | 400 |
| | | 300 |
| HELLENISTIC AGE SELEUCID EMPIRE | HELLENISTIC AGE 330, Persepolis falls to Alexander SELEUCID EMPIRE | 200 |
| | | 100 |

All dates are B.C.

|  | Central Mexico | Yucatán (Maya) | Highland Guatemala (Maya) | B.C. A.D. |
|---|---|---|---|---|
| PRE-AGRICULTURAL | TEPEXPAN CHALCO (CHUPICUARO) |  |  | 10,000 |
| FORMATIVE | COPILCO-ZACATENCO CUICUILCO-TICOMAN TEOTIHUACÁN I | MAMOM CHICANEL | LAS CHARCAS MIRAFLORES | 1000 |
| FLORESCENT | TEOTIHUACÁN III IV | OLD EMPIRE   328, Stele 9— Uaxactún—earliest dated Maya stele<br>Tzakol 328–633<br>Tepeu 633–987   909, latest long-count date in the Old Empire | ESPERANZA PAMPLONA-AMATLE | 1000 |
| FUSIONAL | TOLTEC (TULA) | NEW EMPIRE   MEXICAN OCCUPATION 987–1204<br>987, Chichén reoccupied by Itzás; Mayapan founded<br>1007, Uxmal founded<br>1007–1194, the League of Mayapan<br>1204–1441, ascendancy of Mayapan<br>1441, destruction of Mayapan | QUICHÉ-KAKCHIQUEL | 1200 |
| IMPERIAL-MILITARIST | 1325 Tenochtitlán founded<br>1428–1440, Itzcoatl<br>AZTEC 1440–1469, Moctezuma I<br>1481–1486, Tizoc<br>1503–1520, Moctezuma II<br>(Spanish arrive in 1519) | MEXICAN ABSORPTION 1204–1450<br>1527–1546, Spanish conquer Yucatán |  | 1550 |

TABLE II. MIDDLE AMERICA.

# BIBLIOGRAPHY

## FOR THE CHRONOLOGICAL TABLES

Childe, V. Gordon: *New Light on the Most Ancient East.* 1935.
——: *Dawn of European Civilization.* 4th edn., 1947.
——: *Man Makes Himself.* 1948.
Kroeber, Alfred L.: *Anthropology.* 1948.
Morley, Sylvanus G.: *The Ancient Maya.* 1946.
Robinson, Charles A., Jr.: *Ancient History.* 1951.
Strong, William Duncan: *Cultural Resemblances in Nuclear America: Parallelism or Diffusion?* XXIX International Congress of Americanists.
Vaillant, George C.: *The Aztecs of Mexico.* 1941.
Woolley, Sir Leonard: *Ur of the Chaldees.* 2nd edn., 1950.

Mayan dates are based on the Goodman, Thompson, Martinez correlation.

# BIBLIOGRAPHY

## GENERAL

Bibby, Geoffrey: *Four Thousand Years Ago*. New York, 1961.

Ceram, C. W.: *March of Archæology*. New York, 1958.

Cleator, P. E.: *Lost Languages*. London, 1959.

Daniel, Glyn E.: *A Hundred Years of Archæology*. London, 1950.

Daux, G.: *Les Etapes de l'Archéologie*. 1942.

Frobenius, Leo: *Der Ursprung der afrikanischen Kulturen*. Berlin, 1898.

——: *Kulturgeschichte Afrikas (Prolegomena zu einer historischen Gestaltlehre)*. Zurich, 1933.

Glover, T. R.: *The Ancient World*. Penguin Books, 1948.

Hawkes, Jacquetta, Ed.: *The World of the Past*. 2 vols. New York, 1963.

Heizer, Robert: *The Archæologist at Work: A Source Book in Archæological Method and Interpretation*. New York, 1959.

Hennig, Richard: *Von rätselhaften Ländern*. Munich, 1925.

Hertslet, W. L.: *Der Treppenwitz der Weltgeschichte*. Berlin, 1927.

Jensen, Hans: *Die Schrift*. Gluckstadt, 1935.

Jirku, Anton: *Die Welt der Bibel: Fünf Jahrtausende in Palästina-Syrien*. Stuttgart, 1957.

Kemmerich, Max: *Kulturkuriosa*. 2 vols. Leipzig, 1910.

Koepp, Friedrich: *Archäologie*. 4 vols. Leipzig, 1919–20.

Lübke, Wilhelm: *Die Kunst des Altertums* (Vol. I of *Grundriss der Kunstgeschichte*). Esslingen, 1921.

Meissinger, K. A.: *Roman des Abendlandes*. Leipzig, 1939.

Meyer, Eduard: *Geschichte des Altertums*. 5 vols. Stuttgart and Berlin, 1926–31.

Michaelis, Adolf: *Die archäologischen Entdeckungen des Neunzehnten Jahrhunderts*. Leipzig, 1906.

Oppeln-Bronikowski, Friedrich von: *Archäologische Entdeckungen im 20. Jahrhundert*. Berlin, 1931.

Otto, Walter: *Handbuch der Archäologie*. Munich, 1939–50.

Piggott, Stuart, Ed.: *The Dawn of Civilization*. New York, 1961.

Reinhardt, Ludwig: *Urgeschichte der Welt*. 2 vols. Berlin and Vienna, 1924.

Robert, Carl: *Archäologische Hermeneutik*. Berlin, 1919.

Rodenwaldt, Gerhart: *Die Kunst des Altertums*. 1927.

Schmökel, Hartmut, with Heinrich Otten, Victor Maag, Thomas Beran: *Kulturgeschichte des Alten Orient*. Stuttgart, 1961.

Schuchhardt, Carl: *Die Burg im Wandel der Weltgeschichte*. Potsdam, 1931.

Spengler, Oswald: *Der Untergang des Abendlandes*. 2 vols. Munich, 1920. English translation, 2 vols. New York and London, 1926–8.

Springer, Anton: *Kunstgeschichte*. 5 vols. Leipzig, 1923.

Toynbee, Arnold J.: *A Study of History*. 6 vols. London and New York, 1933–9. Two-volume abridgment by D. C. Somervell, London and New York, 1947, 1957.

Wegner, Max: *Altertumskunde*. Freiburg-Munich, 1951.

Wheeler, Sir Mortimer: *Archæology from the Earth*. London, 1954.

Woolley, C. Leonard: *Digging Up the Past*. New York, 1950.

## I. THE BOOK OF THE STATUES

Bossert, Helmuth Th.: *Alt-Kreta*. Berlin, 1923.

Buschor, Ernst: *Die Plastik der Griechen*. Berlin, 1936.

Corti, Egon Cäsar Conte: *Untergang und Auferstehung von Pompeji und Herkulaneum*. Munich, 1940.

Curtius, Ludwig: *Antike Kunst*. 2 vols. (in the *Handbuch der Kunstwissenschaft*, Athenaion). Potsdam, 1938.

Evans, Arthur: *Scripta Minoa*. Oxford, 1909.

——: *The Palace of Minos*. 7 vols. London, 1964.

Fimmen: *Die kretisch mykenische Kultur*. 1924.

Goethe, Johann Wolfgang von: *Winckelmann und sein Jahrhundert*. 1805.

Hausrath and Marx: *Griechische Märchen*. Jena, 1913.

Holm, Adolf, Wilhelm Deeke, and Wilhelm Soltau: *Kulturgeschichte des klassischen Altertums*. Leipzig, 1897.

Homer, *Iliad* and *Odyssey*.

Justi, Carl: *Winckelmann*. Leipzig, 1866.

Klein, Wilhelm: *Vom antiken Rokoko*. Vienna, 1921.

Lichtenberg, R. von: *Die Ägäische Kultur*. Leipzig, 1911.

Ludwig, Emil: *Schliemann*. Berlin, 1932.

Maiuri, Amedeo: *Pompejo*. Novara, 1956.

Matz, Friedrich: *Kreta, Mykene, Troja*. Stuttgart, 1957.

Meyer, Ernest: *Briefe von Heinrich Schliemann*. Berlin and Leipzig, 1936.

Palmer, Leonard R.: *Mycenaeans and Minoans, Aegean Prehistory in the Light of the Linear B Tablets*. New York, 1963, 1965.

Pendlebury, J. D. S.: *A Handbook to the Palace of Minos, Knossos, with its Dependencies*. London, 1954.

Pfister, Kurt: *Die Etrusker*. Munich, 1940.

Poole, Lynn and Gray: *One Passion, Two Loves. The Story of Heinrich and Sophie Schliemann, Discoverers of Troy*. New York, 1966.

Schliemann, Heinrich: *Ithaka*. Leipzig, 1869.

——: *Mykenä*. Leipzig, 1878.

——: *Ilios*. Leipzig, 1881.

——: *Troja*. Leipzig, 1884.

——: *Tiryns*. Leipzig, 1886.

Schoener, R.: *Pompeji*. Stuttgart, 1876.

Schuchhardt, Karl, and Theodor Wiegand: *Carl Humann*. 1931.

Uhde-Bernays, Hermann Hans: *Winckelmanns kleine Schriften*. Leipzig, 1913.

Vietta, Egon: *Zauberland Kreta*. Vienna-Wiesbaden, 1952.

Winckelmann, Johann Joachim: *Sendschreiben von den herculanischen Entdeckungen*. 1762.

——: *Neue Nachrichten von den neuesten herculanischen Entdeckungen*. 1764.

——: *Geschichte der Kunst des Altertums*. 1764.

——: *Monumenti antichi inediti*. 2 vols. Rome, 1767.

## II. THE BOOK OF THE PYRAMIDS

Breasted, James A.: *Ancient Records of Egypt*. 4 vols. Chicago, 1906–7.

———: A History of Egypt, 1905.

Brugsch, Heinrich: Inscriptio Rosettana. Berlin, 1851.

———: Die Ägyptologie. Leipzig, 1891.

———: Steininschrift und Bibelwort. Berlin, 1891.

Carter, Howard, and A. C. Mace: The Tomb of Tut. Ankh. Amen. Vol. I. New York, 1923.

Carter, Howard: ibid. Vol. II. New York, 1927.

Champollion, Jean François: Lettre à M. Dacier, relative à l'alphabet des hiéroglyphes phonétiques. Paris, 1822.

———: Panthéon égyptien. Paris. 1823.

Desroches-Noblecourt, Christiane: Life and Death of a Pharaoh; Tutankhamen. New York, 1963.

Ebers, Georg: Papyros Ebers. 2 vols. 1875.

———: Eine ägyptische Königstochter (novel). 3 vols. 1884.

Edwards, A. A. B.: Pharaohs, Fellahs and Explorers. 1891.

Edwards, I. E. S.: The Pyramids of Egypt. Penguin Books, 1952.

Erman, Adolf: Die Hieroglyphen. 1917.

———: Die Literatur der Ägypter. Leipzig, 1923.

———: Die Welt am Nil. Leipzig, 1936.

Friedell, Egon: Kulturgeschichte Ägyptens und des Alten Orients. Munich, 1951.

Goneim, Mohammed Zakaria: The Lost Pyramid. New York, 1956.

Hartleben, H.: Champollion. 2 vols. Berlin, 1906.

Lange, Kurt: Pyramiden, Sphinxe, Pharaonen. Munich, 1952.

Ludwig, Emil: Napoleon. Berlin, 1930.

Meier-Graefe, Julius: Pyramide und Tempel. Berlin, 1927.

Mertz, Barbara: Temples, Tombs, and Hieroglyphs. New York, 1964.

Petrie, William M. Flinders: Ten Years' Digging in Egypt. 1881–91.

———: Methods and Aims in Archæology. 1904.

Reybaud, Louis: Histoire scientifique et militaire de l'expédition française en Égypte. 10 vols. 1830–6.

Scharff, Alexander: Ägyptische Sonnenlieder, Berlin, 1922.

———: and Moortgat: Ägypten und Vorderasien im Altertum. Munich, 1950.

Schott, Siegfried: Hieroglyphen, Untersuchungen zum Ursprung der Schrift. Mainz, 1951.

Sethe, Kurt: *Die altägyptischen Pyramidentexte.* 4 vols. 1908–22.

Steindorff, Georg: *Die ägyptischen Gaue und ihre politische Entwicklung.* 1909.

———: *Blütezeit des Pharaonenreiches.* 1926.

Wolf, Walther: *Die Welt der Ägypter.* Stuttgart, 1958.

## III. THE BOOK OF THE TOWERS

Botta, Paul Emile: *Monuments de Ninive découverts et décrits par Botta, mesurés et dessinés par E. Flandin.* 4 vols. Paris, 1847–50.

Ceram, C. W.: *The Secret of the Hittites.* New York, 1956.

Dietz, Ernst: *Entschleiertes Asien.* Berlin, 1943.

Grotefend, Georg Friedrich: *Beiträge zur Erläuterung der persepolitanischen Keilschrift.* Hannover, 1837.

Hedin, Sven: *Bagdad, Babylon, Niniveh.* Leipzig, 1918.

Jordan, Franzis: *In den Tagen des Tammuz.* Munich, 1950.

Kittel, Rudolf: *Die orientalischen Ausgrabungen.* Leipzig, 1908.

Koldewey, Robert: *Das wiedererstehende Babylon.* Leipzig, 1914.

——— and Karl Schuchhardt: *Heitere und ernste Briefe.* Berlin, 1925.

Kramer, Samuel Noah: *History Begins at Sumer.* Garden City, N.Y., 1959.

Kubie, Nora B.: *The Road to Nineveh: The Adventures and Excavations of Sir Austen Henry Layard.* New York, 1961.

Lawrence, T. E.: *The Letters of T. E.* London, n. d.

Layard, Austen Henry: *Nineveh and Its Remains.* 2 vols. London, 1848.

———: *Nineveh and Babylon, Being the Narrative of Discoveries.* London, 1853.

Lloyd, Seton: *Foundations in the Dust.* London, 1949.

Meissner, Bruno: *Babylonien und Assyrien.* 2 vols. 1920–5.

———: *Könige Babyloniens und Assyriens.* Leipzig, 1926.

Parrot, André: *Sumer, the Dawn of Art.* New York, 1961.

Rawlinson, G.: *A Memoir of Major-General Sir Henry Creswicke Rawlinson.* 1938.

Rawlinson, Henry Creswicke: *The Persian Cuneiform Inscriptions at Behistun.* 1846.

———: *Commentary on the Cuneiform Inscriptions of Babylonia and Assyria.* 1850.

———: *Outline of the History of Assyria, as Collected from the Inscriptions Discovered in the Ruins of Nineveh.* London, 1852.

Schmidtke, Friedrich: *Der Aufbau der babylonischen Chronologie.* Münster, 1952.

Schmökel, Hartmut: *Ur, Assur, und Babylon: Drei Jahrtausende im Zweistromland.* Stuttgart, 1955.

Weidner, Ernst F.: *Studien zur assyrisch-babylonischen Chronologie und Geschichte.* 1917.

Woolley, C. Leonard: *Vor 5000 Jahren.* Stuttgart, 1929.

———: *Ur of the Chaldees.* Penguin Books, 1952.

## IV. THE BOOK OF THE TEMPLES

Batres, Leopoldo: *Teotihuacan.* Mexico, 1906.

Bowditch, Charles P.: *A Suggestive Maya Inscription.* Cambridge, Mass., 1903.

———: *Mexican and Central American Antiquities, Calendar Systems and History.* Washington, 1904.

Catherwood, F.: *Views of Ancient Monuments in Central America, Chiapas and Yucatan.* 1844.

Charnay, Désiré: *Ruines américaines.* Paris, 1863.

Collier, John: *Indians of the Americas.* New York, 1948.

Danzel, Theodor-Wilhelm: *Mexiko.* 2 vols. Hagen, 1923.

———: *Mexiko und das Reich der Inkas.* Hamburg, n. d.

Dieseldorff, E. P.: *Kunst und Religion der Mayavölker.* 3 vols. Berlin, 1926–33.

Greene, Graham: *Lawless Roads.* London, 1939. Published in New York (1939) as *Another Mexico.*

Humboldt, Alexander von: *Reise in die Äquinoktialgegenden des neuen Kontinentes.* Stuttgart, 1859–60.

Joyce, T. A.: *Mexican Archæology.* London, 1914.

———: *Central American and West Indian Archæology.* London, 1916.

Kingsborough, Edward Lord: *Antiquities of Mexico.* 9 vols. London, 1831–48.

Kisch, Egon Erwin: *Entdeckungen in Mexiko.* Berlin, 1947.

Landa, Diego de: *Relación de las cosas de Yucatán*. 1566.
(French edition: *Relation des choses de Yucatan*,
published by Brasseur de Bourbourg. Paris, 1864.)

Lehmann, Walter: "*Ergebnisse und Aufgaben der mexi-
kanistischen Forschung*," in *Archiv für Anthropologie*.
Braunschweig, 1907.

Maudslay, Alfred P.: *Biologia Centrali Americana*. 4 vols.
London, 1889–1902.

*Maya Sculptures, Guide to the Maudslay Collection of*.
British Museum, London, 1938.

Morley, Sylvanus G.: *The Rise and Fall of the Maya
Civilization in the Light of the Monuments and the
Native Chronicles*. New York, 1917.

—— and George W. Brainerd: *The Ancient Maya*. 3rd
edn. Stanford, Calif., 1956.

Peterson, Frederick A.: *Ancient Mexico: An Introduction
to the Pre-Hispanic Cultures*. New York, 1959.

Prescott, William H.: *History of the Conquest of Mexico*.
1844.

Radin, Paul: *The Story of the American Indian*. New
York, 1944.

Ricketson, Oliver G., Jr.: *Six Seasons at Uaxactún*. International Congress of Americanists, 1928.

Ruz, Alberto: "An Astonishing Discovery," in *Illustrated
London News* (August 29, 1953).

Sahagún, Bernadino de: *Historia General de las cosas de
Nueva España*. 3 vols. Mexico, 1829. English trans-
lation (1932) by Fanny R. Bandelier: *A History of
Ancient Mexico*.

Schultze Jena, Leonhard: *Gliederung des Alt-Aztekischen
Volks in Familie, Stand und Beruf*. Stuttgart, 1952.

Seler, Eduard: *Gesammelte Abhandlungen zur amerika-
nischen Sprach- und Altertumskunde*. 5 vols. Berlin,
1902–23.

Stephens, John L.: *Incidents of Travel in Central America,
Chiapas and Yucatan*. New York, 1842.

Thompson, Edward Herbert: *People of the Serpent*. London, 1932.

Thompson, J. Eric: *Civilization of the Mayas*. Chicago,
1927.

Vaillant, G. C.: *The Aztecs of Mexico*. Penguin Books,
1951.

Verrill, A. Hyatt and Ruth: *America's Ancient Civiliza-*
    *tions.* New York, 1953.
Westheim, Paul: *Arte antiguo de México.* Mexico, 1950.

# V. BOOKS THAT CANNOT YET BE WRITTEN

Barthel, Thomas: *Grundlagen zur Entzifferung der Os-*
    *terinselschrift.* Abhandlungen aus dem Gebiet der
    Auslandskunde, Band 64. Hamburg, 1958.
Bass, George F.: *Archæology under Water.* London, 1966.
Baudin, Louis: *Les Incas du Pérou.* Paris, 1942.
——: *L'Empire socialiste des Incas.* Paris, 1928.
Biek, Leo: *Archæology and the Microscope.* New York,
    1963.
Brothwell, Don, and Eric Higgs: *Science in Archæology.*
    London, 1963.
Ceram, C. W., and Peter Lyon: "The Blue Museum" in
    *Horizon,* Vol. 1, No. 2, New York (November 1958).
Cousteau, Jacques-Yves: *The Silent World.* New York,
    1950.
Deuel, Leo: *Testaments of Time.* New York, 1965.
Hagen, Victor W. von: *The Desert Kingdoms of Peru.*
    New York, 1965.
Heyerdahl, Thor: *Aku-Aku: The Secret of Easter Island.*
    New York, 1958.
Lerici, Carlo Maurillo: *A Great Adventure of Italian Ar-*
    *chæology: 1955–65, Ten Years of Archæological Pros-*
    *pecting.* Milan, 1965.
Libby, Willard F.: *Radiocarbon Dating.* Chicago, 1952.
Mackay, D. Ed.: *Early Indus Civilizations.* London, 1948.
Mackay, E. J. H.: *Excavations at Mohenjo-Daro.* Delhi,
    1938.
Marshall, John: *Mohenjo-Daro and the Indus Civilizations,*
    I–III. London, 1931.
Mellaart, James: *Catal Hüyük, a Neolithic Town in Ana-*
    *tolia.* New York, 1967.
Piggott, Stuart: *Prehistoric India to 1000 B.C.* Penguin
    Books, 1952.
Poole, Lynn and Gray: *Carbon-14 and Other Science*
    *Methods That Date the Past.* New York, 1961.
Prescott, William H.: *History of the Conquest of Peru.*
    1847.

*Reports of the Norwegian Archæological Expedition to Easter Island and the East Pacific*, Vol. II: *Miscellaneous Papers*. Chicago, 1965.

Spanuth, Jurgen: *Atlantis*. Tübingen, 1965.

Stallings, W. S.: *Dating Pre-Historic Ruins by Tree-Rings*. Tucson, Ariz., 1960.

Ubbelohde-Doering, Heinrich: *Kunst in Reiche der Inca*. Tübingen, 1952.

Wheeler, Sir Mortimer: *Early India and Pakistan*. New York, 1959.

Yadin, Yigael: *Masada*. New York, 1966.

## ABOUT THE AUTHOR

**C. W. CERAM** is a name familiar to everyone interested in archaeology. Born in 1915 in Berlin, he was known for many years under his real name, Kurt W. Marek, as a newspaperman, drama critic, and a leading figure in the publishing world. His first book, *Gods, Graves, and Scholars* (1951), presented here in its second edition, brought world fame to its author—it has now achieved great popular and critical success in twenty-six languages —and immeasurably expanded popular interest and concern for the world's archaeological heritage. He also wrote *The Secret of the Hittites* (1956), the result of an invitation to participate in two digs in Turkey, uncovering the Hittite past; *The March of Archaeology* (1958); in 1961, under his real name, *Yestermorrow: Notes on Man's Progress;* in 1966, *Hands on the Past: The Pioneer Archaeologists Tell Their Own Story;* and in 1971, *First American.*

# 27 million Americans can't read a bedtime story to a child.

It's because 27 million adults in this country simply can't read.

Functional illiteracy has reached one out of five Americans. It robs them of even the simplest of human pleasures, like reading a fairy tale to a child.

You can change all this by joining the fight against illiteracy.

Call the Coalition for Literacy at toll-free **1-800-228-8813** and volunteer.

**Volunteer
Against Illiteracy.
The only degree you need
is a degree of caring.**

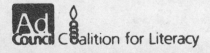